SO-BBH-355

"Worship should take our breath away. And nothing inspires raw, awesome worship like that than meditating on powerful, majestic truths made plain. Steve has done it in this new book!"

JONI EARECKSON TADA
PRESIDENT, JAF MINISTRIES

"I can't think of a better way to invest a few minutes of each day than to thoughtfully consider the awesome attributes of almighty God. I am thankful that Steve Halliday has used his tremendous gift for words to gather and offer these powerful reminders of our Lord's greatness. Surely those who read them cannot help but be changed."

ED YOUNG
PASTOR, SECOND BAPTIST CHURCH OF HOUSTON

"This book truly helps the reader gain a larger vision of the magnificence of God. Thank you for leading me on such an incredible journey into the true greatness of God!"

DAVE DRAVECKY
PRESIDENT, OUTREACH OF HOPE

"This judicious selection of devotional nuggets leads us day after day to the foundation of spiritual life—the adoration of our awesome God."

GEORGE K. BRUSHABER
PRESIDENT, BETHEL COLLEGE AND SEMINARY,
ST. PAUL, MINNESOTA

"Our culture and our churches desperately need a vision of God. The devotionals in this book lift us into His presence, reminding us of His majesty, sovereignty, and love."

THOMAS R. SCHREINER
PROFESSOR OF NEW TESTAMENT,
SOUTHERN BAPTIST THEOLOGICAL SEMINARY

STEVE HALLIDAY &
WILLIAM TRAVIS

HOW GREAT
THOU ART

A DAILY DEVOTIONAL

SELECTIONS FROM
CLASSIC CHRISTIAN AUTHORS

Multnomah® Publishers *Sisters, Oregon*

HOW GREAT THOU ART
published by Multnomah Publishers, Inc.

© 1999 by Steve Halliday and William Travis
International Standard Book Number: 1-59052-978-2 (FCP)

Cover design by Uttley DouPonce DesignWorks
Cover images by Digital Stock

Unless otherwise indicated, Scripture quotations are from *The Holy Bible,*
The New International Version (NIV) © 1973, 1984 by International Bible Society used
by permission of Zondervan Publishing House.

Also quoted:
The American Standard Version (ASV) © 1901
The Holy Bible, King James Version (KJV)
New American Standard Bible (NASB) ©1960, 1977 by the Lockman Foundation
Holy Bible, New Living Translation (NLT) ©1996.
Used by permission of Tyndale House Publishers, Inc. All rights reserved.
The New English Bible (NEB)
The Holy Bible, New King James Version (NKJV) © 1984 by Thomas Nelson, Inc.
Revised Standard Version Bible (RSV) © 1946, 1952
by the Division of Christian Education of the
National Council of Churches of Christ in the United States of America
In some instances, the original writers have paraphrased Scripture quotations.

Printed in the United States of America
ALL RIGHTS RESERVED
No part of this publication may be reproduced, stored in a retrieval system, or transmitted,
in any form or by any means—electronic, mechanical, photocopying, recording, or
otherwise—without prior written permission.

For information:
MULTNOMAH PUBLISHERS, INC.•P.O. BOX 1720•SISTERS, OREGON 97759

Congress Cataloging-in-Publication Data:

How great Thou art: 365 reasons why God is awesome / [compiled by]
    Steve Halliday, William Travis.
        p. cm.
    Includes bibliographical references (p. 407–16)
    ISBN 1-57673-154-5 (alk. paper)
    ISBN 1-57673-838-8 (pb.)
    1. Devotional calendars.   I. Halliday, Steve, 1957–
    II. Travis, William G.
    BV4810.H65   1999
    242'.2—dc21   99-3411 CIP
        06 07 08 09 10 — 10 9 8 7 6 5 4 3

ACKNOWLEDGMENTS

We have personally benefited from our encounter with the readings
reproduced here and the numerous others not used.
Our wives, Lisa and Lucille, gave support, encouragement,
and not a little of their time to the successful conclusion of this project!
Special thanks to Dan Berkland, Bill's teaching assistant,
who spent many hours searching for the right words and phrases
to capture glimpses into the nature of God.
We would also like to thank Dr. John Piper,
who provided the inspiration for this book and whose pen
contributed several of its readings.

～

DEDICATION

*To Robert and Jean Halliday, faithful, loving parents
who even today continue to quietly obey
the delightful command of Psalm 78:4:
"We will tell the next generation the praiseworthy deeds of the Lord,
his power, and the wonders he has done."
Without your guidance, support, and example, this book
would have had to be produced by someone else. I love you!*
STEVE HALLIDAY

*For Phil, Chris, and Bry,
three gifts from God.*
WILLIAM TRAVIS

Contents

Contents

the wonder and majesty that is god

They will speak of the glorious splendor of your majesty,
and I will meditate on your wonderful works.

(PSALM 145:5)

T hrough the ages wise Christians have realized the vital need to know God as He truly is. Jonathan Edwards said it well in the eighteenth century: "It is of exceeding great importance that we should have right notions and conceptions of the nature, attributes, and perfections of God. It is the very foundation of all religion, both doctrinal and practical; it is to no purpose to worship God, except we know what we worship."[1]

For almost twenty centuries the reverent contemplation of the majesty and splendor of God has lifted saints to heights of spiritual insight and delight almost inconceivable to believers of our own day. "When we look back on what the masters of the spiritual life have written and said," wrote one of our contemporaries, "it's hard to escape the conclusion that we have been the victim of a confidence trick in our century. Over the past few decades, the evangelical church has been gripped by a series of issues and concerns that have primarily been marginal, or at best of secondary importance. Conferences, seminars, and books on a whole series of 'vital concerns' have dominated center stage and determined the agenda in many churches and for many individual Christians. *But strikingly absent has been concentration on God Himself.*"[2]

As nothing else, meditating on the glory of God leads to a changed heart and a soaring spirit. Edwards continued: "It is impossible we should love, fear, and obey God as we ought, except we know what He is, and have right ideas of His perfections, that render Him lovely and worthy to be feared and obeyed. . . . It would be greatly to the advantage of our souls if we understood more of the excellency and gloriousness of God. . . . And this is what we hope will be our business to all eternity; to think on, to delight [in], to speak of, and sing forth, the infinite excellencies of the Deity."[3]

Edwards had it right! Knowing God as He has revealed Himself to us in His Word is crucial to our worship—indeed, to our very lives. How could we ever hope to *live* right without first *believing* right? As A.W. Tozer reminded us so well: "History will probably show that no people has ever risen above its religion, and man's spiritual history positively demonstrates that no religion has ever been greater than its idea of God. For this reason the most portentous fact about any person is not what he at a given time may say or do, but what he in his deep heart conceives God to be like.... We do the greatest service to the next generation of Christians by passing on to them undimmed and undiminished that noble concept of God which we received from our Hebrew and Christian fathers of generations past. This will prove of greater value to them than anything that art or science can devise."[4]

Knowing God in all His holiness, sovereignty, wisdom, goodness, power, righteousness, and all other divine attributes is the rich food that best nourishes and strengthens the human soul. That is why John Calvin wrote in the sixteenth century: "This teaching ought to be a subject of daily meditation, and it ought to be something we continually remember. Indeed, all God's blessings which He gives us are intended for this purpose—that His glory might be proclaimed through us."[5]

If this devotional helps even one reader gain a larger vision of the magnificence of God, our labors will have been well spent. We remain more firmly convinced than ever that regular meditation on the excellencies of the Triune God cannot but ground us in the realities of the universe and help us to reflect back to our Maker some small part of the glory He daily showers on us. And when that happens—when we pause to contemplate and enjoy our wonderful Lord—we believe a fresh wind will begin to blow through our churches, sweeping away the dust of apathy and half-heartedness and filling us with a godly passion to be the people God longs for us to be.

To that end we have selected, edited, and presented the following 365 readings, each focused on one of twelve divine characteristics we have chosen to highlight. The language of many of the readings has been updated and even paraphrased to make them more accessible to a modern audience; any loss of meaning from the originals is unintentional and may be attributed solely to our lack of skill.

The spotlight in each section generally moves from insights into God's character to some appropriate response of faith. Although readings are taken from all periods of Christian history, writers from the past two centuries predominate, for the simple reason that these authors usually "connect" more to contemporary concerns than do their more ancient forebears. The inclusion here of any particular author does not, of course, imply our endorsement of every part of his or her ministry or writings. It simply means that, in this excerpt, at least, it seems to us the author has effectively captured some significant morsel of Christian teaching on the glorious Godhead.

We invite you now to turn your heart and mind to a warm-spirited reflection on the glorious nature of our great God, as seen through the eyes of some of the most insightful Christians of the past two thousand years. Of course, we cannot know everything about God. How could the finite ever hope to fully grasp the Infinite? At our best, we know only in part—but that glorious part is vastly more than enough to occupy us from now to eternity!

We hope this book will contribute to that occupation. O, that God would use the following readings to provoke reflection on His excellencies, to encourage trust in and worship of the God of those excellencies, and to promote godly living in the light of His excellencies!

May our Lord be pleased to reveal Himself to you as you ponder the wonder and majesty that is God.

STEVE HALLIDAY
WILLIAM TRAVIS

1. Jonathan Edwards, *Sermons and Discourses, 1720-1723*, *The Works of Jonathan Edwards*, Vol. 10, ed. Wilson Kimnach (New Haven: Yale University Press, 1992), 416–8.

2. Sinclair Ferguson, *A Heart For God* (Colorado Springs, CO: NavPress, 1985), 17–18.

3. Edwards, 417.

4. A.W. Tozer, "A Revealing Question," *Partnership* magazine, May–June 1987, 56, taken from *The Knowledge of the Holy* (San Francisco: Harper & Row, 1961).

5. William E. Keesecker, ed., *A Calvin Reader: Reflections on Living* (Philadelphia: Westminster Press, 1985), 39.

THE MAJESTY
OF GOD

YOURS, O LORD,

IS THE GREATNESS

AND THE POWER

AND THE GLORY

AND THE MAJESTY

AND THE SPLENDOR.

1 CHRONICLES 29:11

who is god?

For who is God besides the LORD? And who is the Rock except our God?

(2 SAMUEL 22:32)

What is God—what, but the Lord God? *For who is the Lord but the Lord? Or who is God save our God?* Most high, most excellent, most powerful, most almighty, most merciful, and most just; most hidden, yet most present; most beautiful, and most strong; stable, yet mysterious; unchangeable, yet changing all things; never new, never old; making all things new and bringing age upon the proud, though they do not know it; always working, yet always at rest; still gathering, yet lacking nothing; sustaining, filling and protecting; creating, nourishing, and maturing; seeking, yet possessing all things.

God loves without passion; He is jealous without anxiety; He repents, yet has no sorrow; is angry, yet serene; changes His ways, yet His plans are unchanged; recovers what He finds, having never lost it; never in need, yet rejoicing in gain; never covetous, yet requiring interest. He receives over and above, that He may owe—yet who has anything that is not His? He pays debts, owing nothing; remits debts, losing nothing.

And what can anyone say when they speak of Him? Yet woe to those who keep silent, since those who say the most are as the mute!

ST. AUGUSTINE OF HIPPO

DAY
I

when tongues fall silent

I know that you can do all things; no plan of yours can be thwarted.... Surely I
spoke of things I did not understand, things too wonderful for me to know.

(JOB 42:2–3)

T he mind of man cannot fittingly conceive how great is God
and how majestic His nature. Nor has human eloquence
the power to express His greatness. For all eloquence is
certainly mute and every mind inadequate to conceive and to utter
His majesty.

Whatever can be thought about Him is less than He; whatever
can be uttered about Him will be less than He when compared with
Him. When we are silent, we can experience Him to some extent, but
we cannot express Him in words as He really is.

DAY
2

If the keen sight of our eyes grows dim by looking at the sun so
that their gaze is overpowered by the bright rays that meet them, so
our mental vision undergoes this very thing in its every thought of God.
The more it endeavors to contemplate God, the more is it blinded by
the light of its own thought.

What can you say about Him that is worthy of Him—He who is
more sublime than all sublimity, loftier than all loftiness, more profound than all profundity, brighter than all light, more brilliant than
all brilliance, more splendid than all splendor, mightier than all might,
more powerful than all power, more beautiful than all beauty, truer
than all truth, stronger than all strength, greater than all majesty, more
potent than all potency, richer than all riches, kinder than all kindness, better than all goodness, more just than all justice, and more
merciful than all mercy? Every kind of virtue must of necessity be less
than He who is the God and Author of them all. Nothing really can be
compared to Him, for He is above everything that can be said of Him.

NOVATIAN

The Thrill above All Thrills

Better is one day in your courts than a thousand elsewhere; I would rather be a doorkeeper in the house of my God than dwell in the tents of the wicked.

(PSALM 84:10)

W e were made to thrill at the panorama of God's power and glory. It is the heart of what the apostles preached: "the light of the knowledge of the glory of God in the face of Christ" (2 Corinthians 4:6). It is the goal of every Christian act: "Whatever you do, do all to the glory of God" (1 Corinthians 10:31, RSV). It is the focus of all Christian hope: "We rejoice in hope of the glory of God" (Romans 5:2). It will some day replace the sun and moon as the light of life: "The city has no need of sun or moon to shine upon it, for the glory of God is its light" (Revelation 21:23, RSV). And even now, before that great day, "the heavens are telling the glory of God" (Psalm 19:1, RSV). When people discover the worth of God's glory—when God says, "Let there be light," and opens the eyes of the blind—they are like people who find a treasure hidden in a field and, full of joy, sell all they have to buy that field. They are like Moses, who cried to the Lord, "I pray thee, show me thy glory" (Exodus 33:18, RSV).

DAY 3

This is the heart-pang of every human being. People everywhere are starving for the enjoyment of God. For, as Jonathan Edwards said, "The enjoyment of God is the only happiness with which our souls can be satisfied. To go to heaven, fully to enjoy God, is infinitely better than the most pleasant accommodations here. Fathers and mothers, husbands, wives, or children, or the company of earthly friends, are but shadows; but God is the substance. These are but scattered beams, but God is the sun. These are but streams. But God is the ocean."

JOHN PIPER

A God Too Big

O LORD, our Lord, how majestic is your name in all the earth!
You have set your glory above the heavens.
From the lips of children and infants you have ordained praise.

(PSALM 8:1–2)

W hen I was a boy, our family often went camping in the High Sierras in California. Traveling along the eastern slopes of those ten- to fourteen-thousand-foot peaks involved several steep grades and dry, desert-like heat. One mountain grade I will never forget. It had a funny name: the "O" grade.

"Why?" I asked my father, "Why is it called that? Is it the next grade after *P*?"

DAY
4

"Just wait," he replied, smiling. "You'll see."

Up and up we climbed on the twisting switchback road through scrub pine and sage. And then—when it seemed we would never get to the top—we did. And spontaneously I cried out, "O!" There in front of us, beyond a diamond-studded lake and framed with quaking aspen, was the jagged, snowy Sierra Crest—higher, more massive, more beautiful, more alive with color than I had dreamed.

We all laughed together at our now-shared secret. *Someday,* I thought, *I will have the chance to say to someone else, "Just wait. You'll see!"*

That time is now. God has ordained that His children respond to the symphony of His majesty, to the vast panorama of His greatness, with a heartfelt, "O!"

God has a limitless store of "O" grades for each of us. Often they will come suddenly, unexpectedly, when we find ourselves confronted with the stark immensity of our most mysterious God—His grace, His forgiveness, His patience, His creativity, His friendship, His judgment. Sometimes they will come at the end of what we feared was an endless "grade" of suffering.

But most of God's "O" grades are ours right now—this moment—when we simply choose to pause and contemplate any of the myriad facets of the character of our awesome God. And bowing low, trembling, we will once more discover *A God Too Big.*

DAVID NEEDHAM

worthy of worship

*Praise the LORD, O my soul.
O LORD my God, you are very great;
you are clothed with splendor and majesty.*

(PSALM 104:1)

W hen we ascribe majesty to someone, we acknowledge greatness in that person and voice our respect for him or her, as when we speak of "Her Majesty" the Queen.

Now, *majesty* is a word which the Bible uses to express the thought of the greatness of God, our Maker and our Lord. "The LORD reigns, he is robed in *majesty*..." (Psalm 93:1). "They will speak of the glorious splendor of your *majesty*" (Psalm 145:5). Peter, recalling his vision of Christ's royal glory at the Transfiguration, says, "We were eyewitnesses of his *majesty*" (2 Peter 1:16). In Hebrews, the phrase "the majesty" twice does duty for "God"; Christ, we are told, at His ascension sat down "at the right hand of *the Majesty* in heaven," "at the right hand of the throne of *the Majesty* in heaven" (Hebrews 1:3; 8:1, italics added).

The word *majesty*, when applied to God, is always a declaration of His greatness and an invitation to worship. The Christian's instincts of trust and worship are stimulated very powerfully by knowledge of the greatness of God.

But this is knowledge which Christians today largely lack: and that is one reason why our faith is so feeble and our worship so flabby. We are modern men, and modern men, though they cherish great thoughts of man, have as a rule small thoughts of God. We are poles apart from our evangelical forefathers at this point, even when we confess our faith in their words. When you start reading Luther, or Edwards, or Whitefield, though your doctrine may be theirs, you soon find yourself wondering whether you have any acquaintance at all with the mighty God whom they knew so intimately.

Yet the Bible never lets us lose sight of God's majesty and His unlimited dominion over all His creatures.

DAY
5

J.I. PACKER

A Broad world, A wide sea

God, the blessed and only Ruler, the King of kings and Lord of lords, who alone is
immortal and who lives in unapproachable light, whom no one has seen or can see.
To him be honor and might forever. Amen.

(1 TIMOTHY 6:15–16)

DAY
6

What a broad world to roam in, what a sea to swim in is this God and Father of our Lord Jesus Christ.

He is *eternal,* which means that He antedates time and is wholly independent of it. Time began in Him and will end in Him. To it He pays no tribute and from it He suffers no change.

He is *immutable,* which means that He has never changed and can never change in any smallest measure. To change He would need to go from better to worse or from worse to better. He cannot do either, for being perfect He cannot become more perfect, and if He were to become less perfect, He would be less than God.

He is *omniscient,* which means that He knows in one free and effortless act all matter, all spirit, all relationships, all events. He has no past and He has no future. He *is,* and none of the limiting and qualifying terms used of creatures can apply to Him.

Love and *mercy* and *righteousness* are His, and *holiness* so unutterable that no comparisons or figures will avail to express it. Only fire can give even a remote conception of it. In fire He appeared at the burning bush; in the pillar of fire He dwelt through all the long wilderness journey; He came at Pentecost as a fiery flame and rested upon each disciple.

Frederick Faber was one whose soul panted after God. Of God the Father he sings:

> *Only to sit and think of God,*
> *Oh, what a joy it is!*
> *To think the thought, to breathe the Name;*
> *Earth has no higher bliss.*
> *Father of Jesus, love's reward!*
> *What rapture it will be,*
> *Prostrate before Thy throne to lie,*
> *And gaze and gaze on Thee!*

A. W. TOZER

Boundless Grandeur

O LORD, our LORD, how majestic is your name in all the earth!
You have set your glory above the heavens.

(PSALM 8:1)

No heart can measure, no tongue can utter, the half of the greatness of God. The whole creation is full of His glory and radiant with the excellency of His power. His goodness and His wisdom are displayed on every hand. The countless hosts of terrestrial beings, from man the head to the creeping worm at the foot, are all supported and nourished by the Divine bounty. The solid fabric of the universe leans upon His eternal arm.

Universally is He present, and everywhere is His name excellent. God works always and everywhere. *There is no place where God is not.* God is there in a thousand wonders, upholding rocky barriers, filling the flowercups with their perfume, and refreshing the lonely pines with the breath of His mouth. Descend, if you will, into the lowest depths of the ocean, where the water sleeps undisturbed and the very sand is motionless in unbroken quiet—but the glory of the Lord is there, revealing its excellence in the silent palace of the sea. Borrow the wings of the morning and fly to the uttermost parts of the sea—but God is there.

Nor on earth alone is God extolled, for His brightness shines forth in the skies above the earth and His glory exceeds the splendor of the starry heavens. Above the region of the stars He has immovably set His everlasting throne, and there He dwells in light indescribable. Let us adore Him who "alone stretches out the heavens and treads on the waves of the sea. He is the Maker of the Bear and Orion, the Pleiades and the constellations of the south" (Job 9:8–9).

CHARLES H. SPURGEON

DAY
7

The crowning glory of God

*I the LORD do not change. So you, O descendants of Jacob,
are not destroyed.*

(MALACHI 3:6)

DAY
8
~

T he crowning glory of God is that He never acts out of character. He never falls below His best, He cannot be false to His own blessed nature. Even if you were to come upon Him without clouds and darkness surrounding Him to confuse your mind, blur your vision, and tempt you to imagine things that are not there; if even once you were to meet Him face to face—then you know what He always is. You can depend upon that absolutely and forever.

The wonderful thing about Christ is that as people looked at Him, followed Him, and watched Him, it became apparent to them that this is what God must be like. They concluded that if there is a God at all, then He must have Christ's eyes, Christ's ways, Christ's ever-helpful hands, Christ's character.

Do not forget, says Scripture, that what God is, He always is. Stand upon Calvary and know that if today He loves like that, He always loves like that. Even when our hearts become hot and suspicious of Him or soured and bad tempered toward Him for His ordering of our lives and crossing our wishes, He still loves us.

To be God means always to stoop lower by far than any man could stoop, to bear what never a human heart would dream of bearing, to give Oneself with an abandon of unselfishness that leaves us staring in slackjawed wonder. His love is a hugeness beyond all human reckoning. It is an everlasting Calvary.

Our mood changes, our emotions cool; for us there come dreary seasons of gray skies and dripping spiritual weather. But God does not change. What we saw Him to be, He still is.

ARTHUR JOHN GOSSIP

The one who fills Heaven and Earth

"Can anyone hide in secret places so that I cannot see him?" declares the LORD.
"Do not I fill heaven and earth?" declares the LORD.

(JEREMIAH 23:24)

T here is nowhere in space, whether within or without creation, where God is not. The great God, the eternal, the almighty Spirit, is as limitless in His presence as in His existence and power.

In condescension to our limited understanding, He is said to dwell in heaven. But strictly speaking, the heaven of heavens cannot contain Him. He fills every part of His dominion. The universal God dwells in universal space, so that we may say,

DAY
9

> *Hail, FATHER! who creating all*
> *Unnumber'd worlds attend!*
> *JEHOVAH, comprehending all,*
> *Whom none can comprehend!*

What is the space occupied by a grain of sand, compared to that which is occupied by the starry heavens? It is as a cipher; it is nothing; it vanishes away in comparison.

And what is this grain of sand compared to the whole expanse of space? The whole creation itself, when seen in proportion with the universe, is infinitely less than a grain of sand. And yet this expanse of space, to which the whole creation bears no proportion at all, is infinitely less, in comparison to the great God, than a grain of sand, yes, even a millionth part of it!

This seems to be the plain meaning of those solemn words which God speaks of Himself: "Do I not fill heaven and earth?" God acts everywhere and therefore is everywhere. It is utterly impossible that any being, created or uncreated, should work where it is not. God acts in heaven, in earth, and under the earth—throughout the whole compass of His creation—by sustaining all things. Without Him, everything would in an instant sink into its primitive nothing.

JOHN WESLEY

one eternal now

*Before the mountains were born or you brought forth the earth
and the world, from everlasting to everlasting you are God.*

(PSALM 90:2)

When we reflect on the eternity of God, our tendency is to think that He has "lived a long time." That He is very old. That He has been around for ages. But Scripture says something very different from that. It says that God simply *is*.

With God, there is no succession of moments. There is neither future nor past. He sees everything as one eternal *now*. He can see the whole play of history—all of it—in action right now. He doesn't have to look back. He doesn't need to look ahead. He just sees it, with the end as much immediate to Him as the beginning.

Years ago I watched a football game. Nothing unusual about that—except it was projected at such an extreme speed that I saw the entire game in just *three minutes*. Players ricocheted up and down the field. Cheerleaders fluttered like tiny flags in a stiff breeze. The crowd boiled in the stands. Back and forth and back and forth—a blur of color—and it was over.

If you asked me, "Did you see the game?" I would have to answer, "Yes and no." It was all there, but I am built to comprehend a certain sequence of moments at a certain rate of passage. If you speed that up too fast or stretch it out too slow, I get frustrated. It loses reality for me. I'm not able to live that way.

But God is. God is eternal. In the infinity of His nature, He can see all the succession of moments of all time. He can grasp it all in one moment, without frustration and without effort. God can see all of history from the death of Christ to this very hour in an instant.

DAVID NEEDHAM

The fearful presence

*The LORD Almighty…is the one you are to fear,
he is the one you are to dread, and he will be a sanctuary.*

(ISAIAH 8:13–14)

God's presence is awesome—and not only His presence in general, but His special presence, even His most comfortable and joyous presence. When God comes to bring a soul news of mercy and salvation, even *that* visit, even *that* presence of God, is fearful.

When Jacob went from Beersheba toward Haran, along the way he met with God in a dream. In that dream he saw a ladder set upon the earth whose top reached to heaven. Now from the top of this dream ladder Jacob saw the Lord and heard Him speak to him—not threateningly, not as if the fury of God stormed into his face, but in the most sweet and gracious manner. In fact, the Lord greeted him with promise of goodness after promise of goodness, to a full eight or nine times (Genesis 28:10–17). Yet when Jacob awoke, all the grace he discovered through this heavenly vision could not keep him from dread and fear of God's Majesty:

DAY
11

> When Jacob awoke from his sleep, he thought, "Surely the LORD is in this place, and I was not aware of it." He was afraid and said, "How awesome is this place! This is none other than the house of God; this is the gate of heaven."

At another time Jacob had a memorable visit from God in which the Lord gave him power as a Prince to prevail with Him, and even gave him a name by which to better remember God's favor to him. Yet even then and there such dread of the Majesty of God fell upon him that he went away astonished that his life was preserved (Genesis 32:30).

Man crumbles to dust at the presence of God even though He shows Himself to us in His robes of salvation!

JOHN BUNYAN

A Hush and Tiptoe

Then Samuel called upon the LORD, and that same day the LORD sent thunder and rain. So all the people stood in awe of the LORD.

(1 SAMUEL 12:18)

My landlord in college worked for the electric company. He specialized in repairing the high-tension power cables transporting electricity between cities. As we talked one day, I remarked how dangerous his job sounded. He replied, "As long as you don't forget what you're handling, everything's fine."

Awe and majesty should breed something deeper in the heart of those who know God through Jesus Christ—something tragically missing in much of what passes for Christian worship. The closest thing to a biblical fear of God that many of us can muster is habitual distant respect. But God is no tame, benign presence. Scripture underscores that vividly:

> The fear of the LORD is the beginning of knowledge, but fools despise wisdom and discipline. (Proverbs 1:7)
> The LORD Almighty is the one you are to regard as holy, he is the one you are to fear, he is the one you are to dread. (Isaiah 8:13)
> I tell you, my friends, do not be afraid of those who kill the body and after that can do no more. But I will show you whom you should fear: Fear him who, after the killing of the body, has power to throw you into hell. Yes, I tell you, fear him. (Luke 12:4–5)
> It is a terrifying thing to fall into the hands of the living God. (Hebrews 10:31, NASB)

This is no craven fear that drives us to run and hide from God but a marveling that we inhabit His presence and live—a hush and tiptoe born of keen awareness of where we stand. To embrace God is to reach out to a pillar of living, holy fire. To approach Him in awe and holy fear shows that we see clearly.

DAVID SWARTZ

Three costly Errors

"To whom will you compare me? Or who is my equal?" says the Holy One....
Why do you say, O Jacob, and complain, O Israel, "My way is hidden from the
LORD; my cause is disregarded by my God"? Do you not know? Have you not heard?
The LORD is the everlasting God, the Creator of the ends of the earth.
He will not grow tired or weary.

(ISAIAH 40:25, 27–28)

To whom will you compare me? Or who is my equal?' says the Holy One" (Isaiah 40:25). This question rebukes *wrong thoughts about God.* "Your thoughts of God are too human," said Luther to Erasmus. This is where most of us go astray. Our thoughts of God are not great enough; we fail to reckon with the reality of His limitless wisdom and power. Because we ourselves are limited and weak, we imagine that at some points God is too, and find it hard to believe that He is not. Put this mistake right, says God; learn to acknowledge the full majesty of your incomparable God.

DAY
13

"Why do you say, O Jacob, and complain, O Israel, 'My way is hidden from the LORD; my cause is disregarded by my God'?" (40:27). This question rebukes *wrong thoughts about ourselves.* God has not abandoned us any more than He abandoned Job. He never abandons anyone on whom He has set His love. If you have been resigning yourself to the thought that God has left you high and dry, seek grace to be ashamed of yourself. Such unbelieving pessimism deeply dishonors our great God and Savior.

"Do you not know? Have you not heard? The LORD is the everlasting God, the Creator of the ends of the earth. He will not grow tired or weary" (40:28). This question rebukes *our slowness to believe in God's majesty.* God would shame us out of our unbelief. How slow we are to believe in God *as God,* sovereign, all-seeing, and almighty! How little we make of His majesty! The need for us is to "wait upon the Lord" in meditations of His majesty, till we find our strength renewed through the writing of these things upon our hearts.

J. I. PACKER

The Joy of sweaty palms

The LORD is exalted, for he dwells on high; he will fill Zion with justice and righteousness. He will be the sure foundation for your times, a rich store of salvation and wisdom and knowledge; the fear of the LORD is the key to this treasure.

(ISAIAH 33:5-6)

V isit a church on Sunday morning—almost any will do—and you will likely find a congregation comfortably relating to a deity who fits nicely within precise doctrinal positions, or who lends almighty support to social crusades, or who conforms to individual spiritual experiences. But you will not likely find much awe or sense of mystery. The only sweaty palms will be those of the preacher unsure whether the sermon will go over; the only shaking knees will be those of the soloist about to sing the offertory.

DAY
14

The New Testament warns us, "Worship God acceptably with reverence and awe, for our God is a consuming fire" (Hebrews 12:28–29). But reverence and awe have often been replaced by a yawn of familiarity. The consuming fire has been domesticated into a candle flame, adding a bit of religious atmosphere, perhaps, but no heat, no blinding light, no power for purification.

"Why do people in churches seem like cheerful, brainless tourists on a packaged tour of the Absolute?" asks Annie Dillard.

> Does anyone have the foggiest idea what sort of power we so blithely invoke? Or, as I suspect, does no one believe a word of it? The churches are children playing on the floor with the chemistry sets, mixing up a batch of TNT to kill a Sunday morning. It is madness to wear ladies' straw hats and velvet hats to church; we should all be wearing crash helmets. Ushers should issue life preservers and signal flares; they should lash us to our pews. For the sleeping god may wake some day and take offense, or the waking god may draw us out to where we can never return.

DONALD MCCULLOUGH

The Reality of God's presence

Then I heard every creature in heaven and on earth and under the earth and on the sea, and all that is in them, singing: "To him who sits on the throne and to the Lamb be praise and honor and glory and power, for ever and ever!"

(REVELATION 5:13)

What would happen if, on a given Sunday morning, the people in the congregation would suddenly have their eyes opened to the reality of God's presence, if they were to see the Lord sitting on the platform?

My feeling is that, before too long, numbers of people would quietly drop to their knees. Some might even stretch out prostrate before Christ.

Why? Because these body positions speak the universal language of worship. Even without words, such postures state the obvious: "You are worthy, Lord. I am only Your servant. But I do offer You my praise."

Awe, reverence, adoration, a holy fear, worship—all this is part of an immediate and natural response to our awareness of the Lord's presence in His church. How grateful we would be on that Sunday morning to have the choir sing the overflowing expression of our inner self:

DAY
15

God reveals His presence:
Let us now adore Him,
And with awe appear before Him.
God is in His temple:
All within keep silence,
Prostrate lie with deepest reverence.
Him alone
God we own,
Him our God and Saviour:
Praise His Name for ever!

God reveals His presence:
Hear the harps resounding;
See the crowds the throne surrounding;
"Holy, holy, holy!"
Hear the hymn ascending,
Angels, saints, their voices blending,
Bow Thine ear
To us here;
Hearken, O Lord Jesus,
To our meaner praises.

DAVID MAINS

Drinking in God's Attributes

All the angels were standing around the throne and around the elders and the four living creatures. They fell down on their faces before the throne and worshiped God, saying: "Amen! Praise and glory and wisdom and thanks and honor and power and strength be to our God for ever and ever. Amen!"

(REVELATION 7:11–12)

DAY
16

W hen we truly worship the Lord, we absorb His person. We drink in His attributes. In so doing, He realigns our reality and rearranges our perspective.

Most of us live life for a glory that fades. The next promotion. The big deal. A house or two. A car or three. Yet the glory of it all soon dissipates, a puff of mist gone when touched by the scorch of eternity. Scripture warns us that "all men are like grass, and all their glory is like the flowers of the field; the grass withers and the flowers fall, but the word of the Lord stands forever" (1 Peter 1:24–25).

But when through worship our minds focus on the eternal Lord of heaven, we see that our temporal days are not futile. Our time-shackled nights are not hopeless. The Ancient of Days numbers our days. It is He who transforms our fading glory into surpassing glory. He confirms the work of our hands and gives purpose to our existence. By reminding us that He has made us to live with Him forever, He gives us hope.

By the time Scripture crescendos in John's Revelation of Jesus Christ, the heavenly choir and orchestra are pregnant with worship. The basses boom in glory's basement. The sopranos skip through hallowed halls of majesty. The altos and the baritones blend harmony in the parlor of praise. The instruments of worship tune with the oil of gladness, anxious to express their joy. The conductor raises his hands. And in one swift motion he whisks the participants into a furious rendition. His baton crashes through stanza after stanza, announcing to an audience of starry skies, "The Lamb is worthy!"

Eternity will be filled with the echo of worship. Even now the heavenly host is getting ready. Are you?

RONALD L. JONES

The Excellencies of His Being

*And the twenty-four elders, who were seated on their thrones before God,
fell on their faces and worshiped God, saying: "We give thanks to you,
Lord God Almighty, the One who is and who was, because you have taken
your great power and have begun to reign."*

(REVELATION 11:16–17)

Worship flows from love. Where love is meager, worship will be scant. Where love is deep, worship will overflow. As Paul wrote his letters, his contemplation of the love and glory of God would spontaneously cause his heart to overflow in worship and doxology.

But there can be an element of selfishness even in love. True, we should worship God for the great things He has done for us, but our worship reaches a much higher level when we worship Him simply and solely for what He is, for the excellencies and perfections of His being.

DAY
17

Thomas Goodwin, the Puritan, said, "I have known men who came to God for nothing else but just to come to Him, they so loved Him. They scorned to soil Him and themselves with any other errand than just purely to be alone with Him in His presence." We might say with some justification that that is a little extreme, but it suggests an intimacy with God and desire for fellowship with Him that we might well covet.

Worship is the loving ascription of praise to God, for what He is in Himself and in His providential dealings. It is the bowing of our innermost spirit before Him in deepest humility and reverence.

David implored his soul: "My soul, wait in silence for God only" (Psalm 62:5, NASB). The deepest feelings often cannot find adequate expression in words. Between intimate friends there can be comfortable silences. There are times when words are unnecessary, or even an intrusion. So it is in our communication with God. Sometimes we are awed into silence in the presence of the Eternal.

J. OSWALD SANDERS

muscles to water

Dominion and awe belong to God; he establishes order in the heights of heaven.

(JOB 25:2)

I n the presence of God we may well experience what Mole felt (if I may draw on the wisdom of *The Wind in the Willows*) when a great awe fell upon him, "an awe that turned his muscles to water, bowed his head, and rooted his feet to the ground. It was no panic terror—indeed he felt wonderfully at peace and happy—but it was an awe that smote and held him, and without seeing, he knew it could only mean that some august Presence was very, very near."

DAY
18

A chapel service during my year at Wheaton College had an unforgettable impact on me. The speaker was Dr. V. Raymond Edman, beloved past president of the college. His health had been precarious, so it was a special moment when he stepped into the pulpit.

He wanted us to learn greater reverence before God. Worship is a serious matter, he told us. He recalled visiting Haile Selassie, then emperor of Ethiopia, and described the preliminary briefings, the protocol he had to follow, and the way he bowed with respect as he entered the presence of the king. In the same way, he said, we must prepare ourselves to meet God.

At that moment Dr. Edman slumped onto the pulpit, fell to the floor...and entered the presence of the King of kings. He was dead, but for a few moments we had come to life. The dividing line between heaven and earth suddenly dissolved, and we were no longer restless college students with textbooks on our laps, worried about exams the next hour and dates the next weekend; we had joined angels and archangels around the throne.

When we gather for worship, whether we are immediately aware of it or not, we're about to meet the Wholly Other.

DONALD McCULLOUGH

god is everything,
everything, everything

*Then the end will come, when he hands over the kingdom to God the Father after he
has destroyed all dominion, authority and power....
When he has done this, then the Son himself will be made subject to him who put
everything under him, so that God may be all in all.*

(1 CORINTHIANS 15:24, 28)

After Arturo Toscanini finished conducting a brilliant performance of Beethoven's Fifth Symphony, the audience
rose to its feet and applauded, shouting its delight. But
Toscanini waved his arms violently for it all to stop. He turned to the
orchestra and shouted hoarsely, "You are nothing!" He pointed to himself and shouted, "I am nothing!" Then he shouted, "Beethoven is
everything, everything, everything."

DAY
19

Christian worship must say, "God is everything, everything, everything." What we do on Sunday mornings (or whenever we gather), the
order of events and the manner in which we enact the drama, must
always point to God, must reinforce again and again that God has
taken the initiative and called us together, that God's grace is more
important than our sin, that God's will is more important than our
desires, and that God's glorification is more important than our edifi-
cation.

All worship ought to be ordered *toward* God; services should be
put together in a way that keeps our attention centered on God. As we
look up to the One seated on the throne, we lose sight of everything
else; the Holy God commands and consumes our attention. What we
really need when we show up for worship is for our attention to be
turned toward the glory of God. Only in turning toward the Light can
we do the dance, and only in this joyous but reverent dance before
the Holy One will our deepest needs be met, for only then will we
enter our full humanity as sons and daughters of God.

DONALD MCCULLOUGH

At The Edge of Mystery

O taste and see that the LORD is good.

(PSALM 34:8 NASB)

N o matter how long any of us have walked with God, we are all still beginners. We are still at the edge of mystery. Dare we imagine what lies ahead of us as we climb higher and see farther into the greatness, the wonder of this magnificent God—this God who has invited us to call Him "Father"?

How tragic if we allow the "eyes of our heart" to become dull and nearsighted. What unspeakable loss to allow the Christian life to become a boring, passive thing as the years go by. So many of us have seemed content to paddle around the edges of the comfortable little cove of understanding we've enjoyed all our lives, as though there were nothing more about God waiting to be discovered.

"The attributes of God? Oh, I learned all about that years ago. Heard it in a sermon series. Memorized some definitions for a class in Bible college. Covered it at a seminar. I don't need to go over that material again. I'm ready for something new."

Really? Listen, there is something about knowing God that transcends definitions and theological equations. The Bible tells us, "O taste and see that the LORD is good." And it invites us, "Come, all you who are thirsty, come to the waters;…come, buy and eat!…Listen to me, and eat what is good, and your soul will delight in the richest of fare" (Isaiah 55:1–2).

God, who is aware of the infinity of His person and the impossibility of our ever fully comprehending or describing or defining Him, says, *"Come taste Me!* Just taste Me, My son, My daughter. You'll see that I am good. And once you taste Me, you're not going to worry about definitions quite so much anymore."

DAVID NEEDHAM

utterly Delightful

Worship the LORD with gladness; come before him with joyful songs.
Know that the LORD is God.

(PSALM 100:2–3)

G od is so vastly wonderful, so utterly and completely delightful that He can, without anything other than Himself, meet and overflow the deepest demands of our total nature, mysterious and deep as that nature is. Hearts that are "fit to break" with love for the Godhead are those who have been in the Presence and have looked with opened eye upon the majesty of Deity. Men of breaking hearts had a quality about them not known to or understood by common men. They habitually spoke with spiritual authority. They had been in the Presence of God, and they reported what they saw there. They were prophets, not scribes, for the scribe tells us what he has read, and the prophet tells what he has seen.

The distinction is not an imaginary one. Between the scribe who has read and the prophet who has seen, there is a difference as wide as the sea. We are today overrun with orthodox scribes, but the prophets, where are they? The hard voice of the scribe sounds over evangelicalism, but the church waits for the tender voice of the saint who has penetrated the veil and has gazed with inward eye upon the Wonder that is God. And yet, to penetrate, to push in sensitive living experience into the holy Presence, is a privilege open to every child of God.

The world is perishing for lack of the knowledge of God, and the church is famishing for want of His Presence. The instant cure of most of our religious ills would be to enter the Presence, to become suddenly aware that we are in God and that God is in us. This would lift us out of our pitiful narrowness and cause our hearts to be enlarged.

A. W. TOZER

DAY
21

An Eternity of Discovery

*No eye has seen, no ear has heard, no mind has conceived what
God has prepared for those who love him.*

(1 CORINTHIANS 2:9)

God's glory—the total manifestation of all His attributes—is so unsearchable that it will take all eternity to discover. On earth we know of certain attributes of God, but they constitute only a small part of God's nature. Their function is to relate God's character to us while we are here on earth. Imagine what He is saving for us to discover throughout all eternity! Understanding His glory will become a never-ending adventure.

Suppose you go fishing at a quiet little pond. As you fish, you spend about ten minutes at each spot. After two hours you have fished the entire circumference of the pond, or at least you think you have. As you near the end, you see an outflow of the pond. Looking up in amazement, you see the ocean. All of a sudden you are involved with something that is unsearchable. You laugh over how small you feel in comparison. That little pond was just a small extension of the ocean. That is what God's glory is like. It is unsearchable.

The Bible begins and ends with God's glory. In Genesis we see His glory in creation. It is still true according to Psalm 19:1 that "The heavens *declare the glory of God.*" Any study of the universe, no matter how small the approach, will bring a person to glorify God in some way. God has made it that way. Man can study hydrology, astronomy, meteorology, geology, or even physiology and still find the amazing creative energy of God. God's creation is the greatest visible display of His glory. Yet it is merely a foretaste on earth of what will come later.

DAN DEHAAN

A state of astonished wonder

Oh, the depth of the riches of the wisdom and knowledge of God! How unsearchable
his judgments, and his paths beyond tracing out!
"Who has known the mind of the Lord? Or who has been his counselor?"
"Who has ever given to God, that God should repay him?" For from him and
through him and to him are all things. To him be the glory forever!

(ROMANS 11:33–36)

W hen the apostle Paul came to this point in his letter to the Romans, in effect he dropped his pen, threw up his hands and exclaimed, "Oh! What a God! Who can second-guess Him? Who can begin to grasp the vastness of His truth? Who can predict what He will do? Who can trace out His logic? Who can say, 'Now I've got Him all figured out'?"

DAY
23

This God we worship is most mysterious. Incomprehensible. He refuses to be impressed with our neat theological boxes, as though we could write down a list of statements about God, draw a circle around them, and say we have it all…as though His being and His ways could be bound by the limits of our intelligence.

"My thoughts are not your thoughts," God told Isaiah, "neither are your ways my ways…. As the heavens are higher than the earth, so are my ways higher than your ways and my thoughts than your thoughts" (55:8–9).

Not only is God higher than all our wisdom, but even "the *foolishness* of God is wiser than man's wisdom" (1 Corinthians 1:25, italics added). In other words, if God were capable of a stupid thought—if He were—that thought would be wiser than the wisest thought man has ever conceived.

So many of us struggle with pride at this very point. Somehow we feel we deserve to know and comprehend to the same degree God knows and comprehends. As though He owes us an explanation for His actions! Yet for all eternity, you and I will bow before a God who will always be greater than our greatest thought. His love, His patience, His holiness, His power, His purposes, and His wisdom will forever leave us in a state of astonished wonder.

DAVID NEEDHAM

Like Rafting in whitewater

The Spirit and the bride say, "Come!" And let him who hears say, "Come!"
Whoever is thirsty, let him come; and whoever wishes,
let him take the free gift of the water of life.

(REVELATION 22:17)

I love whitewater. Canoers, kayakers, and rafters can't always put it into words but know it instinctively: The thrill of the ride stands out. Interacting with nature-in-power breeds awe and reverence. This deepens as the paddler learns to read, and therefore respect, the water. Nobody ever really *beats* whitewater. Under that deep roar lies wild power that nothing can tame; it graciously rewards those who know it with almost life-transcending moments.

Embracing God is something like rafting in whitewater. Deeper than the thunder and the force of whitewater, God resonates throughout His being with a wild, fiery love. All those who long to embrace God should expect boulders and whitewater. Sometimes God is better found in turbulence than in security; calm may be a stagnant backwater for the faithless.

But those who embrace God are in for the ride of their life. In heaven we will join with others who made every kind of sacrifice, endured every kind of deprivation and suffering, and lived through every kind of abuse and torture. As we stand before Christ's throne ablaze in His righteousness, we will say, from every corner of the globe and in every language, that embracing Him was worth it.

Others may hold back, stick a toe in the water, or splash around with one bare foot to test the temperature. But let us plunge into God's grace and love that sweeps away into life abundant and eternal. Then we will disappear among the boulders and foam into Christ's embrace that stands open and will never close until we are safely enfolded in its depths.

DAVID SWARTZ

The Rock That Is Higher Than I

From the ends of the earth I call to you, I call as my heart grows faint;
lead me to the rock that is higher than I. For you have been my refuge,
a strong tower against the foe.

(PSALM 61:2–3)

T he world seems a little less crazy after a couple of days on top of a mountain. Those high country panoramas have a way of clearing my head and giving me fresh perspective. The world and its problems seem a little less overwhelming. Pressures seem somehow less pressing. Life begins to look manageable again.

That's why Psalm 61 remains a real favorite for me. I love it when David says, "lead me to the rock that is higher than I."

God is the Rock higher than you and I. And when our world presses in on us, when deadlines circle like vultures, when commitments cut into our shoulders like a ninety-pound pack, we need renewed perspective. We need a vantage point.

DAY
25

By spending time with God in the high places of His power and love, we can gain a better, wider view of our lives. He is the Mountain towering over our smoggy horizons. Life viewed from His heights can clear our minds, help us sort through priorities, and allow us to see how our days can be managed after all.

Maybe, like me, you've had one whirlwind of a month. You face demands from your family, frustrations at work, commitments at church, and expectations from friends. You feel your heart growing fainter with each added pressure.

You may not be able to take time off and head for the mountains (especially if you live in Kansas). But you can still climb that Rock so much higher than you.

Investing solid, concentrated time with your understanding Lord will give you a whole new outlook. From the summit of His love, you'll see things as they really are.

JONI EARECKSON TADA

glory: as close as
your next breath

*Now to him who is able to do immeasurably more than all we ask or imagine,
according to his power that is at work within us, to him be glory in the church and in
Christ Jesus throughout all generations, for ever and ever! Amen.*

(EPHESIANS 3:20–21)

G lory is what God is all about. Whenever we talk about His character or attributes—like holiness, love, compassion, justice, truth, or mercy—that's God's glory. When He reveals Himself in any of those qualities, we say that He is "glorifying Himself." And I have discovered He does this most often in the course of daily life, not in the blaze of a supernova.

DAY
26

Not long ago I entered a friend's home and immediately sensed the glory of God. My impression was not based on some heebie-jeebie feeling or superspiritual instinct, nor did it come from the Christian plaques I spotted hanging in the hallway. A peace and orderliness pervaded that home. Joy and music hung in the air. Although the kids were normal, active youngsters, everyone's activity seemed to dovetail—the home had direction, the kids really cared about each other, the parents put love into action.

After dinner I left that home refreshed. It was a place where God's essential being was on display. His kindness, His love, His justice. That home was filled with God's glory.

You and I glorify God every time we reveal His attributes in the course of our daily lives. His glory isn't reserved for a temple of stone or some heavenly vista. It can shine out clearly while we're changing a flat on the freeway, or counseling an angry coworker, or lying in a hospital bed, or balancing two crying babies in the church nursery. Whenever those around us see God's character displayed in our attitudes and responses, we are displaying His glory.

Far from being some spacey concept out of a theology text, *glory* is as close as your next breath, as real as a smile on a dark day, as warm as the clasp of a caring hand.

JONI EARECKSON TADA

Enjoying God's Being God

He determines the number of the stars, he gives to all of them their names.

(PSALM 147:4, RSV)

T he earth, where we live, is a small planet revolving around a star called the sun, which has a volume 1.3 million times that of the earth. There are about a hundred billion stars in our galaxy, the Milky Way, which is one hundred thousand light years across. The sun travels about 155 miles per second, and so it would take two hundred million years to make a single revolution on its orbit in the Milky Way. There are millions of other galaxies besides ours.

And yet God determined the number of all the stars. Not only that, He named them all. Like naming hamsters or puppies or bunnies. You look them over, note their distinctives, and then think up something to call them that fits.

Now what would impress a God like this? Psalm 147:10–11 (RSV) tells us very plainly:

> *His delight is not in the strength of the horse,*
> *nor his pleasure in the legs of a man;*
> *But the LORD takes pleasure in those who fear him,*
> *in those who hope in his steadfast love.*

Imagine some Olympic weightlifter feeling proud that he had picked up five hundred pounds. Or imagine some scientist feeling proud that he had figured out how some molecule is affected by another. It takes no genius to know that God is not impressed.

The good news for those who enjoy God's being God is that *He* enjoys *them*. He delights in those who hope in His immeasurable power. O, may the truth grip us that God is God and that He works omnipotently for those who wait for Him (Isaiah 64:4), hope in Him (Psalm 147:11), and love Him (Romans 8:28). He loves to be God for the weak and childlike, who look to Him for all they need.

JOHN PIPER

no sacrifice too great

Even Lebanon is not enough to burn, nor its beasts enough for a burnt offering.

(ISAIAH 40:16, NASB)

T he closer we draw to God, the more we are awed by His greatness and majesty. The prophet Isaiah recorded how his vision of the transcendent God affected him: "Woe is me, for I am ruined!…for my eyes have seen the King, the LORD of hosts" (Isaiah 6:5, NASB). The Lord graciously cleansed him, drew him into a closer intimacy than he had ever before experienced, and entrusted him with amazing insight into the divine character.

In the latter half of his prophecy, Isaiah depicted to the discouraged exiles a God who is incredibly great and majestic, but who yearns over His people and tenderly woos them back into fellowship with Himself.

Isaiah 40 has been termed one of the noblest pieces of prose ever created. It combines in a unique way a simplicity and majesty that compels us to realize the inadequacy of our conception of God. Its theme, the awesome transcendence and tender love of God, is worthily expressed in the Swedish hymn:

> *Oh Lord my God, when I in awesome wonder,*
> *Consider all the worlds Thy hands have made,*
> *I see the stars, I hear the rolling thunder,*
> *Thy power throughout the universe displayed:*
> *Then sings my soul, my Savior God to Thee,*
> *How great Thou art!*

What adequate and worthy response can we make to a God so great, so holy, so transcendent? Isaiah 40:16 tells us that using all the cedars of Lebanon to kindle an altar fire to consume all the cattle on its slopes, would be no extravagance. Our debt to Him is so great that no conceivable sacrifice would be too great to make for Him, since sacrifice is "the ecstasy of giving the best we have to the One we love the most."

J. OSWALD SANDERS

starving for the greatness of god

*In the year that king Uzziah died I saw the LORD sitting upon a throne, high
and lifted up; and his train filled the temple. Above him stood the seraphim; each
had six wings: with two he covered his face, and with two he covered his feet, and
with two he flew. And one called to another and said:
"Holy, holy, holy is the LORD of hosts; the whole earth is full of his glory."*

(ISAIAH 6:1-3, RSV)

P eople are starving for the greatness of God. But most of
them would not give this diagnosis of their troubled lives.
The majesty of God is an unknown cure. There are far
more popular prescriptions on the market, but the benefit of any
other remedy is brief and shallow. Solutions that do not have the
aroma of God's greatness may entertain for a season, but they will not
touch the hidden cry of the soul: "Show me Thy glory!"

DAY
29

Years ago during the January prayer week at our church, I decided
to preach on the holiness of God from Isaiah 6. I did my best to display
the majesty and glory of such a great and holy God. I gave not one
word of application to the lives of the people. Application is essential
in the normal course of preaching, but I felt led that day to make a
test: Would the passionate portrayal of the greatness of God in and of
itself meet the needs of people?

Not long before this Sunday one of the families of our church discovered their child was being sexually abused by a close relative. They
were there that Sunday and heard that message. Some weeks later the
husband took me aside and said, "John, these have been the hardest
months of our lives. Do you know what has gotten me through? The
vision of the greatness of God's holiness that you gave me the first
week of January. It has been the rock we could stand on."

The greatness and the glory of God *are* relevant. It does not matter if surveys turn up a list of perceived needs that does not include
the supreme greatness of the sovereign God of grace. That is the deepest need. People are starving for God.

JOHN PIPER

seeing the unseen god

Blessed are the pure in heart, for they will see God.

(MATTHEW 5:8)

T hough the Bible speaks of the "face" of God, it uses the term figuratively. To speak of God's face is to describe Him in human terms. In reality, God has no face. He has no lips, nose, eyebrows, forehead, or ears. He is the "immortal, invisible, the only God" (1 Timothy 1:17).

When Jesus promised that the pure in heart would see God, He did not mean that it would be a physical perception. No optic nerve is potent enough to enable a human being, even a glorified human being, to physically perceive the invisible God. The promise of the beatific vision is not to those with strong eyes but to those with pure hearts. It is the pure in heart, and only the pure in heart, who receive the promise: "Blessed are the pure in heart; for they will see God."

In the enjoyment of this beatific vision the soul finally reaches the goal of its supreme quest. At last we enter into that haven where we find our peace and rest. The warfare between flesh and spirit ends. Peace that transcends anything in this world fills the heart. We reach heights of excellency and sweetness only dreamed of in this mortal flesh. We shall see Him as He is. No veil, no shield will hide His face. The immediate and direct vision will flood the soul from the well-spring on high. The highest joy, the greatest pleasure, the purest delight will be ours without mixture and without end.

One taste of this felicity will erase all painful memories and heal each dreadful wound. No scar will remain. The pilgrim's progress will be complete. The body of death, the burden of sin, will vaporize the moment we behold His face.

R. C. SPROUL

choosing the other world

Whoever has my commands and obeys them, he is the one who loves me. He who loves me will be loved by my Father, and I too will love him and show myself to him.

(JOHN 14:21)

I f we truly want to follow God we must seek to be other-worldly. This I say knowing well that that word has been used with scorn and applied to the Christian as a badge of reproach. So be it. Every man must choose his world.

If we who follow Christ deliberately choose the Kingdom of God as our sphere of interest, I see no reason why anyone should object. If we lose by it, the loss is our own; if we gain, we rob no one by so doing. The "other world," which is the object of this world's disdain and the subject of mocking song, is our carefully chosen goal and the object of our holiest longing.

DAY
31

As we begin to focus upon God, the things of the spirit will take shape before our inner eyes. Obedience to the word of Christ will bring an inward revelation of the Godhead (John 14:21–23). It will give acute perception enabling us to see God even as is promised to the pure in heart. A new God-consciousness will seize upon us, and we shall begin to taste and hear and inwardly feel the God who is our life and our all. There will be seen the constant shining of the light that lighteth every man that cometh into the world. More and more, as our faculties grow sharper and more sure, God will become to us the great All, and His Presence the glory and wonder of our lives.

> *O God, quicken to life every power within me,*
> *that I may lay hold on eternal things.*
> *Open my eyes that I may see; enable me to taste Thee*
> *and know that Thou art good.*
> *Make heaven more real to me than any*
> *earthly thing has ever been.*
> *Amen.*

A. W. TOZER

THE HOLINESS
OF GOD

WHO WILL NOT FEAR YOU,

O LORD, AND BRING GLORY

TO YOUR NAME?

FOR YOU ALONE ARE HOLY.

REVELATION 15:4

The separate one

Holy, holy, holy is the Lord God Almighty, who was, and is, and is to come.

(REVELATION 4:8)

Holy is the most intimately divine word in the Bible. It is that attribute in God which marks Him off as God. To say that He is holy is to say that He is God. Holiness, in Scripture, is the fundamental attribute of God that conditions and qualifies all other attributes.

Holy apparently comes from a Semitic root that means "to cut." Hence its most basic meaning is "to separate" or "to make distinct" (as in "to cut off"). Most fundamentally, as a divine attribute it claims that God is other and set apart from everything else, that He is in a class by Himself. God is not just quantitatively greater than us, but qualitatively different in His greatness. He is transcendent, infinitely above or beyond us. The true God is distinct, set apart, from all that He has made as the only truly self-sufficient Being. All His creatures depend on Him; He alone exists from within Himself.

DAY
32

And the true God is distinct, set apart, from all that is evil. His moral perfection is absolute. His character as expressed in His will forms the absolute standard of moral excellence. God is holy, the absolute point of reference for all that exists and is good. Across the board He is to be contrasted with His creatures. At heart He is a glowing white center of absolute purity.

The Holy One is high and exalted, great beyond our imagining, the uncreated Creator of all that is, the sovereign Lord of all. Further, the Holy One is perfect in goodness, a lover of justice and righteousness whose wrath goes out against all that is evil and whose mercy reaches out to deliver the poor, the helpless, and the needy. As such He alone is worthy of the praise of all His creatures.

THOMAS L. TREVETHAN

fourfold Holiness

Who among the gods is like you, O LORD? Who is like you—majestic in holiness,
awesome in glory, working wonders?

(EXODUS 15:11)

H oliness, the characteristic of God that sets Him apart from His creation, has at least four elements.

The first is *majesty*. Majesty is "dignity," "stateliness," or "grandeur." It is the proper characteristic of monarchs and is supremely the attribute of the One who is Monarch over all. The element of majesty links the idea of holiness to sovereignty.

Second is *will*. Apart from this the idea of holiness becomes abstract, impersonal, and static, rather than concrete, personal, and active. God's will is predominantly set on proclaiming Himself as the "Wholly Other," whose glory must never be slighted by human arrogance and willful rebellion. God is not indifferent to how men and women regard Him. He does not go His solitary way heedless of their rejection of Him. Rather, He wills and acts to see that His glory is recognized.

Third is *wrath*. Wrath is an essential part of God's holiness, but we must not compare it to the human emotion of anger. It is, rather, the necessary and proper stance of a holy God to all that opposes Him. It means that He takes the matter of being God so seriously that He will not allow any thing or personality to aspire to His place. When Satan sought to do that, Satan was judged (and will yet be judged). When men and women refuse to take the place that God has given to them, they will be judged also.

Last is *righteousness*. When we ask, "What is right? What is moral?" we answer not by appealing to some independent moral standard, as if there could be a standard for anything apart from God, but rather by appealing to the will and nature of God Himself. The right is what God is and reveals to us.

JAMES MONTGOMERY BOICE

DAY
33

The god-ness of god

Your ways, O God, are holy.
What god is so great as our God?

(PSALM 77:13)

Holy is the word which the Bible uses to express all that is distinctive and transcendent in the revealed nature and character of the Creator, all that brings home to us the infinite distance and difference that there is between Him and ourselves. Holiness in this sense means, quite comprehensively, the "God-ness" of God, everything about Him which sets Him apart from man.

When God is called "holy," the thought conveyed is of those qualities of deity which mark out the infinite superiority of the Triune Jehovah over mankind, in respect to both powers and perfections. The Word points to God as standing above and apart from men, a different kind of being on a higher plane of existence. It focuses attention on everything in God that makes Him a proper object of awe and worship and relevant fear, and that serves to remind His human creatures how ungodlike they really are.

Thus, it denotes, *first,* God's infinite greatness and power, contrasted with the smallness and weakness of men and women; *second,* it denotes His perfect purity and uprightness, which stands in glaring contrast with the unrighteousness and uncleanness of sinful humanity, and which call forth from Him that inflexible retributive reaction to sin which the Bible calls His "wrath" and "judgment"; *third,* it denotes His determination to maintain His own righteous rule, however much it may be resisted and opposed—a resolve which makes it certain that all sin will eventually receive its due reward. The biblical idea of God's holiness involves all this.

J. I. PACKER

Nothing so positive

Holy and awesome is his name.

(PSALM 111:9)

DAY
35

W hen we call God holy, the central idea concerns His absolute and complete separation from sin and uncleanness. Not that the idea is primarily negative. There is no idea so positive as that of holiness; it is the very climax of positiveness, simply because this idea is above any synonym we might choose. Holiness is more than sinlessness, though it, of course, includes the idea of sinlessness. It is more than righteousness, although again it includes the idea of righteousness. It is more than wholeness, complete soundness and integrity and rightness, though, of course, again it includes these ideas. It is more than high simplicity and guilelessness, though it includes this too. It is more than purity, though, of course, it includes this too.

Holiness includes all these and more. It is God's whole, entire, absolute, inconceivable, and, therefore, inexpressible completeness and perfection of separation from and opposition to and indescribable revulsion of all that is evil in any sense or degree.

We fall back at last on this negative description of holiness just because language has no positive word which can reach up to the unscalable heights of this one highest word, holiness. It is the crown of God, as mercy is His treasure; as grace is His riches, this is His glory. Who is like God, majestic in holiness?

The holiness of God is a conception peculiar to the religion of the Bible. None of the gods of the nations was like our God in this, the crown and climax of His glory. But it is just this perfection that He calls us to imitate. It is just His exhibition of this glory that He trusts to create in us an unquenchable thirst to be like Him.

BENJAMIN B. WARFIELD

The Door Unlocked

The Mighty One has done great things for me—holy is his name.

(LUKE 1:49)

God's holiness unlocks the door to understanding and making sense out of everything else about Him. This attribute infiltrates all the other attributes. His love is holy love. His omniscience is holy omniscience. His omnipresence is holy omnipresence. Everything has been infiltrated by this defining attribute of God called holiness.

God even calls Himself by that name. Throughout the Old and New Testaments He is called "The Holy One." When Mary was reciting her praise to God at the news that she would be the mother of the Savior, she said in Luke 1:49: "The Mighty One has done great things for me—holy is his name."

If we are going to be serious about walking with God, we have to understand who He is and who we are in light of Him. We must go low because He sits high. We must hallow His name. We must worship Him seriously. We must stop playing church, stop playing Christianity.

God's holiness is central to understanding who and what He is. Nowhere in Scripture is God called "love, love, love"; "eternal, eternal, eternal"; or "truth, truth, truth." He is never emphatically called by any name except one: "Holy, holy, holy is the LORD Almighty" (Isaiah 6:3). Whenever you see three words like this, you are reading an emphatic statement that shouts, "This is a centerpiece, this is key, this is something you don't want to miss."

God swears by His holiness (Psalm 89:35). Why? Because it is the fullest expression of His character, because it fully explains who He is. The Bible declares that God is holy in all of His being (Leviticus 19:2). Holiness is the defining point of God's character. At the heart of who God is, is His holiness.

TONY EVANS

scintillating Light

God is light; in him there is no darkness at all.

(1 JOHN 1:5)

S uddenly the screen went stark white. And it stayed white for five or six seconds. It was 1970 and I was watching a film, but my thoughts flashed back to the original event, captured by ultra high-speed cameras protected by concrete bunkers and leaded glass. Only milliseconds before, there had been ships in a lagoon formed by a coral atoll called Bikini. Now there was only blinding light. Some of the ships, part of the sea, and one of the little islands were vaporized in a flash of awesome whiteness.

DAY
37

The film was taken in 1954 when the first hydrogen fusion weapon was tested in the South Pacific. The whiteness of that screen remains, for me, the most powerful illustration of the way biblical writers express God's holiness:

God is light; in him there is no darkness at all. (1 John 1:5)

God, the blessed and only Ruler, the King of kings and Lord of lords, who alone is immortal and who lives in unapproachable light. (1 Timothy 6:15–16)

Our God is a consuming fire. (Hebrews 12:29)

God's moral purity—His inherent personal righteousness and holiness—is symbolized in Scripture as light: blinding, unending, undiminishing, dazzling whiteness. Even the newest believer has read in John 1:5 that with the coming of the Lord Jesus, the light of God was made to shine in the darkness on this island in space called earth. But few of us consider the implications of God's light for human holiness. As John 1:5 goes on to say, "The darkness has not understood it." Comprehending holiness is difficult, yet life changing.

God is *not* a crotchety, self-righteous prude who delights in never doing anything wrong. He is a living, dynamic Being actively involved in making wrong right. He is scintillating light.

W. BINGHAM HUNTER

The Beauty of Holiness

There is no one holy like the LORD.

(1 SAMUEL 2 : 2)

O f all the perfections of God, none is more worthy of His nature and so uniquely admirable as His infinite purity. God's holiness outshines every other attribute and gives a luster to all the rest.

Without holiness, wisdom degenerates into craft, power into tyranny, and mercy loses its nature. God swears by holiness as His supreme excellency: "Once for all, I have sworn by my holiness—and I will not lie to David" (Psalm 89:35). Holiness is the most revered divine attribute, and heaven praises God for it in joyful harmony. The angels and saints both are reported to express their ecstasy and rapture at the beauty of God's holiness: "Holy, holy, holy is the LORD Almighty; the whole earth is full of his glory" (Isaiah 6:3; see Revelation 4:8).

DAY
38

It is this attribute alone which God especially loves and values in His creatures. Why? Because it alone mirrors His most divine and sweet perfection. Inferior creations may reflect other divine attributes: the winds and thunder display God's power; the ancient rocks and the enduring vastness of the heavens offer a vague and incomplete impression of His unchanging nature. But holiness, the most priceless pearl in the crown of heaven, shines only in creatures of reason. That is why man alone is said to be formed in the image of God.

Of course, there are men who reflect other attributes of God who yet are not entitled to His special love. Princes may reflect a shadow of His sovereignty, even as they are objects of His displeasure. But anyone who reflects even a small measure of God's holiness at once attracts His eye and heart. The one who partakes of God's holiness finds himself infinitely endeared to the Holy One.

REV. W. BATES

angry at evil

Your eyes are too pure to look on evil; you cannot tolerate wrong.

(HABAKKUK 1:13)

G od is angry at evil.

For many, this is a revelation. Some assume God is a harried high school principal, too busy monitoring the planets to notice us.

He's not.

Others assume He is a doting parent, blind to the evil of His children.

Wrong.

Still others insist He loves us so much, He cannot be angry at our evil.

They don't understand that love is *always* angry at evil.

Many don't understand God's anger because they confuse the wrath of God with the wrath of man. The two have little in common. Human anger is typically self-driven and prone to explosions of temper and violent deeds. We get ticked off because we've been overlooked, neglected, or cheated. This is the anger of man. It is not, however, the anger of God.

God doesn't get angry because He doesn't get His way. He gets angry because disobedience always results in self-destruction. What kind of father sits by and watches his child hurt himself?

What kind of God would do the same? Do we think He giggles at adultery or snickers at murder? Do we think He looks the other way when we produce television talk shows based on perverse pleasures? Does He shake His head and say, "Humans will be humans"?

I don't think so. Mark it down and underline it in red. God is rightfully angry. God is a holy God. Our sins are an affront to His holiness. His eyes "are too pure to look on evil; [He] cannot tolerate wrong" (Habakkuk 1:13).

God is angry at the evil that ruins His children. "As long as God is God," Anders Nygren wrote in his *Commentary on Romans,* "He cannot behold with indifference that His creation is destroyed and His holy will trodden underfoot."

MAX LUCADO

good, not safe

Our God is a consuming fire.

(HEBREWS 12:29)

G od is definitely not safe. To appear before the Wholly Other with steady knees—well, it would be foolhardy, to say the least. In the presence of this One, human indifference gets slapped to alert attention and human pretension gets knocked on its backside. One may appear before other gods with confidence, with no sense of being threatened. They will stay put; they don't stray from places assigned to them by human egos desperately trying to maintain control. But the God revealed in Jesus Christ is holy, and a holy God cannot be contained or tamed.

"Our God is a consuming fire." As children we were told not to play with matches, and as adults we treat fire with caution. We must. Fire demands respect for its regal estate: It will not be touched; it will be approached with care; and it wields its scepter for ill or for good. With one spark it can condemn a forest to ashes and a home to memory as ghostly as the smoke rising from the charred remains of the family album. Or with a single flame it can crown a candle with power to warm a romance and set to dancing a fireplace blaze that defends against the cold. Fire is dangerous, to be sure, but we cannot live without it; fire destroys but also sustains life.

The blaze of God's holiness admits no disrespect; its boundaries cannot be trespassed. But this very distinctness is the fire that thaws our frozen hearts, the fire that draws us into relationship with God and one another, the fire that cleanses even as it purges.

God is *not* safe—but God is good, very good.

DONALD McCULLOUGH

NO HUMAN INVENTION

"You thought I was altogether like you.
But I will rebuke you and accuse you to your face. Consider this, you who forget
God, or I will tear you to pieces, with none to rescue."

(PSALM 50:21-22)

Unbelievers do not really believe in the holiness of God. Their conception of His character is altogether one-sided. They fondly hope that His mercy will override everything else. "You thought I was altogether like you," God scolds them (Psalm 50:21). They think only of a "god" patterned after their own evil hearts and so they continue in a course of mad folly.

DAY
41

But the holiness ascribed to God in the Scriptures clearly demonstrates its superhuman origin. The character attributed to the "gods" of the ancients and of modern non-Christian religions is the very opposite of that immaculate purity which belongs to the true God. None of Adam's fallen descendants ever invented an inexpressibly holy God who utterly abhors all sin! The fact is that nothing makes more obvious the terrible depravity of the human heart and human hatred for the living God than to have set before it One who is infinitely and unchangeably holy. Our own idea of *sin* is practically limited to what the world calls "crime." Anything short of that, mankind sugarcoats as "defects," "mistakes," "weakness," etc. And even where sin is admitted, excuses and extenuations are made for it. The "god" which many professing Christians love is very much like an indulgent old man who leniently winks at the "indiscretions" of youth.

But the Word says of God, "You hate all who do wrong" (Psalm 5:5). And again, God "expresses his wrath every day" (Psalm 7:11). Still men and women refuse to believe in *this* God and gnash their teeth when His hatred of sin is faithfully brought to their attention.

The truth is, sinful man was no more likely to devise a holy God than to create the lake of fire in which he will be tormented forever and ever.

ARTHUR W. PINK

what god expects

"I am the LORD your God; consecrate yourselves and be holy, because I am holy."

(LEVITICUS 11:44)

W hen the Israelites accepted God's covenant, God again called Moses to the mountaintop where He made one of the most remarkable promises in the Bible: "I will consecrate the Tent of Meeting and the altar and…I will dwell among the Israelites" (Exodus 29:44–45). What a staggering thought! The sovereign God of the universe promised to pitch His tent, *actually* to dwell in the midst of His chosen people.

Many are tempted to skip over these chapters of Exodus and Leviticus that describe in such detail the construction of the tabernacle, the forms of worship, and the like. Altars and acacia wood and cubits sound irrelevant today, superseded by the atonement of Christ. But this is a perfect example of the necessity of taking the Word of God in its entirety. For the prescriptions for the place wherein God was to dwell and be worshiped reveal the very character of God Himself.

DAY
42

The tabernacle reflects a holy God, a God set apart, unique, utterly unstained by the sin of the world. No wonder God specified rules of cleanliness for those who worshiped there. It was not because He had some obsession with personal hygiene, but because in every way possible His people were to be clean, set apart—holy—as they entered to worship in the place where He, a holy God, *actually* dwelt.

This is indeed the very heart of the relationship God demands with His people, expressed in the covenant: "I am the LORD your God; consecrate yourselves and *be holy, because I am holy"* (Leviticus 11:44, italics added). Understanding this basic covenant, the character of God, and what He expects is essential to understanding the New Covenant. For the character of God has not changed, nor has His expectation of holiness from His people.

CHARLES COLSON

the way god is

Do not profane my holy name. I must be acknowledged as holy by the Israelites.
I am the LORD, who makes you holy.

(LEVITICUS 22:32)

U ntil we have seen ourselves as God sees us, we are not likely to be much disturbed over conditions around us. We have learned to live with unholiness and have come to look upon it as the natural and expected thing. We are not disappointed that we do not find all truth in our teachers or faithfulness in our politicians or complete honesty in our merchants or full trustworthiness in our friends. That we may continue to exist, we make such laws as are necessary to protect us from our fellow men and let it go at that.

DAY
43

Neither the writer nor the reader of these words is qualified to appreciate the holiness of God. Quite literally a new channel must be cut through the desert of our minds to allow the sweet waters of truth that will heal our great sickness to flow in. We cannot grasp the true meaning of the divine holiness by thinking of someone or something very pure and then raising the concept to the highest degree possible. God's holiness is not simply the best we know, infinitely bettered. We know nothing like the divine holiness. It stands apart, unique, unapproachable, incomprehensible, and unattainable. The natural man is blind to it. He may fear God's power and admire His wisdom, but His holiness he cannot even imagine.

Holy is the way God is. To be holy He does not conform to a standard. He *is* that standard. He is absolutely holy with an infinite, incomprehensible fullness of purity that is incapable of being other than it is. Because He is holy, all His attributes are holy; that is, whatever we think of as belonging to God must be thought of as holy.

A. W. TOZER

A strong but Necessary word

To fear the LORD is to hate evil.

(PROVERBS 8:13)

Hate is such a strong word we dislike using it. We reprove our children for saying they hate someone. Yet when it comes to God's attitude toward sin, only a strong word such as *hate* conveys an adequate depth of meaning. Speaking of various sins in Israel, God says, "I hate all this" (Zechariah 8:17). Hatred is a legitimate emotion when it comes to sin. Because God is holy, He hates sin.

We often say, "God hates the sin but loves the sinner." This is blessedly true, but too often we quickly rush over the first half of this statement to get to the second. We cannot escape the fact that God hates our sins. We may trifle with our sins or excuse them, but God hates them.

DAY
44

Therefore every time we sin, we are doing something God hates. He hates our lustful thoughts, our pride and jealousy, our outbursts of temper, and our rationalization that the end justifies the means. We need to be gripped by the fact that God hates all these things. We become so accustomed to our sins we sometimes lapse into a state of peaceful coexistence with them, but God never ceases to hate them. God, being infinitely holy, has an infinite hatred of sin.

We need to cultivate in our own hearts the same hatred of sin God has. The more we ourselves grow in holiness, the more we too hate sin. David said, "I gain understanding from your precepts; therefore I hate every wrong path" (Psalm 119:104). As we grow in holiness, we grow in hatred of sin. Hatred of sin as sin, not just as something disquieting or defeating to ourselves but displeasing to God, lies at the root of all true holiness.

JERRY BRIDGES

Holiness upon the Throne

The LORD reigns, let the nations tremble;…he is holy…he is holy…
for the LORD our God is holy.

(PSALM 99:1, 3, 5, 9)

DAY
45

T he LORD reigns, let the nations tremble," writes the psalmist. Why? "He is holy," answers the first stanza. "He is holy," answers the second stanza. "For the LORD our God is holy," answers the third stanza. Put the two statements together, "The LORD reigns…the LORD our God is holy," and what do you get? You get *holiness upon the throne.*

To believe that God is on the throne, working out His own holy and perfect and acceptable will, maintaining and asserting the eternal law of righteousness—is there not enough in that to fill the hearts of sinful men with "godly fear"? Is there not enough in that to make us "tremble"?

We are constantly deploring our lack of the sense of sin. Is that because we have obscured God's holiness? Sometimes I wonder whether the very emphasis we have laid on the tenderness and gentleness and patience of God's fatherly love has made it easy for men to sin. We have made God's forgiveness so cheap that sin has come to appear a light and trivial matter.

If that is so, let us this day remind ourselves of the holiness of God; let us lift up our eyes to the shining peaks of His "awful purity." Let us remind ourselves that this Holy God is on the throne—and that He is on the throne to maintain purity and righteousness. The Will that rules is a holy will. The Power that governs is a holy power.

All who sin bring themselves into collision with the sovereign will and power of the universe. No wonder our Lord said, "Whosoever shall fall on this stone shall be broken, but on whomsoever it shall fall, it will grind him to powder" (Matthew 21:44, KJV).

JOHN DANIEL JONES

The Facts of Existence

*Go into the rocks, hide in the ground from dread of
the LORD and the splendor of his majesty!*

(ISAIAH 2:10)

C hristian appreciation for God's astounding gift of love, forgiveness, and reconciliation in Christ has been allowed to
consume the awesome reality of His terrible holiness. God
has become our "buddy." It seems foreign to speak about God as
Isaiah did.

We have turned statements about freedom to speak openly during prayer (what the New Testament calls "confidence") into license
for flippancy, and we have made remarks about the privilege of access
to God through Christ (what the New Testament calls "boldness") into
sanctions for arrogance. Somehow we have forgotten that Jesus, who
taught us to call God *Abba* (Dear Father), also called Him *Holy* Father,
Righteous Father and *Lord* of heaven and earth.

Many of the arguments against holy terror are based on faulty
theological systems ("the 'fearful' image of God belongs to the dispen-
sation of Law"), imprecise exegesis ("God has not given us a spirit of
fear"), or the existence of psychopathology ("some Christians do have
phobias about God"). But without a sense of God's awesome holiness,
and the consequent "fear," we simply do not have biblical religion,
either positively—"The fear of the LORD is the beginning of wisdom"
(Psalm 111:10)—or negatively—"Concerning the sinfulness of the
wicked: There is no fear of God before his eyes" (Psalm 36:1).

Fearing God is not irrational. It is the only course open to a
thinking Christian. Those who do not fear God in the biblical sense
either do not understand, or find themselves forced to deny, the facts
of existence.

W. BINGHAM HUNTER

DAY
46

No place for mocking

Among those who approach me I will show myself holy;
in the sight of all the people I will be honored.

(LEVITICUS 10:3)

T he holiness of God must fill us with a sense of our uncleanness and deepen our humiliation. When Isaiah heard the seraphim cry, "Holy, holy, holy is the LORD Almighty; the whole earth is full of his glory" (Isaiah 6:3), he said, "Woe to me!...I am ruined! For I am a man of unclean lips, and I live among a people of unclean lips, and my eyes have seen the King, the LORD Almighty" (v. 5).

The holiness of God must cause us to walk continually in the fear of the Lord and to take careful inventory of all the complex desires of our hearts—and even to how we behave when we come near to Him in holy worship. Remember what happened to the Bethshemites for looking irreverently into the holy ark (1 Samuel 6:19), and to Uzzah for merely touching it! And what a dreadful example is that of the two sons of Aaron, who were slain by a devouring fire from the LORD for offering unauthorized fire before Him (Leviticus 10:1–2). Remember, too, that immediately afterward Aaron was awed into silence when God told him, "Among those who approach me I will show myself holy; in the sight of all the people I will be honored."

Be careful that you bring neither irreverence, nor deadness, nor cold, heartless, worldly service before a holy God. Beware of hypocritical, carnal worship! The holy God will not be mocked with compliments and shows.

RICHARD BAXTER

DAY
47

# of Greenland Glaciers

The LORD takes pleasure in those who fear him,
in those who hope in his steadfast love.

(PSALM 147:11, RSV)

Does it strike you as strange that we should be encouraged to *fear* and *hope* at the same time and in the same person? It's usually the other way around: If we fear a person, we hope that someone *else* will come and help us. But here we are supposed to fear the one we hope in and hope in the one we fear. What does this mean?

Suppose you were exploring an unknown Greenland glacier in the dead of winter. Just as you reach a sheer cliff with a spectacular view of miles of jagged ice and mountains of snow, a terrible storm breaks in. The wind is so strong that the fear rises in your heart that it might blow you over the cliff. But in the midst of the storm you discover a cleft in the ice where you can hide. Here you feel secure. But, even though secure, the awesome might of the storm rages on, and you watch it with a kind of trembling pleasure as it surges out across the distant glaciers. Not everything we call fear vanishes from your heart, only the life-threatening part. There remains the trembling, the awe, the wonder, the feeling that you would never want to tangle with such a storm or be the adversary of such a power.

DAY
48

And so it is with God. The fear of God is what is left of the storm when you have a safe place to watch right in the middle of it. Hope turns fear into a trembling and peaceful wonder; and fear takes everything trivial out of hope and makes it earnest and profound. The terrors of God make the pleasures of His people intense. The fireside fellowship is all the sweeter when the storm is howling outside the cottage.

JOHN PIPER

Dangerous Thinking

But just as he who called you is holy, so be holy in all you do; for it is written:
"Be holy, because I am holy."

(1 PETER 1:15–16)

I n the deceitfulness of our hearts, we sometimes play with temptation by entertaining the thought that we can always later confess and ask forgiveness. Such thinking is exceedingly dangerous. God's judgment is without partiality. He never overlooks our sin. He never decides not to bother since the sin is only a small one. No, God hates sin intensely whenever and wherever He finds it, in saint and sinner alike.

DAY
49

David was a man after God's own heart (Acts 13:22), yet after his sin against Uriah, he was told, "Now, therefore, the sword will never depart from your house" (2 Samuel 12:10). Moses, for one act of unbelief, was excluded from the land of Canaan despite many years of faithful service. Jonah, for his disobedience, was cast into a horrible prison in the stomach of a giant fish for three days and nights, that he might learn not to run from the command of God.

Frequent contemplation on the holiness of God and His consequent hatred of sin is a strong deterrent against trifling with sin. We are told to live our lives on earth as strangers in reverence and fear (1 Peter 1:17). Granted, the love of God to us through Jesus Christ should be our primary motivation to holiness. But a motivation prompted by God's hatred of sin and His consequent judgment on it is no less biblical.

The holiness of God is an exceedingly high standard, a perfect standard. But it is nevertheless one that He holds us to. He cannot do less. While it is true that He accepts us solely through the merit of Christ, God's standard for our character, our attitudes, affections, and actions is, "Be holy, because I am holy." We must take this seriously if we are to grow in holiness.

JERRY BRIDGES

walking in the light

"Be holy because I, the LORD your God, am holy."

(LEVITICUS 19:2)

W hen God says to His people, "Be holy because I, the LORD your God, am holy" (Leviticus 19:2), He is not asking us to do the impossible. God's holiness is the standard; as believers we are expected to walk in the way He illuminates for us; yet we are not expected to accomplish this process on our own.

So how do we become more holy? We do so by slowly yet faithfully walking in the light God has revealed to us. We are given the Scriptures as a written guide to personal holiness, and we are given the Holy Spirit as an indwelling Guide on this journey into conformity with the image of God. Fortunately, our Father lights more of the path as we grow.

DAY
50

God is asking us to begin to walk His way in little steps. He asks us not to cheat on our taxes, our spouses, or our employers. He asks us to care for widows and orphans. He wants us to make the right choices, not the expedient ones. He implores us to choose to be different as He works in us to sanctify us.

I like what *The New Bible Dictionary* says about our chances for holiness: "The Bible holds out the promise that the holiness of God will sweep the universe clean, and create new heavens and a new earth in which righteousness will dwell."

So take heart! Our great and holy God does not plan to leave us wallowing in our sin in the midst of a decaying world. Instead He gives us light by which to walk, and through a very human disciple, He challenges us to "live holy and godly lives as [we] look forward to the day of God and speed its coming" (2 Peter 3:11–12).

JIM KILLION

An Installment Buying Plan

It is because of him that you are in Christ Jesus, who has become for us wisdom from God—that is, our righteousness, holiness and redemption.

(1 CORINTHIANS 1:30)

T he Christian life comes on the installment buying plan. There is a down payment of righteousness and a daily installment of holiness—one required for entrance into eternal life and the other for enjoying its fellowship and blessings. Just as God has provided Christ as the down payment, so He has provided Christ as the continuing payment of holiness. The second must be appropriated by faith even as the first. "[He] has become for us...righteousness, holiness and redemption" (1 Corinthians 1:30). The Holy Spirit brings righteousness at the new birth, and He applies righteousness to us every hour of our life. The provision is fully made, and thus are the demands of holiness met.

DAY
51

One of the most holy men of the nineteenth century was Robert Murray M'Cheyne. His diary reveals that he maintained this holiness in the middle of a city where godlessness ran rampant and churches bickered among themselves. The true church was fighting for its very life, and many ministers were cold, if not dead; those who were channels of divine power were criticized for believing in the Lord's coming, for being young men, and for being fanatical. Furthermore, he maintained his personal holiness in the midst of great physical weakness which finally drew the spirit from his frail body at an age of only twenty-nine years.

Holiness is offered to every believer. If we are not living in Christ, we should examine ourselves to see if we actually believe in the faith. The man or woman who lives in constant sin has cause to ask whether the wheat of the Lord or the tares of Satan were planted in his or her heart. God is so ready to maintain us in holiness!

DONALD GREY BARNHOUSE

The Reason for Christ's Death

*God made him who had no sin to be sin for us, so that
in him we might become the righteousness of God.*

(2 CORINTHIANS 5:21)

The Bible states that God is not only a Spirit and a Person, but also a *Holy and Righteous Being.* From Genesis to Revelation, God reveals Himself as a Holy God. He is utterly perfect and absolute in every detail. He is too holy to tolerate sinful man, too holy to endure sinful living.

If we could envision the true picture of His majestic righteousness, what a difference it would make in the way we live! If we could but realize the tremendous gulf that separates unrighteous man from God's perfect righteousness! The Scripture declares Him to be the Light in whom there is no darkness at all—the one Supreme Being without flaw or blemish.

DAY
52

This is a difficult concept for imperfect man to understand. We, whose faults and weaknesses are everywhere apparent, can scarcely imagine the overwhelming holiness of God—but we must recognize it if we are to understand and benefit from the Bible.

Man is a sinner, powerless to change his position, powerless to reach the pure ear of God unless he sincerely cries out for mercy. Man would have remained forever lost if God in His infinite mercy had not sent His Son to earth to bridge this gulf.

It is in God's holiness that we find the reason for the death of Christ. Jesus was the only one good enough, pure enough, strong enough, to bear the sins of the whole world. God's holiness demanded the most exacting penalty for sin, and His love provided Jesus Christ to pay this penalty and provide man with salvation. Because the God we worship is a pure God, a holy God, a just and righteous God, He sent us His only begotten Son to make it possible for us to have access to Him.

BILLY GRAHAM

worship at His footstool

Exalt the LORD our God and worship at his footstool; he is holy.

(PSALM 99:5)

DAY
53
↗

B ecause God is holy, He could never accept us on the basis of anything we might do. A fallen creature could sooner create a world than produce that which would meet the approval of infinite Purity. Can darkness dwell with Light? Can the Immaculate One take pleasure in "filthy rags" (Isaiah 64:6)?

Because God is holy, we must approach Him with the utmost reverence: "In the council of the holy ones God is greatly feared; he is more awesome than all who surround him" (Psalm 89:7). Then "Exalt the LORD our God and worship at his footstool; he is holy" (Psalm 99:5). Yes, "at his footstool," in the lowest posture of humility, prostrate before Him. When Moses began to approach the burning bush, God said, "Take off your sandals" (Exodus 3:5). He is to be served "with fear" (Psalm 2:11). He told Israel, "Among those who approach me I will show myself holy; in the sight of all the people I will be honored" (Leviticus 10:3). The more our hearts are awed by His indescribable holiness, the more acceptably will we approach Him.

Because God is holy we should desire to be conformed to Him. He commands us, "Be holy, because I am holy" (1 Peter 1:16). We are not commanded to be omnipotent or omniscient as God is, but we are to be holy, and that "in *all* you do" (1 Peter 1:15).

As God alone is the Source and Fount of holiness, let us earnestly seek holiness from Him. Let your daily prayer be that He may "sanctify you through and through. May your whole spirit, soul and body be kept blameless at the coming of our Lord Jesus Christ" (1 Thessalonians 5:23).

ARTHUR W. PINK

so what?

Christ loved the church and gave himself up for her to make her holy
cleansing her by the washing with water through the word,
and to present her to himself as a radiant church, without stain or wrinkle
or any other blemish, but holy and blameless.

(EPHESIANS 5:25–27)

T here will be several consequences for those who come to the knowledge of the Holy.

First, they will learn to hate sin. We generally love sin and are loath to part with it. But we must learn to hate sin, or else we will learn to hate God. We see a great tension during the lifetime of the Lord Jesus Christ. Some who saw His holiness came to hate sin and became His followers. Others who saw Him came to hate Him and eventually crucified Him.

DAY
54

Second, those who have come to the knowledge of the Holy One through faith in the Lord Jesus Christ will learn to love righteousness and strive for it. The apostle Peter wrote, "But just as he who called you is holy, so be holy in all you do; for it is written: 'Be holy, because I am holy'" (1 Peter 1:15–16). It does not say, "Be holy *as* I am holy." None of us could do that. We cannot be holy in the same sense that God is holy. But we can be holy in the area of a righteous and upright walk before Him.

Third, we must look to the day when God will be fully known in His holiness by all men and women, and we can rejoice in anticipation of that day. If we had not come to God through faith in Christ, that day would be terrible. It would mean the exposure of our sin and judgment. Having come, it means rather the completion of our salvation in that we shall be made like Jesus. We shall be like Him, in holiness and in every other way, "for we shall see him as he is" (1 John 3:2).

JAMES MONTGOMERY BOICE

god by your bed

Test me, O LORD, and try me, examine my heart and my mind;…
See if there is any offensive way in me, and lead me in the way everlasting.

(PSALM 26:2; 139:24)

I f you believe that God is by your bed as well as by your work place and that He observes all your actions, then take care not to do the least thing, not to speak the least word, not to indulge the least thought, that you think would offend Him.

Suppose an angel were now standing right next to you. Wouldn't you take care to abstain from every word or action that you knew would offend him? Or suppose that a very godly man were to be watching you. Wouldn't you be extremely cautious how you conducted yourself, both in word and action?

DAY
55

How much more cautious ought you to be when you know that not a godly man, not an angel of God, but God Himself, the Holy One "who inhabits eternity," is every moment inspecting your heart, your tongue, your hands! He Himself will surely bring you into judgment for all you think and speak and act.

Since there is not a word on your tongue nor a syllable you speak but He "knows it completely," how careful you should be in setting a guard over your mouth and in keeping watch over the door of your lips! (Psalm 141:3). You should be cautious in all your conversations, for you have been forewarned by your Judge that "by your words you will be acquitted, and by your words you will be condemned" (Matthew 12:37).

If God always sees our hearts as well as our hands; if He understands our thoughts long before they are clothed with words—then how earnestly we should echo that petition, "Test me, O LORD, and try me, examine my heart and my mind;…See if there is any offensive way in me, and lead me in the way everlasting" (Psalm 26:2; 139:24).

JOHN WESLEY

The Tender Walk

Make every effort to live in peace with all men and to be holy;
without holiness no one will see the Lord.

(HEBREWS 12:14)

My dear friends, you must keep up a tender, close walk with the Lord Jesus Christ. Many of us lose our peace by our careless walk; something or other gets between Christ and us and we fall into darkness. Something or other steals our hearts from God and grieves the Holy Ghost, who leaves us to ourselves. Let me, therefore, exhort you who have found peace with God, to take care that you do not lose this peace.

I have paid dearly for backsliding! Our hearts are so wicked that if you fail to keep a constant watch, your wicked heart will deceive you and draw you aside. How sad to come under the lash of a correcting Father! Recall the experiences of Job, David, and other saints in Scripture.

DAY
56

I am grieved with the casual spiritual walk of some professing Christians. There is so little difference between them and other people that I scarcely know which is the true Christian. Such Christians are afraid to speak for God; they run with the crowd and talk of the world as if they were in their element. This you did not do when you first discovered Christ's love! When the candle of the Lord first shined upon your soul, you could talk forever of Christ's love. There was a time when you had something to say for your dear Lord; but today, although you can speak of worldly things boldly enough, you are afraid of being laughed at if you speak for Jesus Christ.

Take care not to be conformed to the world! What have Christians to do with the world? You should be singularly good and bold for your Lord, so that everyone who sees you may take note that you have been with Jesus.

GEORGE WHITEFIELD

How to Love a Holy God

I love you, O LORD, my strength.... As for God,
his way is perfect; the word of the LORD is flawless.

(PSALM 18:1, 30)

DAY

57

How can we love a holy God? The simplest answer is that we can't. Loving a holy God is beyond our moral power. The only kind of God we can love by our sinful nature is an unholy god, an idol made by our own hands. Unless we are born of the Spirit of God, unless God sheds His holy love in our hearts, unless He stoops in His grace to change our hearts, we will not love Him. He is the One who takes the initiative to restore our souls. Without Him we can do nothing of righteousness. Without Him we would be doomed to everlasting alienation from His holiness. We can love Him only because He first loved us. To love a holy God requires grace, grace strong enough to pierce our hardened hearts and awaken our moribund souls.

If we are in Christ, we have been awakened already. We have been raised from spiritual death unto spiritual life. But we still have "sleepers" in our eyes, and at times we walk about like zombies. We retain a certain fear of drawing near to God. We still tremble at the foot of His holy mountain.

Yet as we grow in our knowledge of Him, we gain a deeper love for His purity and sense a deeper dependence upon His grace. We learn that He is altogether worthy of our adoration. The fruit of our growing love for Him is the increase of reverence for His name. We love Him now because we see His loveliness. We adore Him now because we see His majesty. We obey Him now because His Holy Spirit dwells within us. He is holy, holy, holy.

R. C. SPROUL

sing to the Lord

Sing to the LORD, you saints of his;
praise his holy name.

(PSALM 30:4)

R obert Murray M'Cheyne, the great Scottish preacher, had no inconsiderable knowledge of music and his voice was frequently heard in praise to God. Those who lived with him were frequently awakened early in the morning as he began the day with a psalm of praise.

In his diary—one of the outstanding documents of its kind in Christian literature—we see the growth of this great soul as he so earnestly sought after God's own holiness. One day he sought to prepare his heart for the next day of preaching. He wrote, "Is it the desire of my heart to be made altogether holy? Is there any sin I wish to retain? Is sin a grief to me, the sudden risings and overcoming thereof especially? Lord, Thou knowest all things. Thou knowest that I hate all sin and desire to be made altogether *like Thee*...Felt much deadness, and much grief that I cannot grieve for this deadness. Towards evening revived. Got a calm spirit through psalmody and prayer."

DAY
58

Here is the experience of a heavy heart singing its way to peace. When M'Cheyne was spiritually cold, he sang the praises of God until his heart grew warm.

Are you despondent or discouraged? If so, speak now to the Lord who dwells within your heart. Say to Him that you know you have been redeemed. Acknowledge His presence and His character as being more than worthy of praise. Ask Him to kindle the song. Have it on your lips even if you do not feel it in your heart. Ask Him to give you a realization of the truth of your singing, for then praise will go to your heart as you yield to your song of praise to the Lord.

DONALD GREY BARNHOUSE

The soul's final feast

Be still and know that I am God!

(PSALM 46:10, RSV)

Perhaps the first response of the heart at seeing the majestic holiness of God is stunned silence. "Be still and know that I am God!" (Psalm 46:10, RSV). In the silence rises a sense of awe and reverence and wonder at the sheer magnitude of God. "Let all the earth fear the LORD, let all the inhabitants of the world stand in awe of him" (Psalm 33:8, RSV).

And because we are all sinners there is in our reverence a holy dread of God's righteous power. "The LORD of hosts, him you shall regard as holy, let him be your fear, and let him be your dread" (Isaiah 8:13, RSV). But this dread is not a paralyzing fright full of resentment against God's absolute authority. It finds release in brokenness and contrition and grief for our ungodliness. "Thus says the high and lofty One who inhabits eternity, whose name is Holy: 'I dwell in the high and holy place, and also with him who is of a contrite and humble spirit, to revive the spirit of the humble, and to revive the heart of the contrite'" (Isaiah 57:15, RSV).

Mingled with the feeling of genuine brokenness and contrition there arises a longing for God. "As a hart longs for the flowing streams, so longs my soul for thee, O God. My soul thirsts for God, for the living God" (Psalm 42:1–2, RSV).

God is not unresponsive to the contrite longing of the soul. He comes and lifts the load of sin and fills our heart with gladness and gratitude. "Thou hast turned for me my mourning into dancing; thou hast loosed my sackcloth and girded me with gladness, that my soul may praise thee and not be silent" (Psalm 30:11–12, RSV).

In the end the heart longs not for any of God's good gifts, but for God Himself. To see Him and know Him and be in His presence is the soul's final feast. Beyond this there is no quest. Words fail. We call it pleasure, joy, delight. But these are weak pointers to the unspeakable experience.

JOHN PIPER

THE
LOVE OF GOD

WHOEVER IS WISE, LET HIM

HEED THESE THINGS

AND

CONSIDER THE GREAT LOVE

OF THE LORD.

PSALM 107:43

The Great Giver

For God so loved the world that he gave....

(JOHN 3:16)

God gives in an immeasurable way. He does not give as a deserved and fair payment for services rendered, but out of love. Therefore, He is a Giver who gives from the heart and out of unfathomable and divine love, as Christ says: "God so loved the world" (John 3:16).

Now among the virtues none is greater than love. Patience, purity, moderation, etc., are all fine virtues, but they are trivial when compared with love. Love includes all other virtues and brings them in its train. Where there is love, a person gives his entire self and is willing and eager to do anything for which he may be needed.

Our heart should expand and all sadness disappear when we look at the unfathomable love in God's heart. Imagine! God is the supreme and greatest Giver and His giving flows out of love, the sublimest of virtues.

DAY
60

But what is the reason behind His giving? What moves Him to give? Nothing but inexpressible love! For He does not give because He is bound to do so or because someone has asked and begged Him to give. He gives because He is moved by His own goodness. He is a Lord who is glad to give and whose love and delight is in giving, entirely for nothing, without any petition.

So He must really be a good God, and His love must be a great, incomprehensible fire, much greater than the fire which Moses saw in the bush—indeed, much greater than the fire of hell! Since this is God's disposition toward the world, who would now despair? This love is too sublime; I cannot do justice to it. I cannot enlarge upon it nor treat it as exhaustively as it deserves.

MARTIN LUTHER

infinite love

How wide and long and high and deep is the love of Christ,
and to know this love that surpasses knowledge.

(EPHESIANS 3:18–19)

T he Bible teaches that God's love is infinite. This is not the same as saying that God's love is great; the distinguishing mark is its inexpendability. It cannot be exhausted, nor even fully understood. Paul captures this idea when he prays that those to whom he is writing "may have power, together with all the saints, to grasp how wide and long and high and deep is the love of Christ, and to know this love that surpasses knowledge" (Ephesians 3:18–19). Logically analyzed, his words are contradictory; Paul prays that Christians might know the unknowable. That is Paul's way of emphasizing that he wants them to enter more deeply into the knowledge of God's infinite love.

DAY
61

How can we comprehend the infinite love of God? We can know it, but only in part. We have been touched by it, yet its fullness lies forever beyond us—just as the infinity of the universe lies beyond the probing human eye.

One hymn puts this aspect of God's love in memorable language. It was written by F. M. Lehman, but the final stanza (perhaps the best) was added later after it was found written on the wall of a room in an asylum by a man said to be insane but who had obviously come to know God's love.

Oh, love of God, how rich and pure!
How measureless and strong!
It shall forevermore endure—
The saints' and angels' song.
Could we with ink the ocean fill,
And were the skies
of parchment made;

Were every stalk on earth a quill,
And every man a scribe by trade;
To write the love of God above
Would drain the oceans dry;
Nor could the scroll
contain the whole,
Though stretched from sky to sky.

JAMES MONTGOMERY BOICE

fiery love

We love him, because he first loved us.

(1 JOHN 4:19, KJV)

G od being who and what He is, must love Himself with pure and perfect love.

The Persons of the Godhead love each other with a love so fiery, so tender, that it is all a burning flame of intense desire inexpressible.

God is Himself the only being whom He can love directly; all else that He loves is for His own sake and because He finds some reflection of Himself there.

God loves His mute creation because He sees in it an imperfect representation of His own wisdom and power. He loves the angels and seraphim because He sees in them some likeness of His holiness. He loves men because He beholds in them a fallen relic of His own image.

DAY 62

It is hard for a sinful man to believe that God loves him. His own accusing conscience tells him it could not be so. He knows that he is an enemy of God and alienated in his mind through wicked works, and he sees in himself a thousand moral discrepancies that disqualify him for the just enjoyment of so pure a love. Yet the whole Bible proclaims the love of God for sinful men. We must believe in His love because He declares it and avail ourselves of the sanctifying grace of Christ in order to receive and enjoy that love to the full.

God is love, and is for that reason the source of all the love there is. He has set as the first of all commandments that we love Him with all our hearts, but He knows that the desired love can never originate with us. "We love him, because he first loved us," is the scriptural and psychological pattern. We can love Him as we ought only as He inflames our minds with holy desire.

A. W. TOZER

spontaneous love

*The LORD did not set his affection on you and choose you because you were more
numerous than other peoples, for you were the fewest of all peoples.
But it was because the LORD loved you.*

(DEUTERONOMY 7:7–8)

T he love which one creature has for another is because of
something in them; but the love of God is free, spontaneous, uncaused. The only reason God loves any is found
in His own sovereign will. "The LORD did not set his affection on you
and choose you because you were more numerous than other peoples,
for you were the fewest of all peoples. But it was because the LORD
loved you" (Deuteronomy 7:7–8). God has loved His people from
eternity, and therefore nothing in the creature could be the cause of
what has always existed. He loves from Himself, "because of his own
purpose and grace" (2 Timothy 1:9).

DAY
63

"We love him, because he first loved us" (1 John 4:19, KJV). God
did not love us because we loved Him, but He loved us before we had
a particle of love for Him. Had God loved us in return for ours, then it
would not be spontaneous on His part; but because He loved us when
we were loveless, it is clear that His love was uninfluenced.

It is highly important if God is to be honored and the heart of His
child established, that we should be clear on this precious truth. God's
love for me, and for each of "His own," was entirely unmoved by anything in us. What was there in me to attract the heart of God?
Absolutely nothing. But, to the contrary, everything to repel Him,
everything calculated to make Him loathe me—sinful, depraved, a
mass of corruption, with "no good thing" in me.

> *What was there in me that could merit esteem,*
> *Or give the Creator delight?*
> *'Twas even so, Father, I ever must sing,*
> *Because it seemed good in Thy sight.*

ARTHUR W. PINK

great love

But because of his great love for us, God, who is rich in mercy,
made us alive with Christ even when we were dead in transgressions
—it is by grace you have been saved.

(EPHESIANS 2:4–5)

W hat can we say about the love of God for His creatures, a love out of which they are not only created and redeemed but also preserved for an eternity of fellowship with Him? Obviously, nothing we could say could exhaust the full measure of His love. God's love is always infinitely deeper than our awareness or expression of it.

The Bible is simple when it speaks about God's love, and one of the simple things it says is that God's love is *great*. "But because of his great love for us, God…" (Ephesians 2:4). John 3:16 implies as much by the little word *so*: "For God *so* loved the world that…" Of course, when God says that His love is great, He is not using the word as we do when we say that some relatively normal thing is great—as a great concert or a great dinner. God is a master of understatement. So when He says His love is great, He is really saying it is so stupendous that it goes far beyond our understanding.

DAY
64

A person once captured this idea on a card on which John 3:16 was arranged in such a way that the greatness of each part of the verse was evident. It looked like this:

God	the greatest Lover
so loved	the greatest degree
the world	the greatest company
that he gave	the greatest act
his only begotten Son,	the greatest gift
that whosoever	the greatest opportunity
believeth	the greatest simplicity
in him	the greatest attraction
should not perish,	the greatest promise
but	the greatest difference
have	the greatest certainty
everlasting life.	the greatest possession

JAMES MONTGOMERY BOICE

unfailing love

But God demonstrates his own love for us in this:
while we were still sinners, Christ died for us.

(ROMANS 5:8)

T he central characteristic of divine love is not that God lays down His life for His friends, but that He lays down His life for His enemies (Romans 5:10).

That is not human love. It does not mean that no human being has ever laid down his life for his enemies, but it does mean that no human being ever did so without having received the divine nature through the redemption of our Lord.

DAY
65

It is easy to say that human love and divine love are one and the same thing; actually they are very far from being the same. It is also easy to say that human virtues and God's nature are one and the same thing; but this, too, is far from the truth. We must square our thinking with facts. Sin has come in and made a gap between human and divine love, between human virtues and God's nature, and what we see now in human nature is only the remnant and refraction of the divine.

Human relationships may be used to illustrate God's love—the love of father, mother, wife, lover—but illustration is not identity. Human love may illustrate the divine, but it is not identical with it because of sin. God's own love is so strange to our natural conceptions that we see no love in it; not until we are awakened by the conviction of our sin and anarchy do we realize God's great love toward us— "while we were still sinners."

The self-expenditure of God for His enemies in the life and death of our Lord Jesus Christ becomes the great bridge over the gulf of sin by which human love may cross over and be embraced by the divine love, the love that never fails.

OSWALD CHAMBERS

The Right Emphasis

God is love.

(1 JOHN 4:8)

T he sentence "God is love" is to be read with the emphasis on the word *God,* whereas we have fallen into the habit of emphasizing the word *love. God* is love; that is to say not a human attitude, a conviction, or a deed, but God Himself is love.

Only he who knows God knows what love is; it is not the other way around. It is not that we first of all by nature know what love is and therefore know also what God is. No one knows God unless God reveals Himself to him. And so no one knows what love is except in the self-revelation of God. Love, then, is the revelation of God. And the revelation of God is Jesus Christ. "This is how God showed his love among us: He sent his one and only Son into the world that we might live through him" (1 John 4:9).

God's revelation in Jesus Christ—God's revelation of His love—precedes all our love toward Him. Love has its origin not in us but in God. Love is not an attitude of men but an attitude of God. "This is love: not that we loved God, but that he loved us and sent his Son as an atoning sacrifice for our sins" (1 John 4:10). Only in Jesus Christ do we know what love is, namely, in His deed for us. "This is how we know what love is: Jesus Christ laid down his life for us" (1 John 3:16).

Love is not what He *does* and what He *suffers,* but it is what *He* does and what *He* suffers. Love is always He Himself. Love is always God Himself. Love is always the revelation of God in Jesus Christ.

DIETRICH BONHOEFFER

DAY
66

Love in its Fullness

But when the kindness and love of God our Savior appeared, he saved us, not because of righteous things we had done, but because of his mercy.

(TITUS 3:4–5)

T he very coming of the Son of God into this world is a great demonstration of the love of God—that He should ever have humbled Himself, that the Father should ever have asked Him to do so, that He should have been born of a virgin, that He should have lived in this world at all and grown up as a little boy and worked as a carpenter, using the fingers and the hands that, as it were, had made the universe, to make ordinary things—and so too all He said and all He did is a demonstration of that same love.

DAY
67

But we do not really see the love of God even in such facts. The love of God is seen in its fullness in Christ's death upon the cross, in His giving Himself even unto death. Death is the last act, it is final, there is nothing beyond it. And not only that, there is also the particular form of death, the death on the cross, the shame, the insult, the ignominy connected with it and attached to it. It is here we really see the depth and the height of the love of God.

Our Lord's death on the cross is the supreme manifestation of the love of God. As you look at that cross on Calvary's hill, what do you feel? Isaac Watts has told us what he felt:

> When I survey the wondrous Cross,
> On which the Prince of glory died,
> My richest gain I count but loss,
> And pour contempt on all my pride.
> Were the whole realm of nature mine,
> That were an offering far too small;
> Love so amazing, so divine,
> Demands my soul, my life, my all!

D. M. LLOYD-JONES

unspeakable love

God so loved the world that he gave his one and only Son,
that whoever believes in him shall not perish but have eternal life.

(JOHN 3:16)

T hough our Lord spoke as no man ever spoke, yet even He could not describe God's love except by its effects! Jesus did not say, "God loved the world fervently, greatly, immeasurably"; for all of these expressions utterly fail to show the depth of God's love. Nor did He say, "God so loved the world that He preserves, supports, and fills it with His blessings"; for although these benefits prove His goodness, they are as nothing by comparison. So He says, "God so loved the world that he gave his one and only Son," thus implying that God's love can be described only by the greatness of its effects.

You parents—how deeply would you have to love a person in order to exchange your child's life for the life of that person? Yet God's love for His Son infinitely surpasses that of the most affectionate parent.

We are told that God is love, and we find that He can love even His enemies. For He causes His sun to shine and His showers to descend on the evil and the unthankful. If He can so love His enemies, how infinitely must He love His innocent, holy Son, who is at the Father's side and who always does what pleases Him! And how He must love the world, since for its redemption He gave up His beloved Son to the agonies of the cross!

But in vain do I attempt to give you any idea of this love. I sink under its weight. With the apostle, I can say only, "What manner of love is this?" Well may it be called an unspeakable love!

REV. EDWARD PAYSON

DAY
68

praiseworthy Love

For he has rescued us from the dominion of darkness and
brought us into the kingdom of the Son he loves.

(COLOSSIANS 1:13)

During a famine in Germany, a poor family was about to perish from hunger. The husband suggested to his wife that they should sell one of their children for bread, to save themselves and the rest of the family. After a long pause the wife agreed that they should do so. But when they began to think which of the four should be sold, they ran into difficulty.

When the eldest was named, they both refused to part with their firstborn and the beginning of their strength. So they came to the second—but they could not imagine selling him, as he was the very picture and image of the father. The third was named, but that child closely resembled the mother. And how could they sell their youngest? He was their Benjamin, the child of their old age. So they decided to perish together in the famine rather than to part with any of their children.

What is a child, but a piece of the parent wrapped up in another skin? And yet our dearest children are but strangers to us in comparison to the unspeakable dearness that existed between the Father and Christ!

Consider how near and dear Jesus Christ was to the Father. He was his Son, "his only Son," the Son of His love, the darling of His Soul; His other Self, indeed, one with Himself, the express image of His person, the brightness of His Father's glory. In parting with Christ, God parted with His own heart. So in Scripture is Jesus called "the Son he loves" (Colossians 1:13).

Now, that God should ever have been content to part with His Son—His one and only Son—is such a demonstration of love that it will be praised to all eternity.

JOHN FLAVEL

fatherly Love

*The Father himself loves you because you have loved
me and have believed that I came from God.*

(JOHN 16:27)

I remember that for the first few years after I was converted,
I had a good deal more love for Christ than for God the
Father. I looked upon God as the stern Judge, while I
regarded Christ as the Mediator who had come between me and that
stern Judge to appease His wrath. But when I got a little better
acquainted with my Bible, those views all fled.

After I became a father and woke up to the realization of what it
cost God to have His Son die, I began to see that God was to be loved
just as much as His Son was. Why, it took more love for God to give
His Son to die than it would to die Himself. You would a thousand
times sooner die yourself in your son's place than have him taken
away. If the executioner were about to take your son to the gallows,
you would say, "Let me die in his stead; let my son be spared."

Oh, think of the love God must have had for this world, that He
gave His only begotten Son to die for it! And that is what I want you
to understand. "The Father himself loves you because you have loved
me." If a man has loved Christ, God will set His love upon him.

D. L. MOODY

DAY
70

wonderful love

*This is love: not that we loved God, but that he loved us and
sent his Son as an atoning sacrifice for our sins.*

(1 JOHN 4:10)

W e aren't always sure what we mean when we use the term
love. That word has become one of the most widely mis-
used terms in our language. We use the word to describe
the most degraded as well as the most exalted of human relationships.
We say we "love" to travel; we "love" to eat chocolate cake; we "love"
our new car, or the pattern in the wallpaper in our home. No wonder
we don't have a very clear idea of what the Bible means when it says:
"God is love."

DAY
71
Don't make the mistake of thinking that because God is Love that
everything is going to be sweet, beautiful, and happy and that no one
will be punished for his sins. God's holiness demands that all sin be
punished—but God's love provides the plan and way of redemption
for sinful man. God's love provided the cross of Jesus, by which man
can have forgiveness and cleansing. It was the love of God that sent
Jesus Christ to the cross!

Never question God's great love, for it is as unchangeable a part of
God as is His holiness. No matter how terrible your sins, God loves
you. Were it not for the love of God, none of us would ever have a
chance in the future life. But God is Love! And His love for us is everlasting!

The promises of God's love and forgiveness are as real and as sure
as human words can make them. But like describing the ocean, its
total beauty cannot be understood until it is actually seen. Until you
actually accept it, until you actually experience it, until you actually
possess true peace with God, no one can describe its wonders to you.

BILLY GRAHAM

personal love

I, even I, am he who comforts you.

(ISAIAH 51:12)

A loving Personality dominates the Bible, walking among the trees of the garden and breathing fragrance over every scene. Always a living Person is present, speaking, pleading, loving, working, and manifesting Himself whenever and wherever His people have the receptivity necessary to receive the manifestation.

The Bible assumes that we can know God with at least the same degree of immediacy as we know any other person or thing that comes within the field of our experience. The same terms used to express the knowledge of God are used to express knowledge of physical things. "O *taste* and see that the LORD is good." "All your garments *smell* of myrrh, and aloes, and cassia, out of the ivory palaces." "My sheep *hear* my voice." "Blessed are the pure in heart, for they shall *see* God." These are but four of countless such passages from the Word of God. And more important than any proof text is that the whole weight of Scripture affirms this belief.

DAY
72

What can all this mean except that we have in our hearts organs which can enable us to know God as certainly as we know material things through our familiar five senses? Faith enables our spiritual sense to function. The soul has eyes with which to see and ears with which to hear. Feeble they may be from long disuse, but by the life-giving touch of Christ, alive now and capable of sharpest sight and most sensitive hearing.

A spiritual kingdom lies all about us, enclosing us, embracing us, altogether within reach of our inner selves, waiting for us to recognize it. God Himself is here awaiting our response to His Presence. This eternal world will come alive to us the moment we begin to reckon upon its reality.

A. W. TOZER

an eternal spring

He does not treat us as our sins deserve or repay us according to our iniquities.
For as high as the heavens are above the earth,
so great is his love for those who fear him.

(PSALM 103:10–11)

G od's love is an ancient love whose spring is in eternity itself. Believer, God is your ancient Friend, who foresaw and loved you before you were born—indeed, before this world came into being. You gather the fruit of His love in time, but the root that produces them existed before all time. The love of God was planning and providing the best of mercies in Christ for us before anyone walked on this world, even before there was a world prepared to receive us.

DAY
73

The love of God to His people is a free and altogether undeserved love, as David makes clear: "He does not treat us as our sins deserve or repay us according to our iniquities. For as high as the heavens are above the earth, so great is his love for those who fear him" (Psalm 103:10–11). We cannot find one stone of our merit in the foundation of this love; for those whom it embraces in its arms are ill-deserving as well as undeserving. God loved us before we were lovely in ourselves. He freely pitched His love upon us; we did not purchase it.

The love of God to believers is a bountiful love, continually streaming forth in blessings both innumerable and invaluable to their souls and bodies. Christian, it would quickly weary your arm—indeed, the arm of an angel—to write down even the thousandth part of the blessings which already have flowed out of this precious fountain to you. And yet all you have received in this world is but the beginning of His mercy, the firstfruits of God's love to you! The love of God daily loads you with blessings. And if you are daily loaded with blessings, what a heap of blessings will your whole life bring?

JOHN FLAVEL

A Deliberate Choice

He who did not spare his own Son, but gave him up for us all—
how will he not also, along with him, graciously give us all things?

(ROMANS 8:32)

Agape is one of several Greek words translated into one English word, *love*. It is by far the most common "love" word in the New Testament. It is a kind of love that has nothing to do with the quality of the ones being loved (how lovable we are), but everything to do with the quality of the Lover. It is not first a feeling, but rather a deliberate choice—an act of the will. It is God saying to you, "I commit Myself to actively give you all that I am." God gave Himself for us and to us.

Many years ago a missionary to China found it necessary to leave his family for an extended time. Aware that his absence would not be understood by his youngest daughter, he placed in his coat pocket a rare treat in that part of China—a bright red apple—to give her as he boarded the train.

Finally the moment came. He embraced his wife and then each of the older children. At last it was his little girl's turn. Picking her up in his arms, he pressed the apple into her chubby hand, hoping that this special gift would soften the impact of his leaving. But instead, as he looked back from the slowly departing train, he saw the apple slip from her hand and roll across the platform. Tears streaming down her face, she ran alongside the train sobbing, "Daddy, I don't want what you give—I want *you!*"

That's it! That is the wonder of God's love! He does not simply give us "things." He gives us Himself. God is the Inventor of father-daughter love, mother-son love, brother-brother love, parent-child love, husband-wife love, friend-to-friend love, even boy-to-dog love. He invented them all.

And the Inventor says, "I love *you!*"

DAVID NEEDHAM

DAY
74

stronger than Death

Love is as strong as death, its jealousy unyielding as the grave.
It burns like blazing fire, like a mighty flame. Many waters cannot quench love;
rivers cannot wash it away.

(SONG OF SONGS 8:6–7A)

Love is not an attribute, but the very essence of God's nature, the center around which all His glorious attributes gather. It was because He was love that He was the Father, and that there was a Son. Love needs an object to whom it can give itself away, in whom it can lose itself, with whom it can make itself one. Because God is love, there must be a Father and a Son. The love of the Father to the Son is that divine passion which He delights in the Son, and speaks, "My beloved Son, in whom I am well pleased." The divine love is like a burning fire; in all its intensity and infinity it has but one object and but one joy, and that is the only-begotten Son. When we gather all the attributes of God—His infinity, His perfection, His immensity, His majesty, His omnipotence—and consider them but as the rays of the glory of His love, we still fail to form any conception of what that love must be. It is a love that surpasses knowledge.

And yet this love of God to His Son must serve as the glass in which you are to learn how Jesus loves you. As one of His redeemed ones, you are His delight, and all His desire is to you, with the longing of a love which is stronger than death and which many waters cannot quench. His heart yearns after you, seeking your fellowship and your love. Were it needed, He could die again to possess you. As the Father loved the Son and could not live without Him—so Jesus loves you. His life is bound up in yours; you are to Him inexpressibly more indispensable and precious than you ever can know.

ANDREW MURRAY

DAY
75

never too far down

But where sin increased, grace increased all the more, so that,
just as sin reigned in death, so also grace might reign through
righteousness to bring eternal life through Jesus Christ our Lord.

(ROMANS 5:20–21)

H oly love, crystalline love, goes down and down into human necessity, never afraid of the taint. As sunbeams can move among sewage and not be defiled, so can the brilliant, holy love of God minister in the deepest depths of human need.

One night, when I was crossing the Atlantic, an officer of our boat told me that we had just passed over the spot where the *Titanic* went down. I thought of all that life and wreckage beyond the power of man to recover and redeem. I thought of the great bed of the deep sea, with all its guarded treasure, too far down for man to reach and restore.

DAY
76

"Too far down!" And then I thought of all the human wreckage engulfed and sunk in oceanic depths of nameless sin. Too far gone! For what? Not too far down for the love of God!

Listen to this: "He descended into hell" (Ephesians 4:9) and He will descend again if you are there: "If I make my bed in hell, behold, thou art there" (Psalm 139:8, KJV). "Where sin increased, grace increased all the more" (Romans 5:20). "He himself bore our sins" (1 Peter 2:24); then He got down to it and beneath it. There is no human wreckage, lying in the ooze of the deepest sea in iniquity, that His deep love cannot reach and redeem.

What a gospel! However far down, God's love can get beneath it!

Stronger His love than death or hell,
Its riches are unsearchable:
The firstborn sons of light
Desire in vain its depths to see,
They cannot tell the mystery,
The length, and breadth, and height!

JOHN HENRY JOWETT

A Tear-wiping God

And I heard a loud voice from the throne saying, "Now the dwelling of God is with men, and he will live with them. They will be his people, and God himself will be with them and be their God. He will wipe every tear from their eyes."

(REVELATION 21:3–4A)

What mystery! A God so vast, so beyond, so incomprehensible—somehow wants me. And He wants you. This very fact underlines that God's message of forgiveness—of life and hope for the human race—is more than simply a proposition to be accepted or rejected. It is rather an offer of a love relationship to be enjoyed or forfeited.

DAY
77

For this to be so requires something we easily take for granted. Our God is a genuine, full-fledged *Person*. He is far more than "the Force" or "Love" or any other mere *thing*; He is a Person who relates to us personally.

Near the end of the Bible John records one of the most intimate, tender expressions of God's personal relationship with us: "And I heard a loud voice from the throne saying, 'Now the dwelling of God is with men, and he will live with them. They will be his people, and God himself will be with them and be their God. He will wipe every tear from their eyes'" (Revelation 21:3–4).

I can't think of anything that expresses the love and tenderness we feel toward our young children more than this act of wiping away tears. At this very moment I can look back over the years and see my little daughter running to me with tears streaming down her face. Squeezing her close, I would gently wipe away those tears with my hand. And wipe and wipe until at last the tears were gone.

God will not delegate any "tear wiping" committee when we arrive in heaven. No! "He Himself...shall wipe away every tear." He is my—your—*personal* Savior. He has chosen to share a closeness of relationship that will take an eternity to fulfill. And He wants to start with me, with you, today.

DAVID NEEDHAM

The persistent voice

You see, at just the right time, when we were still powerless,
Christ died for the ungodly.

(ROMANS 5:6)

G od is continually trying to teach you that He loves you, to win you to Himself by a cross of love. All the burdens He has placed upon men and women have been out of pure love, to bring them to Himself. Those who do not believe that God is love are under the power of the Evil One. He has blinded them and they have been deceived with his lies.

God has dealt with us always with love, love, love—from the fall of Adam to the present hour. Adam's calamity brought down God's love. No sooner did the news reach heaven than God came down after Adam with His love. The voice that rang through Eden was the voice of love, hunting after the fallen one—"Adam, where are you?" For all these thousands of years that voice of love has sounded down the ages. Out of His love He made a way of escape for Adam. God saved him out of His pity and love.

I hear you say, "I do not see, I do not understand how it is that He loves us." What more proof do you want that God loves you? You say, "I am not worthy to be loved." That is true; I will admit that. But He does not love you because you deserve it.

Because you do not deserve it, God offers it to you. You may say, "If I could get rid of my sins, God would love me." But how can you get rid of them until you come to Him? He takes us to His own side, and then He cleanses us from sin. He has shed His blood for you. He wants you, and He will redeem you today if you will let Him.

D. L. MOODY

DAY
78

The Incurably Blessed Soul

I pray also for those who will believe in me through their message,
that all of them may be one, Father, just as you are in me
and I am in you. May they also be in us.

(JOHN 17:20–21)

I ncurably blessed is that soul loved by God. Blessed, too, is the soul on whom the triune God acts in such a way that he is able not only to love God, but does so for God's own sake. Loving and approving as God Himself does, the soul loves in God. Or to put it another way, it loves only what the Creator Himself loves.

Thus love is not the private property of any creature as a personal right, but as God's alone. God is so worthy of love, for He is true love. We know this is the will of God's Son for us when we hear His prayer to God on our behalf: "Father...may they also be in us" (John 17:21). This is the goal, the consummation, and the perfection. This is the peace, the joy in the Holy Spirit (Romans 14:17), and the silence in heaven (Revelation 8:1).

Here below we are sometimes given this love to enjoy, like the silence of an inexpressible peace that mirrors the silence of heaven. While this peace remains briefly, for perhaps an hour or two the thoughts of it are enough to provide a perennial feast. But in the blessed and eternal life to come, it shall be said: "Enter into the joy of your master" (Matthew 25:21, NASB). Then, and there alone, we shall find perfect and perpetual enjoyment. The bliss then will be proportionately greater to all the obstacles and hindrances we now suffer, for they will all be done away. Then the security of the soul's love will be eternally assured, with untouchable perfection and incorruptible bliss.

BERNARD OF CLAIRVAUX

DAY
79

A SUN THAT NEVER SETS

Who shall separate us from the love of Christ?
Shall trouble or hardship or persecution or famine
or nakedness or danger or sword?

(ROMANS 8:35)

T hink of the glory of a midsummer day, in that hushed hour of noon when everything is still, and the sun blazes down in its midday splendor until every nook and cranny lies saturated and soaked through and through with warmth and light. Ah! but the sun dips, and the shadows lengthen, and the chill of evening comes, and then the dark.

But God's love is a sun that never sets. It is always, always, at its full noonday glory! He can never fall below His best; He cannot be untrue to His own nature.

DAY
80

If only we could be quite sure of that and always certain of God's Christlikeness, would not a mass of difficulties be as good as over! Sometimes we are quite sure that God is love—and then one of the grim facts of life knocks at our door, wilting and withering our faith like a wild flower suddenly touched by the scythe's sharpness. Or perhaps the web of our days grows sad, colored, and gray. We doubtingly ask, "Can hands that were pierced for us really weave such a cloth as this?" Clouds rise from our own frightened minds, and we cry desperately that the sun has been extinguished.

If only we could understand that whenever and wherever God meets us, we are dealing with the heart we see on Calvary! If only we would see that whatever comes to us, it is He who gave His Son, His best, His all, who sends it to us. Then, if facing trouble, we could say with Fraser of Brea, "This is a harsh-featured messenger, yet he comes to me from God; what kindness does he bring me?"

ARTHUR JOHN GOSSIP

abiding in His love

I pray that you, being rooted and established in love, may have power,
together with all the saints, to grasp how wide and long and high
and deep is the love of Christ, and to know this love that surpasses
knowledge—that you may be filled to the measure of all the fullness of God.

(EPHESIANS 3:17–19)

L ove gives all, but asks all. It does so, not because it begrudges us anything, but because without this it cannot get possession of us to fill us with itself. In the love of the Father and the Son, it was so. In the love of Jesus to us, it was so. In our entering into His love to abide there, it must be so too; our surrender to it must have no other measure than its surrender to us.

DAY
81

O that we understood how the love that calls us has infinite riches and fullness of joy for us, and that what we give up for its sake will be rewarded a hundredfold in this life! Or rather, would that we understood that it is a LOVE with a height and a depth and a length and a breadth that passes knowledge! How all thought of sacrifice or surrender would pass away, and our souls be filled with wonder at the unspeakable privilege of being loved with such a love, of being allowed to come and abide in it forever.

But is it possible always to abide in His love? Listen how that love itself supplies the only means for abiding in Him: It is faith in that love which will enable us to abide in it. If this love be indeed so divine, such an intense and burning passion, then surely I can depend on it to keep me and to hold me fast. Then surely all my unworthiness and feebleness can be no hindrance. With infinite power at its command, surely I have a right to trust that it is stronger than my weakness and that with its almighty arm it will clasp me to its bosom and suffer me to go out no more.

ANDREW MURRAY

The strength of His Determined Love

I waited patiently for the LORD; he turned to me and heard my cry.
He lifted me out of the slimy pit, out of the mud and mire;
he set my feet on a rock and gave me a firm place to stand.

(PSALM 40:1–2)

hen I stumbled headlong into my first big trial as a new Christian, I wondered just where the love of God had gone.

People spoke of God's love helping me through hard times, yet I couldn't shake a mental image of Him leaning against some ivory wall in heaven, casually thumbing in the direction of the cross. "That says it all," I imagined Him saying.

DAY
82

I soon discovered I wasn't alone in that attitude. I've talked to a number of people over the years who imagine a bored, lethargic God, a God only passively interested in our circumstances—and slightly irritated if pushed to demonstrate His present-day love. Some describe Him as little more than a cosmic Warehouse Clerk, filling mail order prayer requests. Others feel God abandons them when some other "more obedient" Christian catches His attention.

Even those of us who view Him as a powerful, caring God easily underestimate the strength of His determined love.

God does not observe our lives at a cool distance. He is neither apathetic nor detached. He is on the move. He is involved. God is not the sort to casually murmur, "Well, sure I love you." And He constantly shows us how much.

In a day when it's fashionable to appear cool, bored, uncaring, and detached, we can't afford to doubt the enthusiastic, all-encompassing love of God. His compelling love surrounds us every minute. He's in front of us, behind us, relentlessly pouring His love into our lives. What madness! What a passion for our souls! How can we be half-hearted toward our circumstances—toward others—when He loves us so?

May we pursue our God with even a fraction of the energy with which He pursues us.

JONI EARECKSON TADA

The Grandest Fact

And so we know and rely on the love God has for us. God is love.
Whoever lives in love lives in God, and God in him.

(1 JOHN 4:16)

L ook back over your own history as revealed to you by grace, and you will see one central fact growing large: God is love. No matter how often your faith in such an announcement was clouded, no matter how the pain and suffering of the moment made you speak in a wrong mood, still this statement has borne its own evidence along with it most persistently. God is love.

DAY
83
~

In the future, when trials and difficulties await you, do not be fearful. Let not this faith slip from you: God is love. Whisper it not only to your heart in its hour of darkness, but here in the corner of God's earth. Live in the belief of it; preach it by your sweetened, chastened, happy life; sing it in consecrated moments of peaceful joy, sing until the world around you "is wrought to sympathy with hopes and fears it heeded not."

The world does not invite you to sing, but God does. Song is the sign of an unburdened heart; so sing your songs of love uninvited, rising ever higher and higher into a fuller concept of the greatest, grandest fact on the stage of life: God is love.

But words and emotions pass, precious as their influence may be for the time. So when the duller moments come and the mind needs something more certain and sure to consider than the memory of mere emotions and stirring sentiments, consider this revelation: the eternal fact that God is love—not, God is loving.

We must keep ourselves in the love of God by meditating on this fact; then we shall not despair for long. The love of God performs a miracle of grace in graceless human hearts. God is love. One brief sentence; it is the gospel.

OSWALD CHAMBERS

not if god drives

*Can a mother forget the baby at her breast and have no
compassion on the child she has borne? Though she may forget,
I will not forget you! See, I have engraved you on the palms of my hands.*

(ISAIAH 49:15–16)

Seasons of doubt and distress and discouragement sometimes overcome us, days when the morning dawns outside
but not within our hearts. Life is all gloom for us. The
solid ground seems to be slipping from beneath us and we struggle for
a foothold. We feel as though we are walking on a narrow ridge in the
darkness and a single misstep will plunge us to destruction. We need
help—but who can help us? *There is no help,* we think, and we resign
ourselves to darkness and despair.

Can it be that the God of all the earth is mindful of us? That God,
whom we have been shunning, fearing, and dreading, has written our
name where He can see it day by day—on His hands, the hands
which do the work of the universe?

It seems absurd to think that God, who holds the stars in the
hollow of His hand, should hold me also; that He who guides ten
thousand worlds should wish to guide me and help me and deliver
me. But He *does* wish it; to prove this He has inscribed my name on
the palms of His hands. And He calls in tenderest tones, "Do not fear,"
"Take courage," and "In all things God works for the good of those
who love him."

If we love God, then we are to trust Him, and in due time we
shall see how even disappointment and sickness work for our good.
Then we shall be like the boy who was reading to his brother about
how Elijah was taken up to heaven in a chariot of fire. "Wouldn't you
be afraid to ride in a chariot of fire, Billy?" the brother asked. "No!"
was the triumphant answer, "not if God drives!"

JOHN T. FARIS

his face toward me

Let your face shine on your servant; save me in your unfailing love.

(PSALM 31:16)

O ne night while discouraged and unable to sleep, I left our home in a southern California coastal resort town and found myself minutes later standing as close to the sea as the incoming waves would allow. In spite of myself, I could not help noticing the full moon hanging over the ocean. For a long time I simply looked and listened to the thunder of the surf. I noticed that sometimes when a series of huge breakers rolled in, the moonlight would dance across the phosphorescent foam, tumbling upon itself, swishing far up the sand. And then, as though spent, the sea would calm, and the streak of light from the moon would lie flat with a brilliant sheen all the way across the wet sand to my feet.

That's amazing! I thought. *Since the sea on either side of that streak appears dark, it is as though the moon is putting on a private show for* me. *Just for me.*

Just for the fun of it, I ran down the beach. The streak of light kept right with me. It never stopped. It was never too late. It never got there before I did. It was just there—wherever I stood. It was as though the whole moon concentrated its radiance straight through the vault of space, across the vast Pacific...*to me.*

Then I thought, *Well, David, this is what God is to you, isn't it?*

The Lord taught me through that late night object lesson. It was as though He were saying, "David, My *face* is your way. You can run as fast as you can. You can travel as far as you like. You can hide as long as you will. My *face* will be toward you. I will never turn away."

DAVID NEEDHAM

DAY
85

The Essence of Loving God

Because your love is better than life, my lips will glorify you.

(PSALM 63:3)

T ragically, most of us have been taught that duty, not delight, is the way to glorify God. We have not been taught that delight in God is our duty! Being satisfied in God is not an optional add-on to the real stuff of Christian duty. It is the most basic demand of all. "Delight yourself in the LORD" (Psalm 37:4) is not a suggestion, but a command. So are: "Serve the LORD with gladness" (Psalm 100:2), and "Rejoice in the Lord always" (Philippians 4:4).

Scripture says that the "steadfast love [of the Lord] is better than life" (Psalm 63:3, RSV). If it is better than life, it is better than all that life in this world offers. What satisfies are not the gifts of God, but the glory of God—the glory of His love, the glory of His power, the glory of His wisdom, holiness, justice, goodness, and truth.

DAY
86

We do not honor the refreshing, self-replenishing, pure water of a mountain spring by lugging buckets of water up the path to make our contributions from the ponds below. We honor the spring by feeling thirsty, getting down on our knees, and drinking with joy. Then we say, "Ahhhh!" (that's worship!), and we go on our journey in the strength of the fountain (that's service!). The mountain spring is glorified most when we are most satisfied with its water.

To be satisfied in God is the essence of what it means to love God. Loving God may include obeying all His commands; it may include believing all His Word; it may include thanking Him for all His gifts; but the *essence* of loving God is enjoying all He is. It is this enjoyment of God that glorifies His worth most fully, especially when all around our soul gives way.

JOHN PIPER

LET US LOVE HIM

Love the LORD your God with all your heart and with
all your soul and with all your strength.

(DEUTERONOMY 6:5)

G od deserves to be loved because He gave Himself for us, unworthy of it as we are. Yet, being God, what greater gift could He give than Himself? Hence this is surely the greatest claim that God has upon us. He thus deserves our love in return.

Who is so worthy to be loved? Surely it is He of whom the Spirit confesses, "You are my LORD; apart from you I have no good thing" (Psalm 16:2). This then is the true love of the majestic God, who does not seek His own advantage (1 Corinthians 13:5).

And to whom did God direct such pure love? "When we were God's enemies, we were reconciled to him" (Romans 5:10). Thus did God love us. Freely!

And to what measure did God love us? John tells us: "God so loved the world that he gave his one and only Son" (John 3:16). Paul adds: "He…did not spare his own Son, but gave him up for us all" (Romans 8:32). The Son declared of Himself: "Greater love has no one than this, that one lay down his life for his friends" (John 15:13).

Some may argue that while this is true of mankind, it is not true of the angels—but it is also true that the angels did not need it. He who helped men in their need preserved angels from having such a need. So the same God—who loves in equal measure—rescued man *from his sin* while keeping the angels *from sinning*. In both ways, God revealed His love. This, then, is the claim which the Holy One has upon the guilty, and the Supreme Being has upon all mankind.

BERNARD OF CLAIRVAUX

The River of God's Delights

*Father, I desire that they also, whom you have given me, may be with me where I
am, to behold my glory which you have given me in your love for me before the
foundation of the world.... I made known to them your name, and I will make it
known, that the love with which you have loved me may be in them and I in them.*

(JOHN 17:24, 26, RSV)

The great hope of all the holiest people is not only that they
might see the glory of God, but that they might somehow
be given a new strength to savor it with infinite satisfaction—not the partial delights of this world, but, if possible, with the
very infinite delight of God Himself.

And this highest of hopes is exactly what Jesus prays will happen
to His people. Jesus asks the Father that we might see His glory. But
more than that! He asks that the very love that the Father has for the
Son might be in us. Jesus prays for the highest imaginable privilege
and pleasure—that we might be so filled with the fullness of God that
the pleasure of God in the beauty of His Son might fill us and be our
pleasure in the Son. He prays that the Son Himself might be in us and
thus fill us with the infinite delight He has in His Father.

DAY
88

This is the soul's end—the blessing beyond which no better can
be imagined or conceived: an infinite, eternal, mutual, holy energy of
love and pleasure between God the Father and God the Son flowing
out in the Person of God the Spirit, and filling the souls of the
redeemed with immeasurable and everlasting joy.

Surely this is the river of God's delights. This is the water of life
that wells up to eternal life and satisfies forever. And the river is free. It
is our Father's pleasure to give it. "The Spirit and the Bride say,
'Come.'...Let him who is thirsty come, let him who desires take the
water of life without price" (Revelation 22:17, RSV).

JOHN PIPER

what are you afraid of?

For I am convinced that neither death nor life, neither angels nor demons,
neither the present nor the future, nor any powers, neither height
nor depth, nor anything else in all creation, will be able to separate us
from the love of God that is in Christ Jesus our Lord.

(ROMANS 8:38–39)

he question which the gospel of grace puts to us is simply this: Who shall separate you from the love of Christ? What are you afraid of?

Are you afraid that your weakness could separate you from the love of Christ? It can't.

Are you afraid that your inadequacies could separate you from the love of Christ? They can't.

Are you afraid that your inner poverty could separate you from the love of Christ? It can't.

Difficult marriage, loneliness, anxiety over the children's future? They can't.

Negative self-image? It can't.

Economic hardship, racial hatred, street crime? They can't.

Rejection by loved ones or the suffering of loved ones? They can't.

Persecution by authorities, going to jail? They can't.

Nuclear war? It can't.

Mistakes, fears, uncertainties? They can't.

The gospel of grace calls out: Nothing can ever separate you from the love of God made visible in Christ Jesus our Lord.

You must be convinced of this, trust it, and never forget to remember. Everything else will pass away, but the love of Christ is the same yesterday, today, and forever. Faith will become vision, hope will become possession, but the love of Jesus Christ that is stronger than death endures forever. In the end, it is the one thing you can hang onto.

BRENNAN MANNING

DAY
89

Lord, Love Yourself in us

You did not receive a spirit that makes you a slave again to fear
but you received the Spirit of sonship. And by him we cry, "Abba, Father."

(ROMANS 8:15)

O Sovereign Father of Light, love Yourself in us that we may love You through us! Then are we made one with You and made worthy of Your love, only when we participate in that holy union. For we are your people, Lord, the people of God as the apostle says (Acts 17:28). Thus are the words of the pagan poet made into a perfume jar that allows only the scent of that good thought to be inhaled. We are indeed God's "offspring," children of the Most High (Psalm 82:6). In such a spiritual kinship we claim a closer relationship with You, because by the Spirit of adoption (Romans 8:15) Your Son does not disdain to take our name (Hebrews 2:11). In His divine school He teaches us to boldly say: "Our Father in heaven" (Matthew 6:9).

DAY
90

Thus, You love us by making us lovers of Yourself. We love You as we receive Your Spirit, who is Your Love. You let Him penetrate and wholly possess all the most intimate affections of our hearts. You change them into the perfect purity of Your Truth and bond them into full accord with Your Love. From such a wonderful union there is great enjoyment of our sweetness, expressed in the words of Your Son our Savior: "that they may be one in us" (John 17:21). Great, then, is the dignity of this union! Great is its glory that He should add: "as You and I are one" (John 17:11).

O the joy, the glory, and the exaltation of it! No wonder wisdom can say: "With me are riches and honor, enduring wealth and prosperity" (Proverbs 8:18).

BERNARD OF CLAIRVAUX

THE
SOVEREIGNTY
OF GOD

How great you are,

O Sovereign Lord!

There is no one like you, and

there is no God but you.

2 Samuel 7:22

subject to none

"My purpose will stand, and I will do all that I please."

(ISAIAH 46:10)

T he sovereignty of God may be defined as the *exercise of His supremacy*. Being infinitely elevated above the highest creature, He is the Most High, Lord of heaven and earth. Subject to none, commanded by none, absolutely independent; God does as He pleases, only as He pleases, always as He pleases. So His own Word expressly declares: "My purpose will stand, and I will do all that I please" (Isaiah 46:10). Divine sovereignty means that God is on the throne of the universe, directing all things, working all things "according to the plan of him who works out everything in conformity with the purpose of his will" (Ephesians 1:11). Rightly did Charles Haddon Spurgeon say in his sermon on Matthew 20:15,

> There is no attribute more comforting to His children than that of God's sovereignty. Under the most adverse circumstances, in the most severe trials, they believe that sovereignty has ordained their afflictions, that sovereignty overrules them, and that sovereignty will sanctify them all. There is nothing for which the children ought more earnestly to contend than the doctrine of the Master over all creation— the Kingship of God over all the works of His own hands— the throne of God and His right to sit upon that throne. We proclaim an *enthroned* God and His right to do as He wills with His own, to dispose of His creatures as He thinks best, without consulting them. It is God upon the throne that we love to preach. It is God upon His throne whom we trust.

"The LORD does whatever pleases him, in the heavens and on the earth, in the seas and all their depths" (Psalm 135:6). Such is the imperial Monarch revealed in Holy Scripture—unrivaled in majesty, unlimited in power, undirected by anything outside Himself.

ARTHUR W. PINK

Long Ago He Planned It

He does as he pleases with the powers of heaven and the peoples of the earth.
No one can hold back his hand or say to him: "What have you done?"

(DANIEL 4:35)

O ur God is both omnipotent and sovereign. The psalmist says, "He does whatever pleases him" (Psalm 115:3). The theme is amplified in Daniel 4:35: "He does as he pleases with the powers of heaven and the peoples of the earth. No one can hold back his hand or say to him: 'What have you done?'"

And God's power and authority are eternal: "Your kingdom is an everlasting kingdom, and your dominion endures through all generations" (Psalm 145:13).

DAY
92

Christians pray to a God whose omnipotence and sovereignty is coupled with His goodness and moral perfection. Every act of God is always kind; He does nothing from mere whim or arbitrary caprice. Thus Jesus says,

> Which of you, if his son asks for bread, will give him a stone? Or if he asks for a fish, will give him a snake? If you, then, though you are evil, know how to give good gifts to your children, how much more will your Father in heaven give good gifts to those who ask him! (Matthew 7:9–11)

The ideas of God's omnipotence, sovereignty, and goodness are the primary basis for what Christian scholars call providence. Because of God's providential care for His creation, ultimately, there is no such thing as luck. What is more, from God's perspective, there are no accidents, surprises, or "curious turns of history." What we call chance doesn't exist.

Sound extreme? Yes, it does. But these ideas are straightforward consequences of verses like Proverbs 16:33: "The lot is cast into the lap, but its every decision is from the Lord" (NASB). From a biblical perspective, your world history book should be prefaced with 2 Kings 19:25, "Have you not heard? Long ago I ordained it. In days of old I planned it; now I have brought it to pass."

W. BINGHAM HUNTER

A Happy God

Our God is in the heavens; he does whatever he pleases.

(PSALM 115:3, RSV)

C an you imagine what it would be like if the God who ruled the world were not happy? What if God were given to grumbling and pouting and depression, like some Jack-and-the-Beanstalk giant in the sky? What if God were frustrated and despondent and gloomy and dismal and discontented and dejected? Could we join David and say, "O God, thou art my God, I seek thee; my soul thirsts for thee; my flesh faints for thee, as in a dry and weary land where no water is" (Psalm 63:1, RSV)?

I don't think so. We would all relate to God like little children who have a frustrated, gloomy, dismal, discontented father. They can't enjoy him. They can only try not to bother him, and maybe to work for him to earn some little favor.

DAY 93

But God is not like that; the foundation of the happiness of God is the sovereignty of God: "Our God is in the heavens; he does whatever he pleases." If God were not sovereign, if the world He made were out of control, frustrating His design again and again—God would not be happy.

Just as our joy is based on the promise that God is strong enough and wise enough to make all things work together for our good, so God's joy is based on that same sovereign control: He makes all things work together for His glory.

So if our Father's heart is full of deep and unshakable happiness, we may be sure that when we seek our happiness in Him we will not find Him "out of sorts" when we come. We will not find a frustrated, gloomy, irritable Father who wants to be left alone, but instead a Father whose heart is so full of joy it spills over onto all the thirsty.

JOHN PIPER

absolute freedom

"This is what the LORD says—Israel's King and Redeemer, the LORD Almighty:
I am the first and I am the last; apart from me there is no God."

(ISAIAH 44:6)

G od is absolutely free, which means simply that He must be free to do whatever He wills to do, anywhere at any time, to carry out His eternal purpose in every single detail, without interference. Were He less than free He must be less than sovereign.

DAY 94

To grasp the idea of unqualified freedom requires a vigorous effort of the mind. We are not psychologically conditioned to understand freedom except in its imperfect forms. Our concepts of it have been shaped in a world where no absolute freedom exists. Here each natural object is dependent upon many other objects, and that dependence limits its freedom.

Yet God is said to be absolutely free because no one and no thing can hinder Him or compel Him or stop Him. He is able to do as He pleases always, everywhere, forever. To be thus free means also that He must possess universal authority. That He has unlimited power we know from the Scriptures and may deduce from certain other of His attributes. But what about His authority?

Even to discuss the authority of Almighty God seems a bit meaningless, and to question it would be absurd. Can we imagine the Lord God of Hosts having to request permission of anyone or to apply for anything to a higher body? To whom would God go for permission? Who is higher than the Highest? Who is mightier than the Almighty? Whose position antedates that of the Eternal? At whose throne would God kneel? Where is the greater one to whom He must appeal? "This is what the LORD says—Israel's King and Redeemer, the Lord Almighty: I am the first and I am the last; apart from me there is no God."

A. W. TOZER

absolute control

Now listen, you who say, "Today or tomorrow we will go to this or that city,
spend a year there, carry on business and make money." Why, you do not even
know what will happen tomorrow. What is your life? You are a mist that
appears for a little while and then vanishes. Instead, you ought to say,
"If it is the Lord's will, we will live and do this or that."

(JAMES 4:13–15)

I n 1902, a young English boy came down to breakfast to find his father reading the newspaper which carried news of preparations for the first coronation in Britain in sixty-four years. In the middle of breakfast the father turned to his wife and said, "Oh, I am sorry to see this worded like that. Here is a proclamation that on a certain date Prince Edward will be crowned king at Westminster, and there is no *Deo volente,* 'God willing.'" The words stuck in the young boy's mind for the very reason that on the appointed date the future Edward VII was ill with appendicitis, and the coronation had to be postponed.

DAY
95

At this time, at the end of Queen Victoria's reign, the political, economic, and military power of the British Empire was at its zenith. Yet for all its great might, Great Britain could not carry out its planned coronation on the appointed date.

Was the omission of "God willing" from the proclamation and the subsequent postponement of the coronation merely a coincidence, two events without any relation to one another? Or did God cause Prince Edward to have appendicitis to show that He was "in control"? We don't know why the situation occurred as it did. One thing we do know, however: Whether we acknowledge it with *Deo volente* or not, we cannot carry out any plan apart from God's will.

God is in control; He is sovereign. He does whatever pleases Him and determines whether we can do what we have planned. This is the essence of God's sovereignty; His absolute independence to do as He pleases and His absolute control over the actions of all His creatures. No creature, person, or empire can either thwart His will or act outside the bounds of His will.

JERRY BRIDGES

levi finds his home

[God] works out everything in conformity with the purpose of his will.

(EPHESIANS 1:11)

Since God is infinite, His sovereignty must be absolute. His rule must involve total control of everything in His domain—every circumstance, every situation, every event. God claims responsibility for establishing and removing human rulers, however acceptable or unacceptable we may consider them to be (Daniel 2:20–21). The psalmist said that God controls the weather (Psalm 147:16–18; 148:8). He even holds the life of every creature in His hand (Job 12:10).

DAY
96

Everyone in my family is convinced that God led a collie named Levi to our door. His name was engraved on the tag hanging around his neck when he arrived. Can you imagine a dog named Levi finding the Strauss house? Our youngest son had been praying for a dog for nearly three years, but we had laid down some stringent requirements. He had to be housebroken. He had to be obedient. And he had to be a gentle "people dog" in order to live in a pastor's home where visitors come and go regularly.

When my wife returned the dog to its owner, whose address was engraved on the tag, she said kiddingly, "If you ever want to get rid of this dog, please let us know." The surprising reply was, "I do. I'm looking for a good home for him right now." When the owner brought us his papers, we learned that he had been conceived at the approximate time our son began to pray for a dog, that he was born on my wife's birthday, and that he was an honor graduate of obedience school. No one will ever convince us that Levi's coming was anything other than the gracious work of our sovereign God.

God's sovereignty means that He either directly causes or consciously permits *everything* that happens in human history.

RICHARD STRAUSS

Absolute supremacy

Yours, O LORD, is the greatness and the power and the glory and the majesty and the splendor, for everything in heaven and earth is yours. Yours, O LORD, is the kingdom; you are exalted as head over all.... You are the ruler of all things. In your hands are strength and power to exalt and give strength to all.

(1 CHRONICLES 29:11–12)

A n infinite distance separates the mightiest creatures from the Creator. He is the Potter, they are but the clay in His hands, to be molded into vessels of honor or to be dashed into pieces (Psalm 2:9) as He pleases. Were all the denizens of heaven and all the inhabitants of earth to combine in open revolt against Him, it would cause Him no uneasiness. It would have less effect upon His eternal, unassailable throne than the spray of the Mediterranean's waves has upon the towering rocks of Gibraltar. So powerless is the creature to threaten the Most High, Scripture tells us that when the Gentile heads unite to defy Jehovah and His Christ, "The One enthroned in heaven laughs" (Psalm 2:4).

The absolute and universal supremacy of God is plainly affirmed in many Scriptures. "O Lord, God of our fathers, are you not the God who is in heaven? You rule over all the kingdoms of the nations. Power and might are in your hand, and no one [not even the devil himself] can withstand you" (2 Chronicles 20:6). Before Him presidents and popes, kings and emperors are less than grasshoppers.

"But he stands alone, and who can oppose him? He does whatever he pleases" (Job 23:13). The God of Scripture is no make-believe monarch, no imaginary sovereign, but King of kings and Lord of lords. "I know that you can do all things; no plan of yours can be thwarted" (Job 42:2). All that He has designed, He does. All that He has decreed, He perfects. All that He has promised, He performs. "Our God is in heaven; he does whatever pleases him" (Psalm 115:3). Why has He? Because "There is no wisdom, no insight, no plan that can succeed against the Lord" (Proverbs 21:30).

ARTHUR W. PINK

no such thing as mere coincidence

The lot is cast into the lap, but the decision is wholly from the LORD.

(PROVERBS 16:33, RSV)

P eople lift their hand to rebel against the Most High only to find that their rebellion is unwitting service in the wonderful designs of God. Even sin cannot frustrate the purposes of the Almighty.

When we come to the end of the New Testament and to the end of history in the Revelation of John, we find God in complete control of all the evil kings who wage war. In Revelation 17, John speaks of a harlot sitting on a beast with ten horns. The harlot is Rome, drunk with the blood of the saints; the beast is the antichrist, and the ten horns are ten kings "who give over their power and authority to the beast...[and] make war on the Lamb."

But are these evil kings outside God's control? Are they frustrating God's designs? Far from it. They are unwittingly doing His bidding. "For God has put it in their hearts to carry out his purpose by being of one mind and giving over their royal power to the beast, until the words of God shall be fulfilled" (Revelation 17:17, RSV).

God's sovereignty over men's affairs is not compromised even by the reality of sin and evil in the world. It is not limited to the good acts of men or the pleasant events of nature. The wind belongs to God whether it comforts or whether it kills.

In the end, one must finally come to see that if there is a God in heaven, there is no such thing as mere coincidence, not even in the smallest affairs of life: "The lot is cast into the lap, but the decision is wholly from the LORD" (Proverbs 16:33, RSV). Not one sparrow "will fall to the ground without your Father's will" (Matthew 10:29, RSV).

JOHN PIPER

DAY
98

The Lord Reigns

*The LORD reigns, he is robed in majesty; the LORD is robed
in majesty and is armed with strength.*

(PSALM 93:1)

W hatever opposition may arise, God's throne is unmoved.
He has reigned, does reign, and will reign for ever and
ever. Whatever turmoil and rebellion there may be
beneath the clouds, the eternal King sits above it all in supreme serenity. What can give greater joy to a loyal subject than to see the King in
all His beauty? Let us repeat the proclamation, "the Lord reigns," whis-
pering it in the ears of the despairing and proclaiming it in the face of
the enemy.

God is robed in majesty. Not with symbols of majesty, but with
majesty itself. His is not the mere appearance, but the reality of sovereignty. In nature, providence, and salvation the Lord is infinite in
majesty.

DAY
99

His garments of glory are not His only clothing. He also wears
strength as His sash. He is always strong, but sometimes He displays
His power in a special manner and therefore may be said to be
clothed with it.

As men prepare themselves for running or working, so the Lord
appears in the eyes of His people to be getting ready for action,
clothed with His omnipotence. Strength always dwells in the Lord
Jehovah. But often He hides His power until, in answer to His children's cries, He puts on strength, ascends the throne, and defends His
own.

It should be a constant theme of prayer that in our day the reign
of the Lord may be conspicuous and His power displayed in His
church and on her behalf. *Your kingdom come* should be our daily
prayer. That the Lord Jesus actually *does* reign should be our daily
praise.

CHARLES H. SPURGEON

A true philosophy of History

"Though the mountains be shaken and the hills be removed,
yet my unfailing love for you will not be shaken nor my covenant
of peace be removed," says the LORD, who has compassion on you.

(ISAIAH 54:10)

N o philosophy of history is true which does not take into account the sovereign hand of God controlling all permitted developments. God is still God. He has not abdicated. Neither has He changed. Nor has He slackened His control over the nations. He is yet just as truly God though millions of people are still self-blinded to His sovereign activity.

As the poet said, "When statesmen have had their last parley,/ And despots have made their last threat:/ When prophets are dumb with misgiving,/ And forces of conflict are set:/ When factions misleading and treacherous/ Bring chaos where order prevailed;/ When freedom long-cherished is vanquished,/ And leaders long trusted have failed,/ When God and His Word are derided,/ And men call it useless to pray; Remember that God is still sovereign,/ And *HE* has the last word to say."

For the unbeliever and the wicked, the sovereignty of God may well be terrifying; but to the yielded, trusting Christian it is "joy unspeakable." Commit everything to God even though your world seems shaken to its foundations. Lie still on His bosom, and listen to the heartbeat of that boundless love from which all the demons either inside or outside of Hades can never pluck you.

DAY
100

God is still on the throne,
And He will take care of His own;
Though trials distress us,
And burdens oppress us,
He never will leave us alone:
God is still on the throne,
And He will take care of His own;
His promise is true,
He will see us right through;
God is still on the throne.

J. SIDLOW BAXTER

An inescapable pattern

*The LORD foils the plans of the nations; he thwarts the purposes of the peoples.
But the plans of the LORD stand firm forever,
the purposes of his heart through all generations.*

(PSALM 33:10–11)

World events take on a new dimension when viewed in the light of the Person who controls. Out of the confusion and blunders of men emerges an inescapable pattern of divine direction.

First, *everything fits into a design.* Looking upward and forward, we may say, "For what purpose was this? What good will come from this that will completely justify our present disappointment and grief?" Viewed negatively and judged by our limited insight, the answer is never satisfactory. Viewed positively, however, things tend to fall into place and reveal a marvelous, long-range divine plan.

Second, *God sees what men do not see.* Astronauts on a space journey are confined to cramped quarters. Even when they can look out through tiny windows, what they see tells them little about where they are going. They depend upon their instruments and their contact with Mission Control. Only God knows history from beginning to end. The only logical attitude is to trust His judgment and let Him lead.

Third, *God guides His people, not only by the Spirit and the written Word, but also through what goes on around them.* Instead of making the best of unfortunate circumstances, He actually controls circumstances and brings victory out of what men might have intended as defeat.

Fourth, *the Lord is always present with His people, especially with those who venture out in obedience to the Great Commission.* Following His command, "Go," He says, "I am with you always, to the very end of the age."

God is still in command. He has no need to consult the news media to see what is good news or bad, important or trivial. For Him there are no accidents, no tragedies—all things are under the control of His sovereign hand.

PAUL H. SHEETZ

DAY
101

Nothing Like It in History

*I will surely gather all of you, O Jacob; I will surely bring together the
remnant of Israel. I will bring them together like sheep in a pen,
like a flock in its pasture; the place will throng with people.*

(MICAH 2:12)

I n all the records of kings and nations, is there anything to match the history of the Jews? Never was there any other such high calling with such deep sinning; never such unique privilege with such big responsibility.

Never has any race or nation suffered such recurrent slaughterings and scatterings without disintegrating into extinction. If the Jewish people could have retained at least some small territorial foothold somewhere on earth, there might have been some explanation for their continual survival. But for over two thousand years they had no throne, no kingdom, no colony, no land, no city, no laws of their own. *Yet they are still here!*

From the time of Xerxes about 500 B.C., down to the demon-possessed Adolph Hitler, they have been hounded, tortured, burned alive, or buried alive together in hundreds or thousands by maddened Jew haters determined to stamp them out completely. *Yet they are still here!*

Today they are back in their own land—"Eretz Yizrael"—with their own government, their own laws, their own legal system, their own coins, their own language, and their own institutions. After an historical hiatus of 2,300 years, they are again acknowledged by the nations as a self-governing state. There has never been anything like it in all history.

What does this say to you and me? It says that God is sovereign in history. It says that whatever God may allow to happen in His present, *permissive* will, He overrules all so as ultimately to fulfill His *purposive* will. It says that God does not violate the free will of men and nations, while at the same time He overrules all to a final, righteous outcome. Nothing can ultimately defeat God. His purpose always triumphs in the end.

J. SIDLOW BAXTER

DAY
102

an unknown tongue?

*Yours, O LORD, is the greatness and the power and the glory and the
majesty and the splendor, for everything in heaven and earth is yours.
Yours, O LORD, is the kingdom; you are exalted as head over all.*

(1 CHRONICLES 29:11)

T*he sovereignty of God* is an expression that once was generally understood. It was a phrase commonly used in religious literature. It was a theme frequently expounded in
the pulpit. It was a truth which brought comfort to many hearts and
gave strength and stability to Christian character.

But in many quarters today, to make mention of God's sovereignty
is to speak in an unknown tongue. Were we to announce from the average pulpit that the sermon topic would be the sovereignty of God, it
would sound very much as though we had borrowed a phrase from
one of the dead languages. How sad that the doctrine which is the key
to history, the interpreter of providence, the warp and woof of
Scripture, and the foundation of Christian theology, should be so
sadly neglected and so little understood!

When we speak of the sovereignty of God, we mean the
supremacy of God, the kingship of God, the godhood of God. To
say that God is sovereign is to declare that God *is* God. To say that
God is sovereign is to declare that He is the Most High, who does as
He pleases with the powers of heaven and the peoples of the earth,
so that no one can hold back His hand or say to Him: "What have
you done?" (Daniel 4:35). To say that God is sovereign is to declare
that He is the Almighty, the possessor of all power in heaven and
earth, so that no one can defeat His plans, thwart His purpose, or
resist His will (Psalm 115:3). To say that God is sovereign is to
declare that He is "the blessed and only Ruler, the King of kings and
Lord of lords" (1 Timothy 6:15). Such is the God of the Bible.

ARTHUR W. PINK

He Needs No Counselors

Who has understood the Spirit of the LORD, or instructed him as his counselor?
Whom did the LORD consult to enlighten him, and who taught him the right way?
Who was it that taught him knowledge or showed him the path of understanding?

(ISAIAH 40:13–14)

DAY
104

The bitter news of Dawson Trotman's drowning swept like cold wind across Schroon Lake. Eyewitnesses tell of the profound anxiety, the tears, the helpless disbelief in the faces of those who now looked out across the deep blue water. Everyone's face except one—Lila Trotman, Dawson's widow. As she suddenly walked upon the scene, a close friend shouted, "Oh, Lila…he's gone. Dawson's gone!" To that she replied in calm assurance the words of Psalm 115:3, NASB: "But our God is in the heavens; He does whatever He pleases."

Accept it or not, God's calling the shots. He's running the show. Either He's in *full* control or He's *off* His throne. It's as foolish to say He's "almost sovereign" as it would be to say I'm "almost married" or the surgeon's gloves are "almost sterile."

It was a glorious day when I was liberated from the concentration camp of fear…the fear of saying, "I don't understand the reasons why, but I accept God's hand in what has happened." It was a *greater* day when I realized that nobody expected me to have all the answers…least of all God! If I could figure it all out, I'd qualify as His adviser, and Scripture makes it clear He doesn't need my puny counsel. He wants my unreserved love, my unqualified devotion, my undaunted trust—not my unenlightened analysis of His ways.

One of the marks of spiritual maturity is the quiet confidence that God is in control…without the need to understand why He does what He does. Lila Trotman bore such a mark as she faced the ways of God that were "unsearchable…and unfathomable."

What marks *your* life?

CHARLES R. SWINDOLL

A life of rule and peace

Your throne, O God, will last for ever and ever;
a scepter of justice will be the scepter of your kingdom.

(PSALM 45:6)

W e live in days when the perpetual sovereignty of God is being questioned. In a revolutionary time like this it is well for Christian people, who see so many revered things going, to tighten their grasp upon the conviction that, whatever goes, God's Kingdom will not go. Whatever may be shaken by any storms, the foundation of His throne stands secure.

In the great mosque of Damascus, which was once a Christian church, there may still be read, deeply cut in the stone, "Thy kingdom, O Christ, is an everlasting kingdom." It is true! And one day it shall be known that He is for ever and ever the monarch of the world.

God's rule is no arbitrary sway. He loves righteousness and therefore puts His broad shield of protection over all who love it and seek after it. He hates wickedness and therefore wars against it wherever it is, seeking to draw men and women out of it. His kingdom is the hope of the world.

And that kingdom is offered to us! God rules that He may make us like Himself, lovers of righteousness, and so, like Himself, possessors of unfading joy.

So make Him your King. Let His arrow reach your heart. Bow in submission to His power. Take for your very life His words of graciousness. Lovingly gaze upon His beauty till some reflection of it shines from you. Fight by His side with strength drawn from Him alone. Own and adore Him as the enthroned God. Crown Him with the many crowns of supreme trust, heart-whole love, and glad obedience. And when you do, you shall be honored to share in His triumph.

ALEXANDER MACLAREN

finding hope in the pain

*Now then go, and I, even I, will be with your mouth,
and teach you what you are to say.*

(EXODUS 4:12)

DAY
106

T his conversation between God and Moses has given me hope in the silent pain of physical suffering. The Lord knows Moses' weaknesses better than Moses does. He has already planned to make His strength evident through Moses' speech problems.

When my husband Lloyd and I picked the boy's name for our first child, we had no idea that our infant would have spina bifida. The first night after he was born, as Brian struggled to survive, I recalled that the name Brian literally means "strong." Wondering if it were some kind of cruel joke, I cried out to God. He gently reminded me of His words to Paul, "My power is made perfect in weakness," and Paul's words to us, "For when I am weak, then I am strong" (2 Corinthians 12:9–10).

It seemed like an assurance to me that just as He had told Moses, "I will be with your mouth," He was telling Brian, Lloyd, and me, "I will be your strength." When I think about all that came out of the mouth of Moses, I am amazed: the challenges to Pharaoh...the words that echoed over the Red Sea...the Law of Moses given at Mount Sinai...and his most intimate prayer, "Show me your glory" (Exodus 33:18).

But I caution myself: *Beware of any expectations about what God's strength through your weakness will look like on this earth.* It may not be as glamorous as Moses' eloquence. However, by faith, I believe it will someday be revealed as having just as much power. For our life—our *true* life—is hidden with Christ in God. Those who appear to be last will one day be first.

KATHY OLSEN

nothing but good

And we know that in all things God works for the good of those
who love him, who have been called according to his purpose.

(ROMANS 8:28)

Benjamin B. Warfield was a world-renowned theologian who taught at Princeton Seminary for almost thirty-four years until his death on February 16, 1921. Many people are aware of his famous books, like *The Inspiration and Authority of the Bible*. But what most people don't know is that in 1876, at the age of twenty-five, he married Annie Pierce Kinkead and took a honeymoon to Germany. During a fierce storm Annie was struck by lightning and permanently paralyzed. After caring for her for thirty-nine years, Warfield laid her to rest in 1915. Because of her extraordinary needs, Warfield seldom left his home for more than two hours at a time during all those years of marriage.

DAY
107

Now here was a shattered dream. She was never healed. There was no kingship in Egypt at the end of the story as there was for Joseph—only the spectacular patience and faithfulness of one man to one woman through thirty-nine years of what was never planned—at least, not planned by man.

But when Warfield came to write his thoughts on Romans 8:28, he said, "The fundamental thought is the universal government of God. All that comes to you is under His controlling hand. The secondary thought is the favor of God to those that love Him. If He governs all, then nothing but good can befall those to whom He would do good…. Though we are too weak to help ourselves and too blind to ask for what we need, and can only groan in unformed longings, He is the author in us of these very longings…and He will so govern all things that we shall reap only good from all that befalls us."

JOHN PIPER

The most precious commodity in the universe

As he went along, he saw a man blind from birth. His disciples asked him,
"Rabbi, who sinned, this man or his parents, that he was born blind?"
"Neither this man nor his parents sinned," said Jesus, "but this happened so that the
work of God might be displayed in his life."..."Go," he told him,
"wash in the Pool of Siloam" (this word means Sent).

(JOHN 9:1–3, 7)

DAY
108

T he blind man in John 9 was not healed for his benefit alone; God had divinely arranged the circumstances of his life to accomplish something of infinitely greater importance. God used this miraculous event to demonstrate several crucial truths:

1. God's power is greater than any of our misfortunes; even a man born blind can receive sight when God gives the order.

2. God is the Potter, we are the clay; He has the right to shape our circumstances however He pleases for His good purposes.

3. God often connects His work in our lives with some physical reminder of that work. Jesus *sent* the blind man to a pool whose name means *sent;* ever afterward, the pool itself would remind him both of God's great mercy and how he found that mercy.

4. Jesus was a unique vessel through Whom God displayed His dazzling glory.

5. Jesus proved Himself to be the Messiah by coupling His claim to be the light of the world with His giving light to the eyes of the blind man.

This incident shows as clearly as any in the Bible that God is not primarily concerned with our comfort or our prosperity. The most comfortable and prosperous people in the world often have no interest in God and His glory. But to the believer, God's glory is the most precious commodity in the universe. That's another way of saying that *God Himself* is our ultimate treasure: His power, His holiness, His love, His justice and promises and intellect and faithfulness and mercy and grace and truth, all combine into infinite perfection to proclaim His unsurpassed glory and worth.

STEVE HALLIDAY

some through the fire

When you pass through the waters, I will be with you; and when you pass through the rivers, they will not sweep over you. When you walk through the fire, you will not be burned; the flames will not set you ablaze. For I am the LORD, your God, the Holy One of Israel, your Savior.

(ISAIAH 43:2–3)

Some through the fire, some through the flood—that is the way God leads His dear children along. That is His method. He will send His own into a storm. But always remember that He will not let you fall.

There have been many times in my life when I have been pushed to the edge of the cliff, and I was sure there would be a crash. But there wasn't.

In college I knew that God had called me to the ministry, but I had very little faith in Him. I had a notion that He would take me to a certain height and drop me off, let me go.

When I graduated from college, I was the unhappiest person there. After having received my degree, I returned to my room in the dormitory, still in cap and gown, and sat dejectedly on the edge of my bed. My roommate came in and asked, "What in the world—did somebody die?" I said, "Might just as well have. I thought God called me to the ministry. I'm through college, the Depression has hit, and I do not even have a job this summer. I haven't a dime to go to seminary next year."

Without going into details, let me just say that when I went to bed that night, I had checks that totalled $750 which had come from people whom I never dreamed would be interested in seeing me go to seminary. And $750 the year the Depression hit, brother, was a whole lot of money!

I thought He was going to drop me. He did, but He did not let me fall.

J. VERNON MCGEE

A firm and unshakable confidence

Shadrach, Meshach and Abednego replied to the king, "O Nebuchadnezzar, we do not need to defend ourselves before you in this matter. If we are thrown into the blazing furnace, the God we serve is able to save us from it, and he will rescue us from your hand, O king. But even if he does not, we want you to know, O king, that we will not serve your gods or worship the image of gold you have set up."

(DANIEL 3:16–18)

DAY
110

T he perseverance of Shadrach, Meshach, and Abednego was based upon two reasons: Their firm conviction that God was the guardian of their life and would free them from imminent death by His power if He so chose, and also their determination to die boldly and fearlessly if God called upon them to make such a sacrifice.

What Daniel relates of these three men can be applied to us all. Experience teaches us how many individuals turn away from God and their profession of faith because they do not feel confident in God's power to liberate them. Yet it may be said truthfully of us all—God does take care of us since our life is placed in His hand and will. Still, scarcely one in a hundred holds such a conviction deeply and surely fixed in the heart, for most people depend on themselves to preserve their life, as if God were not the least bit interested in them.

Only those individuals who have learned to place their life in God's care and to consider it safe under His protection have made some progress in God's Word. This one feeling frees them from all fear and trembling since God can extricate His servants from a thousand deaths, as it is said in Psalm 68:20: "Our God is a God who saves; from the Sovereign LORD comes escape from death." So this conviction ought to inspire us with a firm and unshakeable confidence.

JOHN CALVIN

a life was spared

Unless the LORD had given me help, I would soon have dwelt in the silence of death. When I said, "My foot is slipping," your love, O LORD, supported me.

(PSALM 94:17–18)

O ne dark night many years ago, a vessel grounded on a harbor bar in only sixteen feet of water. A seaman went out on the footropes of the vessel's jibboom, but because he was a heavy man, the rope broke and he plunged into the sea. He could not swim. After breaking the surface several times, he sank to rise no more and was carried by the current some distance away from the vessel. The captain and two others sprang into a longboat in which lay a steering oar sixteen feet long. That night the water was "firing"— when stirred, it produced a phosphorescent glow. The sharp eyes of the captain soon saw a phosphorescent gleam where bubbles were rising from the drowning man and immediately plunged down the long oar, touching the man's shoulder. Despite his semicomatose condition, the seaman knew enough to grasp it and so was pulled to the surface.

DAY
III

Had the water not been "firing" that night, had not the oar's length matched the depth of the water on the bar, had not the man's cry been heard when he went overboard, these lines would never have been written and fifty other persons would never have lived. This incident happened in the life of my father several years before his marriage. It is a testament to the sovereignty of God.

How often through history the brittle thread of life has threatened to snap—but God's great purposes held and a life was spared. Why? Because God's blessed sovereignty was ruling and overruling all the time. In this way human lives fulfill His sovereign plans and glorious purposes.

JOHN B. CHAMPION

A Deep and central calm

The LORD reigns, let the earth be glad;
let the distant shores rejoice.

(PSALM 97:1)

G od directs our path; He is acquainted with all our ways; He orders our steps. The temptations, the trials, the joys, the sorrows of our lives—He ordains them all. The niche we occupy, the sphere we try to fill, the work we seek to do—He appoints them all.

This is one of the obvious facts of our faith, but it is one of those facts that desperately needs to be revitalized. When we try to account for our trials and difficulties and hardships—if we believe in the living God at all—we ultimately come to this: They happen to us because they are God's will for us. But that will is a loving will, a perfect will. Once we realize this, we will arrive at Paul's sunny faith that in all things God works for the good of those who love God (Romans 8:28).

Our lives get broken and harassed precisely because we forget that the Lord reigns. "Be still," says one of the psalmists, "and know that I am God" (46:10). Once we realize that He who gave His Son for us is on the throne, we will find it easier to be still, even in life's many perplexities.

To believe this is to possess a deep and central calm which neither sorrow nor pain nor trouble nor even death can disturb, for we will know that underneath us are the everlasting arms. We will be able to make the lines of Whittier our own and say:

DAY
112

I know not what the future hath
Of marvel or surprise,
Assured alone that life and death
His mercy underlies.
I know not where His islands lift
Their fronded palms in air;
I only know I cannot drift
Beyond His love and care.

JOHN DANIEL JONES

HOW CAN WE BE AFRAID?

The LORD is my light and my salvation—whom shall I fear?
The LORD is the stronghold of my life—of whom shall I be afraid?

(PSALM 27:1)

T he world's opinion of God is that He sits in heaven, an idle and unconcerned spectator of passing events. Is it any wonder that people tremble under every misfortune that befalls them when they thus believe themselves to be the victims of blind chance? None of us can feel secure unless we satisfy ourselves of the truth that God superintends everything that happens in this world, and that we can commit our lives and everything we have to the hands of God.

If we are to enjoy a deep conviction that our Lord is a sure refuge for those who cast themselves upon His care, the first thing we must do is to bank on His power. Along with this we must place full confidence in His mercy to prevent those anxious thoughts which might otherwise trouble our minds. God's power and mercy are the two pillars on which we rest and by which may resist the surges of temptation.

DAY
113

In short, does danger spring up from any quarter? Then let us quickly call to mind the divine power which can send far away every evil force intent on causing us harm.

Why should we fear, how can we be afraid, when the God who covers us with the shadow of His wings is the same One who rules the universe with His nod, holds in secret chains the devil and all the wicked, and effectively overrules their schemes and intrigues?

JOHN CALVIN

Beyond the Big Things

During the last watch of the night the LORD looked down from the pillar of fire and cloud at the Egyptian army and threw it into confusion. He made the wheels of their chariots come off so that they had difficulty driving. And the Egyptians said, "Let's get away from the Israelites! The LORD is fighting for them against Egypt."

(EXODUS 14:24–25)

T he Bible insists that God's control extends beyond the "big things" of life. We all know the Lord has His hand in the monumental decisions of our lives, overseeing our dreams and destiny. But Scripture also tells us the Lord gets down into the nuts and bolts of little things.

For example, my comfort and independence rest heavily on bits and pieces of adaptive equipment. When that equipment fails—a buckle on a corset snap or a clamp on a leg bag—it really gets to me.

DAY
114

I was explaining this to a friend not long ago as I wheeled into my van. I cranked the engine and was about to push the control to close the electric-powered door, when my friend reached over, grabbed the handle, and—before I could cry "Stop!"—slammed the door shut. With one good yank, my friend snapped the delicate door chain. He was thoroughly embarrassed, and I was almost irritated.

You probably feel the same way when your washing machine gets rusty joints, when the printer on your computer freezes up, or your car's air conditioner takes a vacation. Take heart! If God can make axheads float (2 Kings 6) or cause the wheels to fall off Egyptian chariots (Exodus 14), then God must be in control of the springs and hinges and widgets that seem to break down at the wrong time.

I try hard to remember that whenever my wheelchair batteries konk out on me, leaving me stranded where I don't want to be, God is still in control!

The next time you have to call a plumber or have a mechanic look under your hood, remember that the King's sovereignty extends to such lowly, utilitarian objects as refrigerators, toasters, transistors, and oil filters. Even in these, He is Lord.

JONI EARECKSON TADA

Nothing but wise, good, and Happy

Whether you turn to the right or to the left, your ears
will hear a voice behind you, saying, "This is the way; walk in it."

(ISAIAH 30:21)

T he infinitely wise, great, and glorious Benefactor of the universe has offered to take you by the hand, lead you through the journey of life, and bring you to His own house in heaven. Trust His Word, therefore, with undoubting confidence. Take His hand with humble gratitude, and obey His voice with all your heart. Then everywhere you go you will hear Him say, "This is the way; walk in it."

In sickness and in health, by night and by day, at home and in public, He will watch over you with a tenderness beyond description. He will make you lie down in green pastures, lead you beside the still waters, and guide you in paths of righteousness for His name's sake. He will prepare a table before you in the presence of your enemies and cause your cup to run over with blessings. From their home in heaven He will direct those charming twin sisters, Goodness and Mercy, to descend and "follow you all your days."

But if you wish God to be your Guide and your Friend, you must do what pleases Him. Certainly you cannot wonder that the infinitely wise Father should prefer His own wisdom to yours and that He should choose for His children their place in life, rather than leave the choice to themselves. The Scriptures tell us what pleases Him. And the whole plan of God is laid out for us in plain, easy, profitable, and delightful terms. Every part and principle of the whole is designed to lead you to God, and following it will make you nothing but wise, good, and happy.

TIMOTHY DWIGHT

DAY
115

A Vision That Transforms

In the year that King Uzziah died, I saw the Lord seated on a throne,
high and exalted, and the train of his robe filled the temple.

(ISAIAH 6:1)

DAY
116

We find true freedom when we accept reality as it is (including God's rightful and effective sovereignty over all His creation) and when we allow Him to make us into all that He would have us be. The doctrine of God's sovereignty, far from being an offense to us, can bring us great and wonderful blessings.

A realization of God's sovereignty inevitably *deepens our reverence of the living and true God.* Without an understanding and appreciation of this truth, it is questionable whether we know the God of the Old and New Testaments at all. For what is a god whose power is constantly being thwarted by the designs of people and Satan? Who can worship such a truncated and pitiable deity? Pink says, "A 'god' whose will is resisted, whose designs are frustrated, whose purpose is checkmated, possesses no title to Deity, and so far from being a fit object of worship, merits nothing but contempt." On the other hand, a God who truly rules His universe is a God to be joyfully sought after, worshiped, and obeyed.

Such is the God whom Isaiah saw: "In the year that King Uzziah died, I saw the Lord seated on a throne, high and exalted, and the train of his robe filled the temple. Above him were seraphs, each with six wings: With two wings they covered their faces, with two they covered their feet, and with two they were flying. And they were calling to one another: 'Holy, holy, holy is the Lord Almighty; the whole earth is full of his glory'" (Isaiah 6:1–3).

Such is the God of the Scriptures. It was a vision of Him, not of a lesser god, that transformed Isaiah's ministry.

JAMES MONTGOMERY BOICE

Recovering our sense of awe

Dominion and awe belong to God;
he establishes order in the heights of heaven.

(JOB 25:2)

W hen we focus on the sovereignty of God, we gain a *new sense of awe.* There was a note of seriousness and solemnity about the religion of the Puritans that is all too often lacking in the religion of today. It was born of their sense of the sovereignty of God. It has passed away because, to a large extent, that doctrine has lost its hold upon us.

We have almost forgotten that cherubim and seraphim, with veiled faces, continually cry, "Holy, holy, holy is the Lord Almighty." In our absorption in the thought of God as Father we have almost lost sight of the fact that He is the Holy Sovereign, ruling the world in righteousness. The result has been that, to a large extent, we have lost the sense of *religious awe,* of *reverence,* and of *godly fear.* There is a verse in a hymn in which the writer says:

DAY
117

> *Oh, how I fear Thee, living God,*
> *With deepest, tenderest fears;*
> *And worship Thee with trembling hope,*
> *And penitential tears.*

That verse is almost foreign to our modern religious experience. We do not "fear" God. We do not "tremble" in His presence. We do not worship Him with "penitential tears." We have lost our sense of God's holy sovereignty, and the awe has passed out of our religion. The seriousness and the solemnity have gone out of it.

To make our religious life deep and strong again, we need to recover that lost sense of awe. We need to be taught afresh the fear of the Lord. And to recover that lost sense of awe, to create within us the feeling of reverence, we need a new vision of God as the Holy Sovereign.

JOHN DANIEL JONES

comfort in the midst of trials

*God is our refuge and strength, an ever present help in trouble. Therefore we will not
fear, though the earth give way and the mountains fall into the heart of the sea,
though its waters roar and foam and the mountains quake with their surging.*

(PSALM 46:1–3)

A knowledge of God in His sovereignty gives us *comfort in the
midst of trials, temptation, or sorrow.* Temptations and sorrows
come to Christians and non-Christians alike. The
question is: How shall we meet them? Clearly, if we must face them
with no clear certainty that they are controlled by God and are permitted for His good purposes, then they are meaningless and life is a
tragedy. That is precisely what many existentialists say. But if God is
still in control, then such circumstances are known to Him and have
their purpose.

DAY
118

We don't know all God's purposes, of course. To know that, we
would have to be God. Nevertheless, we can know some of them
because God reveals them to us. For example, the aged apostle Peter
writes to some who had endured great trials, reminding them that the
end is not yet—Jesus will return—and that in the meantime God is
strengthening and purifying them through their struggles. "In this you
greatly rejoice, though now for a little while you may have had to suffer
grief in all kinds of trials. These have come so that your faith—of greater
worth than gold, which perishes even though refined by fire—may be
proved genuine and may result in praise, glory and honor when Jesus
Christ is revealed" (1 Peter 1:6–7).

Similarly, Paul writes to those at Thessalonica who had lost loved
ones through death, reminding them that the Lord Jesus Christ will
return and will at that time reunite all who are living with their
deceased loved ones. He concludes, "Therefore encourage each other
with these words" (1 Thessalonians 4:18).

Encouraging words indeed! But the encouragement they bring
depends entirely on the truth of God's sovereignty.

JAMES MONTGOMERY BOICE

without a claw mark

When Daniel was lifted from the den, no wound was
found on him, because he had trusted in his God.

(DANIEL 6:23)

T he biblical doctrine of God's sovereignty should both challenge and solidly comfort us. Let me mention four ways in which we should respond to it.

First, let us thoroughly believe it and speak of it. Perhaps more than we suspect in these days when things seem to have gone badly askew, people want to be reminded that the reins are in higher hands than those of human governments. Others who may not *want* to hear it are all the more in *need* of hearing somebody say it. It is the missing note which we must keep sounding.

Second, let us not be swept off our feet by the lengths to which anti-God powers may be permitted to go during this closing stretch of the present age. The Bible has forewarned us. We will enjoy more inward stability and composure if we continually keep in mind our heavenly Keeper's all-control.

Third, there is still the possibility of a large-scale spiritual revival. So long as God remains sovereign, and promises like 2 Chronicles 7:14, John 14:13, and others are in the Bible, mighty visitations may come from our prayer-answering God. So long as the throne in heaven is a "throne of *grace*," big answers may be expected by way of great spiritual awakenings.

Fourth, more than ever, let us *rest* in the sovereignty of God. God is sovereign even when His presence seems least real and the agents of Satan seem unrestrained. If we have to go through the lions' den, our God will bring us out without a claw mark on us. If we must go through the furnace heated seven times hotter than usual, we shall meet the risen Lord there, and He will bring us out without even the smell of the fire upon us.

J. SIDLOW BAXTER

The unbreakable chain

Do you not know? Have you not heard? The LORD is the everlasting God,
the Creator of the ends of the earth. He will not grow tired
or weary, and his understanding no one can fathom.
He gives strength to the weary and increases the power of the weak.

(ISAIAH 40:28–29)

Are you weak? Remember that God is strong. Do your days of service seem short? God is eternal and He will take care of your work. Are you sick with hope long deferred? Hope in God; He will yet send help. Have troubles driven happiness from you? Return to your rest, for the Lord will rescue you. Are you depressed because your strength is almost gone? Remember the unwearied God who works omnipotently on your behalf. Nothing can break the golden chain that binds you to God's throne.

Sometimes God takes away earthly things from us in order that He might be our all and in all. When the earth is made poor for us, the heavens may become rich. God closed the eyes of Milton to the beauty of land and sea and sky, that he might see the companies of angels marching on the hills of God. He closed the ears of Beethoven, that he might hear the music of St. Cecilia falling over heaven's battlements. He gave Isaiah a slave's hut, that he might ponder the house not made with hands, eternal in the heavens.

Look up today; be comforted once more. From this moment on, work in hope. Live like a prince. Scatter sunshine. Let happiness brighten your face. If troubles come, let them be the dark background that throws your hope and faith into bolder relief.

God has set His heart upon you to deliver you! Though your strength fail and the tool of deliverance fall from your hand, the eternal God does not faint or grow weary. He will bring you to victory, immortalize your good deeds, and crown your life with everlasting renown.

NEWELL DWIGHT HILLIS

DAY
120

THE GOODNESS
OF GOD

PRAISE THE LORD,

FOR THE LORD IS GOOD.

PSALM 135:3

summum bonum

You are good, and what you do is good.

(PSALM 119:68)

s God is perfect in every part of His nature, so is He perfect in goodness: "God is light; in him there is no darkness at all" (1 John 1:5). As Thomas Manton wrote:

> He is originally good, good of Himself, which nothing else is; for all creatures are good only by participation in and inter-action with God. He is essentially good; not only good, but goodness itself; the creature's good is a superadded quality; in God it is His essence. He is infinitely good; the creature's good is but a drop. But in God there is an infinite ocean or gathering together of good. He is eternally and immutably good, for He cannot be less good than He is. As there can be no addition made to Him, so can nothing be subtracted from Him.

DAY
121

God is *summum bonum,* the chiefest good.

The original Saxon meaning of our English word *God* is "The Good." God is not only the greatest of all beings, but the best. All the goodness in any creature has been imparted from the Creator; but God's goodness is underived, for it is the essence of His eternal nature. As God was infinite in power from all eternity even before He displayed any of that power, so He was eternally good before He made any expression of His bounty. "You are good, and what you do is good" (Psalm 119:68). God has in Himself an infinite and inexhaustible treasure of all blessedness enough to fill all things.

ARTHUR W. PINK

The foundation stone

For the LORD is good and his love endures forever;
his faithfulness continues through all generations.

(PSALM 100:5)

W hen Christian theology says that God is good, it is not the same as saying that He is righteous or holy. The goodness of God is that which disposes Him to be kind, cordial, benevolent, and full of goodwill toward men. He is tenderhearted and of quick sympathy, and His unfailing attitude toward all moral beings is open, frank, and friendly. By His nature He is inclined to bestow blessedness, and He takes holy pleasure in the happiness of His people.

That God is good is taught or implied on every page of the Bible and must be received as an article of faith as impregnable as the throne of God. It is a foundation stone for all sound thought about God and is necessary to moral sanity. If God is not good, then there can be no distinction between kindness and cruelty, and heaven can be hell and hell, heaven.

The goodness of God is the drive behind all the blessings He daily bestows upon us. God created us because He felt good in His heart, and He redeemed us for the same reason. All our religious activities and every means of grace, however right and useful they may be, are nothing until we understand that the unmerited, spontaneous goodness of God is back of all and underneath all His acts.

Divine goodness is self-caused, infinite, perfect, and eternal. Since God is immutable, He never varies in the intensity of His lovingkindness. He has never been kinder than He now is, nor will He ever be less kind. He is no respecter of persons but makes His sun to shine on the evil as well as on the good and sends His rain on the just and on the unjust.

A. W. TOZER

goodness without parallel

His divine power has given us everything we need for life and godliness
through our knowledge of him who called us by his own glory and goodness.

(2 PETER 1:3)

G od is infinitely exalted above all created beings in goodness. Goodness and royal generosity, mercy, and forgiveness is the glory of earthly monarchs and princes, but in this attribute the Lord, our God, is infinitely exalted above them. God delights in the welfare and prosperity of His creatures; He delights in making them exceedingly happy and blessed, if only they will accept the happiness which He offers.

All creatures continually live upon the generosity of God; He maintains the whole creation through His mere goodness. And every good thing that is enjoyed is a part of His generosity.

When kings are generous and dispense good things to their subjects, they give only what the Almighty has already given to them. God is so merciful and so full of compassion that when miserable man—whom God had no need of, who did Him no good, nor could he do Him any favors—had made himself miserable by rebelling against God, the Lord took such pity on him that He sent His only Son to suffer his torment in his place, so that he might be delivered and set free. And now, on His Son's account, God freely offers to grant these rebels complete and perfect happiness for all eternity.

Never was there such an example of goodness, mercy, pity, and compassion since the world began! All the mercy and goodness of creatures fall infinitely short of it. This is goodness that never was, never will, and never can be paralleled by any other.

JONATHAN EDWARDS

DAY
123

Not Like the Morning Clouds

The earth is full of the goodness of the LORD.

(PSALM 33:5, KJV)

finite minds cannot comprehend the infinite goodness of God. It is so perfect that nothing can be added to it—it is immutable and eternal. The goodness of creatures is like the morning clouds and early dew, but the goodness of God is invariably the same and lasts forever. And although God always has and continues to lavish His goodness on us, it stays the same as ever and remains an inexhaustible fountain.

God is good, and He does good: "The earth is full of the goodness of the LORD" (Psalm 33:5, KJV), and there is not a creature that does not partake of it. This attribute belongs to each divine person, Father, Son, and Spirit.

The goodness of God, like His love and mercy, may be considered both in general and special terms. His general goodness is as extensive as His mercy: "The LORD is good to all" (Psalm 145:9). All creatures as they came from His hand are *very good,* and all share in His goodness in a thousand ways.

His special goodness is extended only to unfallen angels and redeemed men and women. God is good to the unfallen angels in preserving them from apostasy, confirming them in their holy state, and in many other blessings. The angels that sinned, on the other hand, He does not spare but has reserved for judgment. Redeemed men and women also share in His special goodness, yet in this world they each display that goodness in varying ways. For example, some have greater spiritual gifts than others; and while all enjoy the same grace, they do not possess it to the same degree. All such differences must be attributed to His sovereign good will and pleasure.

JOHN GILL

Different Names, same Delight

They will celebrate your abundant goodness and joyfully sing of your righteousness.
The LORD is gracious and compassionate, slow to anger and rich in love.

(PSALM 145:7-8)

T he goodness of God spills over into all His other attributes. All the acts of God are nothing but the outpouring of His goodness, distinguished by various names—just as the oceans of the world are really one body of water, distinguished by several names depending upon what shore their waves touch.

When Moses longed to see God's glory, the Lord told him He would grant him a vision of His goodness: "I will cause all my goodness to pass in front of you" (Exodus 33:19). God's goodness is His glory. The whole catalog of mercy, grace, patience, and faithfulness proclaimed in Exodus 34:6 is summed up in this one word. All are streams from this one fountain; God could be none of these things if He were not first good.

DAY
125

When His goodness confers happiness without merit, it is grace; when it bestows happiness against merit, it is mercy; when He endures rebels, it is patience; when He keeps His promise, it is faithfulness; when it consoles a distressed person, it is pity; when it provides for a destitute person, it is generosity; when it helps an innocent person, it is righteousness.

This attribute is so full of God that it deifies all the rest and broadcasts His infinite delightfulness. His wisdom might strategize against us, His power crush us, His holiness terrify us—but His goodness directs them all for our good and makes them all kind to us.

Whatever beauty or comfort we enjoy in this world, we are indebted for them all to His goodness. It is God's goodness that makes His wisdom plan for us and His power to act for us. It is His goodness that prevents His holiness from making us afraid and His goodness that sends His mercy to relieve us.

STEPHEN CHARNOCK

your father's pleasure

Fear not, little flock, for it is your Father's pleasure to give you the kingdom.

(LUKE 12:32, RSV)

DAY
126

J esus will not sit by and let us disbelieve without a fight. He takes up the weapon of the Word and speaks it with power for all who struggle to believe. His aim is to defeat the fear that God is not the kind of God who really wants to be good to us—that He is not really generous and helpful and kind and tender, but is basically irked with us—ill-disposed and angry.

Sometimes, even if we believe in our heads that God is good to us, we may feel in our hearts that His goodness is somehow forced or constrained, perhaps like a judge who has been maneuvered by a clever attorney into a corner on some technicality, so he has to dismiss the charges against the prisoner whom he would rather send to jail. But Jesus is at pains to help us not feel that way about God. He is striving in this verse to describe for us God's indescribable excellency by showing the unbridled pleasure He takes in giving us the kingdom.

Every little word of this stunning sentence is intended to help take away the fear that Jesus knows we struggle with, namely, that God begrudges His benefits; that He is constrained and out of character when He does nice things; that at bottom He is angry and loves to vent His anger. This is a sentence about the nature of God. It's about the kind of heart God has. It's a verse about what makes God glad—not merely about what God *will* do or what He *has* to do, but what He *delights* to do, what He *loves* to do and takes *pleasure* in doing. Every word counts: "Fear not, little flock, for it is your Father's pleasure to give you the kingdom."

JOHN PIPER

A variety of pleasures

The LORD is good to all; he has compassion on all he has made.

(PSALM 145:9)

All that emanates from God—His decrees, His creation, His laws, His providences—cannot be otherwise than good; as it is written, "God saw all that he had made, and it was *very good*" (Genesis 1:31). Thus, the more closely the creature is studied, the more the beneficence of its Creator becomes apparent.

Consider the highest of God's earthly creatures, man. For abundant reasons the psalmist says, "I praise you because I am fearfully and wonderfully made; your works are wonderful, I know that full well" (139:14). Everything about the structure of our bodies attests to the goodness of their Maker.

DAY
127

The goodness of God can also be seen in the variety of natural pleasures which He has provided for His creatures. God might have been pleased to satisfy our hunger without the food pleasing our palates. But how His benevolence is displayed in the varied flavors which He has given to meats, vegetables, and fruits! God has not only given us senses, but also that which gratifies them; and this too reveals His goodness. The earth might have been as fertile as it is without its surface being so delightfully kaleidoscopic. Our physical lives could have been sustained without beautiful flowers to regale our eyes with their colors, and our nostrils with their sweet perfumes. We might have walked the fields without our ears being serenaded by the music of the birds.

From where, then, did all this loveliness, this charm—so freely distributed over the face of nature—come from? Truly, "The LORD is good to all; he has compassion on all he has made" (Psalm 145:9).

ARTHUR W. PINK

A wondrously carved cabinet

God saw all that he had made, and it was very good.

(GENESIS 1:31)

DAY
128

No other attribute of God's nature is so clearly visible in the whole realm of nature as is the Lord's goodness. His goodness is what caused Him to make anything, while His wisdom enabled Him to make everything in complete order and harmony. Here the goodness of God shines with a glorious luster.

All the creatures which He made express His goodness in a wild variety of ways. It was nothing but great goodness to create beings outside of Himself, to dream up such a multitude of beasts from the depths of nothing, and to give life and breath to these creatures. Divine goodness formed their natures and beautified and adorned them with their diverse appearances and traits. In this way everything was enabled to act for the good of the physical world. Every creature under heaven reflects some aspect of God's goodness. The whole world is a map to represent and a herald to proclaim this wondrous perfection of God.

But the goodness of God is especially displayed in the creation of man. God raised him from the dust by His almighty power, placed him in a more exalted position, and gave him nobler rights and duties than the rest of the creatures. Man's soul and body is like a wondrously carved cabinet, inset with rich and precious gems! God has made him a summary of the whole creation: he links two worlds, heaven and earth. He interacts with the earth in the dust of his body, and he participates with heaven in the spirit of his soul. The life of angels blooms in his reason, and that of animals in his physical senses.

THOMAS BOSTON

A perfect Life

Now the LORD God had planted a garden in the east, in Eden; and there he put the man he had formed. And the LORD God made all kinds of trees grow out of the ground—trees that were pleasing to the eye and good for food. In the middle of the garden were the tree of life and the tree of the knowledge of good and evil.

(GENESIS 2:8–9)

ollowing the mighty creation of Genesis 1 came the triumphant unveiling of God's ultimate and perfect blueprint of life within his newly created family—the majestic glory of Genesis 2. Here was *life* as God intended it—*good* life!

In a sense, Genesis 2 details perfection. It opens with rest, with a holy day, because creation was fully accomplished...and fully good. It then goes on to describe in detail the kind of life God intended to enjoy with His creatures. A beautiful Garden was to be their home. Trees were planted that were pleasing to look at and pleasing to eat. What provision! Not mere trees, but good and pleasing trees. Not just some trees...*all* kinds of trees!

DAY
129

Did Adam and Eve need to eat of the tree of the knowledge of good and evil? Of course not. They had every other kind of tree imaginable, as well as every other generous provision.

Life with God in the Garden was anything but dull. It was a life of constantly receiving good from the hands of God. God gave and gave and gave...and everything He gave was very good!

He gave Adam a helper, Eve. He gave both of them all they needed. He gave them the privilege of working with Him to tend the Garden. He gave them food. He gave them freedom. He gave them pleasure. He gave them wisdom and knowledge. He gave them dominion over the earth. He gave them innocence.

Most of all, He gave them fellowship with Himself, the God who had made them. He gave them nothing less than a *perfect* life.

MICHAEL PHILLIPS

monuments to the goodness of god

The God who made the world and everything in it is the Lord of
heaven and earth and does not live in temples built by hands.
And he is not served by human hands, as if he needed anything,
because he himself gives all men life and breath and everything else.

(ACTS 17:24–25)

DAY
130

G od is good in Himself, fully, totally good without any min-
gling of evil. He is the source of all good; from Him come
all the goods which charm and delight us. His goodness is
infinite, His liberality inexhaustible.

It is God who enlightens us with the sun, which cheers us with
its pleasant warmth and delights us with the varied beauties of field
and forest. God's goodness is shown in the endless supplies of our
teeming earth. His hand paints the petals of the flowers, shapes their
tiny leaves, and fills their cups with honeyed fragrances.

And what are we in soul and body, but living monuments to
attest the goodness of God? Our souls are His gifts; they live and act;
they know and feel through Him. Our eyes see with His sight; our
tongues speak with His motion; our hands labor and our feet walk
with His power, for "in Him we live and move and have our being"
(Acts 17:28).

In all His works God acts in order to communicate His generosity.
He desires the good of His creatures, especially His rational creatures. To
suppose the contrary would be to deny the infinite perfection of the
divine Being.

Of course, this world is not as perfect as it might be, and we do
not always see the "why?" behind this or that physical evil. But should
we wonder at this, that our reason—like the human eye, whose range
of vision is limited—should not be able to see beyond its narrow hori-
zon and comprehend the full extent of the divine counsels? But such
as it is, the world is ruled by a Being infinitely perfect and infinitely
good.

REV. W. DEVIVIER

A change of outlook

The LORD is my helper; I will not be afraid.

(HEBREWS 13:6)

T he whole outlook of mankind might be changed if we could all believe that we dwell under a friendly sky and that the God of heaven, though exalted in power and majesty, is eager to be friends with us.

But sin has made us timid and self-conscious, as well it might. Years of rebellion against God have bred in us a fear that cannot be overcome in a day. The captured rebel does not enter willingly the presence of the king he has so long fought unsuccessfully to overthrow. But if he is truly penitent he may come, trusting only in the loving-kindness of his lord, and the past will not be held against him.

Though the kindness of God is an infinite, overflowing fountain of cordiality, God will not force His attention upon us. If we would be welcomed as the Prodigal was, we must come as the Prodigal came; and when we so come, even though the Pharisees and the legalists sulk without, there will be a feast of welcome within, and music and dancing as the Father takes His child again to His heart.

The greatness of God rouses fear within us, but His goodness encourages us not to be afraid of Him. To fear and not be afraid—that is the paradox of faith.

DAY
131

O God, my hope, my heavenly rest,
My all of happiness below,
Grant my importunate request,
To me, to me, Thy goodness show;
Thy beatific face display,
The brightness of eternal day.
Before my faith's enlightened eyes,

Make all Thy gracious
goodness pass;
Thy goodness is the sight I prize;
O might I see Thy smiling face:
Thy nature my soul proclaim,
Reveal Thy love, Thy glorious name.

Charles Wesley

A. W. TOZER

A good Master

How great is your goodness, which you have stored up for those who fear you,
which you bestow in the sight of men on those who take refuge in you.

(PSALM 31:19)

DAY
132

W hen faith led David to his God, she set him singing at once. He does not describe for us the greatness of God's goodness, for he could not. Yet if we cannot measure, we can marvel. Though we may not calculate with accuracy, we can adore with passion.

In the treasury of the covenant, in the field of redemption, in the banks of the promises, in the granaries of providence, the Lord has provided for all the needs which can possibly arise for His chosen. We should often consider the laid-up goodness of God which has not yet been distributed to the chosen, but is already provided for them. If we are frequently meditating on these things, we will soon feel devout gratitude such as glowed in the heart of David.

Heavenly mercy is not all hidden in the storehouse. In a thousand ways it has already revealed itself on behalf of those who are bold to proclaim their confidence in God. Before their contemporaries this goodness of the Lord has been displayed, so that a faithless generation might stand rebuked. The proofs of the Lord's favor to believers are overwhelming. History teems with amazing examples and our own lives are full of marvels of grace. We serve a good Master!

Faith receives a large reward even now, but looks for her full inheritance in the future. Who would not desire to cast his lot with the servants of a Master whose boundless love fills all holy minds with astonishment?

CHARLES H. SPURGEON

why goodness hates evil

The Lord examines the righteous, but the wicked
and those who love violence his soul hates.

(PSALM 11:5)

S ince it is part of God's goodness that He loves what is excellent and what reflects His character, shouldn't He also hate what is bad and unworthy? If God were to love a gigantic vice as passionately as a noble virtue, how could we possibly call Him divine? Would He really be God if He treated the guilty just as He treats the godly? Could you call Him "good" if it gave Him pleasure to observe evil, or if He always allowed the innocent to be abused and never threatened to punish their oppressors?

How would we know the goodness of God and His passion to be good to His creatures, if He never demonstrated His unbending hostility toward sin and His eagerness to preserve the good order of the world? If sinful creatures were always exempt from the effects of His wrath, He would declare Himself not to be infinitely good because He would not really be righteous.

No one thinks it a defect in the sun that its scorching heat can dry up and consume the unwholesome vapors of the air. In the same way, God's demonstrations of His justice cannot be considered blots upon His goodness since they defend and glorify His holiness and preserve the beauty and order of the world.

When Abel's blood cried out for vengeance against Cain, it spoke a good thing (Hebrews 12:24). So if it was a good thing that his innocent blood demanded justice, how could it be a bad thing that the Sovereign of the world executed it? How could God continue to be a good and righteous Judge if He did not preserve human society? And how could it be preserved unless He were to make public judgments against public wrongs?

STEPHEN CHARNOCK

DAY
133

pushed to repentance

*Do you show contempt for the riches of his kindness,
tolerance and patience, not realizing that
God's kindness leads you toward repentance?*

(ROMANS 2:4)

C ontemplating the kindness and goodness of God always leads us to repentance. I was thinking about that a few days before last Easter. I read through the story of the Crucifixion to prepare my heart for Easter morning. But I spent more than a few hours deliberating over the words of Christ when He cried in anguish from the cross, "My God, my God, why have you forsaken me?"

The reply was silence. Cold, accusing silence. Heaven itself accused Jesus of sins in those horrible moments: lusting and lying, cheating and coveting, murder and hypocrisy, cruelty and deceit. Of course, Christ had never committed any of those sins, *but we have*. And every one of your sins and mine was racked up on His account right there on that cross.

So where was God's goodness in treating Christ so? Where was the Father's kindness in turning His back on His only Son—while Jesus cried out in horror and grief?

On that terrible, wonderful day, God's goodness and kindness were directed toward you. God forsook His own Son...so that He would never have to forsake you!

As I pondered that amazing thought, I felt ashamed. The goodness of God was, indeed, leading me to repentance. To think that God's anger for my sins was poured out on Christ—and that He has no anger left for me!

Unlike Christ, I will *never* have to agonize over separation from my Father. And neither will you. God poured the full measure of His wrath—the terrors of eternal hell—on His own Son...so that you and I could be adopted into His very family. That's how good He is. And that's how his goodness has a way of pushing us to repentance.

JONI EARECKSON TADA

DAY
134

He Means Us Good

*Perhaps the reason he was separated from you for a
little while was that you might have him back for good—
no longer as a slave, but better than a slave, as a dear brother.*

(PHILEMON 15-16)

T radition has it that Paul's letters were first collected and circulated by the church in Ephesus, which first recognized that these epistles had lasting and universal value. And who do you suppose was most responsible for collecting and distributing these letters? Most biblical scholars attribute this to the work of the bishop of that place—a man named Onesimus, a former runaway slave.

Had it not been for Onesimus, we might not have had the letters of Paul in our New Testament. And if he had not run away, he would have never met Paul. And if Paul had not seen him as a brother and not a slave, he would have never been converted. If he had not gone back to face his owner, he would have never really been free.

Friends, we do not know enough to pass final judgment on the things that are happening to us. We do not have the capacity to eat of "the Tree of Knowledge of good and evil." That food is beyond us.

But for all we do not know, here is what we do know: "In all things, the seemingly good and the seemingly bad, God is at work for good!" Life is like a circus and every day is like those little cars that appear so tiny, yet, out of which emerge a thousand clowns. It is too early to come to a conclusion about any event. But it is not too early to live in hope, in faith, in confident openness. Our God is a Mystery, to be sure, but count on it—He means us good and in all things is at work to bring it to pass. Therefore, bet your life on it, stake your whole future on it. He loves us and means us good!

JOHN R. CLAYPOOL

A Hedge Around Us

*"Does Job fear God for nothing?" Satan replied. "Have you not put
a hedge around him and his household and everything he has?"*

(JOB 1:9–10)

G od has put a hedge around the life of every believer. The thorns that seem to hem us in are in reality placed there to close us in to God Himself, to protect us from evil, to provide us with sanctuary in the midst of a troubled world.

For most of His children, God's hedges do not seemingly entail suffering, but only protection. For some, however, they mean unending pain and weakness, disappointment and sorrow, varying in degree to total imprisonment. Why this must be so, we may not know; sufficient for us to know that God Himself has hedged us in, and God's hedges are always hedges of protection and blessing. And God Himself, living there both with us and in us, longs to make of our thorny wall a thing of wonder to men and angels and demons, a thing that will one day bring forth holy blossom and fruit to our eternal good and His eternal glory.

DAY
136

Fragrance and fruit from a thorny hedge—how can it be? Only by His Spirit's enabling: "The fruit of the Spirit is love, joy, peace, patience, kindness, goodness, faithfulness, gentleness and self-control" (Galatians 5:22–23); and that fruit may be borne on any tree if Christ is there. Did not the thorniest tree of all bring forth the holy flower of redemption and the fruit of everlasting life because of Him who gave Himself there for us? How then can we doubt His power to so enrich our thorn that it, too, may blossom?

God does not ask His children to endure anything that He Himself has not first endured. In Jesus Christ the almighty God suffered Himself to be hedged about in a manner we shall never be able to comprehend, let alone be called upon to undergo.

MARGARET CLARKSON

HIS DEEP WORK

He is the LORD; let him do what is good in his eyes.

(1 SAMUEL 3:18)

God gives only good; His will and His ways are perfect. If we believe these things implicitly, we must learn to make use of the strength they can impart. We must say them repeatedly to ourselves in our hours of darkness, laying them on our hearts as a healing balm, even though we may not feel their truth being borne out in our experience.

Feeling, in fact, has nothing to do with it; we cling to naked truth and stake our all on that. We repeat these truths, blindly believing with a faith that refuses to be daunted, until one day we discover, often to our own surprise, that there is no longer any shadow of doubt in our hearts—we know the truths to which we have been clinging so desperately; at last we have the unshakeable assurance that these things are so. God has wrought His work of faith in us and given us the grace of a great acceptance, which cannot be taken from us.

DAY
137

Such an experience may take place within a short time; more likely it will take months, even years. Always it is initiated by an act of the will on our part; we set ourselves to believe in the overruling goodness, providence, and sovereignty of God and refuse to turn aside no matter what may come, no matter how we feel.

God honors such faith and holy purpose, and sooner or later He "sets in pain the jewel of His joy" and gives His gift of an acceptance so deep that peace will be ours forever. For no matter how deep the pain or sorrow, His work in us is deeper, and "everything God does will endure forever" (Ecclesiastes 3:14).

MARGARET CLARKSON

The Thought That Most Pleases God

*I am still confident of this: I will see the goodness
of the LORD in the land of the living.*

(PSALM 27:13)

J ulian of Norwich, who lived six hundred years ago, saw clearly that the ground of all blessedness is the goodness of God. Chapter 6 of her incredibly beautiful and perceptive little classic, *Revelations of Divine Love,* begins, "This showing was made to teach our souls to cleave wisely to the goodness of God." Then she lists some of the mighty deeds God has wrought in our behalf, and after each one she adds "of His goodness." She also writes:

DAY
138

> All of the strength that may come through prayer comes from the goodness of God, for He is the goodness of everything. Just as our flesh is covered by clothing and our blood is covered by our flesh, so are we, soul and body, covered and enclosed by the goodness of God.
>
> God desires only that our soul cling to Him with all of its strength, and in particular, that it clings to His goodness. For of all of the things our minds can think about God, it is thinking upon His goodness that pleases Him most and brings the most profit to our soul. For we are so preciously loved by God that we cannot even comprehend it. No created being can ever know how much and how sweetly and tenderly God loves them. It is only with the help of His grace that we are able to persevere in spiritual contemplation with endless wonder at His high, surpassing, immeasurable love which our Lord in His goodness has for us.

A. W. TOZER AND JULIAN OF NORWICH

A place to Belong

Let us then approach the throne of grace with confidence, so that we may receive mercy and find grace to help us in our time of need.

(HEBREWS 4:16)

M any years ago when my wife and I were first married, we looked with surprise out of the kitchen window one day at a blur of black and white as it zipped around the corner of our home. In days to come we discovered that the "blur" was actually a frightened stray dog. In time she would dare to drink our water and eat our food—but never when we were around. The moment she caught a glance of us, she would run away as though she knew she didn't belong. Certainly she was in no way worthy of us. How could she trust our invitations to come closer?

DAY
139

Gradually her fears subsided, and instead of running she would simply sit a ways off and cock her little head. She so much wanted to belong, to be close. But could she, would she, trust our gentle words? No, they were too good to be true. To think that anyone would consider her to be of value—that someone would truly desire her!

Finally, one day her rigid pose and cocked head changed in an instant into that familiar black and white blur of speed we had so often seen. But this time it ended in one huge leap right into our arms. She belonged! She was safe. In the months that followed, little "Hurry" entered into all the rights and privileges befitting a member of our family. Closeness would be hers the rest of her life. She had taken us at our word.

Can we take God at His word, incredibly good as it seems? Can we believe Him and respond to Him as He offers invitation after invitation through His Word? When we pray, we too come home. Do we truly belong there? God's answer is "Yes, you do! Forever!"

DAVID NEEDHAM

Don't miss god's extras

You do not have, because you do not ask God.

(JAMES 4:2)

T he Bible tells us that we do not have because we do not ask. Many added blessings could be ours, but we live without them because we do not ask and receive. I am convinced that our Father would grant us far more than our daily requirement of grace if we came boldly to His throne to receive it.

> *O what peace we often forfeit,*
> *O what needless pain we bear—*
> *all because we do not carry*
> *everything to God in prayer!*

DAY
140

Do not be satisfied with the daily run of average requirements. There are extras, for our Father's storehouse is well stocked and the cupboard will never be bare. He is pleased that we ask for special favors. We honor Him when we expect great things from Him. He is able to do exceeding abundantly above all that we ask or think.

> *His love has no limit, His grace has no measure,*
> *His power no boundary known unto men;*
> *For out of His infinite riches in Jesus*
> *He giveth and giveth and giveth again.*

Even among us mortals down here we have bonuses, and the worker sometimes receives extra pay from the boss. Surely our heavenly Father is not a hard master, doling out bare necessities. He is our *Father* and delights to make glad the hearts of His children. We are not to love Him for His gifts, but we must not be afraid to ask for more than our daily allowance. There is more, much more, in His abundance that could be ours, but we do not have because we do not ask. Don't miss God's extras!

VANCE HAVNER

The source of greatness

Thy gentleness has made me great.

(PSALM 18:35, KJV)

T he word translated "gentleness" here can also be rendered "goodness," as in "Thy *goodness* has made me great." David saw that God had been tremendously benevolent to him, and he gratefully ascribed all his greatness not to his own goodness, but to the goodness of God. "Thy providence" is another possible reading—which indeed is nothing more than goodness in action. Goodness is the bud, providence the flower; or goodness is the seed, providence the harvest. Some translate it "thy help," which is but another word for providence. Providence is the faithful ally of the saints, aiding them in the service of their Lord. Some other scholars tell us that the text means "thy humility" has made me great.

DAY
141

Perhaps the most comprehensive reading is "thy condescension," as it combines all the ideas already mentioned, as well as that of humility. It is God's making Himself little in order to make us great. We are so little that if God should reveal His greatness without condescension, we would be trampled under His feet. But God, who must stoop to view the skies and bow to see what angels do, looks to the lowly and contrite and makes them great.

While these translations have all been suggested for the original text, we find that the Septuagint, the ancient Greek version of the Hebrew Old Testament, reads "thy discipline"—thy fatherly correction—has made me great. David ascribes all his own greatness to the condescending goodness and graciousness of his Father in heaven.

However we translate the verse, let us all feel David's sentiment in our hearts and confess that whatever goodness or greatness God may have bestowed upon us, we must cast our crowns at His feet and cry, "Thy goodness has made me great!"

CHARLES H. SPURGEON

I'D TELL HIM HE LIED!

O taste and see that the LORD is good.

(PSALM 34:8, NASB)

A pastor told the children of his communion class about a troubled man who declared that God is not good. Turning to a bright boy of fourteen, the pastor asked: "What would you say if you heard anyone make such a statement?"

Instantly, his eyes flashing, his fists clenched, indignation in his voice, the boy replied: "I'd tell him he lied!"

Perhaps his answer was not as polite as it might have been, but the boy had the right idea. It was refreshing to note the certainty of his convictions about God and to feel that some day he would be ready to repeat the more peaceful challenge of the psalmist: "O taste and see that the LORD is good."

How much that old Saxon word *good* expresses! Every one of its many meanings describes an aspect of God's goodness, goodness so great that human beings cannot conceive it. Even those who wrote our sweetest hymns of praise could only look up in adoration and sing, "Surely God is good to Israel" (Psalm 73:1); "O give thanks to the LORD, for He is good" (1 Chronicles 16:34); "O taste and see that the LORD is good." Goodness—goodness—goodness—this is the keynote of the most beautiful of the Psalms.

How those praises of the Lord are echoed by the Christian whose personal experience enables him or her to bear testimony to the goodness of God! Frequently that testimony will be given by someone lying on a bed of suffering. But there is no doubt in his heart. He knows that God is good, and whatever his trials may be, his one triumphant thought is, *God's in His heaven; All's right with the world.*

JOHN T. FARIS

DAY
142

A priceless Heritage

I will praise you forever for what you have done;
in your name I will hope, for your name is good.

(PSALM 52:9)

A young man who was putting himself through college sometimes did not know where he would get the money to pay his bills, and he was worried. One dark day when he feared he would have to leave college and abandon his cherished career plans, he received a letter from a friend. The writer, powerless to help in any other way, pointed the student to God and reminded him of the Father's goodness. He said, in substance:

> The covenant which enfolds you is a priceless heritage; expect great things from it, to the degree you make this possible by honoring it yourself. "Those who honor Me I will honor" is not the catch phrase of a cheap bargain, but the memorial of a great and gracious opportunity. Hold to it with a deathless grip—that is, the grip of faith. As I grow older, I find it inexpressibly restful and invigorating, and also unutterably sweet, to rest on this. God is good—good—good. He is gentleness itself, shaping Himself to our state, even our weaknesses; with infinite and most gracious pliability, fitting Himself to our deformed figures and crooked ways with untold affection and unspeakable skill. Trust Him wholly, and make loyalty to Him and to your purposes, shaped by His providence, the cardinal rule of life. This will pay a thousandfold, in a thousand ways, beyond all expectation.

DAY
143

That letter was penned by a man who, at the moment of writing, was passing through an experience which would test the faith of anyone. But his faith remained firm because he knew that the Lord is good.

It is this certainty of the goodness of God which enables the Christian to live in fulness of joy and to sing His praises night and day.

JOHN T. FARIS

The Required Response

*Oh, that men would praise the LORD for his goodness,
and for his wonderful works to the children of men!*

(PSALM 107:8, KJV)

G ratitude is the required response of those upon whom God has showered His goodness. Yet it is often withheld simply because God's goodness is so constant and so abundant. It is lightly esteemed because it is exercised toward us in the everyday course of events. It is not felt because we daily experience it.

"Do you show contempt for the riches of his kindness?" asks Paul in Romans 2:4. God's goodness is held in contempt when it is not used as a means to lead men to repentance, but instead serves to harden them in the erroneous belief that God entirely overlooks their sin.

The goodness of God is the life of the believer's trust. It is this excellency in God which most appeals to our hearts. Because His goodness endures forever, we ought never to be discouraged: "The LORD is good, a refuge in times of trouble. He cares for those who trust in him." As Charles Spurgeon said:

> When others behave badly to us, it should only stir us up the more heartily to give thanks to the Lord, because He is good. And when we ourselves are conscious that we are far from being good, we should only the more reverently bless Him that He is good. We must never tolerate an instant's unbelief as to the goodness of the Lord. Whatever else may be questioned, this is absolutely certain, that God is good. His gifts may vary, but His nature is always the same.

ARTHUR W. PINK

DAY
144

Give Thanks to the Lord

Give thanks to the LORD, for he is good.

(PSALM 136:1)

Psalm 107 opens with the statement, "Give thanks to the LORD, for he is good." The psalm then presents us with four scenes, each depicting human need in some form: the plight of a man on his journey by land (vv. 4–9); the plight of a prisoner enslaved (10–16); the plight of one who is sick (17–22); the plight of the sea voyager in a storm (23–32). In each instance we see the goodness of God in deliverance.

The goodness which God displays here is no ordinary, common, run-of-the-mill goodness. Here is divine goodness shown toward the tired and bewildered traveler, the enslaved captive, the sick and the dying, the sailor being battered and tossed about on the sea of life. The entire Old Testament resounds with the praiseful refrain, "He is good." And rightly so!

DAY
145

We should thank God daily for all of the good things of life and enjoy them in moderation. But are we as passionate and regular as we should be in giving thanks to God for them? When we humbly and gratefully offer thanks to God for the things He provides, they acquire a holy quality as His gifts to us. Indeed the Lord is good! What a variety of natural pleasures He has provided for His creatures! The first recorded lie of the devil was his calling into question the goodness of God.

Who is there among us who can deny that God has been good? Then let us not delay to praise Him for His goodness.

LEHMAN STRAUSS

songs of praise

With praise and thanksgiving they sang to the LORD: "He is good; his love to Israel endures forever." And all the people gave a great shout of praise to the LORD.

(EZRA 3:11)

W hen we become aware of God's goodness, it should elicit a certain kind of response from us. We see the proper response in a group of weary exiles who had made their way back to their promised land after seventy years of Babylonian captivity. Their goal was to rebuild the temple of God. Progress was slow, but in the second year of their restoration the foundation was finally completed. Those who had lived long enough to remember Solomon's temple knew that this one could not begin to compare with it in size or beauty. But that made little difference to them. They were back in their land, and their temple was under way. "With praise and thanksgiving they sang to the LORD: 'He is good; his love to Israel endures forever.' And all the people gave a great shout of praise to the LORD" (Ezra 3:11). God's goodness prompted songs of praise and thanksgiving. And that is exactly what it should do for us.

DAY
146

The word *praise* comes from a root that means "to be boastful." When we praise God, we are boasting in the good things He has done, not necessarily because He has done them for us, but simply because they demonstrate who He is. People who know a good God have no cause to grumble and complain. Praise becomes a way of life for them.

Our response to God's goodness is not only praise, but also thanksgiving. If we take a few minutes each day to do nothing but thank God for some of the good things He has done, we may never get depressed again. So take a thanksgiving break! Thanksgiving is like a tonic that brightens the entire complexion of our lives. Learn to practice it.

RICHARD STRAUSS

NO GREATER REASON

Praise be to the LORD, the God of Israel, from everlasting to everlasting.
Then all the people said "Amen" and "Praise the LORD."

(1 CHRONICLES 16:36)

T he Lord is good; but good not in the way that the things He has made are good. Indeed, God made all things very good. Heaven and earth and all that is in them—He made them good, and He made them very good.

But if all these things that He made are good, what is He who made them like? It was He who made all things good; but no one made the good which He is. He is good by virtue of His own goodness, not by participation in any other goodness. He needed no one to make Him good, but other things needed Him to make them good. The Lord Jesus Christ said, "No one is good—except God alone" (Mark 10:18). So how good is that good from which all goods are derived!

Whatever you praise, you praise it because it is good. Only a madman praises what is not good. If you praise an unjust man on account of his injustice, will you not also be unjust? If you praise a thief because he is a thief, will not you also be his accomplice? On the other hand, if you praise a just man on account of his justice, will not you also have a share in his justice through praising him?

So then, whatever else we praise, we praise because it is good. And you can have no greater, better, or surer reason for praising God than that He is good. Therefore, praise the Lord, for He is good.

ST. AUGUSTINE OF HIPPO

DAY
147

just celebrate!

Worship the LORD your God; it is he who will
deliver you from the hand of all your enemies.

(2 KINGS 17:39)

DAY
148

W henever we come to worship, we come to celebrate. Worship is not intended to be a quiet, regal, dignified event where the Spirit of God is kept locked up in our hearts. Rather, it is a joyful celebration of God's goodness and salvation. All of us have some reason to celebrate something that God has done in our lives. It may be a victory over defeatism or over spiritual shyness. We may have been delivered from enemies. Deliverance from poverty. Deliverance from ignorance. Deliverance from frustration. Deliverance from temptation. Deliverance from substance abuse. Deliverance from a failed marriage. Deliverance from senseless spending habits. Deliverance from fears and anxiety. Deliverance from venomous speech. But most of all, each of us can celebrate being delivered from the hand of spiritual and eternal death. Our good God has set us free!

Therefore, when we gather for worship, it's not a funeral. It's not a morbid gathering of morbid people, but a gathering of vibrant, animated, dynamic, lively, spirited, intense, and red-hot people who understand that it was God's grace that woke them up in the morning. It was grace that kept them all week long. It was grace that brought them to the house of worship.

Worship is for celebrating the goodness and grace of God. It is for celebrating what He has done in the past and what He is doing right now. And if you want to shout, then shout. If you want to run, then run. If you want to dance, then dance. If you want to cry, then cry. If you want to hold up your hands, then hold them up. If you want to jump up and down, then jump up and down. If you want to wave your arms, then wave your arms. Just celebrate!

GEOFFREY V. GUNS

The Master's Touch

All who touched him were healed.

(MARK 6:56)

By the time I met Pop Trombero in the mid 1960s, he had long since retired as a successful jockey and master horse trainer. Once when Pop came to our farm, my sister asked me to let him ride my horse, Tumbleweed. I protested. Listen, that horse was *mine,* and I didn't want anyone else riding her—even if he was an "expert."

After a few minutes, however, I gave in. While we rode, I stuck close to Pop and Tumbleweed—just to make sure he didn't jerk on her bridle or tug at her reigns.

After a few minutes, I realized I had nothing to worry about. In fact, I grudgingly realized I had a few things to learn. He was so...*tender* with Tumbleweed. Constantly talking to her. Continually stroking her neck. Always giving her his undivided attention. No matter how interesting the trail, Pop's focus never diverted from that horse for a moment.

And you wouldn't believe the way Tumbleweed responded. She became a different horse! Her ears pricked up. She listened to his commands, never balked, obeyed instantly. It seemed her joy to do Pop's bidding. I was amazed!

I learned that day that wonderful things happen when a master like Pop touches a horse. He knows how to guide. He knows how to bring out the best.

In the same way, wonderful things happen when the Master touches our lives. Mark 6:56 tells us that "all who touched him were healed."

God's attention never diverts from you for a moment. His touch in your life is constant, unchanging, always tender. The Lord God knows how to guide you as no one else. He knows how to bring out your best. It's simply a matter of yielding to the Master's touch.

JONI EARECKSON TADA

DAY
149

touch our hearts

*Saul also went to his home in Gibeah; accompanied
by valiant men whose hearts God had touched.*

(1 SAMUEL 10:26)

T he touch of God on one's heart is an awesome thing. It is awesome because the heart is so precious to us—so deep and intimate and personal. When the heart is touched, we are deeply touched. Someone has gotten through protective layers to the center. We have been known. We have been uncovered and seen.

The touch of God is an awesome thing because God is God. Just think of what is being said here! *God* touched them. Not a wife. Not a child. Not a parent. Not a counselor. But God. The One with infinite authority, infinite wisdom, infinite love, infinite goodness, infinite purity, and infinite justice. *That* One touched their hearts. How does the circumference of Jupiter touch the edge of a molecule, let alone penetrate to its nucleus?

The touch of God is awesome because it is a touch. It is a real connection. God, with infinite condescension, touched their hearts. God was that close. And they were not consumed.

I love that touch. I want it more and more. I want it for myself and for all of God's people. I pray that God would touch me and all His church in a new, deep way for His glory. If it comes with fire, so be it. If it comes with water, so be it. If it comes with wind, let it come, O God. If it comes with thunder and lightning, let us bow before it. O Lord, come. Come close enough to touch. Shield us with the asbestos of grace, but no more. Pass through all the way to the heart, and touch. Burn and soak and blow and crash. Or, in a still, small voice. Whatever the means, come. Come all the way and touch our hearts.

JOHN PIPER

Through All Eternity

Surely goodness and love will follow me all the days of my life,
and I will dwell in the house of the LORD forever.

(PSALM 23:6)

ord of hosts! The final fruit for those who know You is that their souls shall dwell among the good and in the paradise of their God.

They slumber without fear, for You are their strength and shield. They rest under the shelter of Your wing, for they belong to You. They do not suffer the cold, for You warm them with the fiery rays of Your love. They do not hunger, for You feed them with the bread of life. They do not thirst, for You give them the waters of the Holy Spirit. They are not in need, for You are their treasure and riches and they live in the house of peace, in confident rest under the cover of Your righteousness.

DAY
151

They wash the feet of their souls in the clear and sparkling waters of Your truth. They study their consciences in the clear mirror of Your wisdom. Their souls dwell in the fullness of Your goodness and the mist of Your grace is upon them. Nothing can stand in their way, for they are partakers of Your Spirit and have tasted its sweetness. Their house is built on the solid rock. They are as pillars in Your holy temple. They have tasted the secrets of the bread of heaven.

Praise to You, Lord! Fear of You remains before their eyes and they walk in Your way. Therefore, their souls shall dwell in Your fullness and their seed, born of the Holy Spirit and the Word, will possess the land of the living where You and Your chosen ones will reign in joyous glory through all of eternity.

MENNO SIMONS

THE
RIGHTEOUSNESS
AND JUSTICE
OF GOD

HE IS THE ROCK,

HIS WORKS ARE PERFECT,

AND ALL HIS

WAYS ARE JUST.

DEUTERONOMY 32:4

mercy, yes!
But also justice

But thou, O LORD, art a God full of compassion, and gracious,
long-suffering, and plenteous in mercy and truth.

(PSALM 86:15, KJV)

A ll sinners and lovers of this world are delighted to hear the Lord is merciful and compassionate, that He is longsuffering and very merciful. But we should not forget that although He is so merciful, yet too He is true!

If the Lord had told us only of His mercy and compassion, we might devote ourselves to our sins, feeling secure and free to pursue wickedness with impunity. We might practice every evil that appealed to us, we might enjoy the world's pleasures as much as we were allowed to (or as much as our lusts dictated to us). And if anyone tried to scold or frighten us with some good advice about restraining ourselves from the wild pursuit of our own degraded desires and warned us about our abandonment of God, we would stand there among the scolding voices and quote from the Lord's own book: "Why are you trying to scare me about our God? He is merciful and compassionate and very merciful!"

DAY
152

To stop us from saying that sort of thing, God added one phrase at the end of this passage in Psalms: *and true*. Thus He ruled out the smugness of presumptuous sin and prompted in us instead the sorrow for sin. Yes, our God is lavish with His mercy in this age; but so is He severe with His threat of punishment in the age to come!

Let us by all means rejoice at the Lord's mercy—but let us also fear the Lord's judgment! He spares, but He doesn't say nothing. Yes, He does say nothing, but He won't always say nothing. Listen to Him while He is refraining from saying nothing in words, or you will have no time to listen while He is refraining from saying nothing in judgment.

ST. AUGUSTINE OF HIPPO

A straightness about Him

When they came to the threshing floor of Nacon, Uzzah reached out and took hold of the ark of God, because the oxen stumbled.
The LORD'S anger burned against Uzzah because of his irreverent act; therefore God struck him down and he died there beside the ark of God.

(2 SAMUEL 6:6–7)

T here is a consistency in God, a "straightness" about Him. Often man's unrighteousness is described in terms of our being not straight. We are crooked. It is not by accident that we often refer to criminals as "crooks." Crooks are so called because they are crooked. They are not straight. God is straight. His straightness is seen in His outward behavior, His external righteousness. In all eternity God has never done a crooked thing. Yes, He killed Nadab and Abihu. He killed Uzzah. He did the same thing to Ananias and Sapphira in the New Testament. But these were all righteous acts of judgment.

DAY
153

The Bible clearly teaches that God is the Supreme Judge of the universe. The question we ask after reading about Uzzah is this: Is God qualified for the job? To function as the Supreme Judge of heaven and earth, He ought to be just. If the Supreme Judge is unjust, we have no hope of justice ever prevailing. We know that earthly judges can be corrupt. They take bribes; they show partiality; at times they act from ignorance. They make mistakes.

Not so with God. There is no corruption in Him. No one can bribe Him. He refuses to show partiality. He is no respecter of persons. He never acts out of ignorance. He does not make mistakes. Bumper stickers in this world may demand, "Impeach the President," but only a fool asks for the impeachment of God.

God's justice is never divorced from His righteousness. He never condemns the innocent. He never clears the guilty. He never punishes with undo severity. He never fails to reward righteousness. His justice is perfect justice.

R. C. SPROUL

The Marriage of Justice and Benevolence

Great and marvelous are your deeds, Lord God Almighty.
Just and true are your ways, King of the ages.

(REVELATION 15:3)

Many seem to be afraid to contemplate justice as an attribute of benevolence. Any demonstration of it among men causes them to recoil and shudder as if they saw a demon. But let it have its place in the glorious circle of God's moral attributes. It must have. It will have. It cannot have otherwise.

Justice executes law. It aims to produce commercial honesty, public and private integrity, and tranquility. It says to violence, disorder, and injustice, "Peace, be still," and brings about a great calm.

DAY
154

We see the evidences and the illustrations of this attribute of God in the thunderings of Sinai and in the agony of Calvary. We hear it in the wail of the world when the fountains of the great deep were broken up, when the windows of heaven were opened and the floods descended and the population of a globe was swallowed up. We see it exhibited in the destruction of Sodom and Gomorrah; and last, we shall forever see its bright but awful and glorious displays in the dark and curling folds of that pillar of smoke of the torment of the damned that ascends up before God forever and ever.

Seeing justice as an attribute of benevolence will prevent the punishment of the finally impenitent sinner from taking away from the happiness of God and of holy beings. They will never delight in misery for its own sake. But they will take pleasure in the administration of justice. When the smoke of the torment of the damned comes up in the sight of heaven, they will, just as they are represented, shout, "Hallelujah! For our Lord God Almighty reigns. Just and true are your ways, King of the ages!"

CHARLES G. FINNEY

goodness shines in justice

He does not leave the guilty unpunished.

(EXODUS 34:7)

T he justice of God is a part of His goodness. God Himself thought so when He told Moses He would make all His goodness pass before him (Exodus 33:19). Included in that "goodness" was His unwillingness to clear the guilty (Exodus 34:7). Since it is a property of goodness to hate evil, it is also a property of goodness to punish it. It is no less righteous to punish a person for his sins than it is to reward a person who obeys God's will. Whatever is righteous is good; since sin is evil, whatever opposes it is good. God's goodness shines in His justice, for without being just He could not be good.

DAY
155
⤳

Sin is a moral disorder in the world and every sin is injustice. Since injustice breaks God's moral order, justice demands that the world be put back in order. Punishing an offender accomplishes this; if a person refuses to obey God, then he must suffer to uphold God's honor. At the beginning when God pronounced all things good, they all existed in perfect order and thus mutually benefitted and helped one another. When this order is disturbed, the goodness of the creature ceases.

So if it is a bad thing to spoil this order, would it not be a part of divine goodness to restore it, and thereby restore some measure of the creature's goodness? Do we ever consider a governor less good because he is strict in his justice and punishes whatever brings disorder to his jurisdiction? If not, how could we ever imagine that it diminishes God's goodness to punish that which brings disorder into His creation? As wisdom without goodness would be nothing but devilish cunning resulting in destruction, so goodness without justice would be impotent indulgence, resulting in confusion everywhere.

STEPHEN CHARNOCK

A moral world

He is the Rock, his works are perfect, and all his ways are just.
A faithful God who does no wrong, upright and just is he.

(DEUTERONOMY 32:4)

T he way of modern men and women is to turn a blind eye to all wrongdoing as long as they safely can. They tolerate it in others, feeling that there, but for the accident of circumstances, go they themselves. Parents hesitate to correct their children, and teachers to punish their pupils, and the public puts up with vandalism and antisocial behavior of all sorts with scarcely a murmur. The accepted maxim seems to be that as long as evil can be ignored, it should be; one should punish only as a last resort, and then only so far as is necessary to prevent the evil from having grievous social consequences. Willingness to tolerate and indulge evil up to the limit is seen as a virtue, while living by fixed principles of right and wrong is censured as morally doubtful.

DAY 156

In our pagan way, we take it for granted that God feels as we do. The idea that retribution might be the moral law of God's world and an expression of His holy character seems to us quite fantastic. Those who uphold it find themselves accused of projecting onto God their own pathological impulses of rage and vindictiveness. Yet the Bible insists throughout that this world which God in His goodness has made is a moral world, one in which retribution is as basic a fact as breathing.

God is the Judge of all the earth, and He will do right, vindicating the innocent, but punishing lawbreakers. God is not true to Himself unless He punishes sin. And unless one knows and feels the truth of this fact, that wrongdoers have no natural hope of anything from God but retributive judgment, one can never share the biblical faith in divine grace.

J. I. PACKER

can god be angry?

But the LORD is the true God; he is the living God, the eternal King.
When he is angry, the earth trembles; the nations cannot endure his wrath.

(JEREMIAH 10:10)

W e tend to be taken aback by the thought that God could be angry. How can a deity who is perfect and loving ever be angry? Just look at us—we manage to be very understanding and accepting of our flaws. We take pride in our tolerance of the excesses of others. So what is God's problem?

Of course, the Bible never suggests that God's anger is lightly provoked. Or that God is ready to pounce at the first misstep. On the contrary, we are told He is "slow to anger" (Exodus 34:6). Nor does His anger come from having a bad temper. Indeed, God's anger issues from the intensity and depth of His love for us, as well as the height of His moral perfection and His outrage against evil. Nor does God's anger come from feeling slighted or ignored. God's anger is a just anger and from perfect motives.

Think of how we feel when we see someone we love ravaged by unwise actions or relationships. Do we respond with benign tolerance as we might toward strangers? Far from it. We are dead against whatever is destroying the one we love.

Love detests what destroys the beloved. Real love stands against the deception, the lie, the sin that destroys. If God were not angry over how we are destroying ourselves, then He wouldn't be good, and He certainly wouldn't be loving. Anger isn't the opposite of love. Hate is, and the final form of hate is indifference.

To be truly good one has to be outraged by evil and utterly and implacably hostile to injustice. No one can call himself good and have an iota of indifference to evil of any sort. And that is precisely what the Bible tells us about God.

REBECCA MANLEY PIPPERT

DAY
157

unworthy of god?

Whoever rejects the Son will not see life,
for God's wrath remains on him.

(JOHN 3:36)

M any of us harbor a disquieting suspicion that ideas of wrath are in one way or another unworthy of God. To some, wrath suggests a loss of self-control, an outburst of "seeing red" which is partly if not wholly irrational. To others it suggests the rage of conscious impotence, wounded pride, or plain bad temper. Surely, it is said, it would be wrong to ascribe to God such attitudes as these!

The reply is: Indeed it would, but the Bible does not ask us to do this. There seems to be here a misunderstanding of the biblical habit of describing God's attitudes and affections in terms ordinarily used for human beings. The basis of this habit is the fact that God made us in His own image, so that human personality and character are more like the being of God than anything else we know. But when Scripture speaks of God in human terms, it does not imply that our limitations and imperfections also belong to our holy Creator; rather, it takes for granted that they do not.

DAY
158

Thus, God's wrath in the Bible is never the capricious, self-indulgent, irritable, morally ignoble thing that human anger so often is. It is, instead, a right and necessary reaction to moral evil. God is angry only where anger is called for. Even among humans, there is such a thing as *righteous* indignation. But all God's indignation is righteous. It is precisely this adverse reaction to evil, which is a necessary part of moral perfection, that the Bible has in view when it speaks of God's wrath.

J. I. PACKER

Be careful where you put the period

*Since you call on a Father who judges each man's work impartially,
live your lives as strangers here in reverent fear.*

(1 PETER 1:17)

A ny discussion of God's character that does not include His wrath is incomplete. Worse yet, it may be an errant study because one of the very real, inescapable truths about our great God is that *He is a God of wrath.*

The issue is not whether we like it, want it, or agree with it. The Bible has more to say about God's wrath than it does about His love. Of course God is good, kind, loving, and forgiving. But if you put a period there, you don't have the complete story. God's wrath must be taken seriously.

The wrath of God is His necessary, just, and righteous retribution against sin. Because of the justice of His law and the righteousness of His character, God must judge sin. He takes no pleasure in punishing the unrighteous (Ezekiel 33:11), but He will, because He is a God of wrath.

Psalm 18:8 puts it this way: "Smoke rose from [God's] nostrils" as He huffed with anger at the presence of sin. In Deuteronomy 32:41, Moses records God's declaration that "I will take vengeance on my adversaries." Peter reminds us that God is impartial and will judge all men according to their deeds (1 Peter 1:17).

We can find no way around it, nowhere to run from it. God is a God of wrath. The Greek words for *wrath* indicate God's intense displeasure at sin and His judgment against it. God does not throw temper tantrums. He doesn't pitch fits, but He has intense anger against sin.

In fact, God takes torrid displeasure at sin: big sin, little sin, medium-sized sin. He does not make a distinction between white and black lies, between felonies and misdemeanors. Because He is a holy God, all sin is repulsive to Him.

TONY EVANS

Edwards' still-Angry god

*If your eye causes you to sin, pluck it out. It is better for you to enter
the kingdom of God with one eye than to have two eyes and be thrown
into hell, where "their worm does not die, and the fire is not quenched."*

(MARK 9:47–48)

O
ne might easily conclude today that the wrath of God is
fiction. No longer are churches aflame with a lively sense
of God's anger against sin. Some churchmen feel the need
to apologize for any stress on divine wrath, and many theologians are
inclined to moderate or even to reinterpret it.

That the justice of God demands the punishment of the wicked,
and that only Jesus Christ quells the wrath of God toward sinners and
secures their forgiveness, was a great theme of Jonathan Edwards. In
his famous sermon, "Sinners in the Hands of an Angry God," Edwards
spoke unhesitatingly of "the wrath of the infinite God" and of "the
vengeance of God on the wicked."

DAY
160

Modern men need to hear again the echo of Edwards' message,
for in it they will detect the warnings and pleadings of the holy
prophets and apostles: "Nothing...keeps wicked men at any one
moment out of hell, but the [sovereign] pleasure of God.... They
deserve to be cast into hell; so that divine justice...calls aloud for an
infinite punishment of their sins.... They are already under a sentence
of condemnation to hell.... The devil stands ready to...seize them...."

These are strong words, but they reflect the biblical teaching of
man's precarious position outside of Christ. Perhaps the fervent declaration of this warning will stir some to repentance as no other appeal
can.

Righteousness and love are equally infinite in the Godhead. The
wrath of God, mediation, atonement, sacrifice, propitiation are part of
the biblical doctrine of redemption. Sinners with hearts uncleansed by
the purifying blood of Christ will discover polluted blood unwashed
from their guilty hands. Jonathan Edwards' God is still angry.

A CHRISTIANITY TODAY READER

The slender Thread

I tell you, my friends, do not be afraid of those who kill the body and after that can do no more. But I will show you whom you should fear: Fear him who, after the killing of the body, has power to throw you into hell. Yes, I tell you, fear him.

(LUKE 12:4–5)

T he wrath of kings is deeply dreaded, especially that of absolute monarchs who hold the possessions and lives of their subjects wholly in their power, to do with them what they will. So Proverbs 20:2 says, "A king's wrath is like the roar of a lion; he who angers him forfeits his life." The poor subject who enrages an arbitrary ruler is liable to suffer the most extreme torments that human art can invent or human power can inflict.

DAY
161

But the greatest earthly monarchs, in their greatest majesty and strength and even when they threaten their greatest terrors, are but feeble, despicable worms in comparison to the great and almighty Creator and King of heaven and earth. Before God all the kings of the earth are as grasshoppers; they are nothing and less than nothing. Both their love and their hatred are to be despised. As the majesty of the King of kings is greater than theirs, so is His wrath infinitely more terrible.

O sinner! Consider the fearful danger you are in. It is a great furnace of wrath, a wide and bottomless pit, full of the fire of wrath, over which you are held in the hand of God. His wrath is provoked and enraged as much against you as against many of the damned in hell. You hang by a slender thread, with the flames of divine wrath flashing about it, every moment ready to singe it and burn it to pieces. And you have no mediator to plead your case, nothing to lay hold of to save yourself, nothing to keep away the flames of wrath, nothing of your own, nothing that you ever have done, nothing that you can do, to persuade God to spare you even one moment.

JONATHAN EDWARDS

A Necessary Day

The present heavens and earth are reserved for fire, being kept
for the day of judgment and destruction of ungodly men.

(2 PETER 3:7)

G od intends to glorify every one of His divine attributes. Since the righteousness of God is as infinite as His other attributes, and all the others have their day, the justice and righteousness of God require that there be a day of judgment.

The power of God had its day when He made the world out of nothing by the word of His power. The Bible says His creation work shows forth His eternal power and Godhead.

The love and mercy of God had a day when He redeemed the world in giving Christ to die for us. Then was love and mercy made visible: "God so loved the world that he gave his one and only Son, that whoever believes in him shall not perish but have eternal life" (John 3:16).

The patience of God has its day. Now is the time of God's patience, when He bears with sinners and their wicked provocations. He waits for them to repent and return and believe. God uses all the time we live on this side of the grave to exercise His patience toward sinners. The earthly life of man is nothing but the season of God's patience in which He waits for him and calls to him to believe and repent for the benefit of his soul.

In this way all the other attributes of God have had their day—so shall not the justice and righteousness of God have a day, too? How else shall His righteousness be made known and proclaimed? It cannot be known in this world, where the wicked prosper and the righteous are afflicted. Therefore a day of judgment is highly necessary, for that is "the day of the revelation of the righteous judgment of God." The justice of God makes this necessary for both believers and sinners alike.

DAY
162

MATTHEW MEAD

The wise course

You have heard that it was said to the people long ago, "Do not murder,
and anyone who murders will be subject to judgment." But I tell you
that anyone who is angry with his brother will be subject to judgment.
Again, anyone who says to his brother, "Raca," is answerable to the Sanhedrin.
But anyone who says, "You fool!" will be in danger of the fire of hell.

(MATTHEW 5:21–22)

DAY
163

T he almighty and sovereign Creator is infinite in holiness. Therefore His "law is holy, and the commandment is holy, righteous and good" (Romans 7:12). Sin is ruinous, reprehensible and damning: in fact, it is the most awful thing in the universe.

Sin separates and estranges the sinner from God. He becomes an enemy of God through his wicked deeds (Romans 8:7), has no peace (Isaiah 57:21), no rest (Isaiah 57:20), is polluted (Ephesians 4:17–19), condemned (John 3:18), and without hope (Ephesians 2:12). Oh, the curse and ruin of sin!

If the sinner refuses to repent and believe, the future holds for him, first, unyielding and awful judgment (see Matthew 25:30–46). Second, the wrath of God (John 3:36). Third, eternal torment (Matthew 22:11–13).

Anyone who ignores these three awful and unchanging truths— be he ever so faithful in holding to other truth—believes an emasculated gospel. Whoever declares the love of God to the exclusion of God's justice and wrath proclaims little but idle sentiment. No one will ever truly desire salvation unless he first realizes that there is something to be saved *from*. "By faith Noah, when warned about things not yet seen, in holy fear built an ark to save his family" (Hebrews 11:7)—which symbolizes the sinner's condition, need, motive, and hope.

While He walked among men, our Lord had far more to say about the doom of the finally unrepentant than about love and heaven. Is it not wise and safe to follow the example of Him who said, "These words you hear are not my own; they belong to the Father who sent me" (John 14:24)? How can we wonder at our difficulties if we fail to imitate the Master at this point?

L. W. MUNHALL

pity yourself
in time

For with fire and with his sword the LORD will execute judgment
upon all men, and many will be those slain by the LORD.

(ISAIAH 66:16)

W e may guess at the severity of the Judge by the lesser strokes of judgment He sends upon sinners to make them afraid of the horrible pains of doomsday—I mean the torments of an uneasy conscience, the confusion and guilt felt by some in this world.

I have seen individuals surprised in an evil act, caught redhanded before they were ready with an excuse. Their color changed, their speech faltered, their tongue stammered, their eyes wandered and fixed nowhere, until shame made them sink into their hollow eye-pits. They lost their wits, their reason, and their composure, and they neither saw, nor felt, nor thought as they normally did, but collapsed under the strain of a minor stroke of judgment and a lesser lash of hell.

We can estimate the severity of our Judge by the unbearable weight of a guilty conscience. If guilt can make a person despair, and despair can lead to madness such that the guilty one feels, hears, and sees nothing but ghosts and illusions, devils and frightful dreams, and shrieks with fear, and looks pale and distracted, like a hopeless man dazed by the horrors and confusions of a lost battle upon which all his hopes rested—then at the day of judgment the wicked must expect strange and fearful things which no language can now express and no patience can then endure.

For on that day He will be both inflexible and immovable. No prayers will move Him, no groans will cause Him to pity you. Therefore pity yourself in time, that when the Judge comes, you may be found among the children of eternal mercy, to whom pity belongs as part of their rightful inheritance.

DAY
164

JEREMY TAYLOR

payday—some day

If a man digs a pit, he will fall into it;
if a man rolls a stone, it will roll back on him.

(PROVERBS 26:27)

Payday comes as certainly as night follows day because sin carries in itself the seed of its own fatal penalty. The fathers sow the wind and the children reap the whirlwind. One generation labors to scatter tares, and the next generation reaps tares and retribution immeasureable.

To the individual who refuses to go the direction God points, a terrible payday comes. To the nation which forgets God, payday will come in the awful realization that the nations that forget God shall be turned into hell (see Psalm 9:17, KJV). When nations trample on the principles of the Almighty, the result is that the world is beaten with many stripes. We have seen nations slide into Gehenna—and the smoke of their torment has gone up before our eyes day and night.

DAY
165

The certainty of payday—some day for all who disregard God is set forth in the words of an unknown poet:

> *You'll pay. The knowledge of your acts will weigh*
> *Heavier on your mind each day,*
> *The more you climb, the more you gain,*
> *The more you'll feel the nagging strain.*
> *Success will cower at the threat*
> *of retribution. Fear will fret*
> *Your peace arid bleed you for the debt*
> *Conscience collects from every crook*
> *More than the worth of what he took.*
> *You only thought you got away*
> *But in the night you'll pay and pay.*

All these statements are but verification of Bible truth: "If a man digs a pit, he will fall into it; if a man rolls a stone, it will roll back on him" (Proverbs 26:27).

"As I have observed, those who plow evil and those who sow trouble reap it" (Job 4:8).

R. G. LEE

Death of a female Demon

When they went out to bury her, they found nothing except her skull, her feet and
her hands. They went back and told Jehu, who said, "This is the word of the LORD
that he spoke through his servant Elijah the Tishbite: On the plot of ground at
Jezreel dogs will devour Jezebel's flesh. Jezebel's body will be like refuse on the
ground in the plot at Jezreel, so that no one will be able to say, 'This is Jezebel.'"

(2 KINGS 9:35–37)

G od Almighty saw to it that the hungry dogs despised the brains that conceived the plot that took Naboth's life. God Almighty saw to it that the mangy, lean dogs of the back alleys despised the hands that wrote the plot that took Naboth's life. God Almighty saw to it that the lousy dogs which ate carrion despised the feet that walked in Baal's courts and then in Naboth's vineyard. Thus perished a female demon, the most infamous queen to ever wear a royal diadem.

DAY
166

God said it—and it was done! From this we learn the power and certainty of God in carrying out His own retributive providence, that we might know His justice does not sleep. Even though the mill of God grinds slowly, it grinds to powder; "and though His judgments have leaden heels, they have iron hands."

When I see the dogs eating Jezebel by the walls of Jezreel, I say, as the Scripture says: "If only you had paid attention to my commands, your peace would have been like a river, your righteousness like the waves of the sea" (Isaiah 48:18). And as I remember that the profits of ungodliness are weighed down with the curse of God, I ask you: "Why spend money on what is not bread, and your labor on what does not satisfy?" (Isaiah 55:2).

The only way I know for any man or woman on earth to escape the sinner's payday on earth and the sinner's hell beyond is through Christ Jesus, who took the sinner's place upon the cross, becoming for all sinners all that God *must* judge, so that sinners through faith in Christ Jesus might become all that God *cannot* judge.

R. G. LEE

justice cries out

Cut it down! Why should it use up the soil?

(LUKE 13:7)

G od does not lack the power to cast wicked men into hell at any moment. Men's hands cannot be strong when God rises up; the strongest have no power to resist Him, nor can anyone deliver out of His hands.

He is not only *able* to cast wicked men into hell, but He can most *easily* do it. Sometimes an earthly ruler has trouble subduing a rebel who has fortified himself and gathered large numbers of followers. Not so with God. No fortress provides any defense from the power of God. Though vast multitudes of God's enemies combine and gather together, they are easily broken in pieces; they are like great heaps of light chaff before the whirlwind, or large quantities of dry stubble before devouring flames.

We find it easy to step on and crush a worm crawling on the ground, or to cut or singe a slender thread by which some object is suspended. It is just that easy for God to cast His enemies down to hell. Who are we, that we should dare to stand before Him—He, at whose rebuke the earth trembles and before whom the rocks are thrown down?

Divine justice never stands in the way or makes any objection against God's using His power at any moment to destroy the wicked. On the contrary, justice cries out for an infinite punishment of their sins. Divine justice says of the tree that brings forth grapes of Sodom, "Cut it down! Why should it use up the soil?" (Luke 13:7). The sword of divine justice is brandished every moment over their heads, and nothing but the hand of mercy and God's sovereign will holds it back.

JONATHAN EDWARDS

HOW will They Answer?

The accuser of our brothers, who accuses them before our God day and night, has been hurled down.... Woe to the earth and the sea, because the devil has gone down to you! He is filled with fury, because he knows that his time is short.

(REVELATION 12:10B, 12)

How will the wicked answer on the day of judgment when they are told they despised God's mercies and did not fear His angry judgments; that they disregarded His Word and did not love His excellencies; that they were not persuaded by His promises nor alarmed by His threatenings; and that they would accept neither His rule nor His blessings?

Cannot the devil truly say to the Judge concerning them, "They were Yours by creation, but mine by their own choice; You certainly redeemed them, but they sold themselves to me for a trifle; You died for them, but they obeyed my commandments; I gave them nothing, I promised them nothing but the filthy pleasures of a night, or the joys of madness, or the delights of a disease; I never hung upon the cross three long hours for them, nor endured for their sake thirty-three years of impoverished labor; when they were Yours by the merit of Your death, they quickly became mine by the demerit of their ingratitude; and when You had clothed their soul with Your robe and adorned them by Your graces, we stripped them naked as their shame and put on a robe of darkness. Yet they thought they were secure and went dancing to their grave, like a drunkard to a fight or a fly to a candle. Therefore, they who joined us in our faults must share with us in our wages and fearful interest."

We must remember that he who tempts us will one day accuse us, and what he calls pleasant now he will then say was nothing. All the pleasures that now invite us to choose emptiness he will say were nothing but the seeds of folly, with a harvest of pain and sorrow and eternal shame.

DAY
168

JEREMY TAYLOR

TOO LATE

For the LORD your God is a consuming fire, a jealous God.

(DEUTERONOMY 4:24)

Would to God that the world believed and considered it true that God is a consuming fire! Because it does not, people lead a "wild and woolly" life in this world. Everybody acts contrary to God's command and lets God scold and threaten as He pleases. People do not consider God a consuming fire, but rather some sort of stubble, a wisp of straw, or a little drop of cold water.

This is why the world is so chaotic. One steals and robs, another cheats and lies; this one fornicates, that one hates, another is greedy, etc. And yet it does not seem as if such a life were bound to be destroyed and perish! As the prophet Jeremiah complains, "Why does the way of the wicked prosper?" (Jeremiah 12:1). And so sinners seem to have success…for a time.

Pious people and the prophets have taken great offense at this contradiction, that sinners should have a superabundance of everything. St. Paul, too, observed this contradiction. Hence the thought arises, *Surely, if God were a consuming, devouring fire, zealous and angry, He would not put up with such conduct!* To the world God seems to be nothing but a sleepy, yawning fellow, or a deceived husband who allows another man to sleep with his wife and acts as if he did not see it.

Moses refutes these thoughts when he says, "Beware, for you have a God who is a consuming fire—a God who will devour you and wipe you out if you are ungodly, a God who is zealous, who devours and reduces to dust and ashes."

But alas, you cannot convince people this is true. They will not believe it until experience has taught them. But then they will have waited too long.

MARTIN LUTHER

DAY 169

None would be left

*In the past God overlooked such ignorance, but now he
commands all people everywhere to repent.*

(ACTS 17:30)

o one, living or dead, can escape the judgment of God. He
has power both to cast down the living from on high and
to inflict eternal tortures upon the dead.

"But if that is true," someone objects, "if God is really angry with
sinners, then He ought to immediately punish each person according
to what he has done."

But if He did this, no one would be left! For there is no one who
does nothing wrong, and there are many things which incite people to
sin: age, drunkenness, need, opportunity, reward. The frailty of our
flesh is prone to sin to such an extent that, unless God for a time overlooked this compulsion, perhaps too few would be living. Public laws
condemn those who are obviously guilty, but there are very many
whose sins are concealed; very many who silence the accuser either by
appeal or bribe; very many who elude trials by favor or influence. And
if divine censure should condemn all those who escape human punishment, there would be but a few odd men, or even none at all on
the earth.

DAY
170

For this reason, God is most patient and He restrains His wrath.
Because virtue in Him is perfect, it is necessary that His patience also
be perfect since it is itself a virtue.

And think of this: How many who were depraved in early life
and condemned by common judgment, afterwards turned out to be
laudable! This certainly would not be the case if punishment followed
every offense.

LACTANTIUS

TO MαKE BαD
PEOPLE GOOD

The sins of some men are obvious, reaching the place of
judgment ahead of them; the sins of others trail behind them.

(1 TIMOTHY 5:24)

DAY
171
⅍

nyone should be able to observe that when God wants to, He takes notice of human sin and judges it; He doesn't defer for a moment. On the other hand, when He wants to, He does defer judgment. Why is this?

Because if He *never* judged in the present time, God would be thought not to exist; but if He judged *everything* in the present time, nothing would be left for the judgment.

The reason many things are reserved for future judgment, while some things are judged here and now, is that those whose cases are deferred might learn to fear and thus be converted. For God loves saving, not condemning, and therefore He is patient with bad people in order to make them into good people. Thus He admonishes and rebukes the contemptuous man and says, "Do you show contempt for the riches of his kindness, tolerance and patience?" (Romans 2:4).

Yet because God is good to you, because He is patient, because He is kind to you, because He reproves you and doesn't remove you, you disdain Him and think nothing about the judgment of God. You ignore the fact that "God's kindness leads you toward repentance. But because of your stubbornness and your unrepentant heart, you are storing up wrath against yourself for the day of God's wrath, when his righteous judgment will be revealed. God 'will give to each person according to what he has done'" (Romans 2:4–6).

ST. AUGUSTINE OF HIPPO

"Lord, how could you be like that?"

Far be it from you to do such a thing—to kill the righteous with the wicked,
treating the righteous and the wicked alike. Far be it from you!
Will not the Judge of all the earth do right?

(GENESIS 18:25)

I f there is one thing Abraham had built his life on, it was the justice and the faithfulness of God. Yet with dismay he sees standing before him a God he no longer understands. God has become alien to him. Who would have thought that God would turn out to be a monster?

You cannot have a relationship with God without standing, at one time or another, precisely where Abraham stood. I stood there late one night as I grappled with the apparent injustice of a God who chose Jacob and rejected Esau. I stood there another time as in my morning devotions I read of God's deadly anger against Uzzah whose only fault had been to reach out to prevent the ark of the covenant from tumbling off a cart (2 Samuel 6:6). I remember kneeling on the boards of an old church hall, begging God to show me that He was not the God of 2 Samuel 6. How could I preach of His saving mercy if He were in fact a petulant tyrant?

God has never defended Himself when I have come to Him in my perplexity. I can well understand Abraham's torment, for it is a torment I have felt. I loved God and wanted Him to go on being the God I had always known. I was frightened both by what I seemed to be seeing, and by my own temerity in daring to question the Judge of the universe. Yet with tears and sweat the question had to come, "Lord, how could you *be* like that?" And His answer has always been to show me more of Himself than I had seen before, so that my tears and perplexity gave place to awe and worship.

DAY
172

JOHN WHITE

what about the heathen?

God will judge men's secrets through Jesus Christ, as my gospel declares.

(ROMANS 2:16)

What about the person who has never heard of Jesus Christ?" many people ask. "Will he be condemned to hell?" To begin with, we must acknowledge that we don't have the whole story here. Certain things are known to God alone. Deuteronomy 29:29 says, "The secret things belong to the LORD our God, but the things revealed belong to us and to our children for ever." However, Scripture does offer some clear points to keep in mind.

DAY
173

First, God is just. All the evidence indicates that we can have confidence in His character. We can trust that whatever He does with those who have never heard of Jesus Christ will be fair.

Second, no person will be condemned for rejecting Jesus Christ of whom he has never heard; instead, he will be condemned for violating his own moral standard, however high or low it has been (see Romans 2:12–16).

Third, Scripture indicates that everyone has enough information from creation to know that God exists. And from Matthew 7:7–11 and Jeremiah 29:13 we may conclude that if someone responds to the light he has and seeks God, God will give him a chance to hear the truth about Jesus Christ.

Fourth, there is no indication in the Bible that anyone can be saved apart from Jesus Christ. Our Lord Himself declared in John 14:6, "I am the way and the truth and the life. No one comes to the Father except through me."

Last, the Bible is absolutely clear concerning the judgment which awaits the individual who *has* heard the gospel. When that person faces God, the issue will not be the heathen. He will have to account for what he personally has done with Jesus Christ.

PAUL E. LITTLE

over and above this world

Is God unjust? Not at all! For he says to Moses, "I will have mercy on whom I have mercy, and I will have compassion on whom I have compassion."

(ROMANS 9:14-15)

S tanding over and above this world is the Great Judge of all. Though men may mistreat me, God never does. That God allows a human being to mistreat me unjustly is just of God. While I may complain to God about the human justice I have suffered, I cannot rise up and accuse God of committing an injustice by allowing the human injustice to befall me. God would be perfectly just to allow me to be thrown in prison for life for a crime I didn't commit. I may be innocent before men, but I am guilty before God.

We often blame God for injustices done to us and harbor in our souls the bitter feeling that God has not been fair toward us. Even if we recognize that He is gracious, we think that He has not been gracious enough. We deserve more grace.

DAY
174

Please read that last sentence again: We *deserve* more grace. What is wrong with that sentence? Grammatically it is fine. It has a subject, a verb, and a direct object. There is no need for the editor's red pencil in that regard. But there is something seriously wrong with the content, with the meaning of the sentence.

It is impossible for anyone, anywhere, anytime to *deserve* grace. Grace by definition is undeserved. As soon as we talk about deserving something, we are no longer talking about grace; we are talking about justice. Only justice can be deserved. God is never obligated to be merciful. Mercy and grace must be voluntary or they are no longer mercy and grace. God never "owes" grace. He reminds us more than once, "I will have mercy on whom I will have mercy." This is the divine prerogative. God reserves for Himself the supreme right of executive clemency.

R. C. SPROUL

perfect government

The LORD reigns forever; he has established his throne for judgment.
He will judge the world in righteousness; he will govern the peoples with justice.

(PSALM 9:7-8)

T he justice of God is not to be understood along the lines it is commonly represented. Those who represent God's justice as if it were in opposition to His mercy—as in the proverb, "I appeal from justice to mercy"—are in error. The Scripture speaks of it very differently. Justice is to be understood as that faithful protection of God by which He defends and preserves His own people. And judgment is the rigor which He exercises against the transgressors of His law.

"Judgment and justice." When these two words are joined together, they express perfect government.

So if we find it strange that God treats us with too great strictness and we do not see the reason why He does it; if we are puzzled why God does not spare us in our weakness, that He does not pity us as we think He ought—let us not give in to such fantasies or believe their lies, but let us always remember this: God is just, whatever else He is.

It is true that we shall not understand the reason for everything He does. But the reason for this is easily traceable to our finite and weak condition. Must we measure the justice of God by our own feeble senses? Where would that lead? And what would be the purpose of it?

So then, let us learn to glorify God in all that He does. And although His hand may be rough to us, let us never cease to confess, "Alas! Lord, if I enter into judgment with You, I know very well that my case is lost."

JOHN CALVIN

wait for the Day

Therefore judge nothing before the appointed time; wait till the Lord comes. He will bring to light what is hidden in darkness and will expose the motives of men's hearts.

(1 CORINTHIANS 4:5)

W e cannot know what secret decree of God's justice makes this good man poor and that bad man rich; why this man, whose immoral life should cause him to be torn with grief, is, in fact, quite happy; why that man, whose praiseworthy life should bring him joy, is instead sad of soul; why this innocent party leaves the courtroom not just unavenged but actually condemned, unfairly treated by a corrupt judge or overwhelmed by lying testimony, while his guilty opponent not merely gets off unpunished but goes gloating over his vindication. Here we have an irreligious man in excellent health, there a holy man wasting away to a shadow with disease.

DAY
176

Even though we cannot understand what kind of divine judgment can positively or even permissively will such inequalities—since God is omnipotent, all-wise, all-just, and in no way weak, rash, or unfair—it is good for our souls to learn to attach no importance to the good or ill fortune which we see granted without distinction upon the good and the bad. We learn, too, to seek the good things that are meant for the good, and to avoid at all costs the evil things that are fit for the bad.

When, however, we come to "judgment day" or "the day of the Lord," we shall see that all God's judgments are perfectly just: those reserved for that occasion; all those that He had made from the beginning; and those, too, He is to make between now and then. On that day it will be shown plainly how just is that divine decree which makes practically all of God's judgments lie beyond the present understanding of men, even though devout men may know by faith that God's hidden judgments are most surely just.

ST. AUGUSTINE OF HIPPO

sinai before calvary

Against you, you only, have I sinned and done what is evil in your sight,
so that you are proved right when you speak and justified when you judge.

(PSALM 51:4)

N o one will ever go to Christ for a blessing until he feels himself burdened with the curse. The hoarse, stern voice of justice must be heard from Sinai, pronouncing our condemnation, before we will listen to the "still small voice" of love from Calvary, declaring our justification. Until the soul feels its lost condition, it will hear no music in the name of Jesus.

Many years ago a German prince visiting France went to see the place where many convicts were being confined. In deference to his rank, he was permitted to commemorate his visit by granting liberty to one of the convicts. He spoke to one man whose intelligent look attracted his notice and asked him for what crime he was incarcerated. The convict began to tell him the most unlikely story of his innocence and how false witnesses had testified against him. The prince left him and asked the same question of another, who also denied his guilt and claimed that he had been mistaken for another man. The same question was put to several others, with the same result. At last the prince came to a man whose solemn and melancholy demeanor attracted his attention.

The man told the prince, "I have been a vile wretch and have deserved far more than my present punishment. I have openly defied the laws both of God and men, and am not fit to look upon God's blue heaven or the green earth." The prince, turning to his attendants, said, "Set this man free; he is in a proper state of mind to make a wise use of his liberty."

In just this way the Prince of Peace receives and pardons the sinner who is ready to justify God and condemn himself.

ROBERT BOYD

DAY
177

freedom from fear

There is no fear in love. But perfect love drives out fear, because fear has to do with punishment. The one who fears is not made perfect in love.

(1 JOHN 4:18)

Are we then forever subject to fear? Is there nothing for us sinners but a certain, fearful expectation of judgment? Jesus came to tell us, No! He came to deliver us from fear. He did not do so by concealing facts; He painted no false picture of a complacent God who negotiated with sin; He encouraged no flattering illusions about the power of man. Jesus did not abandon the realm of divine justice and establish in its place a realm of love. But He introduced unity into the world by His redeeming work. He died not to abolish, but to satisfy, divine justice. Today we look back to what has already been accomplished. Our joy is in salvation already attained, and our boasting is in the cross.

DAY
178
↬

Even the Christian must fear God. But it is another kind of fear, a fear of what might have been rather than of what is; a fear of what would come if we were not in Christ. Without such fear there can be no true love, for love of the Savior is proportionate to one's horror of the punishment from which we have been saved. How strong are the lives saturated with such a love! They are brave, not because they ignored the realities of life, but because they have first been faced— lives founded upon the solid foundation of God's grace. May such lives be ours!

Perfect love casts out fear. But if our love casts out fear, it is only in response to the loving act of God. "This is love: not that we loved God, but that he loved us and sent his Son as an atoning sacrifice for our sins" (1 John 4:10). There is the culmination and the transformation of fear.

J. GRESHAM MACHEN

A Judge who Rules

*God is a righteous judge, a God who
expChresses his wrath every day.*

(PSALM 7:11)

I n our day the word *judge* has only one meaning—one who
rules in a court and decides the merits of a case according
to the relevant points of law. In the Word of God there is
another type of judge. In the Book of Judges, the Hebrew word translated *judge* means to "put right" and then "rule." The world needs this
type of judge.

Many men desire to rule and there are numerous dictators in the
world today; but there is no man with the power to put things right.
Ten thousand men will give you ten thousand different explanations
of all that is wrong, and will suggest as many remedies. Nothing
works out, however, for no man has the power to deal with sin in the
human heart. Until a man comes who can do this, the world must
wait in agony.

We cannot put things right and rule; the Lord Jesus alone can do
this. It is not even in line with His purpose and grace to do this now,
for when He *puts right* it will be with a "rod of iron." Our business is
"to serve the living and true God" by doing only what He wants done.
He has revealed His purpose, which is "taking out a people for His
name." If we work in line with this purpose, success will crown our
efforts and we shall be blessed. When the last individual is brought
out of the world—the last living stone added to complete the edi-
fice—then He, the Lord Jesus Christ, the righteous *Judge,* will come to
put right and *rule.* He alone can do it, and He can do it alone.

DONALD GREY BARNHOUSE

The Judge, our savior

God presented him as a sacrifice of atonement, through faith in his blood. He did this to demonstrate his justice, because in his forbearance he had left the sins committed beforehand unpunished—he did it to demonstrate his justice at the present time, so as to be just and the one who justifies those who have faith in Jesus.

(ROMANS 3:25–26)

A judge had a reputation for extreme severity. It was said that he "sat like a graven image on a case, seldom opened his mouth, and had a cold eye, which seemed to look into the very heart of a witness."

Everybody feared him. Even the reporters dreaded him—or they used to. That is all over now. Once these reporters were accused of accepting bribes to withhold publication of the names of certain prominent people who had appeared in court. The charge was false, but the reporters didn't know how to clear themselves.

DAY 180

Help came from an unexpected source. The judge rose in his place and said that for years he had watched the reporters, knowing they would be tempted by bribes; yet he was convinced they had done their work honestly, and he could not remain silent while honest men were publicly charged with fraud. His statement was printed next day, and the charges were immediately withdrawn.

Afterwards the judge became as silent as ever, and many people feared him as before. But the reporters no longer feared him, for they had learned that his searching eye was their protection; they read the man's heart and knew his kindness to them.

As the reporters misread the character of the judge, so we sometimes mistake the character of God. We think of Him as a harsh, uncaring judge, aware of us only when we sin and earn His rebuke and punishment. We hope to forget God and be forgotten ourselves.

But all the time God has been trying to attract our attention. He looks upon us and calls to us. And when we finally look to Him, we find that He, the Judge, has acted to clear our names in the name and for the sake of His Son.

JOHN T. FARIS

I Rest My Case

We also rejoice in God through our Lord Jesus Christ,
through whom we have now received reconciliation.

(ROMANS 5:11)

I understand God's justice because I remember rebellion—ten-year-old rebellion. My father was the dispenser of justice. "No swimming in the creek today," he said. I had plenty of excuses: "Jimmy went in." "I am so hot." "It isn't fair when everybody else's dad lets them go."

Excuses didn't matter because the standard had been violated. The penalty was swift and sure. Justice was done. But then the father who had just administered justice reached for his big white handkerchief and wiped the tears from my eyes. That day, justice and love were forever linked in my mind.

DAY
181

My father's actions pointed me toward a heavenly Father who sits in the hall of justice, calls His creation to accountability, but weeps over waywardness even as He pronounces sentence. "O Jerusalem, Jerusalem,...how often I have longed to gather your children together, as a hen gathers her chicks under her wings, but you were not willing!" (Luke 13:34). Justice and love exist in the same person.

Sin contaminates all and grace is available to all, no matter who stands before the bar. I can be at peace about God's system of justice, for I have confidence in the Judge. There will be no payoffs. He judges clean.

As a sinner who knew where to find grace, I know God today not as my judge but as a loving Father who continually calls me to accountability. One day He was my judge. But I can almost see a white handkerchief dabbing tears as He wept over my rebellion, issued the sentence, and then took my penalty upon Himself. I am acquitted. Justice has been done. My debt has been paid. I can rest my case.

RUTH SENTER

THE GRACE
AND FORGIVENESS
OF GOD

YOU ARE A FORGIVING GOD,

GRACIOUS AND

COMPASSIONATE,

SLOW TO ANGER AND

ABOUNDING IN LOVE.

NEHEMIAH 9:17

where are you?

But the LORD God called to the man, "Where are you?"

(GENESIS 3:9)

S uppose, after we had sinned, God had given up on us and let us lie where we had fallen. Then none of us ever would have been saved.

But God does not act that way. He loves men; He is kind to them; He desires their salvation above all things. And so He looks out for them even after they have sinned.

He put Adam on his guard even before he sinned. He said to Adam: "You are free to eat from any tree in the garden; but you must not eat from the tree of the knowledge of good and evil, for when you eat of it you will surely die" (Genesis 2:16–17).

God looked out for Adam very carefully; He instructed him, exhorted him, and gave him many blessings. But even so, Adam disregarded His command and fell into sin. Still God did not say: "What good will it do now? What is the use of helping now? He ate the fruit, he fell into sin, he transgressed the law, he believed the devil, he dishonored My commandment, he was wounded, he became subject to death and died, he came under the judgment. What need have I to speak to him now?"

But God said none of those things. Rather, He came immediately to Adam, spoke to him, and consoled him. Again God gave Adam another remedy—the remedy of toil and sweat. God kept right on doing everything and exerting Himself until He raised up fallen man, rescued him from death, led him by the hand to heaven, and gave him greater blessings than he had lost.

ST. JOHN CHRYSOSTOM

DAY
182

grace upon grace

Thanks be to God for his indescribable gift!

(2 CORINTHIANS 9:15)

E very blessing God ever lavished upon mankind sprang from His grace, generosity, or favor—favor free and altogether undeserved. We can lay no claim to even the least of His mercies. Through His free and gracious choice God "formed the man from the dust of the ground and breathed into his nostrils the breath of life," stamped upon that soul the image of God, and "put everything under his feet" (Psalm 8:6). The same free grace continues to us today in every breath we take and every good thing we enjoy. Nothing we are or have or do can deserve the least thing from God's hand. "All that we have accomplished you have done for us" (Isaiah 26:12). Life itself demonstrates God's free mercy toward us. And beyond that, whatever righteousness may be found in us, is also the gift of God.

DAY
183

How then shall sinful people atone for even the least of their sins? With their own works? No. Even if their works were both holy and beyond count, they would belong to God, not them. And the truth is our works are both unholy and sinful, so that every one of them needs a fresh atonement. Corrupt trees bear nothing but corrupt fruit. Our hearts are altogether corrupt and abominable, falling "short of the glory of God," the glorious righteousness at first stamped on our souls after the image of our great Creator. Therefore, having nothing—neither righteousness nor works to plead—our mouths are utterly stopped before God.

If then sinful people are to find favor with God, it is nothing but "grace upon grace"! If God still pours fresh blessings upon us—even the greatest of all blessings, salvation—how can we respond but with, "Thanks be to God for his indescribable gift!"

JOHN WESLEY

Here Is Love

For this is what the LORD says: "I will extend peace to her like a river."

(ISAIAH 66:12)

W ill you, my fellow debtor, stand still awhile, and contemplate the abundant mercy of our blessed God?

A river deep and broad lies in front of you. Track it to its fountain head; see it welling up in the covenant of grace, in the eternal purposes of infinite wisdom. The secret source is no small spring, no mere bubbling fountain; it is a very Geyser, leaping high in fullness of power. Not even an angel could fathom the springs of eternal love or measure the depths of infinite grace.

Now follow the stream. See how it widens and deepens, how at the foot of the cross it expands into a measureless river! See how the filthy come and wash; observe how each polluted one comes up milky-white! Note how the dead are brought to be bathed in this sacred stream, and witness how they live the moment they touch its wave.

DAY
184

See how on either bank rich, green foliage blankets the land! Wherever this stream flows, all is life and happiness. Observe along the shoreline the many trees whose leaves never wither, and whose fruits always ripen in season; all of these draw their life from this flood and drink from this river of God.

Do not fail to note the thousand ships with beautiful sails which skim along the mighty river, colors flying, each vessel laden with joy. Behold how happily they are borne along by the current of mercy to the ocean of infinite bliss!

Now we reach the mighty source of mercy. No shoreline marks the boundary of that great deep, no voice proclaims its length and breadth. But from its lowest deeps and all along its smooth surface I hear a voice that says, "Here is love."

CHARLES H. SPURGEON

An inexhaustible fountain

*I will have mercy on the whole house of Israel;
and I shall be jealous for My holy name.*

(EZEKIEL 39:25)

G race is free because God is jealous to be seen as an inexhaustible fountain of self-replenishing life and power and joy. He is jealous for the world to see that He has no deficiencies which we humans could supply with our works or our distinctives. He is always the benefactor, and we are always the beneficiary. He is never constrained by what He has made. He remains free. This is what it means to be God. This is what He is jealous to preserve and display for the endless enjoyment of all who trust Him.

Paul speaks of the "riches of his grace." His point is that the free overflow of God's inexhaustible, self-replenishing fullness is immeasurably great. There is no end to grace because there is no bottom to the well from which it comes. This is what Paul is getting at in Ephesians 2:6–7, NASB (italics added), "[God] raised us up with Him, and seated us with Him in the heavenly places, in Christ Jesus, *in order that in ages to come He might show the surpassing riches of His grace* in kindness toward us in Christ Jesus."

There are two astonishing things here. One is that the purpose of our salvation is for God to lavish the riches of His grace on us. The other is that it will take Him forever to do it. This is a mighty thought. God made us alive and secured us in Christ so that He could make us the beneficiaries of everlasting kindness from infinite riches of grace. Grace is eternal because it will take that long for God to expend inexhaustible stores of goodness on us. Grace is free because God would not be the infinite, self-sufficient God He is if He were constrained by anything outside Himself.

JOHN PIPER

you can't save yourself

*When the kindness and love of God our Savior appeared, he saved us,
not because of righteous things we had done, but because of his mercy.*

(TITUS 3:4)

Y ou can know God in many capacities: Father, Creator,
Maker, Judge, Sustainer, Shepherd, and so on. But you
must know Him as Savior, the One who intervened in
your affairs and did something about your sins.

Why did He do it? Because you deserved it? No. Because it was
your idea that He should do it? No. Why then did He do it? Because
of loving-kindness and tender mercy and unmerited grace. Being
changed from what you were into what you are is attributable to God
and to God alone. Get this straight if you've never gotten it straight
before. You can't save yourself!

I remember some bored kids in a conference I had for teenagers
in England some years ago. It was a typical English summer's day, with
lots of liquid sunshine pouring out of the skies. We had about five
hundred kids just hanging around and looking out at the rain, bored
to tears. I figured I had to do something, so I brought a bucket into
the middle of the room. Then I said there was a nice, crisp, green
pound note for the first kid who could stand in the bucket and lift
himself off the ground. They thought that was the easiest pound they
would ever earn. Kept them happy all afternoon, trying to earn their
pound. And I've still got the pound because you can't lift yourself off
the ground standing in your own bucket. Neither can you save yourself. It's an act of God, who intervenes.

God in His loving-kindness, tender mercy and capacity as Savior
has moved into our lives and has done something for us we couldn't
do for ourselves.

STUART BRISCOE

DAY
186

for His own sake

For my own sake, for my own sake, I do this.

(ISAIAH 48:11)

God finds His supreme motive in Himself. Note how strongly He insists on it: "For my own name's sake I delay my wrath; for the sake of my praise I hold it back from you" (Isaiah 48:9). Surely this is a matter for extreme comfort.

If God had saved us because of some trait of natural beauty and attractiveness in us, He might turn from us when it faded through the touch of years. The woman whose only claim to attention and honor is her face, who has no other qualities to command and retain respect, must dread the inevitable effect of time. It would be therefore a cause of perpetual unrest to us if God's motive sprang only from pity or complacency.

But God's motive is His character, His name and nature, the maintenance of His honor. In the face of a universe of intelligent beings, He is too deeply involved in our salvation to show signs of variableness or the shadow of turning. He did not begin to save us because we were worthy or lovely, but because He chose to; and therefore He will not give up because we prove ourselves weak and worthless and difficult to save.

There are times when we all can do nothing but cast ourselves on His infinite grace and say, "Save me for Your own name's sake." And when we have been overcome by sin, it is good to go to Him and say, "Father, I have nothing to plead but Your own nature and name declared in Jesus; for His sake, because you have made a promise to Him and to me in Him; for Your glory's sake defer Your anger, forgive my sins; save me for Your own name's sake."

F. B. MEYER

DAY
187

one act, not two

Grace, mercy and peace from God the Father and from
Jesus Christ, the Father's Son, will be with us in truth and love.

(2 JOHN 1:3)

Since sin entered the world, the experience of grace has been different for all of us. Adam and Eve did not *deserve* grace, but their lack of desert was not yet accompanied by misery. Now that sin has entered the world, however, everyone who does not deserve God's goodness is also in a miserable plight. "The wages of sin is *death*" (Romans 6:23).

Since sin always brings misery, and misery is always experienced by sinners, therefore all of God's acts of grace are also acts of mercy, and all His acts of mercy are also acts of grace. It never makes sense to say that sometimes God shows us mercy and sometimes He shows us grace. Whenever He shows one He is showing the other. The difference is whether the act of goodness is viewed in relation to our sin or in relation to our misery.

In a courtroom you might look at the same act of acquittal from two angles. From behind the judge you might see his black robe and huge bench and all the papers with convicting evidence spread out before him. This would make the acquittal look like an amazing act of grace. Sin and justice call for conviction, not acquittal. But if you moved around to the front of the bench and saw the tears in the judge's eyes and noticed the utterly miserable plight of the criminal, this would make the acquittal look like an act of *mercy*. The act of goodness is one act, not two. What changes is the angle from which we view it.

JOHN PIPER

DAY
188

flowing like a River

*If the many died by the trespass of the one man, how much
more did God's grace and the gift that came by the grace of
the one man, Jesus Christ, overflow to the many!*

(ROMANS 5:15)

DAY
189

People talk about grace, but, as a rule, they know very little about it. Let a businessman visit a banker to borrow a few thousand dollars for sixty or ninety days; if he is well able to pay, the banker will perhaps lend him the money if he can get another responsible man to cosign the note. They give what they call "three days' grace" after the sixty or ninety days have expired; but they will make the borrower pay interest on the money during these three days, and if he does not return both principal and interest at the appointed time, they will sell his possessions. They will perhaps evict him from his house and take the last piece of furniture he owns.

That is not grace at all, but it fairly illustrates man's idea of it. Real grace not only frees you from payment of the interest, but of the principal as well.

For many years men tried to find the source of the Nile. The river of grace has been flowing through this dark earth for six thousand years, and we certainly ought to be more anxious to find that than to discover the source of the Nile.

I remember being in Texas a few years ago, in a place where the country was very dry and parched. In that dry country there is a beautiful river that springs right out of the ground. It flows along and on both sides of the river you find life and vegetation. Grace flows like that river, and you can trace its source right up to the very heart of God.

D. L. MOODY

awake, o sword

He...did not spare his own Son,
but gave him up for us all.

(ROMANS 8:32)

W e delight to think of the Christ, whose love was stronger than death and who deemed no suffering too great to undergo for His people. But what must it have meant to the heart of the Father when His Beloved left His heavenly home! God is love and nothing is so sensitive as love. Deity is not emotionless and stoic as represented by the schoolmen of the middle ages. The Father deeply felt the departure of His Son; it was a real sacrifice on His part.

Weigh well the solemn fact underlying the promise that God "did not spare his own Son"! Expressive, profound, melting words! Knowing as only He could, all that redemption involved: the Law, rigid and unbending, insisting on perfect obedience and demanding death for transgressors; Justice, stern and inexorable, requiring full satisfaction, refusing to "clear the guilty." Yet God did not withhold the only suitable sacrifice.

Though He knew full well the humiliation and shame of Bethlehem's manger, the ingratitude of men, the lack of any place to lay His head, the hatred and opposition of the ungodly, the malice and loathing of Satan—yet He did not hesitate. God did not relax any of the holy requirements of His throne nor moderate one particle of the awful curse. No, He "did not spare his own Son." The last cent must be levied; the final dregs in the cup of wrath must be drained. Even when His Beloved cried from the garden, "If it is possible, may this cup be taken from me" (Matthew 26:39), God did not spare Him. Even when vile hands nailed Him to the tree, God cried, "Awake, O sword, against my shepherd, against the man who is close to me! Strike the shepherd" (Zechariah 13:7).

ARTHUR W. PINK

The Bible Message

Here is a trustworthy saying that deserves full acceptance:
Christ Jesus came into the world to save sinners.

(1 TIMOTHY 1:15)

I n a word, here is the Bible message: The divine Creator seeks to rescue lost and doomed sinners from the guilt and penalty of sin—that is, from the pangs of hell—and seeks to restore them to fellowship with the living God and to holiness.

The gospel deals with us as sinners in the sure grip of a righteous God, as sinners offered salvation at tremendous price, as sinners for whom Christ has died and risen. There is no deliverer but Jesus only, no other name whereby man can and must be saved. The crucified and risen Christ alone spares men from the guilt and penalty of sin and gives them heart and power for the right.

The gospel, the good news, is not simply that Jesus Christ was crucified, not simply that He rose from the dead; its center is that Jesus Christ died to rescue doomed sinners and that He lives to restore them completely to God's high and holy will. Paul reminds the Corinthians: "First and foremost, I handed on to you the facts which had been imparted to me: that Christ died for our sins, in accordance with the scriptures; that he was buried; that he was raised to life on the third day, according to the scriptures" (1 Corinthians 15:3–4, NEB). "I thank God," he writes to the Romans, "there *is* a way out through Jesus Christ our Lord."

And to Timothy he writes, "Here is a trustworthy saying that deserves full acceptance: Christ Jesus came into the world to save sinners" (1 Timothy 1:15). "Deserves full acceptance"! Have you accepted Jesus Christ, crucified and risen, as the Savior and Lord of life? "Deserves full acceptance"! That is man's basic decision.

CARL F. H. HENRY

DAY
191

Retrieving the Hope we Lost

Create in me a clean heart, O God,
and renew a right spirit within me.

(PSALM 51:10, KJV)

This is a psalm of a repentant heart, the words of someone wishing to retrieve the hope he had lost, lying where he had fallen, begging the Lord to give him a hand to raise him up again. He is like someone quite capable of injuring himself but not of healing himself.

We can stab and wound our own flesh whenever we want, but to heal it we look for a doctor. In the same way, the soul is perfectly able to sin all by itself, but to heal the hurt it has caused by sinning, it implores the helping hand of God.

That's why the psalmist says in another psalm, "I said, 'O Lord, have mercy on me; heal me, for I have sinned against you'" (Psalm 41:4). The reason he says that he himself said it, is to thrust before our eyes the fact that the will and the decision to sin arises from the soul. We are fully capable of destroying ourselves, but it takes God to seek that which was lost and to save that which has wounded itself. "For the Son of Man came to seek and to save what was lost" (Luke 19:10). It is to Him that we pour out our prayers and say, "Create in me a clean heart, O God, and renew a right spirit within me."

Let the soul that has sinned say this, or it may perish twice over through despair, having lost itself once already by its delinquency.

ST. AUGUSTINE OF HIPPO

DAY
192
乑

tears of joy

To all who received him, to those who believed in his name,
he gave the right to become children of God.

(JOHN 1:12)

I t ought to break your heart to hear of God's love, and it ought to bring you right to Him. You may say you do not deserve it, and that is true. But because you do not deserve it, God offers it to you.

Some people say, "You must turn away from sin and then Christ will love you." But how can you get rid of it until you come to Him? He takes us into His own embrace, then He cleanses us from sin.

Many years ago a boy was kidnapped in London. Through the months and years his mother prayed and prayed for his safe return, but all her efforts had failed. But while others gave up all hope, this mother did not quite give up her hope.

One day the boy was sent to a neighbor's house to sweep the chimney. By some mistake he went down the wrong chimney into what had been his own home. His memory began to travel back through the years, and he thought things looked strangely familiar; scenes of his early days of youth were dawning upon him. As he stood there surveying the place, his mother came into the room.

Did she wait until she had sent him to be washed before she rushed and took him in her arms? He stood there, covered with rags and soot. No, indeed; *it was her own boy!* She took him to her arms, all black and sooty, hugged him to her breast, and shed tears of joy on his head.

You may have wandered very far from God, and there may not be a sound spot on you. But if you will come to God, He will forgive and receive you.

D. L. MOODY

But I'm Not Worthy!

This man welcomes sinners and eats with them.

(LUKE 15:2)

S ome say, "I am not worthy to come." I never knew anyone yet who was worthy. Why, God does not profess to save worthy men and women; He saves sinners. As a man once said, "He didn't come to save make-believe sinners into painted sinners, but real sinners. A man doesn't want to draw his filthy rags of self-righteousness about him when he comes to God."

The only thing a sinner has that God wants is his sin. You need not bring your tears, your prayers, your good works, or deeds; you must come to Him as a sinner, and He will clothe you in a garment fit to come before Him.

The rulers of this earth gather around them the wealthy and influential people of their nations; but when Christ came down here He called the outcasts, the tax collectors, the sinners. And that was the principal fault the people found with Him. Those self-righteous Pharisees were not going to associate with prostitutes and tax collectors! They complained, "This man welcomes sinners and eats with them" (Luke 15:2).

Who would welcome such a man as John Bunyan? A mere tinker from Bedford, he couldn't get inside one of the princely castles. I was very much amused during a visit to England one time when a monument erected to Bunyan was unveiled by lords and dukes and great men. But while he was on earth, they wouldn't allow him inside the walls of their strongholds! Yet God used him as a mighty instrument to spread the gospel. No book ever written comes so near the Bible as Bunyan's *Pilgrim's Progress.*

So it is with God. He picks up some poor, lost tramp, and makes him an instrument to turn hundreds and thousands to Christ.

D. L. MOODY

DAY
194

The constant search

I revealed myself to those who did not ask for me;
I was found by those who did not seek me.
To a nation that did not call on my name, I said, "Here am I, here am I."

(ISAIAH 65:1)

Many years ago a young man left for Chicago to sell his father's grain. When the time came for him to come home, the boy did not return. The father and mother stayed up all night, but still he did not come. The father, a preacher, became so uneasy that he went into the stable, saddled his horse, and departed for Chicago.

DAY
195
࿔

When he reached the city, he discovered that his son had sold the grain but had not been seen since. He concluded he had been murdered. After investigating, however, he found the boy had lost all the money at a gambling house. After a fruitless search, the father went home and told his wife what he had learned. He did not settle down but went from one place to another, preaching in various churches and always telling the congregation that he had a boy dearer to him than life. He always left his address and urged them if ever they heard anything about his boy to let him know.

At last, he learned his son had gone to California. Immediately he started for the Pacific coast to find his boy. When the father reached San Francisco, he put a notice in the papers, trusting that it might reach his son. After preaching a sermon one Sunday, he noticed a single person who remained after the benediction. It was his boy! He did not reprimand him or judge him, but put his loving arms around him, drew him close, and took him home.

This is what God wants to do for us. He offers us His love and His forgiveness. This is what God has been doing for you. There has not been a day, an hour, or a moment, but God has been searching for *you*.

D. L. MOODY

like a log from a Burning fire

*For it is by grace you have been saved, through faith—
and this is not from yourselves, it is the gift of God—
not by works, so that no one can boast.*

(EPHESIANS 2:8-9)

T o be saved does not mean just to be a little encouraged, a little comforted, a little relieved. It means to be pulled out like a log from a burning fire. You have been saved! We are not told that you may be saved sometime, or a little bit. No, you have been saved, totally and for all times. *You!*

This is so because Jesus Christ, through His life and death, has become our Savior who has wrought our salvation. He is the word of God for us. And this word is: "By grace you have been saved"!

Have you heard the legend of the rider who crossed a frozen lake by night without knowing it? When he reached the opposite shore and was told from where he came, he broke down, horrified. We are like that terrified rider. When we hear this word we involuntarily look back, asking ourselves: *Where have I been?* (Over an abyss, in mortal danger!) *What did I do?* (The most foolish thing I ever attempted!) *What happened?* (I was doomed and miraculously escaped, and now I am safe!) You ask: "Do we really live in such danger?" Yes, we live on the brink of death. But we have been saved.

Look at our Savior and at our salvation! Look at Jesus Christ on the cross, accused, sentenced, and punished instead of us! Do you know for whose sake He is hanging there? For our sake—because of our sin—sharing our captivity—burdened with our suffering! He nails our life to the cross. This is how God had to deal with us. From this darkness He has saved us. He who is not shattered after hearing this news may not yet have grasped the word of God: "By grace you have been saved"!

KARL BARTH

DAY
196

An Eternal pardon

Therefore, there is now no condemnation
for those who are in Christ Jesus.

(ROMANS 8:1)

hen God forgives a sinner for any single sin in the present, He also forgives him for all the sins he will ever commit afterwards. This is a mighty mystery!

This is a way of pardoning sin belonging to God alone. No creature pardons the offense of another as God does. That is why the prophet cries out in Micah 7:18, "Who is a God like you, who pardons sin and forgives the transgression of the remnant of his inheritance?"

Who is a God like You? Who in all the world can pardon sin as God does? No father pardons the sin of a child, no prince pardons the sin of a subject like God does—for when God pardons the first sin, He issues a pardon for all the sins that person will commit afterwards.

When the apostle says, "There is now no condemnation for those who are in Christ Jesus," he means that there is no instant in time when it can be said of any justified person that he or she is in a state of condemnation. Though a person may fall into sin after being justified, yet at the moment of sin God applies a pardon that was secured at the very beginning. Whenever any new sin is committed, this pardon is applied by God Himself. If this were not so, there could be no point in time when a believer was *not* under condemnation, since there is no point in time when a believer does not sin against God in some way or another.

JEREMIAH BURROUGHS

DAY
197

East from west

*As far as the east is from the west, so far has
he removed our transgressions from us.*

(PSALM 103:12)

How far is the east from the west? If you start due north at any point on earth, you would eventually cross over the North Pole and start going south, but that is not true when you go east or west. If you start west and continue in that direction, you will always be going west. North and south meet at the North Pole, but east and west never meet. In a sense, they are an infinite distance apart. So when God says He removes our transgressions from us as far as the east is from the west, He is saying they have been removed an infinite distance from us. But how can we get a "handle" on this rather abstract truth in such a way that it becomes meaningful in our lives?

DAY
198

When God uses this expression to describe the extent of His forgiveness, He is saying His forgiveness is total, complete, and unconditional. He is saying He is not keeping score with regard to our sins. I know it seems too good to be true. I confess I almost hesitate to write those words because they are so foreign to our innate concepts of reward and punishment.

But those gracious words are right in the Bible, and they are God's words. How can God possibly do this? The answer is by His grace through Jesus Christ. God laid our sins on Christ, and He bore the penalty we should have borne. Because of Christ's death in our place, God's justice is now completely satisfied. God can now, without violating His justice or His moral law, forgive us freely, completely, and absolutely. He can now extend His grace to us; He can show favor to those who, in themselves, deserve only wrath.

JERRY BRIDGES

Hurled into the sea

You will tread our sins underfoot and hurl
our iniquities into the depths of the sea.

(MICAH 7:19)

W hen I was a naval officer I had an experience in which equipment was lost in the depths of the sea through a small boat accident. I know what it is to drag grappling hooks across the bottom of the sea all day in a vain effort to recover the equipment. That ship's gear was lost forever.

So it is with our sins. God has hurled them into the depths of the sea to be lost forever, never to be recovered, never to be held against us. He says He will *hurl* our sins into the depths of the sea; they will not "fall overboard." He wants them to be lost forever because He has fully dealt with them in His Son, Jesus Christ.

Do you begin to get the picture? Are you realizing that God's forgiveness is complete and irreversible? Have you started to understand that regardless of how "bad" you have been or how many times you have committed the same sin, God completely and freely forgives you because of Christ? Do you see that, because God has already dealt with your sins in Christ, you do not have to do penance or fulfill some probationary term before God can bless you or use you again?

I once heard someone say he felt he could no longer claim God's gracious promise of forgiveness because he had sinned so many times he had used up all his "credit" with God. I believe many Christians think that way. But if we insist on thinking in terms of "credit" before God, we must think only of Christ's credit, for we have *none* of our own. And how much does He have? An infinite amount.

JERRY BRIDGES

DAY
199

Divine forgetfulness

*I will forgive their wickedness and
will remember their sins no more.*

(JEREMIAH 31:34B)

There will never be even the least mention of a believer's sins before God, either now nor hereafter. Ezekiel writes of every godly man who turns to God and believes, "None of the offenses he has committed will be remembered against him" (Ezekiel 18:22).

By the way, let men be careful how they chide the people of God for any of their former sins. Perhaps you knew such a person before his conversion, and you say he was a liar or a drunkard. But now God has revealed His mercy to him in the pardon of his sins, and God says He will not mention them anymore. Take care how you cast their sins, committed in their times of ignorance, in their teeth, saying, "Oh, you are so holy now. But not very long ago I knew you when you were something else." Shall the God of heaven say He will not mention their sins any more, and yet you *will* do it? God will not take such insolence lightly!

It should be a great comfort to every believer that God will not remember their sins any more. He would have *you* remember them to humble you and renew your repentance, but *He* will not remember them to rebuke you with them—nor would He have others do it.

Oh, what a comfort and privilege this is! No matter how wicked or despicable you were, God will never remember your sin any more. This may be a mighty encouragement for men and women to believe and turn from all their sins. Although you may have been vile, abominable, and wicked, yet if you will believe, God will never mention any of your wickedness. More than that—they shall never be mentioned because they will have been forgotten.

JEREMIAH BURROUGHS

The only sure
way to Happiness

Blessed is he whose transgressions are forgiven, whose sins are covered.
Blessed is the man whose sin the Lord does not count against him.

(PSALM 32:1-2)

ardoning mercy is of all things in the world most to be prized, for it is the only and sure way to happiness. To hear from God's own Spirit the words, "I forgive you," is joy unspeakable.

Blessedness is here ascribed to a lawbreaker, who by grace most rich and free has been forgiven. Self-righteous Pharisees have no part in this blessedness. The word of welcome is here pronounced over the returning prodigal, and the music and dancing begin. A full, instantaneous, irreversible pardon of transgression turns the poor sinner's hell into a heaven, and makes the heir of wrath a partaker in blessing.

The word rendered *forgiven* in the original means "taken off" or "taken away," as a burden is lifted or a barrier removed. What a lift is here! It cost our Savior a sweat of blood to bear our load—indeed, it cost Him his life to take it away. Samson carried the gates of Gaza, but what was that to the weight which Jesus bore on our behalf?

Whose sins are covered. Covered by God, as the ark was covered by the mercy-seat, as Noah was covered from the flood, as the Egyptians were covered by the depths of the sea. What a cover must it be which hides away for ever from the sight of the all-seeing God all the filthiness of the flesh and of the spirit! Christ's atonement is the propitiation, the covering, the ending of sin. Where this is recognized and trusted in, we know we are accepted in the Beloved and therefore enjoy a foretaste of heaven. It is clear that we may *know* we are pardoned, for how could we enjoy an unknown forgiveness? Such certain knowledge is the ground of comfort.

CHARLES H. SPURGEON

DAY
201

The Joy and Life
of the Soul

Blessed are they whose transgressions are forgiven, whose sins are covered.
Blessed is the man whose sin the Lord will never count against him.

(ROMANS 4:7-8)

God does not forgive by halves. The love of God is so great and the atonement in the blood of Jesus so complete and powerful that God always forgives completely. Take time with God's Word to rest in the certainty that your guilt has been completely removed. God thinks absolutely no more of your sins. "I will forgive their wickedness and will remember their sins no more" (Jeremiah 31:34).

The forgiveness of our sin restores us entirely to the love of God. Not only does God not impute sin anymore—that is but one-half—but He imparts to us the righteousness of Jesus also, so that for His sake we are as dear to God as He is. Not only is wrath turned away from us, but the fullness of love now rests upon us. Forgiveness means access to all the love of God and all the other blessings of redemption.

DAY
202

Live in the full assurance of forgiveness, and let the Holy Spirit fill your heart with the certainty and the blessedness of it, and you will have great confidence in expecting all the blessings from God. Learn from the Word of God, through the Spirit, to know God and to trust Him as the ever-forgiving God. That is His name and His glory.

Yet the certainty of forgiveness must not be a matter only of memory or understanding, but also of the fruit of life—living fellowship with the forgiving Father, with Jesus in whom we have forgiveness. It is not enough to know that I once received forgiveness; my life must remain in the love of God, my living fellowship with Jesus by faith—this makes the forgiveness of sin always new and powerful, the joy and the life of my soul.

ANDREW MURRAY

A puzzle solved

Who will bring any charge against those whom God has chosen? It is God who justifies. Who is he that condemns? Christ Jesus, who died—more than that, who was raised to life—is at the right hand of God and is also interceding for us.

(ROMANS 8:33–34)

W hen God "justifies" a person, He *declares* that person righteous, He does not *make* that person good or holy. Justification does not transfer goodness into a person. It is a pronouncement of the status of a person.

In Romans 8:33–34 the idea of God justifying is contrasted with condemning or accusing. To condemn doesn't mean making a person wicked, sinful, or evil. It is a declaration that the person is already in this condition. Similarly, justification is not a matter of making the person good. It is a declaration that he is acquitted. God both condemns the unjust and justifies the righteous. In each case, it is an act of pronouncement, not of transformation.

Here we find a puzzle. If justification is God's declaration of man's status, and if no one is as perfect as God requires, how can God say, "Good enough!"? Either He must be mistaken in His appraisal or dishonest in His judgment.

The solution to this puzzle is that justification is more than a two-party relationship. If it were just God and I, then I would fail to meet with God's approval. Justification, however, is a three-party transaction, involving God, Jesus, and me. God sees me, but not with my righteousness alone; He sees me with Christ's. Jesus' death is so highly valued because it was voluntary. Consequently, part of His righteousness can be credited to me. It is as if I owe a debt which I am unable to pay. But then a concerned third party with abundant assets offers to pay the debt for me. Now I am "paid up" with my creditor.

Thus God's declaration of my righteousness is based on my actual standing, the righteousness that I genuinely possess, even though it is not my own accomplishment.

MILLARD J. ERICKSON

Every Need Met

*And God is able to make all grace abound to you,
so that in all things at all times, having all that you need,
you will abound in every good work.*

(2 CORINTHIANS 9:8)

I t is the glory of God's grace that it meets every need of the sinner. If the sinner is dead, it gives him life; if he is filthy, it washes him; if he is naked, it gives him clothing. Is the sinner hungry? It feeds him. Is he thirsty? It gives him something to drink. Do the sinner's needs grow even larger after he becomes a saint, or does he gain a broader perception of them? Then the supplies are just as deep as his need. Bottomless mines are the treasures of divine grace:

> *Deep as our helpless miseries are,*
> *And boundless as our sins.*

DAY
204

You will never get to the point where grace will fail you. You never come to a difficulty where you will have to say, "Here, at last, the arm of grace is withered, and I must look elsewhere for help."

Oh no, from this spot to the brink of Jordan and through Jordan and up to the great white throne of judgment, and through the judgment and until body and soul, remarried in a splendid marriage for eternity, shall sit down at the wedding feast above—till then there shall be no failures in grace, nor shall we ever have to think of it as anything other than all-sufficient.

Where the grace of God begins and the human heart is really changed, the work which has been begun will be completed. There will be much opposition from the flesh and from temptations from without and from Satan; but He who began to build is not a shoddy builder who cannot finish.

Bless the Lord, O my soul! You belong to an unchanging Lord! "I the LORD do not change. So you, O descendants of Jacob, are not destroyed" (Malachi 3:6).

CHARLES H. SPURGEON

The Lamb Is a Lion

Come to me, all you who are weary and burdened, and I will give you rest.
Take my yoke upon you and learn from me, for I am gentle and
humble in heart, and you will find rest for your souls.

(MATTHEW 11:28–29)

I f you come to Christ, you need not fear that you might not be accepted, for He is like a lamb to all who come to Him. He receives them with infinite grace and tenderness.

It is true that He has awful majesty; He is the great God and is infinitely high above you. But Christ is a man as well as God; He is a creature as well as the Creator, and He is the most humble and lowly in heart of any creature in heaven or earth.

DAY
205

Whatever your circumstances, you do not need to be afraid to come to such a Savior as this. There is no danger of being despised. For though He is so much greater than you, He is also immensely more humble than you. There is no danger of Christ despising you, if you in your heart come to Him. He will certainly receive you both graciously and meekly. Therefore you can be bold in coming to Him. You need not hesitate one moment, but may run to Him and cast yourself upon Him.

And if Christ accepts you, you need not fear for your safety, for He is a strong lion for your defense. He will appear as a lion to defend you with His glorious power and dominion. All His excellencies shall be yours and shall be used on your behalf and in your defense. He will be like a lion to fight against your enemies. Whoever touches you or offends you will provoke His wrath, like one who stirs up a lion. Unless your enemies can conquer this Lion, they shall not be able to destroy or hurt you. Unless they are stronger than He, they shall not be able to hinder your happiness.

JONATHAN EDWARDS

An ocean of merit

*After this I looked and there before me was a great multitude
that no one could count, from every nation, tribe,
people and language, standing before the throne and in front of the Lamb.*

(REVELATION 7:9)

I n Christ's finished work I see an ocean of merit; my plumb bob finds no bottom, my eye can locate no shore. There must be enough power in the blood of Christ, if God had so willed it, to have saved not only everyone in this world, but everyone in ten thousand worlds, had they transgressed their Maker's law. Once you have admitted infinity into the matter, limit is out of the question. With a divine person for an offering, all talk of "limited value" must be jettisoned. "Bound" and "measure" are terms inapplicable to the divine sacrifice.

DAY
206

Think of the numbers upon whom God has bestowed His grace already. Think of the countless hosts in heaven. If you were introduced there today, you would find it as easy to number the stars or the sands of the sea as to count the multitudes before the throne even now. They have come from the east and from the west, from the north and the south, and they are sitting down with Abraham and Isaac and Jacob in the kingdom of God. And beside those in heaven, think of the saved ones on earth. Blessed be God, His elect on earth are to be counted by millions, and the days are coming when there shall be multitudes upon multitudes who have come to know their Savior and to rejoice in Him.

The Father's love is not for a few only, but for an enormous multitude. "A great multitude that no one could count" will be found in heaven. An individual can count up to very high figures; our mightiest calculators can count great numbers—but God and God alone can count the multitude of His redeemed men and women.

CHARLES H. SPURGEON

More wondrous
Than creation

Even angels long to look into these things.

(1 PETER 1:12)

There is more of God—more of His essential glory displayed in bringing one sinner to repentance and forgiving his sins—than in all the wonders of creation. In this great work, men and angels may see the very heart of God.

From this work, angels themselves have probably learned more of God's moral character than they had ever been able to discover before. They knew that God was wise and powerful, for they had seen Him create a world. They knew He was good, for He had made them perfectly holy and happy. They knew He was just, for they had seen Him cast down their own rebellious associates from heaven to hell for their sins. But until they saw Him give repentance and forgiveness of sins through Christ, they did not know that He was merciful; they did not know that He could pardon a sinner.

And O! What an hour it was in heaven when this great truth was first made known, when the first repentant sinner was pardoned! Then a new song burst from the mouths of heaven's angels. And with indescribable emotions of wonder, love, and praise, they began to sing, their voices swelled to a higher pitch, and they experienced joys unfelt before.

O how did the joyful sounds, "His love endures forever," spread from choir to choir, echo through the high arches of heaven, and thrill through every enraptured angelic breast! And how they cried, with one voice, "Glory to God in the highest, and on earth peace to men on whom his favor rests!"

REV. EDWARD PAYSON

An Impossible Debt

Then the master called the servant in. "You wicked servant," he said,
"I canceled all that debt of yours because you begged me to. Shouldn't you have had
mercy on your fellow servant just as I had on you?" In anger his master
turned him over to the jailers to be tortured, until he should pay back all he owed.

(MATTHEW 18:32–34)

W ith real anger, Jesus told a terrible story of a wicked servant, a man who experienced mercy and yet remained a hard man. At last all mercy was pronounced over the man's debtor, but the dreadful judgment of God over him. In telling this story, Jesus gives us the greatest help He can; He points out the path to real forgiveness.

Does each of us recall a moment in our life when God called us to judgment, when we were lost persons, when our life was at stake, when God demanded an accounting from us, and we had nothing but debts, immeasurably vast debts? Our life was stained and unclean and guilty before God, and we had nothing, nothing at all to show but debts and more debts.

DAY
208

Do we recall how we felt then, how we had nothing to hope for, how lost and senseless everything seemed? We couldn't help ourselves anymore, we were utterly alone, and before us there remained only punishment, well-deserved punishment. Before Him, we could not stand erect. Before God, in front of God the Lord, we sank to our knees in despair and prayed: "Lord, be patient with me"; and all kinds of foolish talk passed our lips, as in the story of the wicked servant: "I will pay you back." So we said, and yet we knew for certain that we would never be able to pay it.

And then, at once, everything changed: God's face was characterized no longer by wrath, but by great sorrow and pain toward us, and God released us from all debt, and we were forgiven. We were free and the fear had been taken away from us; we were joyful again and could look God in the face and thank Him.

DIETRICH BONHOEFFER

The work of god

Then Peter came to Jesus and asked, "Lord, how many times shall I forgive my brother when he sins against me? Up to seven times?"
Jesus answered, "I tell you, not seven times, but seventy-seven times."

(MATTHEW 18:21–22)

O nly God can limitlessly forgive because forgiveness is the work of God. We miss the point when we begin to think about forgiveness as a duty that is ours alone to do. When we conceive of forgiveness as a commodity to be given or withheld, we do not understand forgiveness. Forgiveness is not a right that belongs to the offended party to give or refuse. Forgiveness is not a human activity. Forgiveness is the work of God.

DAY
209
♒

Eugene O'Neill tells the story of a man who killed his wife on the grounds of excessive forgiveness. Every night he would come home drunk, and every night she would tell him that he was the scurviest, most good-for-nothing scum ever to crawl out of the cracks of life. Then she would say, "But, I forgive you." He heard her words, but he also got the message. If the truth were known, there are lots of folk for whom the absolving utterance, "You are forgiven," is belied by the accompanying word of self-righteous judgment.

The gospel reading, however, confronts us with the unwelcome fact that we cannot forgive. It is humanly impossible. The call to forgive our sisters and brothers an unlimited number of times is something we cannot do, yet it is precisely what we must do. When we grasp both our duty and our inability to forgive, we are in a position to give God the glory. Only then are we capable of understanding that forgiveness is God's work, not ours. And only when we recognize that forgiveness is the work of God will we be ready to ask what it might mean to practice forgiveness. Until we recognize forgiveness as the work of God, we cannot practice forgiveness.

CURTIS W. FREEMAN

"More Grace!"

By the grace of God I am what I am.

(1 CORINTHIANS 15:10)

By the grace of God I am what I am!" This is the believer's eternal confession.

Grace found him a rebel—it leaves him a son. Grace found him wandering at the gates of hell—it leads him through the gates of heaven. Grace devised the scheme of redemption: Justice never would; Reason never could. And it is grace which carries out that scheme.

No sinner would ever have sought his God but "by grace." The thickets of Eden would have proved to be Adam's grave, had not grace called him out. Saul would have lived and died a haughty, self-righteous persecutor, had not grace laid him low. The thief would have continued breathing out his blasphemies, had not grace arrested his tongue and tuned it for glory.

DAY 210

"Out of the knottiest timber," said Rutherford, "He can make vessels of mercy for service in the high palace of glory."

"I came, I saw, I conquered," says Toplady, "may be inscribed by the Savior on every monument of grace. 'I came to the sinner; I looked upon him; and with a look of omnipotent love, I conquered.'"

My friend, this day we would have been "wandering stars, to whom is reserved the blackness of darkness"—Christless, hopeless, portionless—had not grace invited us and grace constrained us.

Oh, let us seek to realize our continual dependence on grace every moment! "More grace! More grace!" should be our continual cry. The treasury of grace, though always emptying, is always full; the key of prayer which opens it is always close at hand; and the almighty Giver of the blessings of grace is always waiting to be gracious. The recorded promise never can be canceled or reversed: "My grace is sufficient for you."

D. L. MOODY

A warm welcome

While they were stoning him, Stephen prayed,
"Lord Jesus, receive my spirit."

(ACTS 7:59)

T he moment Christ received us as His own, He stood ready to welcome and greet us with great joy the instant we depart from this world. Poor soul, you were never so welcome to your dearest friend, nor into the arms of a father, a husband, or a wife, as you will be at that moment into the presence and embrace of your Lord!

DAY
211

Even now you hear and read and only partly believe how deeply He loves us, as dearly as a man loves his cherished spouse and his own body, as dearly as he cares for his own flesh and bone. But then you shall *feel* how He loves you—you, in particular!

If the angels of God rejoiced at your conversion, what joy will there be in heaven at your full entrance into the salvation you have received? Surely those angels will shower you with a loud welcome and happily join with Christ in His triumphant joy!

If a returning prodigal finds himself in the arms of his father's love, is welcomed home with kisses, and presented with his own robe and given a great feast, then what welcome may a cleansed and redeemed soul expect when it comes into the presence of God's glorious love! We will be received with amazing demonstrations of love that magnify the love of God, a love which exceeds all human love, as much as omnipotence exceeds our impotence.

Though in the dark here below you may have questioned whether God welcomed you when you came to Him in prayer or when you came to His holy table, yet try to doubt your welcome *then*—if you can!

RICHARD BAXTER

swimming in grace

Remember, O LORD, your great mercy
and love, for they are from of old.

(PSALM 25:6)

L ord of hosts! When I swim in the merciful waters of Your grace I find that I can neither plumb nor measure the depths. Your compassion is the greatest of all Your works. Lord, who ever came to You with a devout heart and was turned away? Who ever sought You and did not find You? Who ever called upon You and was not heard?

Yes, beloved Lord, how many You have received in grace when according to Your strict sense of justice they deserved something else! Adam departed from You and believed the counsel of the serpent. He transgressed Your covenant and became a child of death. But Your fatherly love would not allow him to be thrown aside. In grace You sought after him, you called and admonished him and covered his nakedness with pelts of fur. Paul, Your chosen vessel, was at one time like a roaring lion and a ravaging wolf. Yet You shone Your grace upon him and enlightened his blindness. You called him from heaven and chose him to be an apostle and servant in Your house.

DAY
212

Beloved Lord, I am the greatest of sinners and the least among the saints. I am unworthy to be called Your child or servant, for I have sinned against heaven and before You. There was a time when I opposed Your glorious Word and Your holy will with all my power. I taught and lived according to the flesh and sought my own selfish honor rather than Your justice, honor, truth, and Word. Yet this miserable sinner was never abandoned by Your fatherly grace. Now I also am an inheritor of that promised kingdom with all servants of God and disciples of Christ. So again I say, Your mercy is the greatest of all Your works.

MENNO SIMONS

THE
OMNIPOTENCE
OF GOD

I AM THE LORD,

THE GOD OF

ALL MANKIND.

IS ANYTHING TOO

HARD FOR ME?

JEREMIAH 32:27

power is His name

*You shall see the Son of Man sitting
at the right hand of Power.*

(MARK 14:62, NASB)

P ower is one of the names of God. When Mark says, "You shall see the Son of Man sitting at the right hand of Power," he means "at the right hand of God." God and power are so inseparable that they can be used as synonyms. You do not know God at all if you do not know Him by this name, for power belongs to God.

"God has spoken once, twice I have heard this: that power belongs to God" (Psalm 62:11, NJKV). The psalmist heard it first in the creation of the world, for God made the world by His power. And he heard it for the second time in God's dominion, for the Lord governs by the power of His providence. That is why I say that you cannot rightly understand God if you do not conceive of Him as a God of power, for power is one of His names.

Power is essential to God's nature, and that cannot be said about any creature. Any power a creature may have is derived from somewhere else. In this sense, "There is no power, but of God" (Romans 13:1, KJV). So Solomon says, "Where the word of a king is, there is power" (Ecclesiastes 8:4, KJV). Well, there is and there isn't. He has the power to command, but he does not have the power to make his commands be obeyed. There may be authority where there is no power, and there may be power where there is no authority.

But God has both. He has both the power to reign and the power to maintain His reign. Power is in God originally, and He derives it from no one, for it is of and from Himself.

MATTHEW MEAD

DAY
213

The Arm of God

One thing God has spoken, two things have I heard: that you,
O God, are strong, and that you, O Lord, are loving.

(PSALM 62:11–12)

G od's power brings life and activity to all the other perfections of His nature. How useless would be His eternal counsels if power did not step in to execute them! Without power, His mercy would be a feeble pity, His justice a contemptible scarecrow, and His promises nothing but an empty sound. As holiness is the beauty of all His attributes, so power is their life.

God has the powerful wisdom to accomplish His will, without interruption. He has a powerful mercy to remove our misery, a powerful justice to punish offenders, a powerful truth to fulfill His promises, and an infinite power to bestow rewards and inflict penalties.

Power is the arm and hand of God; through it, all His other attributes appear in their glory. By His power they act and triumph and are made known to the world. Power built the stage for their appearance in creation, providence, and redemption.

This power is originally and essentially in God. The strength and power of great kings is originally in their people and is managed and directed by the authority of the king for the common good. But although a king has the rightful authority to command, he does not have enough strength by himself to make his subjects obey. By himself he cannot conquer countries and increase the population of his kingdom. To overrun other nations and subject them to his dominion, he must rely upon the strength of his own subjects.

But the power of all things is originally and essentially in God. It is not derived from anything outside of Him. Therefore the psalmist says, "Power belongs to God"—that is, to Him and to no one else.

STEPHEN CHARNOCK

DAY
214

The Divine Imperative

You are worthy, our Lord and God, to receive glory and honor and power,
for you created all things, and by your will they were created and have their being.

(REVELATION 4:11)

W e use the term *creativity* to describe the skills of human beings. There are creative inventors, creative problem-solvers, creative artists, and so on. But just how creative are creative people? No human artist or inventor brings something into being from nothing. The artist has a medium through which an artistic creation is shaped or arranged.

An inventor stands before a workbench and with tools and raw material "creates" some new gizmo. But no artist or inventor can create a work of art or an invention by the power of his voice. No artist can speak to his paint and create the *Mona Lisa.* A sculptor would be called a lunatic for standing in front of a mountain and commanding it to turn into Mount Rushmore. Human beings cannot change the course of nature or bring things into existence by sheer talk.

But God can. His voice is almighty.

God spoke. He commanded light to come into existence. And light began to shine. This is what Saint Augustine called the Divine Imperative. The world was created by the sheer power of God's voice, *ex nihilo,* out of nothing.

I am completely baffled by God's power to bring something out of nothing. I know that He does it, but I don't know how He does it. I also know that reason demands that we accept the premise that something, somewhere has the ability to create out of nothing or nothing would exist. I also know that reason shows that it is impossible for something to create itself. We have to have a creator. That creator must be eternal. That creator must have the power to create, or I would not, indeed I could not, be trying to write about this perplexing issue.

R. C. SPROUL

god's whisper

These are but the outer fringe of his works; how faint the whisper we hear of him!
Who then can understand the thunder of his power?

(JOB 26:14)

I used to imagine the voice of God in creation must have been a great cosmic shout reverberating across the universe. But no. Job, after describing God's creative acts, says:

> *And these are but the outer fringe of his works;*
> *how faint the whisper we hear of him!*
> *Who then can understand the thunder of his power?*
> *(Job 26:14)*

DAY
216

I thought, *If all we can see in creation is a product of God's whisper, what would happen if God ROARED?*

I was fascinated some time ago by an astronomy journal account about two stars far to the left of the "belt" in the constellation Orion. Though only one star is seen (Procyon is its name), astronomers using elaborate calculations determined that this star has a tiny twin. By measuring the movements and the distance between these twin stars, they estimated that the smaller star was so compressed, so compacted with power, that a single cubic inch would weigh one hundred tons. Two hundred thousand pounds. Imagine dropping that on your toe!

More recently scientists have discovered such compression is nothing in comparison to what happens when an entire star explodes. In moments, energy is spewed out equal to that of a billion suns, producing what is called a supernova. At the same time, the star collapses in upon itself to produce a small new star, a neutron star. Experts believe these mysterious objects are so compressed that a single cubic centimeter (that's less than a half-inch cube) could weigh at least a hundred billion tons. Maybe a trillion! Some become so dense that the pull of their gravity will not even allow light to escape. We call these black holes.

And Job says, "That is God's whisper."

DAVID NEEDHAM

AS STRONG AS EVER

The LORD is the everlasting God, the Creator of the ends of the earth.
He will not grow tired or weary.

(ISAIAH 40:28)

T he power of God is an everlasting power. Time does not weaken or diminish it, as occurs with all creatures. God has as much power now as He ever did, and He can do for His people now as much as He ever did. Time will decay the power of the strongest creature and make it weak and feeble, but the Creator of the ends of the earth never grows tired or weary. "You remain the same, and your years will never end," says the psalmist in Psalm 102:27.

When God works He never expends any of His strength. He is able to do as much for His church now as ever He did. Whenever He chooses, He can once more bring about any of the glorious deliverances He performed for His people, from the beginning of the world until now. He can do as much for His church today as He did for Israel at the Red Sea.

DAY 217

Upon this ground the church builds its plea: "Awake, awake! Clothe yourself with strength, O arm of the LORD; awake, as in days gone by, as in generations of old. Was it not you who cut Rahab to pieces, who pierced that monster though? Was it not you who dried up the sea, the waters of the great deep, who made a road in the depths of the sea so that the redeemed might cross over?" (Isaiah 51:9–10).

Why should God's people not expect displays of His power as glorious as any of those which occurred in former ages?

JOHN FLAVEL

the world in His Hand

He doeth according to his will in the army of heaven, and among the inhabitants of
the earth: and none can stay his hand, or say unto him, "What doest thou?"

(DANIEL 4:35, KJV)

God's power is infinite and all-sufficient and has no limits except the pleasure and will of God. So Psalm 135:6 says, "The LORD does whatever pleases him, in the heavens and on the earth, in the seas and all their depths." The pleasure of God is the only rule by which divine power exerts itself in the world; that is why we are not to limit and restrain it by our narrow and shallow thoughts, but must believe that He is able to do immeasurably more than all we ask or imagine.

DAY
218

Thus the heroes of Daniel 3:17 by faith exalted the power of God above the power of King Nebuchadnezzar, a mere man: "The God we serve is able to save us from [the blazing furnace], and he will rescue us from your hand, O king." Their faith rested upon the omnipotent power of God, and they expected to be delivered by that power in an extraordinary way.

Of course, it is true that such a miraculous deliverance provides no standing rule for our own faith; nor do we have ground to expect such miraculous salvations. Yet when extraordinary difficulties confront us and the common ways and means of deliverance have disappeared, by faith we ought to exalt the omnipotence of God, glory in His ability to save in miraculous ways, and leave ourselves to His good pleasure—without limiting or narrowing His almighty power according to our weak and inadequate ideas of it. Our apprehension of the power of God is as vastly inferior to His thoughts of it, as the earth is to the heavens.

JOHN FLAVEL

can He do anything?

Nothing is impossible with God.

(LUKE 1:37)

T he word *almighty* causes problems for some. Does it mean that God can do *anything,* including making a triangle with four sides? Or that He can suddenly change His nature and reject those who come to Him in faith and repentance? While it can be fun to explore the logical niceties of these ideas, they aren't of much relevance to the real points at issue! Let's look at some of the important points to be made.

First, we must remember that all power and authority in this world derive from God. Rulers, governments, and Christian leaders all derive authority from God (Romans 13:1–2) and are responsible to Him for the manner in which they exercise it. If you are a Christian leader (or think you might become one), let this be a sobering thought.

Second, realize that things that seem impossible to us are perfectly possible for God. Remember Gabriel's gentle chiding of Mary as she expressed astonishment that she was to bear the Savior of the world: "Nothing is impossible with God" (Luke 1:37). It is very easy for us to underestimate God. But He is able to do far more than we imagine.

Finally, remember that *almighty* does not mean capricious or whimsical. Scripture stresses the *reliability* of God. Having made a promise, God stands by it (Psalm 19:7–10). The Old Testament idea of a covenant—that is, a kind of bond or contract—between God and Israel made this same point: God has committed Himself to us, in word and deed. The fact that He is almighty doesn't mean that He can or will suddenly change His mind about this! In His power and wisdom, God has chosen to achieve our salvation, and has committed Himself to us in this way.

ALISTER MCGRATH

nothing too Hard

Is anything too hard for the LORD?

(GENESIS 18:14)

od likes His people to believe there is nothing too hard for Him.

We talk about Frederick the Great and Alexander the Great, but how very little are these mighty men when we compare them to God! Here is this earth of ours, 7,920 miles across, with its great oceans and its great mountains and its great rivers—yet it is only a little ball that the Lord tosses out of His hand. The astronomers tell us that the sun is twelve thousand times larger than the earth. Besides this, there are millions upon millions of stars. Yet I suppose these are only a few "towns" and "villages" on the outskirts of God's great empire. Now, what folly to try to measure God with our little rulers!

I hear somebody saying, "If God is as great as that, He will not condescend to trouble Himself about such an insignificant creature as I." This is all wrong. Men sometimes get to be so big that they don't care for little things, but God never does.

No obstacle long stands in the way when God rises up to carry on His work. When Mr. Sankey and I first started out, we took for our motto: "Ah! Lord God…there is nothing too hard for thee," and we always had great success. After a while we thought we would take some other motto, but we could make no progress until we came back to this verse: "Is anything too hard for You?"

We are constantly limiting God's power by our own ideas. Let us get our eyes off one another and fix them on God. Nothing is too hard for Him.

D. L. MOODY

who looks at the moon?

Praise him, sun and moon, praise him, all you shining stars.

(PSALM 148:3)

A t 10 P.M. on July 4, Noël, Barnabas, and I walked out onto the Eleventh Avenue bridge and joined our neighbors sitting on the curb. Looking north we could see the fireworks from the Mississippi River. Looking south we could see the fireworks over Powderhorn Park. We were sandwiched in the sky glitz of Independence Night.

About ten minutes into the display, I suddenly noticed a white light behind the trees to the southwest. It was very large and looked full. The moon was politely waiting its turn…but hardly anyone was noticing.

Still, nothing on earth made by man can compare with the moon. Every day the moon takes the oceans of the earth and lifts them quietly—millions upon millions of tons of water silently and irresistibly hoisted into the air. In Boston the tide recedes ten feet. In Eastport, Maine, it recedes nineteen feet. In Nova Scotia, in the Bay of Fundy, the tides vary up to forty-three feet.

The moon is an awesome thing. If you stood in the sunlight on the moon, the fluids in your body would boil; but if you walked into the shadow of a large rock, you would quickly freeze solid.

Think on this, then call this to mind: The moon is but a reflection of the sun, which quietly keeps its ninety-three-million-mile distance lest we be consumed. Then think that the sun is but a medium-size star.

But who sees the moon? Who looks at the moon on Independence Night when there are man-made fireworks to watch?

It is time to read our emotional barometers. Do the amazements and delights of our life correspond to God's reality? Or do they rise and fall on the passing waves of human glitz?

JOHN PIPER

A whole box of apples

I know that you can do all things;
no plan of yours can be thwarted.

(JOB 42:2)

ne Sunday a little boy was standing in the church foyer waiting for his family. The pastor saw him, and knowing that the boy had just come from Sunday school, decided to ask him a few questions. "Young man, if you can tell me something God can do, I will give you a shiny new apple."

The boy looked up at the pastor thoughtfully and said, "Sir, if you can tell me something God *can't* do, I will give you a whole box of apples!"

The challenge is not in finding something God can do, but in trying to find something He can't do. He is absolutely unlimited in power. And yet our limitations make it hard for us to grasp such limitless might.

Did you know that I can lift a ton? You may not believe it, but I can. So now you're going to say, "Show me." All right—just let me hitch a ride on the next space probe that lands on the moon. Then turn on your television and watch me lift a ton.

How can I do that? Because the law of gravity is vastly different on the moon than on the earth. What would be impossible for me on earth is easy on the moon; I'm in a different sphere and have different power. In other words, if you change my environment, I can do things I can't do now.

We have problems with the power of God because we keep Him in our environment. We try to limit Him to what we know on earth, so we "just know" that He can't do this or that. But God lives in a realm far beyond us, and His power operates according to vastly different rules.

TONY EVANS

DAY
222
⌐

A miracle for skeptics?

*If they do not listen to Moses and the Prophets, they will
not be convinced even if someone rises from the dead.*

(LUKE 16:31)

Many times I have wished that God would bare His almighty arm and demonstrate His supernatural power to this skeptical generation in such an overwhelming fashion that everyone would have to admit there is an omnipotent God in heaven. Nothing harmful, you understand, for I would not want Him to scare people. That isn't His style, anyway. When He performs miracles, they are always helpful.

But just once I would love to see our living God demonstrate His existence in such obvious terms that all the world would know that He is THE LORD. I have yearned for and prayed for one awesomely powerful act on the part of God that would settle the question once and for all.

DAY
223

Many of the Hebrew prophets felt the same yearning and said so. Even the rich man Jesus mentioned in Luke 16 meant the same thing when he begged Abraham to send Lazarus back to his father and brothers' house to warn them, lest they come to "this place of torment." He thought that a man brought back from the dead would be able to convince them. We all yearn for that, or some supernatural sign that would prove unmistakably that God does exist.

But that is not His plan. He could easily stop the sun in its orbit, suspend the law of gravity without harmful consequences, or do any number of things to prove His existence—if He chose to do so. But He does not so choose. Instead, we are left with the words of Abraham to Lazarus: "If they do not listen to Moses and the Prophets, they will not be convinced even if someone rises from the dead" (Luke 16:31).

TIM LAHAYE

The Bridle of Divine Power

*"Do you refuse to speak to me?" Pilate asked. "Don't you realize
I have power either to free you or to crucify you?" Jesus answered,
"You would have no power over me if it were not given to you from above."*

(JOHN 19:10–11)

 o creature can move tongue or hand against any of God's people, unless He first commissions them or permits them to do so (even though they do not believe this).

"Don't you realize," said Pilate to Christ, "I have power either to free you or to crucify you?" Proud worm! What an ignorant and insolent boast this was of his own power! And how does Christ spoil and shame it in His answer? "You would have no power over me if it were not given to you from above" (John 19:11).

DAY
224

Wicked men, like wild horses, would run over and trample underfoot all the people of God in the world, were it not that the bridle of Divine Power had a strong rein to restrain them. This world is a raging and wild sea, which severely tosses about the heaven-bound passengers that sail upon it. But this is their comfort and security: "[The Lord] stills the noise of the sea, the noise of the waves, and the tumult of the people" (Psalm 65:7, KJV).

And not only the power of man, but the power of devils is also under the restraint and limitation of God's power. "The devil will put some of you in prison to test you, and you will suffer persecution for ten days" (Revelation 2:10). He would have thrown them into their graves, even into hell if he could, but it must be only into a prison. He would have kept them in prison until they had died and rotted there, but it must be for only ten days. Oh glorious, sovereign power, which in this way keeps the reins of government in its own hand!

JOHN FLAVEL

obedient to every whisper

The foolishness of God is wiser than man's wisdom,
and the weakness of God is stronger than man's strength.

(1 CORINTHIANS 1:25)

G od has declared throughout Scripture that His goal is to showcase before the universe His infinite majesty and glory and power. He has no rivals; He is unique. And He is committed with every ounce of His omnipotence to exalting His own name and humbling all pretenders. "I will not yield my glory to another," He says in Isaiah 48:11.

So what better way to humble human pride than to turn their own, most potent schemes against them? What better way for God to show His strength than to pit His "weakness" against man's "strength"...and win? How better to showcase His glory than to provide example after example that "the foolishness of God is wiser than man's wisdom, and the weakness of God is stronger than man's strength"?

DAY
225

Consider what God did to Pharaoh at the time of the Exodus. Through Moses, God demanded that Pharaoh release the Israelites; time and again, the king refused. Yet even Pharaoh's power was merely a tool in God's hand. "I have raised you up for this very purpose," said the LORD to Pharaoh, "that I might show you my power and that my name might be proclaimed in all the earth" (Exodus 9:16).

Even Pharaoh's stubbornness and pride would in the end serve God's purposes. God knew that immediately after Pharaoh allowed the Israelites to go, the king would change his mind and send his army after them. But even this would play into God's hands: "But I will gain glory for myself through Pharaoh and all his army, and the Egyptians will know that I am the LORD" (Exodus 14:4). Chariots and horses and spears and arrows are no match for a watery torrent obedient to every whisper of God's voice.

STEVE HALLIDAY

completely satisfied

*I know whom I have believed, and I am convinced that he
is able to guard what I have entrusted to him for that day.*

(2 TIMOTHY 1:12)

he Bible is filled with statements of what God is able to do
for His people. Here are seven verses which cover almost
all the fundamental doctrines of Christianity.

1. Hebrews 7:25 declares that Christ "is able to save completely
those who come to God through him." Mel Trotter, an evangelist
whom God called from a life of alcoholism, said this verse proclaimed
God's ability to save a person "from the guttermost to the uttermost."

2. In 2 Timothy 1:12 Paul writes, "I know whom I have believed,
and I am convinced that he is able to guard what I have entrusted to
him for that day." God has the power to keep my spiritual deposits.

3. Second Corinthians 9:8 says, "God is able to make all grace
abound to you, so that in all things at all times, having all that you
need, you will abound in every good work."

4. The Bible says of Jesus, "Because he himself suffered when he
was tempted, he is able to help those who are being tempted"
(Hebrews 2:18).

5. Ephesians 3:20 tells us that God "is able to do immeasurably
more than all we ask or imagine."

6. The Lord Jesus Christ, "by the power that enables him to bring
everything under his control, will transform our lowly bodies so that
they will be like his glorious body" (Philippians 3:21).

7. Jude says the Lord "is able to keep you from falling and to present you before his glorious presence without fault and with great joy"
(Jude 24).

Taken together, these verses declare that God is able to save us for
this life and for eternity, to keep us from falling into sin and temptation, to lead us to the best in human experience, and to satisfy us
completely.

JAMES MONTGOMERY BOICE

DAY
226

Available power

All power is given to Me. Go therefore....
(MATTHEW 28:20, KJV)

God Himself is our source of power. It is His possession. "Power belongs to God," and He employs and displays it according to His sovereign will. Yet He does not do so in an erratic or arbitrary manner, but according to His declared purpose and promises. It is true that our opponents and hindrances are many and mighty, but our God, the living God, is Almighty.

Further, God's power is available power. We are a supernatural people, born again by a supernatural birth, kept by a supernatural power, sustained on supernatural food, taught by a supernatural Teacher from a supernatural Book. We are led by a supernatural Captain on right paths to assured victories. The risen Savior, before He ascended on high, said, "All power is given to Me. Go therefore...." (Matthew 28:20, KJV).

DAY
227

Again, He said to His disciples, "You will receive power when the Holy Spirit comes on you" (Acts 1:8). Not many days after this, in answer to united and continued prayer, the Holy Spirit did come upon them and they were all filled.

Praise God, He remains with us still! The power given is not a gift from the Holy Spirit; He Himself is the power. Today He is as truly available and as mighty in power as He was on the day of Pentecost.

But since the days before Pentecost, has the whole church ever put aside every other work and waited upon God for ten days, that His power might be displayed? We have given too much attention to method and to machinery and to resources, and too little to the true source of power.

JAMES HUDSON TAYLOR

The Bank of Heaven

And my God will meet all your needs according
to his glorious riches in Christ Jesus.

(PHILIPPIANS 4:19)

an is a needy creature. There is not a single exception. The old have needs, as do the young. The rich have needs, as do the poor. We all have needs.

And then, too, there are some things which God sees we need which we ourselves do not recognize. For instance, Joseph needed a prison cell and God provided it; it proved to be a school designed to prepare him for a throne. David needed a cave, and God provided Adullam. Peter needed a great test and he had it, but he learned his lesson. Paul needed a shipwreck and it was supplied, and with it, blessings to himself and to others.

But while man is a needy creature, God is a wealthy Creator, and He is the source of supply for every need—be that need character, wisdom, grace, love, patience, endurance, courage, faith, for the "rainy day," for sickness, for sorrow, for trials—anything and everything that can come into the lives of God's children.

If the Bank of Heaven has never yet failed and the checks which have been issued by it have always been honored, why this woeful lack of faith in God's power and willingness to answer prayer and supply *all* our need? The fact of abundant provision is certain. The way of access is open. He has put the checkbook in our hands. He wants the resources to be used. The only condition and limitation is that they must be used for His glory.

Let us draw our checks, with childlike confidence in His promise to cash them—and every earthly need for our daily lives and every God-given desire to obey His command to give the gospel to the world, will be granted.

THOMAS C. HORTON

DAY
228

A great comfort

To him who is able to keep you from falling and to present you before his glorious presence without fault and with great joy—to the only God our Savior be glory, majesty, power and authority, through Jesus Christ our Lord, before all ages, now and forevermore! Amen.

(JUDE 24–25)

L ike all the other excellencies of God, omnipotence is a great comfort to His children. It is a comfort to them when persecuted and oppressed: "The LORD is my light and my salvation—whom shall I fear? The LORD is the stronghold of my life—of whom shall I be afraid?" (Psalm 27:1).

It is a comfort and encouragement when we are besieged by temptations: "No temptation has seized you except what is common to man. And God is faithful; he will not let you be tempted beyond what you can bear. But when you are tempted, he will also provide a way out so that you can stand up under it" (1 Corinthians 10:13).

God's infinite ability to answer prayer is affirmed by Paul (Ephesians 3:20–21) in a most glorious way. John Stott explains:

DAY
229

(1) He is able to *do,* for He is neither idle, nor inactive, nor dead. (2) He is able to do what we *ask,* for He hears and answers prayer. (3) He is able to do what we ask *or think,* for He reads our thoughts. (4) He is able to do *all* that we ask or think, for He knows it all and can perform it all. (5) He is able to do *more than* all we ask or think, for His expectations are higher than ours. (6) He is able to do much *more abundantly* than all that we ask or think, for He does not give His grace by calculated measure. (7) He is able to do *far more abundantly* than all that we ask or think, for He is a God of super-abundance.

There is yet more! We may be strengthened in knowing that *all* He has promised He *will,* because He *can,* fulfill (Jude 24–25).

C. SAMUEL STORMS

wait for Him

*The eyes of the LORD run to and fro throughout
the whole earth, to show his might on behalf
of those whose heart is blameless toward him.*

(2 CHRONICLES 16:9, RSV)

DAY
230

God aims to exalt Himself by working for those who wait for Him. Prayer is the essential activity of waiting for God: acknowledging our helplessness and His power, calling upon Him for help, seeking His counsel. So it is evident why prayer is so often commanded by God since His purpose in the world is to be exalted for His mercy. Prayer is the antidote for the disease of self-confidence that opposes God's goal of getting glory by working for those who wait for Him.

"The eyes of the LORD run to and fro throughout the whole earth, to show his might on behalf of those whose heart is whole toward him" (2 Chronicles 16:9). God is not looking for people to work for Him, so much as He is looking for people who will let Him work for them. The gospel is not a Help Wanted ad. Neither is the call to Christian service. On the contrary, the gospel commands *us* to give up and hang out a Help Wanted sign (this is the basic meaning of prayer). Then the gospel promises that God will work for us if we do.

The difference between Uncle Sam and Jesus Christ is that Uncle Sam won't enlist you in his service unless you are healthy, and Jesus won't enlist you unless you are sick. "Those who are well have no need of a physician, but those who are sick; I came not to call the righteous, but sinners" (Mark 2:17, RSV). Christianity is fundamentally convalescence ("Pray without ceasing" = Keep buzzing the nurse). Patients do not serve their physicians. They trust them for good prescriptions. The Sermon on the Mount and the Ten Commandments are the Doctor's prescribed health regimen, not the Employer's job description.

JOHN PIPER

turn to the power

*We have not stopped praying for you and asking God to fill you with the
knowledge of his will through all spiritual wisdom and understanding.
And we pray this in order that you may live a life worthy of the Lord and
may please him in every way: bearing fruit in every good work, growing in the
knowledge of God, being strengthened with all power according to his glorious might.*

(COLOSSIANS 1:9–11)

W hat a wonderful prayer for the saints! Were Paul praying
for us today, would he not make the same petition? Do we
not need this prayer in our behalf? Do we not need to reiterate it constantly? Do we not seek the constant renewal of strength
for our bodies day by day, as we use and utilize them in His service?
We are wise if we properly care for our bodies, to avoid unnecessary
waste and depletion; but are we as wise regarding the needs of the
spiritual life?

How comprehensive is the word *all* as used here by Paul: "*all*
spiritual wisdom; with *all* power." This includes every service to
which the Lord may call us.

As we meditate on this theme of the "all-power" of prayer, let us
remember that the power comes from Him to whom we belong and
whom we are to serve. The exercise of this power naturally depends
upon conditions. We must not only be connected with the powerhouse, but the channel must be kept free. Not only is the Lord always
ready to send the power through, but He longs to do so. The limitation lies with us, with our capacity for receiving and using.

The word *power* as used here means "sovereign sway," and in the
New Testament is always associated with the power of God. We have
the privilege of "*being* strengthened," i.e., a *daily* strengthening. Our
natures are naturally weak, and they are further weakened by our
daily toil and stress. But the power of God can fill us constantly and
keep us well-rounded men and women.

It is to this power we must turn as we pray. His glorious power!
His unfailing power! His promised power!

THOMAS C. HORTON

DAY
231

The mightiest force in the world

Pray in the Spirit on all occasions with all kinds of prayers and requests.

(EPHESIANS 6:18)

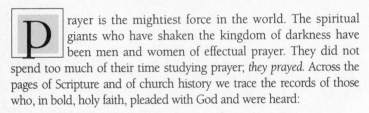

Prayer is the mightiest force in the world. The spiritual giants who have shaken the kingdom of darkness have been men and women of effectual prayer. They did not spend too much of their time studying prayer; *they prayed.* Across the pages of Scripture and of church history we trace the records of those who, in bold, holy faith, pleaded with God and were heard:

DAY
232

- Abraham prayed long for a son: Isaac came.
- Moses prayed: Heaven's wrath was subdued.
- Joshua prayed: Achan was discovered and Ai destroyed.
- Hannah prayed: Samuel was given to her.
- Elijah prayed: The heavens were shut and opened.
- Elisha prayed: Drought came and a dead child lived again.
- David prayed: Ahithophel, the traitor, hanged himself.
- Hezekiah prayed: 185,000 Assyrians were slain.
- Daniel prayed. Archangels were set in motion.

Nor did documentation of the power of prayer disappear when the last page of inspired canon was filled.

- Savonarola prayed: A city was won for God.
- Martin Luther prayed: God broke the spell of ages.
- John Knox prayed: Tyrants were terrified and Scotland was blessed.
- George Whitefield prayed: A thousand souls were saved in one day.
- George Mueller prayed: Hungry orphans were fed.
- Hudson Taylor prayed: Inland China was evangelized.

On we could go, citing thousands of witnesses, all proving the lengths to which God will go when men and women are prepared to lay hold of Him and refuse to let Him go until He blesses. The consistent witness of Bible and church saints is that prayer is the highest resource of the soul.

HERBERT LOCKYER

A failure to know Jesus

*Jesus answered her, "If you knew the gift of God, and who it is
that is saying to you, 'Give me a drink,' you would have
asked him, and he would have given you living water!"*

(JOHN 4:10, RSV)

I f you were a sailor severely afflicted with scurvy, and a generous man came aboard ship with his pockets bulging with vitamin C and asked you for an orange slice, you might give it to him. But if you knew he was generous, and that he carried all you needed to be well, you would turn the tables and ask him for help.

Jesus says to the Samaritan woman in John 4, "If you just knew the gift of God and who I am, you would ask me—you would pray to me!" There is a direct correlation between not knowing Jesus well and not asking much from Him. A failure in our prayer life is generally a failure to know Jesus. "If you knew who was talking to you, you would ask me!" A prayerless Christian is like a bus driver trying alone to push his bus out of a rut because he doesn't know Clark Kent is on board. "If you knew, you would ask." A prayerless Christian is like having your room wallpapered with Sak's Fifth Avenue gift certificates but always shopping at Ragstock because you can't read. "If you knew the gift of God and who it is that speaks to you, you would ask—*you would ask!*"

DAY
233

And the implication is that those who do ask—Christians who spend time in prayer—do it because they see that God is a great Giver and that Christ is wise and merciful and powerful beyond measure. And therefore their prayer glorifies Christ and honors His Father. The chief end of man is to glorify God. Therefore, when we become what God created us to be, we become people of prayer.

JOHN PIPER

power with god

*Elijah was a man just like us. He prayed earnestly that it would
not rain, and it did not rain on the land for three and a half years.
Again he prayed, and the heavens gave rain, and the earth produced its crops.*

(JAMES 5:17–18)

I s it possible that a mere mortal can have power like this with God? It is both possible and true, and forms one of the wonders of His condescending love. Believing prayer takes hold of the Almighty's strength; it has the key that unlocks the treasures of heaven; and it has the power to move the hand that moves all things.

O Christian, whether you are a young man or a mature woman, a person of stature or as poor as a pauper—get the spirit of faith in prayer, and nothing shall be impossible for you. Obstacles of all kinds in the path of duty will be removed or turned into helps; rocks will be split and Red Seas part at your word; and heaven's wonderful treasures will be at your command!

The grand defect of the religion of our day is a lack of strong, unshaken confidence in the power of prayer. There are plenty of public forms of prayer and great activity, but I fear that we lack the strong, wrestling supplication, the giving up of days to plead faithfully with God, and the assured faith that the very things we ask from God will be given.

All people of faith are persons of prayer. They ask what they want directly from God, and get direct answers. They are not troubled with the modern nonsense, held by some, that God does not directly give us anything, but that prayer consists primarily in the effect it has upon our own minds. This is an invention of the enemy to get men to give up prayer altogether—and it is very certain that Satan would not tremble before a million prayers founded upon such a powerless theory.

ROBERT BOYD

power in prayer

*I pray also that the eyes of your heart may be enlightened in order that you
may know the hope to which he has called you, the riches of his glorious
inheritance in the saints, and his incomparably great power for us who believe.*

(EPHESIANS 1:18–19)

L et us prepare ourselves to pray in the power of the Holy
Spirit, so that, as Paul admonishes us in Ephesians
1:18–19: "I pray also that the eyes of your heart may be
enlightened in order that you may know the hope to which he has
called you, the riches of his glorious inheritance in the saints, and his
incomparably great power for us who believe. That power is like the
working of his mighty strength."

What is "his incomparably great power"? We can know it only
through the exercise of faith as God inspires us. The weakness of our
faith is the obstruction which blocks the stream of power flowing
from God to us. The psalmist says: "He turned rivers into a desert,
flowing springs into thirsty ground, and fruitful land into a salt waste,
because of the wickedness of those who lived there" (Psalm 107:33).
But, He also "turned the desert into pools of water and the parched
ground into flowing springs" (Psalm 107:35).

There is a challenge here—a challenge to every child of God, and
especially if you are a Christian leader. It is not an easy thing to be a
real leader for Christ. It is a position fraught with tremendous respon-
sibilities and consequences. No one should seek it unless called and
equipped with the promise of Him who has said: "And I will do whatever you ask in my name, so that the Son may bring glory to the
Father" (John 14:13).

Prayer is a power that reaches the ends of the earth, reaches heaven
itself. It has no limits except those which He Himself has fixed. Let us
consider the subject reverently and lovingly and yield ourselves to the
power of the Holy Spirit, that we may have real "Power in Prayer."

THOMAS C. HORTON

as much of god as we want

That power is like the working of his mighty strength,
which he exerted in Christ when he raised him from the dead.

(EPHESIANS 1:19–20)

T here is an old story about a Christian father, who after torturing himself with theological speculations about the nature of the Trinity, fell asleep and dreamed that he was emptying the ocean with a thimble. Of course, you cannot empty it with a thimble; but you can go to it with one…and will bring away only a thimbleful.

In the same way, the measure of our faith is the measure of God's power given to us. There are two measures of God's divine power. One is the infinite limit of "his incomparably great power for us who believe" (Ephesians 1:19), and the other the practical limit. The *working* measure of our spiritual life is our faith.

In plain English, we can have as much of God as we want. In fact, we *do* have as much as we want. So if we are in touch with the power that can shatter a universe, yet get only a little thrill, scarcely perceptible to ourselves and unnoticed by others—whose fault is that? And if we come to the fountain that laughs at drought and can fill a universe with its waters, yet we take away scarcely a tiny drop or two, barely enough to refresh our parched lips, a mere sip that does nothing to encourage plants of holiness to grow in our gardens—whose fault is that?

The practical measure of God's power in our lives is the measure of our belief and desire. If only we go to Him, as I pray we all may, and continue there, and ask Him to give us strength according to the riches treasured in Jesus Christ, we shall get the old answer: "According to your faith will it be done to you" (Matthew 9:29).

ALEXANDER MACLAREN

DAY
236

NOT BY BRAWN

"Not by might nor by power, but by
my Spirit," says the LORD Almighty.

(ZECHARIAH 4:6)

Y ou could characterize the greatest national force the world
has ever seen with one word: power! Rome was the greatest power machine the world has ever seen. The legions of
Rome marched on every frontier. They were invincible and victorious.
But one day they took into custody a Man who seemed to be very
weak. Pilate said to Him, "Don't you realize I have power either to free
you or to crucify you?" The Lord Jesus answered, "You would have no
power over me if it were not given to you from above."

Today we have a perspective on that. The legions of Rome have
marched into oblivion. As Kipling said, "The tumult and the shouting
die, the captains and the kings depart." They are all gone. But the
gospel of that Man who died on the cross is still being carried by weak
men to the ends of the earth—by men who are as weak as you and I.
His death was a victory.

God is not impressed by brawn and a display of muscle. The
church goes forward today like a little Samson shorn of its locks of
power. It parades up and down, boasting of its accomplishments, and,
like Samson, it does not know that the Spirit of God has departed
from it. The thing that makes this so tragic is that the church could go
forward like a little David with a simple slingshot of the Holy Spirit,
to meet the enemy with all of his stratagems, and come away with a
victory!

Oh, how we need the power of the Holy Spirit! God's work in the
world is not done by brawn. It is accomplished only by His Spirit.

J. VERNON MCGEE

DAY
237

The Real powerhouse

I will not venture to speak of anything except what Christ has accomplished
through me in leading the Gentiles to obey God by what I have said and done
—by the power of signs and miracles, through the power of the Spirit.

(ROMANS 15:18–19)

O h, if we only recognized that we can do nothing in our own strength for God! It would cause us to cast ourselves upon Him and get connected with the real powerhouse, the Holy Spirit. God's will and God's work is instigated, promoted, and carried through to a successful accomplishment by the Holy Spirit, apart from man's ability and help.

God utterly and entirely repudiates the work of the flesh. He will have nothing of it. The day in which we live is impressed by brawn, that which reveals muscle. Well, the dinosaurs were big, but they are not here today. But the little, lowly flea is still with us! Powerful nations flex their muscles. So what? The time will come when God will put them down.

It is man who made the din of the city with its nerve-shattering noises. It is man who made the horn and the siren, the gaudy and garish lights that illuminate the brick and cement canyons of our cities. In contrast, God made the silent depths of the forest with its pleasant shadows.

It is the spring of the year as I write this, traveling through Illinois—oh, what a carpet of green has been laid down! And in Missouri the trees are beginning to leaf out. In Kansas the grain is coming up. Then out on the desert the flowers are unfolding. It is beautiful. Today, my friend, the nitrogen is silently crawling up the stalks and up the limbs, making leaves and flowers. There is enough power being released to blow this little earth to smithereens! God is doing it without any show, without any display. It is not by might; it is not by brawn. "It is by my Spirit," says the Lord.

J. VERNON MCGEE

DAY
238

god's rock
polishing machine

Though he slay me, yet will I hope in him.

(JOB 13:15)

Suppose all the hydroelectric power from all the dams on the Columbia River was channeled into one massive power line. Imagine that instead of lighting and heating cities and running the wheels of vast industries, it was attached to a single rock-polishing machine. Incongruous! The power would be totally out of proportion to the job.

In the same way, it seems to us that omnipotence is not given a chance to flex its muscles when limited to producing in us patience and long-suffering with joyfulness. But "seems" is an important word; for it is much harder to build character than to create a world.

Could it be that we have underestimated the challenge to God's omnipotence? Scripture and history both seem to show that omnipotence is captive to a plan in which the public miracle, the irrefutable demonstration of divine power, is not the order of the day (or age).

Consequently, God's omnipotence is not normally destroying His enemies and rescuing His people in miraculous displays of power. God is rather strengthening the inner man in order that we may endure the hardships of life and say with Job, "Though he slay me, yet will I hope in him" (Job 13:15). And that is indeed a job fit for omnipotence! Especially to make us do it with joyfulness!

The sufferings of Christ which bore in our place the penalty of sin were finished on the cross—never to be repeated.

But the sufferings of the Body of Christ—that mystical organism composed of all true believers in this age—are not yet complete. And so the rock-polishing machine of God continues to turn, producing bright, precious gems fit for the glories of heaven.

WILLARD ALDRICH

LET US BOW DOWN

The LORD, who brought you up out of Egypt with mighty
power and outstretched arm, is the one you must worship.
To him you shall bow down and to him offer sacrifices.

(2 KINGS 17:36)

I f a man makes a clever invention, we honor him for his skill; if another defeats a strong enemy, we admire him for his strength. If this is true, should not the limitless power of God inflame us with praise for His name and perfections? We respect men because of their wisdom and power; so because both are infinite in God, we owe Him our passionate worship and solemn devotion.

DAY
240

We admire rulers with vast empires and great armies, who have the power to conquer their enemies and preserve the peace of their own people. How much more should we pay mighty reverence to God, who without trouble or weariness made and manages this vast empire of the world! How we stand in awe of the thunder's roar, the power of the sun, the storms of the sea! These things—which have no understanding—have struck men with such reverence that many have worshiped them as gods. How much more, then, should we worship and adore God, who is perfect in both power and wisdom!

All religion and worship stands upon two pillars, the goodness and power of God. If either of these were defective, all religion would fade away. We can expect no kindness from Him without goodness, nor any help from Him without power. So before God instructs us to worship Him, He reminds us of the blessings He conferred upon us through His power and goodness. And because His power provides a main foundation of prayer, the Lord's prayer concludes with this doxology: "For yours is the kingdom and the power and the glory forever. Amen." As God is rich and possesses all blessings, so is He powerful to bestow all blessings on us.

STEPHEN CHARNOCK

Reason for comfort

My help comes from the LORD,
the Maker of heaven and earth.

(PSALM 121:2)

I n this verse we find comfort in all our afflictions and distresses. God's power is always greater than our problems. The same power that brought a world out of chaos and put the stars in motion, can bring order out of our confusions and light out of our darkness.

When our Savior was in His greatest distress and saw the face of His Father frowning at Him while He hung upon the cross, even in His complaint to Him, He trusted in His power: *Eloi, Eloi; lama sabachthani?*, "My God, my God, why have you forsaken me?" (Matthew 27:46)—that is, "My strong, my strong." *El* is a name of power belonging to God; Jesus comforts Himself in God's power, even while the Son complains of the Father's frowns.

Follow His pattern and do not forget that power that can scatter the clouds as well as gather them. The psalmist found relief in his distress in the creative power of God.

God's power is strong comfort against all seductive vices and mighty temptations. Through His power we may arm ourselves and be "strong in the power of his might" (Ephesians 6:10). By this we may conquer principalities and powers as dreadful as hell. By this we may triumph over lusts within, too strong for an arm of flesh. By this the battered walls of our souls may be repaired and the Sons of Anak laid flat. The Power that brought light out of darkness and ordered the chaos and set bounds to the ocean and dried up the Red Sea, can still the turmoil in our spirits and level spiritual Goliaths. There is no resistance He cannot overcome, no stronghold He cannot demolish, no tower He cannot level.

STEPHEN CHARNOCK

god can Handle it

*I am the LORD, the God of all mankind.
Is anything too hard for me?*

(JEREMIAH 32:27)

W hen you catch yourself worrying about something, realize there is nothing too great for God to handle. God Himself says to you, "I am the LORD, the God of all mankind. Is anything too hard for me?" Nothing is difficult for Him because His power is infinite. As Stephen Charnock wrote, "As omnipotence is an ocean that cannot be fathomed, so the comforts from it are streams that cannot be exhausted. How comforting to know you have a God who can do what He pleases: there is nothing so difficult that He can't accomplish, nothing so strong that He can't overrule!" Therefore God can handle any problem you have!

DAY
242

God's power is the basis for our spiritual victory. Paul said to "be strong in the Lord and in his mighty power" (Ephesians 6:10). For victory, you are to be like a guard on watch. When the enemy comes, you're not supposed to fight him yourself—you are to tell the commander, and he will lead the battle. God can bring about spiritual victory because "The one who is in you is greater than the one who is in the world" (1 John 4:4). Satan is a powerful enemy, but he is no match for God's power.

What should be our response to God's awesome, majestic, and glorious power? *Humility.* It's easy to be proud if your thoughts are on yourself instead of God. That's why we need to heed this admonition: "Humble yourselves...under God's mighty hand, that he may lift you up in due time" (1 Peter 5:6). We need to humble ourselves before our all-powerful God because, apart from His enabling, we can do nothing (Deuteronomy 6:8–10; John 15:5).

JOHN MACARTHUR JR.

The strength to rescue

Was my arm too short to ransom you?
Do I lack the strength to rescue you?

(ISAIAH 50:2)

We're all sometimes tempted to think that our stumbles, foul-ups, and blunders are somehow too damaging or serious to be overcome—even by the limitless power of God. We grow doubtful that the Holy One of Israel could even stand us, let alone use us.

But when we allow ourselves to descend into that pit, we forget that our God is a God of turnabouts. He delights in taking our silliest, grandest, and even most heinous offenses and transforming them by His wisdom and might into trophies of His boundless grace. Somehow, we fail to recall His indignant questions in Isaiah 50:2:

DAY
243

Was my arm too short to ransom you?
Do I lack the strength to rescue you?

The answers, of course, are no and no.

It's possible you may have just blown it big time. You may feel as though your blunder dooms you to a wretched, hopeless future. But if you are a Christian—if by faith you have entrusted your soul to His tender keeping—it is impossible that any mistake, any blunder, any sin could outstrip His power to reshape it into a brilliant display of His matchless glory.

Because the truth is, as Isaiah well knew, God's arms are so long and so bulging with rippling muscle that the fabric of the universe itself doesn't begin to provide enough material even for a divine warm-up jersey.

STEVE HALLIDAY

THE OMNISCIENCE AND WISDOM OF GOD

OH, THE DEPTH

OF THE RICHES

OF THE WISDOM

AND KNOWLEDGE

OF GOD!

ROMANS 11:33

perfect in knowledge

Do you know how the clouds hang poised,
those wonders of him who is perfect in knowledge?

(JOB 37:16)

G od is infinitely superior to us in knowledge. We are of yesterday and know nothing; our foundation is in the dust. We have little real knowledge of present objects and events, and of the future we are entirely ignorant, except so far as God has been pleased to reveal it.

But God perfectly knows all things. He has a perfect knowledge of the properties and qualities of all creatures, for He made them what they are and sustains them where they are. He knows everything that is now taking place in the universe, for He is everywhere present. He knows everything that ever has occurred or ever will occur, for we are told that He sees the end from the beginning. God "calls things that are not as though they were" (Romans 4:17) and knows all His works from the beginning.

DAY
244

At a single glance God looks through eternity and immensity and sees everything at once—the whole circle of existence. Such perfect knowledge obviously causes His thoughts and ways to be infinitely above our own. Are not the thoughts and ways of a parent above the comprehension of his newborn infant? Do not our own thoughts change, as we gain wisdom and knowledge? How far, then, must the thoughts and ways of the omniscient, infallible God, exceed those of ignorant, shortsighted, and fallible men and women!

REV. EDWARD PAYSON

eyes That penetrate

The eyes of the LORD are everywhere,
keeping watch on the wicked and the good.

(PROVERBS 15:3)

DAY
245

N othing can be hidden from God. He knows our feelings, our desires, our excuses, and our personalities. He knows everything and anything, and He knows it comprehensively. If something can be known, He knows it; and what He knows, He has known from the beginning (Acts 15:18). No angel in heaven could ever throw God a successful surprise party!

Proverbs 15:3 tells us that "The eyes of the LORD are everywhere, keeping watch on the wicked and the good." Nothing can escape His all-encompassing knowledge—not the biggest or the most minute detail. In Matthew 10:29 Jesus said, "Not one [sparrow] will fall to the ground apart from the will of your Father." The legendary Baptist preacher, Dr. Robert G. Lee, once said, "God is the only One who attends a sparrow's funeral." According to Psalm 50:11, God knows every beast and every bird of the air. *That's* comprehensive knowledge!

God sees what's done in secret and what's done in the light. God is the eternal, cosmic X-ray machine. His eyes penetrate. David says in Psalm 139:12 that the day and the night are alike to God. Moses reminds us that our secret sins are brought to light in His presence (Psalm 90:8). *All* of our lives are totally known.

That means you never do anything alone. You may be by yourself, but you are not alone. Whether it's good or bad, the all-knowing eye of God sees it. Many of us don't want such an all-seeing God, so we try to dismiss Him by telling ourselves, "God doesn't know what we're doing" (see Psalm 73:8–11).

But God knows. He knows what's done publicly for all to see and what's done privately for none to see. *He knows.*

TONY EVANS

more Than the Heavenly Head

Lord, you know all things.

(JOHN 21:17)

Some people think a computer provides an apt analogy for God's knowlege because computer "brains" are so big and quick—and no computer ever forgot to pick up a loaf of bread on the way home. But computers are dependent on operator commands and have to be manufactured, programmed, and given data. God has always existed, can never be programmed, and knows all the data innately and intrinsically. Nothing is in memory or storage either: He is simultaneously conscious of everything at the same time. And God does not have to be plugged in.

DAY
246

But most importantly, God is not an electromechanical machine. His knowledge is not a mass of binary numbers, electromagnetic pulses, or synthesized chirps and bleeps. He knows us not as ciphers which originate and terminate, but as children whom He loves. The point is not just that God knows everything, or even that He knows everything *about* us. Rather, it is that He knows *us*—individually and personally—and far better than we know ourselves. You cannot pray to a personal computer no matter how "user friendly" it is.

Nor is God the *Mind*—a disembodied metaphysical deity whose only claim to fame is naked intellect, an infinitely fat head. With such a mind, one may contemplate, seek to merge one's thoughts, or seek fuller and higher levels of esoteric comprehension of the truth. But one cannot communicate with it. Fortunately, God is not just the heavenly Head.

When a Christian says, "Lord, you know all things," the one spoken to *is* infinite Wisdom, Understanding, Intellect, Knowledge, Rationality, and the Source of all Truth. But at the same time He is also the "Wonderful Counselor, Mighty God, Everlasting Father, Prince of Peace" (Isaiah 9:6). And that makes all the difference.

W. BINGHAM HUNTER

He Knows

I know the things that come into your mind, every one of them.
(EZEKIEL 11:5, KJV)

W hat a wondrous Being is the God of Scripture! Each of His glorious attributes should arouse our reverent worship. To learn of His omniscience should cause us to bow before Him in joyful adoration. Yet how little do we meditate upon this divine perfection! Is it because the very thought of it fills us with uneasiness?

How solemn is this fact: Nothing can be concealed from God! "For I know the things that come into your mind, every one of them," He tells Israel through the prophet. Though He is invisible to us, we are not so to Him. Neither the darkness of night, the most dense curtains, nor the deepest dungeon can hide anyone from the eyes of Omniscience. The trees of the Garden of Eden were unable to conceal our first parents. No human eye saw Cain murder his brother, but his Maker witnessed the crime. Sarah might laugh derisively in the seclusion of her tent, yet the Lord heard her snigger. Achan stole a wedge of gold and carefully hid it in the ground, but God brought it to light. David took great care to cover up his sin, but before long the all-seeing God sent one of His servants to say to him, "You are the man!" (2 Samuel 12:7). And to writer and reader it is said, "You may be sure that your sin will find you out" (Numbers 32:23).

While the unredeemed would strip Deity of His omniscience if they could, to the believer, the fact of God's omniscience is a truth brimming with comfort. In times of perplexity we say with Job, "He knows the way that I take" (Job 23:10). My circumstances may be profoundly mysterious to me and quite incomprehensible to my friends, but He knows!

ARTHUR W. PINK

infinite understanding

Whom did the LORD consult to enlighten him,
and who taught him the right way? Who was it that taught him
knowledge or showed him the path of understanding?

(ISAIAH 40:14)

Our knowledge is always arriving to us or flowing from us. We pass from one degree of understanding to another, from worse to better or from better to worse. But God loses nothing by the march of the ages, nor will He gain anything by the ages that are to come.

If there were a variation in the knowledge of God, He would grow wiser than He was—and that would mean He was not perfectly wise before. But God's knowledge does not increase or decrease any more than He does. Since God can never decay into weakness or turn to unfaithfulness, there can be no variation of His knowledge. He knows what He can do and what He will do, and since both these are changeless, His knowledge must also be unchanging. God knows no more now than He did before; and at the end of the world, He shall know no more than He does now. Though things pass into and out of being, the knowledge of God does not vary with them, for He knows them as well before they were as when they are, and knows them as well when they are past as when they are present.

DAY
248

As the sun is continually in the act of shining, so is God perpetually in the act of knowing. And as the sun has never ceased to shine since it was first fixed in the heavens, just so God has never ceased to be in the act of knowing since He was God. And since He always was and always will be God, He always was and always will be in the act of knowing. As His power is coeternal with Him, so is His knowledge. His understanding is infinite.

STEPHEN CHARNOCK

Each of Them by Name

He determines the number of the
stars and calls them each by name.

(PSALM 147:4)

T he stars are so numerous that we cannot count them. Some are visible and known, others lie more distant and undiscovered. They are God's host, which He marshals in the heavens. He knows them more perfectly than we can know anything, even to the point of calling "each of them by name." He knows their characteristics, properties, their different degrees of heat and light, their order and motion—of *all* of them, the least glimmering as well as the most glaring. We cannot do this. As God says to Abraham, "Look at the heavens and count the stars—if indeed you can count them" (Genesis 15:5).

Now He who numbers and names the stars, both those that lie indistinct as well as those that shine clearly, certainly knows each of His people, though they lurk in secret caves. The one is as easy for Him as the other, and He knows the number of the one as accurately as the multitude of the other. Just as He can do what is beyond the power of man to perform, so He understands what is above the skill of man to discover. God knows all His people. He writes them all in His list, even as generals list their soldiers in their troop rosters.

Although God's people may be despised in the eyes of man, all are known and valued by God. Though they are obscure in the world, yet they are the stars of the world. Would God number the inanimate stars in the heavens and not count His living stars on the earth? No. Wherever His people are dispersed, He will not forget them. And however they are afflicted, He will not despise them.

STEPHEN CHARNOCK

the god who sees me

*She gave this name to the LORD who spoke to her:
"You are the God who sees me," for she said, "I have now seen
the One who sees me." That is why the well was called Beer Lahai Roi.*

(GENESIS 16:13–14)

A lone in the wilderness, homeless and friendless, Hagar sat by a well to contemplate her plight. Where could she go? What would she do when the moment arrived to give birth to her child? She had brought this upon herself through her insolent behavior toward Sarai, but now that she was alone she suddenly became aware that there was no one to whom she could turn. She looked about her, and seeing no person who might offer some assistance, she resigned herself to her fate.

Suddenly the Angel of the Lord appeared to her, ministered wise counsel and comfort, and cheered her with a promise. Hagar was so impressed with the fact that God had seen her in her difficulty, she was inspired to call Him *El Roi,* "the God who sees." The name which Hagar gave the well is as rich in meaning as that which she gave to God. She would always remember that place where God saw and met her in her need, where He graciously looked upon her in her affliction. *Beer Lahai Roi* means "the well of Him who lives and sees me."

Yes, the God who sees concerns Himself about our needs. *El Roi* is the God who looks after us, who sees to it that our needs are met. He is not the God of the glaring eye who goes about spying as a detective. While it is true that He sees every sinful thought, word, and deed of all men, the name *El Roi* was first used by a lonely, friendless girl who, in her distress, learned that God saw her plight and treated her with grace and mercy.

LEHMAN STRAUSS

never unaware

Great is our Lord and mighty in power;
his understanding has no limit.

(PSALM 147:5)

T he truth that God always sees us is awesome. Isaac Watts learned this from an old Christian woman when he was just a boy. She had him read the words, "Thou God seest me," from a plaque on her wall, and then she said, "When you are older, my boy, people will tell you that God is always watching to see when you do wrong, in order to punish you. I do not want you to think of it that way. Rather, let these words remind you all through your life that God loves you so much that He cannot take His eyes off of you." These words became for Isaac Watts an incentive to a useful and a beautiful life.

DAY
251

God is infinite, completely unlimited, in understanding and wisdom. He sees the past, the present, and the future with equal clarity. God's knowledge is both complete and intuitive. He knows everything, both actual and possible; He knows what might have been as well as what is actually transpiring.

How comforting it is for believers to realize that God knows everything about the past, the present, and the future! Nothing can ever happen to us that would surprise Him. He is never caught unaware nor is He ever unable to help. Moreover, we have absolute assurance that every prophecy of the Bible will be completely fulfilled. God is aware ahead of time of all the hindrances that will arise. He has the wisdom to deal with them. He has the power to overcome them. Every promise to us as children of God will be fully realized.

RICHARD W. DEHAAN

HE'S THINKING ABOUT ME

How precious to me are your thoughts, O God! How vast is the sum of them!
Were I to count them, they would outnumber the grains of sand.

(PSALM 139:17–18)

L ast night, after Bible study, a few of the girls hung around and started talking as we sipped coffee. But we didn't discuss what we'd just learned—instead we debated the pros and cons of laundry detergent sold in see-through plastic bottles so you can tell when it's near empty. Then we discussed how somebody ought to put a clear plastic strip on the sides of toothpaste pumps so you can tell when they're running low. We discussed the sale at a local department store and why they decaffeinate coffee the way they do.

Little wonder God said to Isaiah, "For my thoughts are not your thoughts, neither are your ways my ways.... As the heavens are higher than the earth, so are my ways higher than your ways and my thoughts than your thoughts" (Isaiah 55:8–9).

Somehow, I don't think God stays up at night worrying about laundry detergent or toothpaste pumps. I can think as much as I please, but my thoughts—limited, finite, and so very human—still leave me on earth.

Ah, but all is not hopeless. Why? Because even though my thoughts cannot bear me up to the Almighty, *He* nevertheless is still thinking about me. *He* bridges the gap. He makes His thoughts available. He puts His thoughts into words we can understand, stooping to make Himself comprehensible. As the psalmist says, "How precious to me are your thoughts, O God! How vast is the sum of them! Were I to count them, they would outnumber the grains of sand" (Psalm 139:17–18).

God's thoughts—at least many of them—*are* within grasp. And when we lay hold of Him and His ideas, then and only then can we be drawn closer to Him.

JONI EARECKSON TADA

DAY
252

A weapon against temptation

*If we had forgotten the name of our God or spread
out our hands to a foreign god, would not God have
discovered it, since he knows the secrets of the heart?*

(PSALM 44:20-21)

People secretly imagine that God does not know what they do, or that He soon forgets—and this makes them bold to sin against Him. How urgently therefore should we strive to keep fresh in our minds the reality of His omniscience! If God "writes us upon the palms of His hands" to remember us, then let us engrave Him upon the tables of our hearts to remember Him.

Will a man easily and delightfully commit some sin, when he realizes a holy God knows all about it? Temptations have no encouragement to draw near to the one who remembers that God records all sins in the book of His omniscience. Who would dare to speak treason against a prince if he were sure the prince heard him, or that it would certainly come to his attention? A recognition of God's infinite understanding would cry *Stop!* to the first glances of our hearts to sin.

Who would come before God with a careless and ignorant attitude, if they kept before their mind His infinite understanding and His penchant for searching the heart? Would we offer to God raw and thoughtless petitions? Would our service be so flat? Would our hearts so often betray us? Would anyone try to pass off a counterfeit humility by hanging down his head like a bent reed? No. Our prayers would be more sound, our devotions more vigorous, our hearts more aflame, our spirits more swift in their eagerness to do good. We would do everything for our Lord with all our might. Let us therefore open the curtain between God and our souls, and remember that we are going before the One who sees and knows us.

STEPHEN CHARNOCK

DAY
253

what if?

To crush underfoot all prisoners in the land,
to deny a man his rights before the Most High,
to deprive a man of justice—would not the Lord see such things?

(LAMENTATIONS 3:34–36)

A s a matter of pure speculative belief, a person may insist that God sees everything; but if such a person can take liberties under the inspection of God which he would not take under the eyes of his human associates, he is little better than an atheist.

Suppose there was one spot somewhere in the universe where God could not look. Would you like to live in such a place? If one country existed where we were as invisible to God as He is to us, would you like to move there? If a place could be discovered where God took no notice of human actions, where Bibles and Sundays were unknown, would you rush to reach that God-forsaken spot?

DAY
254

To godly men and women, the thought of such a place is repulsive. To the godly, living under the solemn, loving eye of God is pure pleasure. It delights them to feel that their work and worship alike fall under the inspection of their heavenly Father. They do not think of the Holy One as a spy looking only to find fault, but rather as a loving friend who watches for their good. They would not, for all worlds, have it otherwise than it is.

If there were one instant when God did not see us, we might fear for our security. We might fear that our enemy would storm over us like a flood, and that we would one day perish by the hand of the evil one. But, praise God, there is no such vacancy where God is not! He is eternally near. The whole universe is full of His presence and even the smallest or most insignificant object in its vast expanse always enjoys His constant attention.

ROBERT BOYD

A Look at the Heart

*Man looks at the outward appearance
but the LORD looks at the heart.*

(1 SAMUEL 16:7)

G od gave us a demonstration of His mind reading, heart searching techniques one day in Bethlehem. The prophet Samuel had arrived to choose Israel's future king. One by one Jesse paraded seven of his sons before Samuel, but God rejected them all. He was looking at something Samuel could not see. As He explained, "Man looks at the outward appearance, but the LORD looks at the heart" (1 Samuel 16:7). God wanted a man whose heart was wholly His, one with a desire to do His will.

DAY
255

He knows whether we have that desire. We can make others believe that we do, when in reality we want our own will. But God knows.

God knew there was something missing from the lives of those seven sons of Jesse. But when the youngest was brought in from keeping his father's sheep, God's spiritual X-ray vision perceived a heart that dearly loved Him and longed to please Him. "Rise and anoint him; he is the one" (1 Samuel 16:12). David had his moments of spiritual failure, as we all do, but few people in Scripture could rival his wholehearted devotion to God. God saw that devotion while David was still a youth.

One of the last things David did before he died was to give this charge to his son Solomon: "And you, my son Solomon, acknowledge the God of your father, and serve him with wholehearted devotion and with a willing mind, for the LORD searches every heart and understands every motive behind the thoughts" (1 Chronicles 28:9). It was a reminder of a truth David knew well, that God knows the secrets of the heart—a good reason to serve Him willingly and keep our thought lives pure and pleasing to Him.

RICHARD STRAUSS

A cause for joy

*For those God foreknew he also predestined
to be conformed to the likeness of his Son.*

(ROMANS 8:29)

T he omniscience of God is a cause of uneasiness and even dread for those who do not have their sin covered with the righteousness of Christ. But for three reasons this omniscience is a great blessing and a cause for joy among Christians.

First, because God knows all things, He knows the *worst about us* and yet has loved us and saved us. We needn't fear that something within us will rise up to startle God, that some forgotten skeleton will come tumbling out of our closet to expose our shameful past. Nothing can happen that isn't already known to God.

Second, God also knows *the best about us,* even though that best may be unknown to any other person. Perhaps things go in a way we didn't intend. Then people say—even our friends—"How could so-and-so do a thing like that? I would have thought better of him." They are critical and nothing we can do or say seems to change their opinion. What then? There is comfort in knowing that God, who knows all things, knows that we really did do our best. And He is patient with us.

Third, God knows *what He is going to make of* us. He knows the end for which we have been made: "For those God foreknew he also predestined to be conformed to the likeness of his Son" (Romans 8:29). God is determined to make us like Jesus Christ.

Sometimes we get discouraged in the Christian life. We take a step forward and fall half a step back. We think God must be discouraged with us. But He isn't. We have a great destiny and in its light all the vaunted achievements of our age and our personal achievements fade into insignificance.

JAMES MONTGOMERY BOICE

Then why pray?

Your Father knows what you need before you ask him.

(MATTHEW 6:8)

W*hat can you tell God, if He already knows everything?*
This is a common thought among Christians, especially in the West, because our pragmatism and logic force us to the certain answer: *nothing*. You can easily envision God being interrupted as He manages the universe and saying into the phone: "It's been good to hear from you, kid. But listen. Next time, don't call Me, I'll call you."

But the Bible is fundamentally a Semitic book written largely by men who were neither pragmatists nor slaves of Western logic. When Jesus the Semite spoke of God's omniscience, He clearly thought it would encourage, *not* discourage, His Semitic disciples to pray. In Matthew 6 He says that our Father already knows what we need before we ask Him, and He concludes: This is how we should pray. Westerners scratch their cerebral lobes at this sort of conclusion. But Jesus' logic is flawless and extremely practical. It is as silly as asking for bananas in a hardware store to ask God for something He doesn't have. Because your heavenly Father knows before you ask, He never gets surprised by your request and finds it necessary to send you a form letter saying your answer is back-ordered. He already has everything you will ever need.

The point is that since God already knows *everything* about you and still loves you, then there is *nothing* you can tell Him that will change His feelings for you. He is obviously not a Self-righteous Celestial Prude, but a loving Father who hugs His children—even when they have jam on their faces. This means you can have absolute *certainty* that nothing you ever tell God will cause Him to turn His back on you. God's omniscience is not a liability, but the source of interpersonal liberation.

W. BINGHAM HUNTER

lay before Him all That we are

You hem me in, behind and before; you have laid your hand upon me.
Such knowledge is too wonderful for me, too lofty for me to attain.

(PSALM 139:5-6)

Many times we miss the essence of communicating with God in prayer. It isn't educating God, and it isn't trying to get God to do something He wouldn't ordinarily do. You see, God is already committed to loving us. The beautiful thing about God is that He listens without interjecting several suggestions and comments before we're through talking. Then when we become quiet and listen, we are able to hear God speaking to us.

A few years ago I was at the Dallas airport to catch a plane to Los Angeles. The elderly lady seated next to me was obviously very uncomfortable with concern over the flight. When we took off, I asked if she wanted to hold my hand so she wouldn't be frightened. She did then and also when we landed. Somehow or other, a hand made all the difference in the world, even a stranger's hand—the touch of someone in the time of struggle.

DAY
258

This is what the psalmist is saying, that God not only knows us totally and perfectly, but also He puts His hand upon us, precedes us, and follows us so that we have no need to be afraid.

Do you see the knowledge of God? It is an awesome thing—but God's knowledge doesn't stay off in the distance somewhere. It comes right down to where He knows us completely. That understanding comforts us, and it goes back to praying. Many times we want to pray and haven't the slightest idea what to say, but God already knows what we're thinking. We can lay before Him all that we are and trust Him to listen and hear, believing that God will never misuse knowing His children totally.

H. PHILLIP HOOK

search me, o god

*Search me, O God, and know my heart; test me and know
my anxious thoughts. See if there is any offensive
way in me, and lead me in the way everlasting.*

(PSALM 139:23–24)

T here is nothing about us that God doesn't know. The beautiful and the ugly. The kind and the cruel. The loving and the lustful. He knows it all.

A disturbing thought? It would seem so. Yet to David that knowledge was precious—"too wonderful." In fact, he valued God's all-knowingness so much that he closed his psalm by inviting God to search the deepest corners of his heart, to know everything to be known, even his anxious thoughts.

Do we really want anyone to know us that well? How would you feel if suddenly some Sunday morning in church all your thoughts were projected on a screen for all to read? How guarded we are in sharing our most private thoughts with anyone—even those closest to us. What then is it about our all-knowing God that will make us feel as safe as David felt?

It is this. David knew that God was more than all-knowing; He was also all-wise. David was not impressed merely that God *knew* his thoughts, but that He *understood* them. That makes all the difference! And if we knew that such a person also loved us, we would find ourselves longing to seek his or her counsel.

Of course there is no one like that...except God! That is why David cried out, "Such knowledge is too wonderful for me." And that is why he closed his psalm, "Search me, O God, and know my heart; test me and know my anxious thoughts. See if there is any offensive way in me, and lead me in the way everlasting" (Psalm 139:23–24).

DAVID NEEDHAM

Approach with confidence

*Let us then approach the throne of grace with
confidence, so that we may receive mercy
and find grace to help us in our time of need.*

(HEBREWS 4:16)

I t is a joy to know that because of God's omniscience our
prayers have a real relationship to His program. He has
urged us to pray and has promised to answer our petitions
according to His will. Hebrews 4:16 exhorts us to come boldly to the
throne of grace, that we may obtain mercy and find grace to help us in
our time of need.

Despite Bible admonitions such as this, some individuals just
cannot see how prayer accomplishes anything. They reason that God's
decrees cannot and will not be changed just because His puny creatures make requests of God. As a result, some of these individuals
place little emphasis upon the value of prayer.

DAY
260

Such an outlook is a tragedy and results from a failure to properly
understand the doctrine of God's omniscience. Since He is aware of
everything from and into all eternity, God knows ahead of time about
our prayers. And, knowing what we would pray under certain circumstances, He has woven our prayers into the fabric of the universe.
Even as the mother of a sick and feverish child anticipates the need of
her little one during the night and has the medication all ready, so
God has framed history in the expectation of our intercession. As our
heavenly Father, He has looked ahead to our prayers and has already
made provision for the answers.

The great truth that God is omniscient should give strength and
encouragement to every true believer. This truth is also precious to
His suffering children, to those who have been misunderstood and
maligned wrongfully. It is good to know that God sees our hearts and
that He understands—even when our friends and loved ones do not.

RICHARD W. DEHAAN

we can be ourselves

*Trust in him at all times, O people; pour out
your hearts to him, for God is our refuge.*

(PSALM 62:8)

I s there anyone you feel you can approach with absolute transparency—with complete honesty? Some couples find it with each other and a few have such a friend. But I am certain that thousands upon thousands feel there is no one whom they can trust enough simply to be themselves.

God *is* such a person—because He knows and loves you and because Jesus died for you. You may feel you must pretend with your priest, your minister, your elder, maybe even your mother. But not so with your heavenly Father.

DAY
261

In our Lord we have someone with whom we can share our anger, joy, fear, frustration, delight, endless struggles with sin, hurt, loneliness—our real selves. This is the powerful, liberating honesty which should result from understanding God's omniscience. With God, we can be somebody: ourself. We don't have to be somebody else. And God also cares about our aspirations—something the twisted self-deprecation which passes among Christians as humility has wrongly convinced us we are not supposed to have. Tell God your dreams, goals, hopes, the desires you have to make something out of yourself. There is no worm so wretched, but what God cannot glorify Himself by making it into a butterfly.

God loves *you* more than you will ever know. Not your image, not your happy face, not your spirituality—but you. The real you. The one you think nobody knows about. No, real love is *not* blind. Because His eyes are open, He can see what you cannot. And He felt what He saw in you was worth dying for. So when you pray, be honest. Tell Him everything.

And if we cannot comprehend the mind of the Lord, we *have* known the love of the Lord. And where there is love, there is hope.

W. BINGHAM HUNTER

infinite in wisdom

*How many are your works, O LORD! In wisdom you
made them all; the earth is full of your creatures.*

(PSALM 104:24)

God is infinitely exalted above all created beings in wisdom. How little do even the wisest of men know! How frequently are they deceived and frustrated, their wisdom turned to foolishness, and their schemes undermined! But when did God's wisdom ever fail? When was He frustrated from accomplishing His purposes, even though all the bleak army of hell continually tries to overturn His will? When was it that God altered His mind and purpose or took a wrong step in His rule of the world?

DAY
262

Solomon realized he needed uncommon and extraordinary wisdom to rule such a kingdom as he had; but what wisdom, what vast knowledge and infinite insight must He have who rules and governs every being in the world? How great is the wisdom of Him who rules every thought, every purpose, every motion and action, not only of angels and men but of every creature, great and small, even to every atom in the whole creation—and that forever and ever! What infinite wisdom and knowledge is necessary in order to do this!

But this is exactly what God does. This He has done and this He will do. All the changes that occur in all the world, whether great or small, He knows them completely, even to the tiniest insect that crawls upon the earth or the dust that flies in the air.

But God's wisdom and omniscience shine clearest of all in His perfect knowledge of Himself. We miserable worms are confounded by the idea that He is eternal, that He has existed from everlasting to everlasting—yet He clearly understands it with the greatest of ease, in one simple view. He also fully comprehends His own infinite greatness and excellency, which no one can do without infinite understanding.

JONATHAN EDWARDS

only wise god

To the only wise God be glory forever
through Jesus Christ! Amen.

(ROMANS 16:27)

W isdom is the property of God alone. He is "only wise." It is an honor peculiar to Him. God does not make Himself wise, any more than He makes Himself God. He can no more be unwise than He can be untrue; for foolishness in the mind is much the same as falsehood in speech.

We gain wisdom through age and experience and instruction and exercise. But the wisdom of God is His by nature. As the sun cannot be without light, and eternity cannot be without immortality, so neither can God be without wisdom. His wisdom is the perfection of His divine nature; it does not come to Him through study or new experiences. He does not reach outside of Himself to find wisdom. He no more needs the brains of creatures in order to plan some purpose of His than He needs their arms to execute it.

God needs no counsel and He receives none from anyone. As Romans 11:34 asks, "Who has been his counselor?" And Isaiah asks, "Whom did the LORD consult to enlighten him, and who taught him the right way? Who was it that taught him knowledge or showed him the path of understanding?" (40:14).

God is the fountain of wisdom to others; what wisdom humans and angels possess, they received from Him. All the wisdom in creation is like a spark of the divine light, like that of the moon borrowed from the sun. Anyone who borrows wisdom from another and does not have it in his own nature, cannot properly be called wise. God is called "the only wise" because all wisdom flows from Him. He is the spring of wisdom to all; no one is the source of wisdom to Him.

STEPHEN CHARNOCK

DAY
263

no second guessing

God is not a man, that he should lie, nor a son of man, that he should change his mind. Does he speak and then not act? Does he promise and not fulfill?

(NUMBERS 23:19)

T he only wise God never second-guesses Himself. Because He is sovereignly wise, He sees no need to reverse anything He has done. And as He is infinitely powerful, He has no superior to hinder Him from executing His will and inviting His people to enjoy the fruit of His wisdom.

In creation He looked back upon the worlds He had made and saw nothing to prompt Him to take up His tools to mend anything He had done. In just that way His promises are made with such infinite wisdom and judgment that what He writes is irreversible and forever, as unchangeable as the decrees of the Medes and Persians. All the words of God are eternal because they are born in righteousness and judgment: "I will betroth you to me forever; I will betroth you in righteousness and justice" (Hosea 2:19).

DAY
264

God does not have a wavering and unstable temperament. If He threatens, He first wisely considers what He threatens. If He promises, He first wisely considers what He promises. Therefore, neither His threats nor His promises change over time.

This is why God is worthy of our trust and confidence. When He promises anything, in His infinite wisdom He sees everything which could hinder it and everything which could promote its fulfillment. He cannot discover anything after the promise has been made that may move Him to second-guess what He has said. He is wiser than to promise anything ridiculous or anything which He knows He cannot accomplish.

Therefore while the truthful God is the *object* of our trust, the wise God is the *foundation* of our trust. God's promises are prompted by mercy and performed by truth, but it is His wisdom that makes sure they are fulfilled.

STEPHEN CHARNOCK

Like the Rainbow

His intent was that now, through the church, the manifold wisdom of God
should be made known to the rulers and authorities in the heavenly realms,
according to his eternal purpose which he accomplished in Christ Jesus our Lord.

(EPHESIANS 3:10–11)

T his is a staggering statement, and we need to pause to reflect on what it says. Paul speaks about the *variety of God's wisdom:* It is manifold. The word he uses means "multi-colored"! God's wisdom is like the rainbow, in symmetry, beauty, and variety. He does not paint scenes merely in black and white, but uses a riot of color from the heavenly palette in order to show the wonder of His wise dealings with His people.

DAY
265

Paul also speaks about the *audience to which God displays His wisdom.* What he says is even more surprising: God shows His wisdom not only for the world to see, but also "to the rulers and authorities in heavenly realms." He gives a cosmic demonstration of His perfect purposes.

But the most interesting aspect of all is *the sphere in which God makes known His wisdom.* Has that ever jumped out of the page at you as you have read Ephesians 3:10? It is important. Because if you are to trust in God's wisdom, where are you to find proof of it? When you look at the world, or the circumstances of your own life and the lives of others, do you not sometimes doubt whether God is really wise?

Paul says that God's wisdom has been, and is being, clearly displayed *in the church.* The church is a theater in which God portrays the drama of His wisdom so clearly that the rulers and authorities in the heavenly realms cannot mistake it! The church, he says, is like a microscope. As we see God bringing it into being we recognize His wisdom. What we cannot discern with the naked eye in our own lives, we can see, living and active, in the church—the wisdom of God!

SINCLAIR FERGUSON

Depth without Bottom

Oh, the depth of the riches both of the wisdom and knowledge of God!
How unsearchable are his judgments, and his ways past finding out!

(ROMANS 11:33, KJV)

T he depth of God's wisdom and knowledge is inexhaustible and inconceivable. No one is capable of investigating the grounds or reasons for God's providential distributions, decisions, and decrees. As a bloodhound who finds it impossible to trace out and track down the scent of an escaped criminal, even so we cannot search out the mind and ways of the Lord. They are "unsearchable...past finding out," that is, they cannot be traced out or tracked down.

DAY
266

As we contemplate God's "mercy upon all," we are carried to new heights, only to discover that while we have arrived at another and higher plateau in pursuit of knowledge, we are unable to sound the depths with the plumb bob of the human mind and words. We can only wonder and adore our great God, who is infinite in His Being, incomprehensible in His judgments, and inexhaustible in knowledge; and then exclaim, "Who has known the mind of the LORD?" We need direction, counsel, and teaching, but He needed no one to direct, counsel, or instruct Him.

The contemplation of God's perfect knowledge is food for the souls of the saints. If I am perplexed at times, "He knows the way that I take" (Job 23:10). In times of weariness and weakness, "He knows how we are formed, he remembers that we are dust" (Psalm 103:14). In times of sorrow and affliction, I hear Him say, "I have indeed seen the misery of my people.... I have heard them crying out because of their slave drivers, and I am concerned about their suffering" (Exodus 3:7). Hallelujah, He is "the only wise God" (1 Timothy 1:17). The contemplation of God's omniscience should fill the soul with holy awe and wonder.

LEHMAN STRAUSS

the goal of god

I cry out to God Most High, to God,
who fulfills his purpose for me.

(PSALM 57:2)

God's almighty wisdom is always active and never fails. All His works of creation and providence and grace display it, and until we can see it in them, we just are not seeing them straight. But we can't recognize God's wisdom unless we know the end for which He is working. Here many go wrong.

Misunderstanding what the Bible means when it says that God is love, they think that God intends a trouble-free life for all, irrespective of their moral and spiritual state, and hence they conclude that anything painful and upsetting (illness, accident, injury, loss of job, the suffering of a loved one) indicates either that God's wisdom, or power, or both have broken down, or that God, after all, does not exist.

But this idea of God's intention is a complete mistake. God's wisdom is not, and never was, pledged to keep a fallen world happy, or to make ungodliness comfortable. Not even to Christians has He promised a trouble-free life; rather the reverse. He has other ends in view for life in this world than simply to make it easy for everyone.

What is He after, then? What is His goal? What does He aim at? When He made man, His purpose was that man should love and honor Him, praising Him for the wonderfully ordered complexity and variety of His world, using it according to His will, and so enjoying both it and Him. God has not abandoned His first purpose. Still He plans that a great host of mankind should come to love and honor Him. His ultimate objective is to bring them to a state in which they please Him entirely and praise Him adequately.

J. I. PACKER

DAY
267

A garment of praise and glory

*In him we have redemption through his blood, the forgiveness of sins,
in accordance with the riches of God's grace that he lavished
on us with all wisdom and understanding.*

(EPHESIANS 1:7–8)

U nless you become familiar with the wisdom of God, you
cannot make much real progress in the Christian life. True
stability over an extended period of discipleship will often
depend on trusting that God is wise in everything He does and in all
His dealings.

The Bible is full of wisdom. Indeed, there are books in the Bible
known collectively as "the wisdom literature." They express the idea
of wisdom (in God or man) in a rich and varied vocabulary. Wisdom
involves training (including correction and instruction); it includes
insight and understanding; it involves practical skill and sensitivity,
shrewdness and discretion, knowledge and right learning. The wise
man is the one who sees his goal, recognizes the best ways to achieve
that goal, and then implements those ways.

DAY
268

The wisdom of God is similar: God puts His glorious purposes
into effect in order to demonstrate His perfect knowledge, sovereign
power, and infinite grace. God's wisdom is evident as He takes the
raw, fallen materials of this world and its history to weave a garment
of praise and glory for His name.

It is fascinating to notice that the wisdom of God is one of the
minor themes of the book of Ephesians. We learn wisdom from God,
and are urged to "Be very careful, then, how you live—not as unwise,
but as wise" (Ephesians 5:15). The child of God is urged to become
like his Father. Paul also tells us that the wisdom of God lies behind
the planning of the gospel: He has lavished grace upon us "with all
wisdom and understanding" (Ephesians 1:8). For men, "wisdom"
often involves caution and frugality. But with God and His expressions
of love, wisdom dictates that grace should be "lavished on us"!

SINCLAIR FERGUSON

The True Way to Wisdom

We do not know what to do,
but our eyes are upon you.

(2 CHRONICLES 20:12)

DAY
269

L et none of us trust in our own wisdom. By seeking for wisdom apart from God, mankind got a cracked head, a wound which has gone unhealed for thousands of years. Ever since then, our own "wisdom and knowledge mislead" us (Isaiah 47:10). To be guided by our own wisdom is to be led by a blind escort and to follow a traitor to God and ourselves.

Those who advance themselves through proud cunning at last prove the greatest fools. God delights to "make foolish the wisdom of this world" (1 Corinthians 1:20). Thus God fooled the devil, the prince of carnal wisdom, into furthering our redemption through the very activities he had designed to hinder it. Carnal acts against divine wisdom never prosper.

The true way to wisdom is to recognize our own folly. "If any one of you thinks he is wise by the standards of this age, he should become a 'fool'" (1 Corinthians 3:18). He who distrusts his own guidance will more successfully follow the counsel of another whom he trusts. The more water is poured out of a glass, the more air enters. In the same way, the more we distrust our own wisdom, the more we will depend upon God's.

Jehoshaphat disowned his own skill and strength when he told God, "We do not know what to do, but our eyes are upon you" (2 Chronicles 20:12). Human prudence is like a spider's web, easily blown away or swept down by a broom. God, by His infinite wisdom, can frustrate the wisdom of man and make a man's own craftiness work against him: "The wisdom of the wise will perish, the intelligence of the intelligent will vanish" (Isaiah 29:14). Let us therefore despise our own understanding so that we may honor the Lord's.

STEPHEN CHARNOCK

ask for wisdom

*If any of you lacks wisdom, he should ask God, who gives
generously to all without finding fault, and it will be given to him.*

(JAMES 1:5)

A sk God for wisdom. The wisdom we have by nature is like the weeds that sprout from untilled earth. Our wisdom since the Fall is the wisdom of the serpent without the innocence of the dove. It flows from self-love and runs to self-interest. It is the wisdom of the flesh and expends itself to satisfy our lusts. Our best wisdom is imperfect, a mere nothing and emptiness, compared to God's. We must go to God for a holy and innocent wisdom and fill our wells from His pure fountain. Remember, the wisdom that was the glory of Solomon came from the Most High.

DAY
270

God grants us the capacity to *understand* at birth, but only by grace does He give us heavenly *wisdom*. Children have a degree of understanding, but they need wise teachers to help them see the right and gain the desire to do the right. "It is the spirit in a man, the breath of the Almighty, that gives him understanding" (Job 32:8).

We must ask God for wisdom. We cannot gain a new understanding except from the Creator. The Spirit of God is the "searcher of the deep things of God," the revealer of them to us, and the enlightener of our minds to grasp them. Therefore He is called a "Spirit of wisdom and revelation" (Ephesians 1:17). Christ has become wisdom to us as well as righteousness.

Seek from God the wisdom which is like the sun, and not the worldly wisdom which is like a shadow. Desire the wisdom whose inward effects are so sweet. Seek it from Him in His Word, the book of divine wisdom: "I gain understanding from your precepts; therefore I hate every wrong path" (Psalm 119:104).

STEPHEN CHARNOCK

Disciples at God's Feet

"For my thoughts are not your thoughts, neither are your ways my ways,"
declares the LORD. "As the heavens are higher than the earth, so are
my ways higher than your ways and my thoughts than your thoughts."

(ISAIAH 55:8–9)

Divine truth is mysterious. For example, as the apostle Paul wrote in Romans 16:25–26, "According to the revelation of the mystery hidden for long ages past," Christ was "manifested in the flesh." The whole scheme of godliness is a mystery.

No man or angel could imagine how two natures, so distant as the divine and human, should be united. Or how the same person could be both criminal and righteous. Or how a just God should be appeased and a sinful man justified. Or how the sin should be punished and the sinner saved.

No one could make up the means of our justification as the apostle lays it out in his epistles. It was a mystery when hidden under the shadows of the law, and a mystery to the prophets even when they spoke of it. They tried to search its depths but were not able to comprehend it: "Concerning this salvation, the prophets, who spoke of the grace that was to come to you, searched intently and with the greatest care, trying to find out the time and circumstances to which the Spirit of Christ in them was pointing when he predicted the sufferings of Christ and the glories that would follow" (1 Peter 1:10–11).

If it is a mystery, then we must humbly submit to it, for mysteries transcend human reason. We must not study God's truth with yawns and a careless attitude. Difficult jobs are not learned by sleeping and nodding; no, diligence is required. We must be disciples at God's feet.

As God is the author of His truth, so He must be our teacher. As God alone revealed His truth, so only He can open our eyes to see the mysteries of Christ in it.

STEPHEN CHARNOCK

DAY
271

unanswered for now

Truly you are a God who hides himself.

(ISAIAH 45:15)

I f you believe God is obligated to explain Himself to us, you ought to examine the following Scriptures. Solomon wrote in Proverbs 25:2, "It is the glory of God to conceal a matter." Isaiah 45:15 states, "Truly you are a God who hides himself." Deuteronomy 29:29 reads, "The secret things belong to the LORD our God." Ecclesiastes 11:5 proclaims, "As you do not know the path of the wind, or how the body is formed in a mother's womb, so you cannot understand the work of God, the Maker of all things." Isaiah 55:8–9 teaches, "'For my thoughts are not your thoughts, neither are your ways my ways,' declares the LORD. 'As the heavens are higher than the earth, so are my ways higher than your ways and my thoughts than your thoughts.'"

DAY 272

Clearly, the Scriptures tell us that we lack the capacity to grasp God's infinite mind or the way He intervenes in our lives. How arrogant of us to think otherwise! Trying to analyze His omnipotence is like an amoeba attempting to comprehend the behavior of man. Romans 11:33 (KJV) indicates that God's judgments are "unsearchable" and his ways "past finding out." Similar language is found in 1 Corinthians 2:16: "For who has known the mind of the Lord that he may instruct him?"

Unless the Lord chooses to explain Himself to us, which often He does not, His motivation and purposes are beyond the reach of mortal man. What this means in practical terms is that many of our questions—especially those that begin with the word *why*—will have to remain unanswered for the time being.

JAMES DOBSON

DO YOU WANT TO KNOW GOD?

*God…made his light shine in our hearts to give us the
light of the knowledge of the glory of God in the face of Christ.*

(2 CORINTHIANS 4:6)

Do you want to know God? Then do what traffic signs at some uncontrolled intersections tell you to do: Stop, look, and listen.

Stop trying to discover God by pursuing thoughts, fancies, and feelings of your own, in disregard of God's revelation. Our knowledge of Him depends upon His revelation to us; you do not have the first without the second.

DAY
273

Look at what God has revealed. The Bible is the window through which you may look to see it, and there are many Christians and guide books that can help you to see what you are looking at and pick out what is important. Because London is the center of England, tourists from overseas put it first on their itineraries. In the same way, Jesus Christ the Lord, who died and is alive forevermore, is the center of Scripture. Whatever else in the Bible catches your eye, do not let it distract you from Him.

Listen to what the Bible tells you about Him, and about our need of Him (which means, your need of Him). The Bible is God's communication to you about Him. Learn from God about the Son of God; respond to all that you are shown. Do that, and one day you will be saying with Paul and many millions more, "God…made his light shine in our hearts to give us the light of the knowledge of the glory of God in the face of Christ" (2 Corinthians 4:6). You will be saying with the once-blind man of Jerusalem, "One thing I do know. I was blind but now I see!" (John 9:25). You will know revelation in the only way that finally counts—namely, from the inside; and in so knowing it, you will know God.

J. I. PACKER

THE
PROVIDENCE
OF GOD

You gave me life and
showed me kindness,
and in your providence
watched over my spirit.

JOB 10:12

god's sustaining word

My Father is always at his work to this
very day, and I, too, am working.

(JOHN 5:17)

God not only created the world and all creatures through the Word, His only begotten Son; but He also constantly governs and sustains them through Him, to the end of the world. Therefore the Son of God is Cocreator of heaven and earth with the Father.

God is not a Master who acts like a carpenter or builder who, when he has prepared, finished, and completed a house or ship, hands over the house to its owner to live in or turns the ship over to the captain and the crew to sail across the sea in it, while he himself leaves and goes wherever he pleases. This is what all other craftsmen do. When they have finished their work or completed their business, they leave and pay no further attention to their work. They are content to depart and to let their product stand as long as it can.

God is not like that. What God the Father has begun and finished through His Word, He constantly sustains by that same Word. He stays with the work He has created until He no longer wants it to exist. This is why Christ says, "My Father is always at his work to this very day, and I, too, am working" (John 5:17). For just as He created us without any cooperation or participation on our part, so too He sustains us through His own power; we cannot preserve ourselves. Therefore as heaven, earth, sun, moon, stars, human beings, and every other living thing was created by the Word in the beginning, so they also are governed and sustained in a marvelous manner by that same Word.

MARTIN LUTHER

DAY
274

They serve our Blessing

If God is for us, who can be against us?

(ROMANS 8:31)

The providence of God is the way in which He governs everything wisely, first for the glory of His own Name, and second for the ultimate blessing of His children. Clearly, the providence of God is closely connected with the wisdom of God. We need to be confident that all things *work together* for our good, if we are to be able to cope with what seem to us to be the "not goods" of life. This is why the Bible teaches us in many different ways that every event of life, every circumstance of each day, is guided by the hand of our Father. He has numbered the hairs on our heads (Matthew 10:30). No detail of our lives is outside of His purpose or control.

This thought causes some Christians difficulties and makes them ask, "If I were to believe that God is universally in control in His providence in the world, wouldn't that paralyze me and make me think that nothing I did really mattered?"

In fact, as the lives of many Christians demonstrate—and as the life of the Lord Jesus Christ most clearly shows—believing in God's complete providence and control has the opposite effect. Instead of discouraging us, it encourages us! That, after all, is why God has taught us about His providence in His Word!

We know that nothing (trouble, hardship, persecution, famine, nakedness, peril, sword—all elements in the world which God providentially rules) can ever separate us from the love of God in Christ. *How* do we know that? Paul's answer is that we know that God has a purpose *through* these things. He is *for us* (Romans 8:31), and therefore, ultimately, none of our difficult circumstances can be against us. They serve God's purpose and must therefore serve our blessing.

SINCLAIR FERGUSON

He Directs the winds and waves

He spoke and stirred up a tempest that lifted high the waves....
He stilled the storm to a whisper; the waves of the sea were hushed.

(PSALM 107:25, 29)

any biblical events prove the special providence of God. God raised a south wind in the desert to bring a large flock of birds to the people (Exodus 16:13; Numbers 11:31). When He wanted Jonah thrown into the sea, He sent a wind to raise a storm (Jonah 1:4).

I conclude from this that no wind ever rises or blows except by the special command of God. Unless He directed the course both of the clouds and of the winds as it pleased Him, displaying in them His awesome power, it would not be true (as the psalmist claims) that He makes the winds His messengers and His ministers a flame of fire, or that He makes the clouds His chariot and rides on the wings of the wind (Psalm 104:3–4).

DAY
276

In the same way we are elsewhere taught that whenever the sea is blown into a tempest by the winds, those disturbances prove the special presence of God. "He spoke and stirred up a tempest that lifted high the waves" of the sea. Then "He stilled the storm to a whisper; the waves of the sea were hushed" (Psalm 107:25, 29). And in another place He proclaims that He struck the people with parching winds (Amos 4:9; Haggai 1:6–11).

Finally, when we hear on the one hand that "The eyes of the LORD are on the righteous and his ears are attentive to their cry," and on the other, that "The face of the LORD is against those who do evil, to cut off the memory of them from the earth" (Psalm 34:15–16), we may be assured that all creatures, above and below, may be used to serve Him in any way He pleases. Hence we conclude that God providentially rules over His creation.

JOHN CALVIN

Every Aspect, Every Moment

He himself gives all men life and breath and everything else....
"For in him we live and move and have our being."

(ACTS 17:25, 28)

T he Bible teaches that God sustains you and me. He supplies our daily food (2 Corinthians 9:10). Our times are in His hands (Psalm 31:15). Every breath we breathe is a gift from God, every bite of food we eat is given to us from His hand, every day we live is determined by Him. He has not left us to our own devices, or the whims of nature, or the malevolent acts of other people. No!

He constantly sustains, provides for, and cares for us every moment of every day. Did your car break down when you could least afford the repairs? Did you miss an important meeting because the plane you were to fly in developed mechanical problems? The God who controls the stars in their courses also controls nuts and bolts and everything on your car and on that plane you were to fly in.

When I was an infant I had a bad case of measles. The virus apparently settled in my eyes and in my right ear, leaving me with monocular vision and deafness in that ear. Was God in control of that virus, or was I simply a victim of a chance childhood disease? God's moment-by-moment sustaining of His universe and everything in it leaves me no choice but to accept that the virus was indeed under His controlling hand. God was not looking the other way when that virus settled in the nerve endings of my ear and the muscles of my eyes.

If we are to trust God, we must learn to see that He is continuously at work in every aspect and every moment of our lives.

JERRY BRIDGES

DAY
277

A WITNESS OF GOD'S LOVE

You open your hand and satisfy the desires of every living thing.

(PSALM 145:16)

T he spring rain falls gently on your tiny backyard vegetable garden. Raindrops bead on the leaves and the green fruit of healthy tomato, zucchini, lettuce, and carrot plants that promise a tasty summer harvest.

You can't get over it. Just a few weeks earlier there was nothing here but dirt. You planted the seeds, watered them, then watched day by day. The warm spring sunlight coaxed green sprouts from the moist earth. Almost before your eyes the tiny seeds had produced a bounty of beautiful vegetables, enough to feed your family with plenty to spare. You think about farmers who grow food by the hundreds of acres and make a good living at it. You think about poor people in Third World countries who grow what little they can just to survive. You wonder if they are also in awe of the miracle of seed, rain, sun, and harvest.

DAY
278

Our experience of living in this world informs us that there is a God who cares about the earth He created and the creatures who live upon it. As Paul preached to the unbelievers at Lystra, God "has not left himself without testimony: He has shown kindness by giving you rain from heaven and crops in their seasons; he provides you with plenty of food and fills your hearts with joy" (Acts 14:17). God promised Noah, "As long as the earth endures, seedtime and harvest, cold and heat, summer and winter, day and night will never cease" (Genesis 8:22).

The earth's abundant and timely fruitfulness, its pleasing blend of symmetry and contrast, its breathtaking sensory beauty, and its intricate design—from the macrocosm of space to the microcosm of the subparticle realm—is a witness of God's love in keeping His promise through the millennia.

JOSH MCDOWELL AND NORM GUISLER

The Master of the House

Ask the LORD for rain in the springtime; it is the LORD who makes the storm clouds.
He gives showers of rain to men, and plants of the field to everyone.

(ZECHARIAH 10:1)

How dependent we are on God's provisions! Without them, there might be nothing but winter to blast us with its frost or summer to scorch us with its heat. Instead, we have the moderate temperatures of autumn and spring to separate winter and summer. This way, the gradual transitions of the year glide by, year after year.

Look also at the sea, bound by the law of its shore. And notice the ocean, with its regular ebb and flow of tides. Look also at the trees, how they are sustained from the depths of the earth. And the fountains, how they gush in perpetual streams. Gaze at the rivers. See how they flow on their same course, year after year.

Or consider the different types of protection provided for animals. Some are armed with horns, others with teeth. Some have claws; others are barbed with stingers. Some escape danger by the swiftness of their feet, others by soaring into the sky with their wings.

God not only cares for the universe as a *whole,* He is equally concerned about its *parts.* For example, Britain doesn't receive much sunshine, but it is refreshed by the warmth of the sea that flows around it. Egypt is dry, but its dryness is tempered by the presence of the Nile River.

Now, if upon entering a house you found everything well arranged and decorated, you would surely believe someone governed the house. You would also recognize this master as greater than all of the things in the house. Therefore, when you look upon the house of the universe—the heavens and the earth, its laws, and its order— believe that there is a Master and Author of the universe far more glorious than the stars themselves and everything else in the universe.

MINUCIUS FELIX OCTAVIUS

the god who fills

*As long as the earth endures, seedtime and harvest, cold and heat,
summer and winter, day and night will never cease.*

(GENESIS 8:22)

God holds in His hands the causes of all things; He both knows them all and connects them all. He is the source of all fertility in seeds, and He put rational souls into the living beings He selected. It is He who gave us the gifts of speech and language.

The God we worship chose certain men and gave them the power of foresight; through them He makes prophecies. To others He gave the gift of healing. He controls the beginnings, progress, and endings of wars, deciding when they are needed for the punishment or reformation of mankind. He rules the power of fire, so vehement and violent, yet so necessary for the equilibrium of nature. He is the Creator and Ruler of all the water of the universe. He made the sun, the brightest of all luminous bodies in our sky, giving it an appropriate energy and motion.

His sovereignty and power reach to the lowest things. All things that grow and sustain animal life, both liquids and solids, He produced and made suitable for different environments. He gave us the earth, the richness of the soil, and foods for men and beast. He gave to the moon its phases, and in the air and on the ground He provided ways for traveling. He instituted mating and marriage for the propagation of life, and to human communities He gave the blessing of fire, to keep them warm and give them light and make their lives easier.

All this belongs to the one true God, who is wholly present everywhere and is confined by no frontiers and bound by no obstacles. Though He needs neither heaven nor earth, He fills them both with His presence and His power.

ST. AUGUSTINE OF HIPPO

DAY
280

with greatest understanding

*I will put my hook in your nose and my bit in your mouth,
and I will make you return by the way you came.*

(2 KINGS 19:28)

od's providence is *holy*. Even though it touches and is fully aware of sinful actions, yet it remains pure—even as the sun does not defile itself even though it shines on a manure pile. God is neither the physical nor moral cause of any evil, any more than he who rides on a lame horse is the cause of the animal's injury. All the evil in any sinful action flows from the wicked agent, not from God, just as the stench of the manure pile does not proceed from the heat of the sun, but from the corrupt matter in the pile.

God's providence is also *wise*. Infinite wisdom always proposes the most excellent ways and methods to accomplish its objectives. However perplexed, confused, and empty of wisdom some of God's providences may appear to us poor mortals, yet they are the result of the highest wisdom and the deepest counsel. They proceed from and are directed by Him whose name is *the only wise God,* who cannot but manage all things with the greatest understanding. The day will come at last when the united voice of the whole assembly and church of the firstborn will say that God has done all things well. Then in every respect the plan of providence will appear to have been most wise, harmonious, and consistent.

Last, God's providence is *powerful.* So the Lord says to Sennacherib, the king of Assyria, "I will put my hook in your nose and my bit in your mouth, and I will make you return by the way you came" (2 Kings 19:28).

Who can resist the will of the Almighty? He never fails to achieve what He desires, and all things take place according to His will.

THOMAS BOSTON

what if we fail?

One night the Lord spoke to Paul in a vision:
"Do not be afraid; keep on speaking, do not be silent. For I am with you, and
no one is going to attack and harm you, because I have many people in this city."

(ACTS 18:9-10)

Many appear almost to imagine that God dispenses His grace with one hand and His providence with the other and does not let His right hand know what His left hand is doing. They think of providence and grace almost as independent forces, working sometimes together, but liable to get out of gear and clog and embarrass one another. Perhaps it would be true to say that some men practically have two gods: a good god of grace and a severe god of providence.

There is, however, only one God, the God of both providence and of grace. The two can never be separated, nor can one suffer for lack of support from the other. God's providence is adequate for all His gracious purposes, however broad and great they may be. He will certainly send His gospel in His providence wherever His grace is pleased to have it.

But what if the church fails in its duty of proclaiming the gospel? What if it withholds the gospel from the world and thus brings down the blood of the perishing on its head? Undoubtedly it may; sadly, it has done so and is doing exactly this. But our faithlessness will never annul the faithfulness of God. Let us remember the philosophy of Mordecai: "If you remain silent at this time, relief and deliverance for the Jews will arise from another place, but you and your father's family will perish" (Esther 4:14). God has not committed His honor to another, neither has He committed the souls of men to the keeping of others. His purposes of mercy will never fail because of our unfaithfulness, for His providence is over all.

BENJAMIN B. WARFIELD

All streams lead to the ocean

*He made known to us the mystery of his will according to his
good pleasure, which he purposed in Christ, to be put into effect
when the times will have reached their fulfillment—to bring all
things in heaven and on earth together under one head, even Christ.*

(EPHESIANS 1:9–10)

T he wheels of providence are not turned round by blind chance, but are full of eyes all around, guided by the Spirit of God (to use Ezekiel's picture). Where the Spirit goes, they go. All God's works of providence through all ages meet at one point, like so many spokes meeting at the center.

DAY
283

God's work of providence is like His work of creation; it is only one work. The events of providence should not be thought of as so many distinct, independent parts of one work; it is all one work, one regular scheme. God's works of providence are not disunited and jumbled without connection or dependence, but are all united, like the various parts of one building. There are many stones, many pieces of timber, but all are joined together in such a way that they make up a single building. They all have one foundation and are united at last in one top stone.

God's providence may be compared to a large and long river with innumerable branches beginning in different regions and at a great distance from each other. They continue for a while in their varied and contrary courses, yet the nearer they approach their common end, the more they gather together. At last they all discharge themselves at one mouth into the same ocean. To us the many streams of this river are apt to appear like mere jumble and confusion, because we cannot see from one branch to another and cannot see the whole at once. Yet if we trace each of them, we see that they all unite at last and all empty themselves at one point into the same great ocean. Not one of all the streams fails to arrive there at last. That is what God's providence is like.

JONATHAN EDWARDS

wait for the prescription

We know that in all things God works for the good of those
who love him, who have been called according to his purpose.

(ROMANS 8:28)

T he events of life are not unrelated. The physician's prescription is compounded of a number of drugs. Taken in isolation, some of them would be poisonous and would do only harm. But blended together under the direction of a skilled and experienced physician, they achieve only good. Barclay renders the verse, "We know that God intermingles all things for good for them that love Him." The experiences of life, when taken in isolation, may seem anything but good—but blended together, the result is only good.

In adverse circumstances unbelief asks, "How can *this* be working for good?" The answer is, "Wait until the Great Physician has finished writing the prescription." Who cannot look back on life to see that things once considered disastrous proved in the end to be blessings in disguise? The artist blends colors which to the unskilled eye seem far removed from his perspective. But wait until he has finished his mixing!

DAY
284

Life has been likened to an elaborate tapestry being woven on the loom. For the beauty of the pattern it is imperative that the colors must not be all of the same hue. Some must be bright and beautiful, others dark and somber. Only as they are all worked together do they contribute to the beauty of the pattern.

> *Not until each loom is silent*
> *And the shuttles cease to fly*
> *Will God unroll the pattern*
> *And explain the reason why;*
> *The dark threads are as needful*
> *In the Weaver's skillful hand,*
> *As the threads of gold and silver*
> *For the pattern He has planned.*

Even if called upon to face the wrath of man or devil, we can confidently rest in the assurance that it will ultimately praise God, and that which cannot do so will be restrained.

J. OSWALD SANDERS

why god tolerates the devil

Then I heard a loud voice in heaven say: "Now have come the salvation and the power and the kingdom of our God, and the authority of his Christ. For the accuser of our brothers, who accuses them before our God day and night, has been hurled down. They overcame him by the blood of the Lamb and by the word of their testimony."

(REVELATION 12:10-11)

The Holy Scripture knows but one God, who rules over all things. Yet in His absolute rule, He tolerates many things that seem out of place.

DAY
285

God rules over idolaters, but out of mercy He allows them the breath to repent. He also rules over heretics who reject and mock Him, putting up with them patiently. Likewise He rules over the devil, tolerating him in His longsuffering. He does so, not because of any lack of divine power, as though He had been defeated! For the devil "is the beginning of the Lord's creation, made to be mocked." Of course, God Himself does not mock the devil, for that would be beneath His dignity; He leaves that task to the angels He made.

But why, we wonder, has He allowed the devil to live? I think there are two main reasons:

1. That the devil might suffer greater shame by his defeat;
2. That men might be crowned with victory.

God has permitted the devil to wrestle with men so that they who conquer him might be crowned, and so that the devil might suffer the greater shame for being defeated by inferiors. Through God's power and providence, men may gain great glory for having triumphed over him who was once an archangel!

O all-wise God, You use even the wicked purposes of the evil one to bring salvation to the faithful. We remember how You used even the brutal actions of Joseph's brothers to carry out Your will, allowing them in their hatred to sell their brother into slavery—yet You took the occasion to make Joseph king over all Egypt. We praise you, Lord, for Your great providence. And we place ourselves in your mighty and gracious hands, confident that nothing can touch us except what You permit.

ST. CYRIL OF JERUSALEM

good out of evil

*You intended to harm me, but God intended it for good
to accomplish what is now being done, the saving of many lives.*

(GENESIS 50:20)

God is an expert at bringing good out of evil. He can strengthen our love and delight in Him and mortify our sins and unbelief through the mystery of providence working through suffering. When Sarah Edwards heard of her husband's death by an inoculation for smallpox, she found her soul strengthened in faith and love for God and not embittered. She wrote to her daughter on receiving the news:

> What shall I say? A holy and good God has covered us with a dark cloud. O that we may kiss the rod, and lay our hands on our mouths! The Lord has done it. He has made me adore his goodness, that we had him so long. But my God lives; and he has my heart. O what a legacy my husband, and your father, has left us! We are all given to God; and there I am, and love to be.

An awareness that God governs all things for His glory and the good of His people, bringing them into glad dependence on Him, has led many of His saints to deepen their delight in Him and see Him for the treasure that He is, even in hours of grief and loss.

I do not know specifically why God works the way He does in His providence or how He will glorify Himself through the deaths in Bangladesh or the ovens of Auschwitz. Yet Christ has spoken to the troubled Philips of this world: "Anyone who has seen me has seen the Father" (John 14:9). I cannot see the blueprints of God's secret decree, but I can see Christ, and in Him I see the Father's rainbow of grace and blessing arching over my turbulent world.

MARK SHAW

food for dark days

*Unless the LORD Almighty had left us some survivors, we would
have become like Sodom, we would have been like Gomorrah.*

(ISAIAH 1:9)

P rovidence is the food our faith lives upon in dark days:
"Unless the LORD Almighty had left us some survivors, we
would have become like Sodom, we would have been like
Gomorrah" (Isaiah 1:9). Based on providences past, saints hope for
new ones to come. So David said, "The LORD who delivered me from
the paw of the lion and the paw of the bear will deliver me from
the hand of this Philistine" (1 Samuel 17:37). And so Paul wrote,
"He has delivered us from such a deadly peril, and he will deliver
us. On him we have set our hope that he will continue to deliver
us" (2 Corinthians 1:10).

The hands of faith hang down when we forget or fail to consider
God's providences. "Do you still not understand?" Jesus once asked
His disciples. "Don't you remember the five loaves for the five thou-
sand, and how many basketfuls you gathered?" (Matthew 16:9).

The saints have often drawn inspiration for their prayers from
God's providence. When Moses asked God to pardon the people, he
argued from the past: "Forgive the sin of these people, just as you
have pardoned them from the time they left Egypt until now"
(Numbers 14:19). The church argues for new providences upon the
same ground: "He who did not spare his own Son, but gave him up
for us all—how will he not also, along with him, graciously give us all
things?" (Romans 8:32).

We can never pray aright for our needs unless we first observe
His providences. That is why we find so much variety in David's
psalms; they vary according to the providences that happened to him.
To pray effectively we must follow his example and be both observant
and careful.

JOHN FLAVEL

when affliction comes calling

*It was good for me to be afflicted so
that I might learn your decrees.*

(PSALM 119:71)

When God allows affliction into your life, set His grace and goodness before you. See Him passing by in the cloudy and dark day, proclaiming His name, "The LORD, the LORD, the compassionate and gracious God" (Exodus 34:6). Remember it is not as bad now as it might be, and that it will be better later on. Has God taken something from you? He might have taken it all. Are we afflicted? It is a mercy we are not destroyed. If we remembered this, we would have reason to welcome mercy rather than to complain of severity!

Second, consider the wisdom of God. See it in the *kind* of your affliction, that it is this, and not another; in its *timing,* that it is now and not later; in the *degree,* that it is to this measure, and not a greater; in the *support* available, that you are not left alone; in the *goal,* that it is to your good, not your ruin.

Third, consider the all-sufficiency of God. His fountain is still as full as ever, although this or that pipe has been broken off. O Christian, cannot you see more in God than in all the comforts you have lost?

Last, consider the immutability of God. Look on Him as the Rock of ages, the Father of lights, who does not change like shifting shadows. Remember that Jesus Christ is the same yesterday, today, and forever.

O, what quietness will this breed! How these views of God can console our hearts in the midst of dark providences! My God will not lose my heart if a rod can prevent it. He would rather hear my groan here than my howl hereafter. Because His love is prudent, not indulgent, He desires my good rather than my comfort.

JOHN FLAVEL

while you are in it

The poor will eat and be satisfied;
they who seek the LORD will praise him—
may your hearts live forever!
All the ends of the earth
will remember and turn to the LORD,
and all the families of the nations
will bow down before him,
for dominion belongs to the LORD
and he rules over the nations.
All the rich of the earth will feast and worship;
all who go down to the dust will kneel before him—
those who cannot keep themselves alive.

(PSALM 22:26–29)

DAY
289

One day many years ago a distinguished man was unable to proceed in his journey because of a fierce storm. That night he was groaning in great mental distress and found himself unable to sleep. His pious servant said, "Master, do you not believe that God governed this world very well before you came into it?"

"Yes," was the reply.

"And do you not believe that He will govern it very well after you leave it?"

"I have no doubt of it," he answered.

"Then, master, can you not believe that He will govern it all right while you are in it?"

To this the man did not reply, but shortly afterwards turned over and went to sleep.

Happy are they who enjoy a firm trust in God and His controlling providence! In great peace shall they possess their souls. Their best Friend sits at the helm of affairs and guides in such a way that all things shall work for their good.

ROBERT BOYD

goodness and love pursue us

Surely goodness and love will follow me all the days of my life, and I will dwell in the house of the LORD forever.

(PSALM 23:6)

W hat a pleasure to see providence turn the very things that seemed to threaten our ruin into great blessings! Little did Joseph think his journey to Egypt would lead to his welfare; yet he lived to acknowledge it with a thankful heart (Genesis 45:5). O what a difference there is between meeting our afflictions and parting from them! We endure them with sighs and tears, but leave them with joy—even blessing God for them as the instruments of our good.

What unspeakable comfort it is for a poor soul, who sees nothing but sin and evil in the mirror, also to see how highly valued he is by the great God! By paying attention to providence, we may see goodness and love following us through all our days (Psalm 23:6). While others pursue good but never overtake it, goodness and love relentlessly follow the people of God. They cannot avoid or escape it; daily it chases them and catches them even when they try to dodge it through their sin.

"What is man," Job asks, "that you make so much of him, that you give him so much attention, that you examine him every morning and test him every moment?" (7:17–18). God's people are His treasure; that is why He does not take His eye off them (Job 36:7). This ought to make us overjoyed!

What in all the world can give a person such joy and comfort as to find himself assisted in his way to heaven? And yet this is exactly what we may discern by carefully observing various providences. However contrary the winds and tides of providence may sometime seem to us, nothing is more certain than that they work together to hurry sanctified souls to God and fit them for glory.

JOHN FLAVEL

we cannot be robbed
of god's providence

*"My son, do not make light of the Lord's discipline, and do not lose heart when he
rebukes you, because the Lord disciplines those he loves, and he punishes everyone
he accepts as a son." Endure hardship as discipline; God is treating you as sons.*

(HEBREWS 12:5–7)

DAY
291

W e cannot be robbed of God's providence." This was one of
the sayings commonly heard in the household of Thomas
Carlyle. In it, the plumb bob is let down to the bottom of
the Christian's confidence and hope. It is because we cannot be
robbed of God's providence that we know, despite whatever encircling
gloom, that all things work together for good to those that love Him.
It is because we cannot be robbed of God's providence that we know
nothing can separate us from the love of Christ—not hardship, nor
anguish, nor persecution, nor famine, nor nakedness, nor peril, nor
sword.

But if God's providence were not over all; if trouble could come
without God permitting it; if Christians could become the prey of this
or the other enemy when God was thinking or resting or on a journey
or sleeping—what certainty of hope could be ours? "Does God send
trouble?" Surely, surely. He and He only. He sends it to the sinner in
punishment and to His children in discipline. To suggest that it does
not always come from His hands is to take away all our comfort. Even
the Unitarian poet knew better than that:

> *These severe afflictions*
> *Not from the ground arise;*
> *But oftentimes celestial benedictions*
> *Assume this dark disguise.*

The world may seem black to us; there may no longer be hope in
men or women; anguish and trouble may be our daily share. But there
is this light that shines through all the darkness: "We cannot be
robbed of God's providence!" So long as the soul keeps firm hold of
this great truth, it will be able to weather all storms.

BENJAMIN B. WARFIELD

faith Rooted in Trust

*After Nathan had gone home, the LORD struck the child that Uriah's wife had borne
to David, and he became ill. David pleaded with God for the child. He fasted and
went into his house and spent the nights lying on the ground.*

(2 SAMUEL 12:15–16)

F or seven days David wrestled with God. He prayed and
fasted and refused to be comforted. When the child died,
his servants were terrified to report it to David, but he
deduced from their whispers that his son had perished. Then he did
something that amazed the servants. David got up, washed, anointed
himself, and went to the house of God.

When God said no to the pleas of David, he immediately went to
church—not to whine or complain, but to worship. David pled his
case before the throne of the Almighty—and lost. Yet he was willing to
bow before the providence of God, to let God be God.

DAY
292

Though David had clearly heard God's declaration that the child
would die, and he did not regard it as an idle threat, he was also aware
of God's actions in the past when He had relented from promised
judgments after the people turned to Him in repentance.

"Who can tell whether the LORD will be gracious to me, that the
child may live?" David had said. The phrase "who can tell?" calls
attention to the "hidden God" whose secret counsel remains unknown
to us. David had heard the words of the "revealed" God, but held out
hope that it was not the entire story. When he discovered that God
had not held any of His plan in reserve, it was enough to satisfy his
soul and submit to God's no.

If we understand the providence of God and love the God of
providence, we are able to worship Him with the sacrifice of praise
even when things occur that bring pain, sorrow, and affliction into our
lives. This understanding of providence is vital to all who would worship God. It is a worship of faith rooted in trust.

R. C. SPROUL

Difficult passages

This is what the wicked are like—always carefree, they increase in wealth. Surely in
vain have I kept my heart pure; in vain have I washed my hands in innocence.
All day long I have been plagued; I have been punished every morning....
When I tried to understand all this, it was oppressive to me.

(PSALM 73:12–16)

DAY
293

D o not pry too curiously into the secrets of providence, nor allow your shallow reason to judge its methods.

There are difficult passages in both the works and Word of God. We are wise if we modestly and humbly respect them and refrain from dogmatizing upon them; a man might easily strain himself by reaching too far. "When I tried to understand all this," said Asaph, "it was oppressive to me" (Psalm 73:16). "I tried to understand all this"—there was reason, arrogantly prying into the arena of providence—"but it was oppressive to me"—it was "useless labor," as Calvin expounds it. Asaph mused so deeply upon that puzzling mystery that it prompted envy toward them and depression in himself (Psalm 73:3, 13). This is all he got by summoning providence to the court of reason. Even Job was guilty of this evil, and was frankly ashamed of it (Job 42:3).

While nothing in the Word or works of God is repugnant to sound reason, there are some things in both which offend carnal reason and transcend right reason. Therefore our reason never shows itself more unreasonable than when it summons providence to the witness stand. Many mischiefs have followed this practice. Sarah laughed at the prophecy that she would bear a son. Why? Because reason contradicted the idea and told her it was naturally impossible (Genesis 18:13–14).

When our reason fills us with a distrust of providence, it naturally prompts us to seek sinful alternatives—and there it leaves us, entangled in traps of our own making. Naked reason often tempts us to try to deliver ourselves by sinful means (Isaiah 30:15–16).

Beware, then, that you do not lean too much on your own reason and understanding! Nothing is more plausible, yet nothing more dangerous.

JOHN FLAVEL

who can explain it?

He performs wonders that cannot be fathomed,
miracles that cannot be numbered.

(JOB 9:10)

We know that God orders everything both in heaven and in earth and that without Him "not a sparrow falls to the ground" nor "a hair from the head of one of His servants."

But will anyone tell me how God overrules the minds of free moral agents in such a way that He always accomplishes His own will without participating in the evils they commit? Our blessed Lord was put to death "by God's set purpose and foreknowledge" (Acts 2:23), yet throughout the entire course of those awful events, the men involved followed the dictates of their own hearts and "with the help of wicked men, put him to death by nailing him to the cross." Will anyone explain to me how this was done?

DAY
294

If we know so little of God's providence, who shall explain to us the wonders of His grace? Will anyone tell me why the world was left for thousands of years before the Savior was sent to redeem it? Or why Abraham was chosen in preference to all others on earth, that the Savior should descend from him? Or why it was through the line of Isaac and Jacob, rather than through the line of Ishmael and Esau, that Christ came? Will anyone explain how the Spirit of God acts upon the souls of some men and women to regenerate, sanctify, and save them, while others never experience these blessings? Can they tell me why some individuals experience His influence, only to aggravate their ultimate, eternal condemnation? Can anyone explain how mind operates upon matter in a single activity of his own body?

If no one can explain these things, then how can anyone presume to judge God, who "performs wonders that cannot be fathomed, miracles that cannot be numbered" (Job 9:10)?

CHARLES SIMEON

no odd pieces

*Are not two sparrows sold for a penny? Yet not one of them
will fall to the ground apart from the will of your Father.*

(MATTHEW 10:29)

W hat did our Lord mean when He said that the sparrow does not fall without our Father's notice? The cynic may say, "But the sparrow falls just the same. We see them lying around almost any day. Small comfort that!"

But something deeper than meets the eye is in this precious word. In this universe everything is known to God, even to the slightest detail. Nothing ever becomes actually nonexistent. It is a law of nature; and any scientist can tell you that things change form, but never cease to be. The burning wood goes up in smoke and is reduced to ashes, but its component elements are still around.

With the child of God no prayer, no tear, *nothing* is lost. All things work together for good to him in the purpose of God. The hairs of our head are numbered. We do not lose our dear ones by death. If they are the Lord's, they are with Him, and in His sight all live somewhere.

God knows what He has in stock in His universe and no item, however small, is unknown to Him. One day in the final restoration of all things we are going to see all things that puzzle us now fitted into a complete picture. Everybody and everything will be where they belong. There will be no odd pieces, no meaningless rubbish. And everyone in heaven, on earth, and under the earth shall confess that Jesus is Lord. That will not mean universal salvation, but it does mean that everybody and everything will be accounted for. God will overlook nothing. How good to know that "His eye is on the sparrow, and I know He watches me!"

VANCE HAVNER

DAY
295

Blessings in Disguise

*Since ancient times no one has heard, no ear has perceived,
no eye has seen any God besides you,
who acts on behalf of those who wait for him.*

(ISAIAH 64:4)

G rant Thorburn, a young Scotch immigrant, landed in New York City. He hoped to make his living by working at his trade, but he soon learned that a new machine had recently been introduced to do his work, and he could find no permanent employment. The future looked bleak. What was he to do? For a time the promises of God, on which he had been depending, seemed to fail.

After a season or two spent in odds and ends of work, he started a small grocery store. A competitor soon drove him out of business. He started a second store with little success. One day he set on the counter a potted rose geranium which he had decorated himself. A customer pleaded for the plant and pot. Thorburn bought a second plant, decorated another pot, and this too quickly sold. Mr. Thorburn was not slow to see his opportunity. He gave up his grocery and started a flower and seed business, which soon developed until he was a man to be reckoned with by others who had been in the business for years.

DAY
296

The lesson? Mr. Thorburn said it well: "You see, what I thought to be misfortunes were only blessings in disguise. When the machines cut me out, I thought it a misfortune. Being cut out of a grocery, I thought that was another misfortune. But this providence was leading me into a more pleasant business."

Why cannot we learn this lesson once for all? Is life hard, in spite of our best efforts? Let us expect the best. When we are distressed and troubled about many things, let us assure ourselves that somehow all these things are for us, not against us. Let us patiently await the outcome.

JOHN T. FARIS

A HAPPY THUNDERSTORM

The LORD thundered from heaven; the voice of the
Most High resounded. He shot his arrows and scattered
the enemies, great bolts of lightning and routed them.

(PSALM 18:13–14)

A theists tell us that because thunder is produced by natural causes, it is childish to be awed by its power. I say such atheism is stupid and wicked, for the great God who makes "a path for the thunderstorm" (Job 38:25) also makes sure that the thunder goes where He directs it (Job 28:26). God determines the path of every lightning bolt under heaven to accomplish His own purposes (Job 37:3, 12).

DAY
297

Good men should meditate on this remarkable truth and so determine to walk humbly with their God, for they never know whether death might come to them suddenly in just this way.

At the same time, those who are in Christ and who strive to live for God do not need to be dismayed at the most terrifying thunder claps any more than a child should be afraid when he hears the voice of his loving father.

The story is told of an unbeliever, an enemy of a very godly man, who while out riding a horse with his wife heard a deafening thunder. The man's wife, a devout Christian, saw him tremble and asked, "Why are you so afraid?"

"Are you not frightened to hear these dreadful thunder claps?" he asked.

"No," she responded, "not at all, for I know it is the voice of my heavenly Father. Should a child be afraid to hear her father's voice?"

The man was amazed at her response and concluded that these Christians possessed a divine secret that gave them peace and serenity when others were filled with fear. He immediately went to see his enemy, begged his pardon and his prayers, and asked what he needed to do to be saved. Ever since that day he has been a very godly man himself.

That was a happy thunderstorm!

INCREASE MATHER

The Lord Has Done Great Things for us

His divine power has given us everything we need for life and godliness
through our knowledge of him who called us by his own glory and goodness.

(2 PETER 1:3)

eter among the apostles is uniquely honored, for everything about him was in some way or other connected with a miracle.

It was by a miracle that he walked on the water, and it was by a miracle that he was saved from drowning when the Savior stretched out His hand and commanded him to stand upon the waves.

There was a miracle in connection with the boat, for it was from that boat that the miraculous catch of fish had been taken and it was filled so full that it began to sink.

DAY
298

There was a miracle in connection with Peter's rusty sword. He used it to cut off the ear of the high priest's servant, but the Master healed the wound that His rash defender inflicted.

Every Christian should be eager to have the hand of God connected with everything he has, so that when he looks at his house, he may see God's providence everywhere. When he looks upon his clothes, he sees the uniform of love; when he observes the food on his table, he sees the daily gift of divine charity. In looking back upon his whole personal history, the believer may see bright spots where the presence of God flames forth and makes the humblest circumstances illustrious.

But above all, it ought to be his prayer that God's hand should be very conspicuous in connection with his relatives, that of every one of them it might be said, "The Lord restored her," or, "The Lord gave him spiritual life in answer to my prayer." May husband, wife, and children all receive healing from "the beloved Physician." May our whole household be "holiness to the Lord," and may all sing for joy because the Lord has done great things for us.

CHARLES H. SPURGEON

why think about it?

Come and see what God has done,
how awesome his works in man's behalf!

(PSALM 66:5)

W hy should we meditate upon God's providence? First, because *God has expressly commanded it.* He has called His people to seriously reflect upon His works, whether of mercy or of judgment. When God's people found themselves about to be exiled because of their apostasy, the Lord urged them to consider Shiloh to see what God did to it (Jeremiah 7:12). In the same way, God calls us to consider and review His mercies: "My people, remember what Balak king of Moab counseled and what Balaam son of Beor answered. Remember your journey from Shittim to Gilgal, that you may know the righteous acts of the LORD" (Micah 6:5). We are called to meditate on God's providence so that we may strengthen our faith (Matthew 6:28).

Second, we are to meditate on God's providence because *to neglect to do so is condemned as a sin.* To be careless and unobservant greatly displeases God: "O LORD, your hand is lifted high, but they do not see it" (Isaiah 26:11). God denounces this sin in His Word (Psalm 28:4–5; Isaiah 5:12–13). Indeed, God strikes men with visible judgments for committing this sin (Job 34:26–27).

For this reason the Holy Spirit frequently affixes special notes of attention—such as "Look!" or "Listen!"—to biblical narratives of God's providential acts. For example, when the daring enemy Rabshakeh was defeated by providence, Scripture prefixed a note of attention to that account: "Listen! I am going to put such a spirit in him..." (2 Kings 19:7). In the book of Revelation, our attention is pointedly drawn to the opening of every seal judgment: "Come and see, come and see" (Revelation 6:1–7). Such notes are useless and superfluous...unless we are instructed to take special note of God's providence.

JOHN FLAVEL

A History of Your Life

I will sing to the LORD,
for he has been good to me.

(PSALM 13:6)

O that we practiced the heavenly spiritual exercise of meditating on the providences of God! How sweet it would make our lives; how light it would make our burdens! You live estranged from the pleasure of the Christian life if you ignore or neglect this discipline.

Fill your heart with thoughts of Him and His ways! Let your meditation be as full and exhaustive as possible. Do not let your thoughts swim like feathers upon the surface of the water, but sink like lead to the bottom. Although we cannot sound the depth of providence by our short line, it is our duty to dive as far as we can and to admire the depth even when we cannot touch the bottom.

DAY
300

Search backward into all the acts of providence throughout your life. That is what Asaph did: "I will remember the deeds of the LORD; yes, I will remember your miracles of long ago. I will meditate on all your works and consider all your mighty deeds" (Psalm 77:11–12). He labored to recover and revive the ancient providences of God's mercies and so coax a fresh sweetness out of them.

There is no more pleasant a history for you to read in all the world as the history of your own life. Sit down and record from the beginning what God has been to you and done for you. What outstanding displays of His mercy, faithfulness, and love have taken place throughout your days? If a single act of providence is so ravishing and thrilling, what would many of them be if they were considered together? If one star is beautiful to behold, what is a constellation? If your heart does not melt before you have recited half that history, it is a hard heart indeed.

JOHN FLAVEL

BE where the provision is

So Abraham called that place The LORD Will Provide. And to this day it is said,
"On the mountain of the LORD it will be provided."

(GENESIS 22:14)

G et near to God if you want to enjoy what He has prepared for you. Live in simple, loving fellowship with Him if you desire to drink in His fulness. And be sure of this: You will have no part in the matter unless you are a child of His house. "On the mountain of the LORD it will be provided," but around it lies a desolate wilderness of famine and death.

DAY
301

Remember, only when Abraham stands with knife in hand, expecting that the next moment it will run red with his son's blood— only then does the call come: "Abraham!" Only then does he notice the ram caught in the thicket.

That is God's way always. Up to the very edge we are driven before He puts out His hand to help us. It is best for us that we should be brought to desperation, to say, "My foot slips" and then, just as our toes feel the ice, help comes and His mercy holds us up. At the last moment—never before it, never until we have discovered how much we need it, and never too late—comes the Helper.

If we want to get our needs supplied, our weakness strengthened, and wisdom to dispel our perplexity, we must be where all the provision is stored. If a man chooses to sit outside the provision shop, he may starve on its threshold. If a woman will not go into the bank, her pockets will remain empty though there may be bursting vaults to which she has a right. If we will not ascend the hill of the Lord and stand in His holy place by simple faith, God's amplest provision will be nothing to us, and we will be empty in the middle of affluence.

ALEXANDER MACLAREN

tearful glory

We are hard pressed on every side, but not crushed; perplexed, but not in despair;
persecuted, but not abandoned; struck down, but not destroyed.
We always carry around in our body the death of Jesus,
so that the life of Jesus may also be revealed in our body.

(2 CORINTHIANS 4:8–9)

G od's providence rules over all, even when illness or natural disasters strike. It's this conviction that can sustain you when you find yourself in the middle of desperate times. In His infinite power and wisdom, God can use even life's worst afflictions to bring Himself glory. Most of the time He gets that glory through you.

Last Sunday my church held a "parent dedication" service. Six couples brought forward their children so that we might pray for the strength, stamina, and wisdom each couple would need. But the usual routine screeched to a halt when the last couple presented their child.

DAY
302

Their one-year-old daughter, born with half a brain, would never develop mentally beyond the age of one or two months. She feeds through a tube and the couple isn't sure how far to utilize medical procedures to keep their child alive.

"I have the same kind of deformity my daughter has," the father confessed, "except mine is in my heart. Sin has affected her physically— my problem is spiritual."

He stopped briefly to collect himself, then described the work of a providential God. No, his daughter wasn't miraculously healed on the platform, and no, his whole extended family hadn't come to faith because of the tragedy.

"But one good thing has come out of all of this," he said while we all wiped away tears. "My wife and I have grown much closer together. I've grown a lot closer to God. And I have learned to depend upon Him completely."

Then we all prayed. Oh, did we pray! Not to the God of our fantasy. Not to the God of never-never land. But to the good God of providence who knows how to turn even the most heart-wrenching tragedies into bits of divine glory.

And as I sat in the pew, I thought, *Even this qualifies.*

STEVE HALLIDAY

what's Left but music?

*I...go about your altar, O LORD, proclaiming aloud your
praise and telling of all your wonderful deeds.*

(PSALM 26:6–7)

Let your mind roam through the whole creation; everywhere the created world will cry out to you: "God made
me."

DAY
303

Whatever pleases you in a work of art brings to your mind the artist
who created it; much more should your consideration of the universe
evoke praise for its Maker. You look on the heavens—they are God's
great work. You behold the earth—God made its numbers of seeds, its
varieties of plants, its multitude of animals. Go round the heavens
again and back to the earth, leave out nothing; on all sides everything
cries out to you of its Author. Indeed, the very forms of created things
are, as it were, the voices which praise their Creator.

But who can fathom the whole creation? Who shall set forth its
praises? Who can adequately praise heaven and earth, the sea, and
everything that is in them? And these indeed are only the visible
things!

Who shall adequately praise the angels, thrones, dominions,
principalities, and powers? Who shall adequately praise that Power
which works actively within ourselves, giving life to the body, giving
movement to its members, bringing the senses into play, embracing so
many things in the memory, distinguishing so many things by the
intelligence? Who can praise it to the degree it so richly deserves?

Now if human language is so at a loss in considering these creatures of God, what is it to do in regard to the Creator Himself? When
words fail, can anything but triumphant music remain? "I proclaim
aloud your praise and tell of all your wonderful deeds!"

ST. AUGUSTINE OF HIPPO

anGels adore Him,
seas bless Him

God has ascended amid shouts of joy, the LORD amid the sounding of trumpets.
Sing praises to God, sing praises; sing praises to our King, sing praises.
For God is the King of all the earth; sing to him a psalm of praise.

(PSALM 47:5–7)

All nature, visible or invisible, gives unceasing witness to God. Angels adore Him, stars wonder at Him, seas bless Him, lands revere Him, and even the lower regions look up at Him. Every human mind is conscious of Him even though it cannot express Him. All things move at His command: Springs gush forth, rivers flow, waves surge, all creatures bring forth their offspring. Winds are compelled to blow, rains come, seas are stirred, all things pour out their fruitfulness everywhere.

DAY
304

He created for our first parents a paradise in the East as a world of eternal life. He saved Noah, a very just man, from the perils of the flood. He took Enoch, admitted Abraham to his friendship, protected Isaac, and made Jacob prosperous. He placed Moses at the head of His people, delivered the groaning children of Israel from the yoke of slavery, wrote the Law, and led the descendants of the patriarchs into the land of promise.

He instructed the prophets by His Spirit and through all of them promised His Son, Christ; and He sent Him at the time He had solemnly promised to give Him. He willed that through Christ we should come to a knowledge of Him; He also lavished upon us the abundant treasures of His mercy by giving His Spirit to enrich the poor and downtrodden.

And because He is so generous, benevolent, and good, lest this whole world should wither after it had despised the streams of His grace, He sent His Son into the entire world, so that poor humanity might acknowledge its Creator. If it should choose to follow Him, the human race would have One whom they could now address in their prayers as Father, instead of God.

NOVATIAN

THE
TRUTHFULNESS
AND FAITHFULNESS
OF GOD

I, THE LORD,

SPEAK THE TRUTH;

I DECLARE WHAT IS RIGHT.

ISAIAH 45:19

THE FAITHFULNESS

OF THE LORD

ENDURES FOREVER.

PSALM 117:2

god the truth

*These are the words of the Amen, the faithful
and true witness, the ruler of God's creation.*

(REVELATION 3:14)

W hatever is said of human beings, God is truth itself. This attribute expresses the reality of His being. He truly and really exists, a fact which every worshiper must believe (Hebrews 11:6).We have but a shadow of being, compared to His (Psalm 39:6). God is true, real, and substantial, the living God in opposition to fictitious deities.

This attribute removes from Him all hint of lying and falsehood. He is not a man, that he should lie; the strength of Israel will not lie. He can neither deceive nor be deceived. This attribute clears God of all insincerity, hypocrisy, and dishonesty. It expresses the faithfulness of God; that is why the terms "true" and "faithful" are joined when the words of God are mentioned (Revelation 22:6).

DAY
305

The truth of God is essential to Him. He is not only called the God of truth, but God the truth (Deuteronomy 32:4), and Christ asserts Himself to be the truth (John 14:6); the Spirit is likewise so called (1 John 5:6). To be false would be to act contrary to His nature, even to deny Himself.

God is true in His written Word. The Scriptures are the Scriptures of truth (Daniel 10:21). They are given by inspiration from God and are the very breath of God; therefore they are to be received, not as the word of man, but as the Word of God. The truth of God is seen in the fulfilment of the predictions, promises, and threats contained in His Word. The truth of God is the foundation of His faithfulness, which is but a branch of it. The words are often used as synonyms for each other, for they signify the same thing.

JOHN GILL

The God of the Amen

Whoever invokes a blessing in the land will do so by the God of truth;
he who takes an oath in the land will swear by the God of truth.

(ISAIAH 65:16)

T he full beauty and significance of these remarkable words are reached only when we consider the literal rendering. As they stand in the original, instead of the vague expression, "The God of truth," they have the singularly picturesque one, "The God of the Amen."

Now, *Amen* is an adjective, which literally means firm, true, reliable. It was the habit of biblical congregations to utter it at the close of prayer or praise. We also find it used at the beginning of a statement in order to confirm some declaration.

These two uses of the expression mean, first, "I tell you it is so," and second, "So may it be!" or "So we believe it is." That is the idea which underlies this grand title which God uses to describe Himself. He is "the God of the Amen," both His Amen and ours—that is, His truth and our faith.

The title emphasizes the absolute truthfulness of every word that comes from His lips. The title implies that He really *has* spoken and declared to us something of His will, His nature, His purposes, and our destiny. He puts the broad seal upon the charter and says, "Amen! Truly it is so, and My word of revelation is no man's imagination. My word of command absolutely unveils human duty and perfection, and a person may rest all his weight upon My word of promise and be safe forever."

God's word is "Amen!" Man's word is "perhaps." No human tongue can expect anyone to accept its confident declarations with nothing behind them but itself. But that is exactly what God does, and He alone has the right to do so. His word—through and through, in every fiber—is absolutely reliable and true.

ALEXANDER MACLAREN

He cannot tell a Lie

Let God be true, and every man a liar.

(ROMANS 3:4)

D oes God tell a lie? He does not; it is impossible for God to tell a lie. Is this an impossibility because of some weakness? Certainly not! How could He be the cause of all things if there were something which He could not cause?

What, then, is impossible for Him? Answer: Not what is difficult for His *power*, but what is contrary to His *nature*. It is impossible, the Scripture says, for Him to tell a lie. The impossibility does not come from weakness, but from His power and greatness. Truth is inconsistent with a lie and God's power can never lead to faithlessness, for "let God be true, and every man a liar" (Romans 3:4).

Truth, therefore, is always in Him. He remains reliable and cannot change or deny Himself. For if He says He is not true, He tells a lie, and a lie can be attributed not to power, but to weakness. Nor can God change Himself because His nature is unmixed with weakness.

The impossibility of God ever lying can be traced to His fullness, which cannot diminish or increase—not from weakness, which is powerless to retard its increasing weakness. For this reason we deduce that this impossibility for God—that He could ever lie—is a very powerful attribute. What is more powerful than the absence of any weakness?

ST. AMBROSE

DAY
307

all truth is
god's truth

I, the LORD, speak the truth; I declare what is right.

(ISAIAH 45:19)

T he early church claimed that all truth is God's truth wherever it be found. The *focus* here is on truth. But the ultimate *locus* of truth is God. If He is the eternal and all-wise Creator of all things, as Christians affirm, then His creative wisdom is the source and norm of all truth about everything. And if God and His wisdom are unchangingly the same, then truth is likewise unchanging and thus *universal*. If all truth is His, and He understands fully its interrelatedness, then truth is *unified* in His perfect understanding.

DAY
308

This claim must be plainly understood. It is a statement primarily about God's understanding, not man's. For man, it is a confession of faith and an essential part of the Christian *credo*. When we recite the Apostles' Creed ("I believe in God the Father Almighty, maker of heaven and earth…"), we tacitly affirm that the Creator of all knows all about His creation so that all truth about everything is His, and He knows it all as a coherent whole. We do not affirm that everything we take to be true is God's truth.

This *credo* about truth extends hope to us that truth is knowable and life ultimately makes sense. It means that men and women created as intelligent beings in God's image can hope to understand in measure a world intelligently made by the most intelligent Being of all. It means that although we know in part and see it all dimly, yet what we see and know will ideally fit together into the intelligible whole that God Himself knows it to be.

ARTHUR F. HOLMES

The Terror of His Enemies

*Because God wanted to make the unchanging nature of his purpose very clear
to the heirs of what was promised, he confirmed it with an oath. God did this
so that, by two unchangeable things in which it is impossible for God to lie, we
who have fled to take hold of the hope offered to us may be greatly encouraged.*

(HEBREWS 6:17–18)

T he truth of God is the terror of His enemies. How happy
would men be if their unbelief could make the threats of
God disappear, or their doubts could make them false!

But the Lord is true and righteous, and "all your words are true;
all your righteous laws are eternal" (Psalm 119:160). Not a word shall
fall to the ground, nor the smallest letter or the least stroke of a pen
pass unfulfilled.

The truth of God is the ground of our faith, the conviction of our
souls, and the rock of all our confidence and comfort. If God were not
true, there would be no difference between a Christian and anyone
else (except, perhaps, in being more deluded). But this is the foundation of all our hopes and the life of our religion. All that we are as
Christians proceeds from this. God's truthfulness animates our faith,
and from that all other graces flow or take root in us.

O Christian, what a treasure is before your eyes when you open
the blessed Book of God! How it should comfort you and enliven
your confidence, to think that all His words are true! All those
descriptions of the everlasting kingdom, all those exceeding precious
promises of this life and that which is to come, and every expression
of the exceeding love of God for His servants—all these are the true
sayings of God. If "a faithful witness will not lie" (Proverbs 14:5, KJV),
much less will the faithful God! Let faith therefore live upon the truth
of God, and let us be strengthened and rejoice in this glorious fact.

RICHARD BAXTER

DAY
309

Living by the Manufacturer's Manual

You will know the truth, and the truth will set you free.

(JOHN 8:32)

I f everything God says in His Word is true, then we are responsible to do what He tells us to do. If a sign says, "Dangerous Curve Ahead, Maximum Safe Speed 15 MPH," and it is true, then we had better reduce our speed to fifteen miles per hour. Truth demands compliance.

Many of us resist that. Some of us reserve the right to live as we please and seek happiness anywhere we think we can find it. But a true God whose Word is truth demands our total submission and faithful obedience. That may sound oppressive and burdensome, but it is the only way our lives can operate smoothly and effectively.

Most products work better when we use them according to the manufacturer's instructions. We are free to ignore the manual if we choose, but that does not always turn out to be true freedom. One of my sons purchased a thirty-five millimeter camera and took it with him on a once-in-a-lifetime trip. But on one roll of film he failed to heed the instructions. By the time he reached forty exposures he realized there was something wrong, but by then it was too late. He had taken forty never-to-be-repeated shots on the same frame. He was free to ignore the instructions, but the end result was frustrating.

Just so, our lives operate most satisfactorily when we live by the principles which our Maker has revealed in His manufacturer's manual, the Bible. To ignore His truth leads not to freedom, but to bondage, frustration, and failure. Jesus said, "And you will know the truth, and the truth will set you free" (John 8:32). By letting His truth find expression in our lives, we can be free to live and grow and become all we were meant to be.

RICHARD STRAUSS

DAY
310

The only Road to Freedom

To the Jews who had believed him, Jesus said,
"If you hold to my teaching, you are really my disciples."

(JOHN 8:31)

T he God of Truth purposes that everyone should come to the knowledge of the truth. This is another facet of His ultimate objective. We know that the truth will make us free. But not just any truth acquired anyhow and any time. The leading of God toward the full light of truth is, like our recognition of Him, a lifelong process, and for this we can be thankful. We move one step at a time, and Christ is the Way and the Truth. He does not drop the whole block of truth into our laps at once, for we could not possibly bear the weight of it.

The words, "You will know the truth, and the truth will set you free," are so familiar that those which precede them are often skipped over entirely: "If you hold to my teaching." This is a very different thing from "If you fully comprehend and are perfectly obedient to all I have said." The promise is to those who go on learning, if only a very little at a time. "If you hold to my teaching, you are really my disciples. Then you will know the truth, and the truth will set you free."

Discipleship, which means discipline, is the only road to freedom. We walk by faith now, for we do not see all the truth. Even Paul admitted that he knew only in part and saw through a glass darkly. But truth is God's objective, and when the day comes for it to be fully revealed, faith will no longer be needed.

ELISABETH ELLIOT

DAY
311

just for us

*You know with all your heart and soul that not one
of all the good promises the LORD your God gave you has failed.
Every promise has been fulfilled; not one has failed.*

(JOSHUA 23:14)

S everal years ago I was preaching for several weeks just outside of London. A woman noted for her saintliness lay at
the point of death. Everyone spoke of her great joy in life
and of her joy in death. She heard of our meetings, and asked, just
before she died, that her study Bible be given to me. A few days later
her earth life span ended, and life indeed began for her.

Today her Bible lies on my table. Her marginal comments have
often delighted me, and I have discovered the secret of her power and
joy. *She believed it was all for her, personally.* On the blank pages at the
back of the book she has lists of promises gathered together over the
years. The headings of the lists are alive with meaning. "How was I
saved?" she wrote, and underneath, "2 Cor. 5:21." Then, for the deeper
Christian life: "A definite act, July 9, 1894, S.E.H." Following this, she
has "Gal. 2:20; Rom. 6:19, a *slave* of God's righteousness." Then are
listed together "Power Tests," "The riches of God's grace," "The root of
holiness," "The Lord's call to praise and joy," and also groups of verses
for "Hours of darkness" and for "Shields against the legal spirit."

She had fortified her soul through God's *revelation*. One feels that
here was holy ground where a soul met God. It breathes the atmosphere of personal contact. It would be a real blessing to many of us if
we would, alone with God, take these headings and, beginning with
"How was I saved?," seek the answers in His Word.

DONALD GREY BARNHOUSE

DAY
312

A Name to Count On

God, who has called you into fellowship with his
Son Jesus Christ our Lord, is faithful.

(1   C O R I N T H I A N S   1 : 9)

A name stands for the total character and resources of an individual. My name is all that I am, your name is all that you are. When my wife took my name in marriage, she literally took me for all I had. It wasn't much! As a matter of fact, we had to cash her bonds to get home from the honeymoon. But whenever I sign my name, "Ray C. Stedman," the whole Stedman fortune, all thirty-five dollars of it, is laid on the line.

Now, the work of Jesus Christ during those thirty-three years of His life was to unveil to us the total resources of the Father, to express His name, so that we might discover what a tremendous, unending resource we have in God. We can never get to the bottom of the barrel. Failure to realize this is exactly where our problem of weakness lies. I see Christians struggling, trying to act by faith, and yet all the time sabotaging their efforts by a flat refusal to believe that God is what He says He is. We believe, essentially, that God is utterly faithless and that He will not do what He says He will do. When we believe that kind of lie, we undermine every effort that God is making to bring us into victory.

God is faithful. How many times does the Scripture say that? The whole work of Jesus Christ is to show us the faithfulness of God. What a glory is manifested in His life as we see how He rested on God's faithfulness! He was not anxious; He was not troubled; He was not disturbed when the clouds of oppression and persecution began to hang heavy over Him, for He rested on the faithful name of God.

DAY
313

RAY C. STEDMAN

all promises fulfilled

He will keep you strong to the end, so that you will be
blameless on the day of our Lord Jesus Christ.

(1 CORINTHIANS 1:8)

God is utterly faithful. God's faithfulness is an attribute closely related to His immutability. It means that God cannot violate His Word. He cannot renege on a promise. "He cannot disown himself" (2 Timothy 2:13).

God's faithfulness does not depend on our own. Second Timothy 2:13 says, "If we are faithless, he will remain faithful." God will not fail to fulfill perfectly all His promises. The Christian's assurance is deeply rooted in the faithfulness of God.

DAY
314

"God is faithful," wrote Paul to the Corinthian church (1 Corinthians 1:9). He is faithful to finish the work that He has begun in you (1:8), and He is faithful to deliver you from the power of temptation: "No temptation has seized you except what is common to man. And God is faithful; he will not let you be tempted beyond what you can bear. But when you are tempted, he will also provide a way out so that you can stand up under it" (1 Corinthians 10:13).

The whole of the Bible is a testimony to the faithfulness of God. God is still fulfilling His promises to the children of Abraham. He fulfilled His promises to Moses, to David, to the prophets, and to the apostles. He is fulfilling His promises in the lives of millions today. We can testify with them that God indeed is faithful.

GEORGE SWEETING

seven pillars of faithfulness

Let us hold unswervingly to the hope we
profess, for he who promised is faithful.

(HEBREWS 10:23)

T he seven pillars of wisdom described in Proverbs 8 and 9 always remind me of seven other wonderful pillars, the seven pillars of the divine faithfulness. The faithfulness of God is like a gigantic archway spanning human history from its beginning to its ending; and that resplendent archway is supported on seven glorious, immovable pillars.

The first is the divine *righteousness*. The faithfulness of God rests on God's absolute fidelity to every obligation which He assumes.

The second is the divine *omnipotence*. Because God is omnipotent, He is able to accomplish all that He sets out to do.

The third is the divine *truth*. God is *the* truth, the shadowless totality of truth, whose every word is truth, who therefore could never possibly be false or faithless.

The fourth is the divine *immutability*. His eternal unchangingness assures us that He never deviates from His perfect goodness, and never withdraws any promise He ever makes.

The fifth is the divine *holiness*. Because God is ethically perfect, all that He ever thinks or says or plans or purposes or promises at any given instant is always faultless. He never has to correct or revise or improve it, which means that He can always be fully faithful to it.

The sixth is the divine *wisdom*. The omniscient wisdom of God guarantees that He not only fulfills His pledged word, but that He always does so in the wisest conceivable way.

The seventh pillar is the divine *love*. As soon as I know that "God is love" and that He loves *me*, I know that all His thoughts toward me emanate from pure love and for my everlasting well-being.

These, then, are the seven magnificent pillars upon which rests the age-to-age faithfulness of our glorious Creator.

J. SIDLOW BAXTER

DAY
315

NO FAILURES

Know therefore that the LORD your
God is God, the faithful God.

(DEUTERONOMY 7:9)

God has declared Himself to be *faithful*. To be faithful is to be absolutely firm and reliable in keeping all one's promises and commitments.

We have all known the hurt of unfaithfulness. We have wondered whom we can depend on. The Scriptures give us great hope by coupling the truth that God is faithful with the fact that He cannot change. "For I the LORD do not change" (Malachi 3:6). God will always be faithful to you because it is impossible for Him to change. For God to be unfaithful even once would cause Him to change. God's very name is "Faithful" (Revelation 19:11), for He is perfect in faithfulness. Imagine, there *is* Someone who will never let you down, who will never break His promise to you!

What does this mean to you? God *will* be, *must* be, faithful to His Word and to every promise He has made to you in it: "Faithful is he that calleth you, who also will do it (1 Thessalonians 5:24, KJV). That means:

Faithful is He who calls you as an encourager to your spouse with his or her unique needs; He will also give you grace to meet those needs.

Faithful is He who calls you as mother or father to your children with their individual physical limitations, temperaments, and mental capacities; He will also enable you to work properly with them.

Faithful is He who calls you to a seemingly impossible task; He will also give you whatever ability you need to accomplish that task (Hebrews 4:16).

Since God is perfect, He cannot fail you even once! What security, what peace, what confidence is now possible for you! God is faithful. He will never fail to keep His promises to you.

MYRNA ALEXANDER

The Unspeakable Blessing

O Lord God Almighty, who is like you? You are mighty,
O Lord, and your faithfulness surrounds you.

(PSALM 89:8)

ow refreshing, how unspeakably blessed, to lift our eyes and behold One who is faithful, faithful in all things, faithful at all times!

This quality is essential to God's being; without it He would not be God. For God to be unfaithful would be to act contrary to His nature, which is impossible: "If we are faithless, he will remain faithful, for he cannot disown himself" (2 Timothy 2:13). Faithfulness is one of the glorious perfections of His being. He is, as it were, clothed with it: "O LORD God Almighty, who is like you? You are mighty, O LORD, and your faithfulness surrounds you" (Psalm 89:8). So too when God became incarnate it was said, "Righteousness will be his belt and faithfulness the sash around his waist" (Isaiah 11:5).

What a word is that in Psalm 36:5, "Your love, O LORD, reaches to the heavens, your faithfulness to the skies." Far above all finite comprehension is the unchanging faithfulness of God. Everything about God is great, vast, incomparable. He never forgets, never fails, never falters, never forfeits His word. To every declaration of promise or prophecy the Lord has exactly adhered, every engagement of covenant or threat He will make good, for "God is not a man, that he should lie, nor a son of man, that he should change his mind. Does he speak and then not act? Does he promise and not fulfill?" (Numbers 23:19). Therefore does the believer exclaim, "His compassions never fail. They are new every morning; great is your faithfulness" (Lamentations 3:22–23).

DAY
317

ARTHUR W. PINK

food for the soul

By faith Abraham, even though he was past age—
and Sarah herself was barren—was enabled to become a father
because he considered him faithful who had made the promise.

(HEBREWS 11:11)

A lthough men become unfaithful out of desire, fear, weakness, loss of interest, or because of some strong influence from without, none of these forces can affect God in any way. He is His own reason for all He is and does.

The faithfulness of God is a datum of sound theology, but to the believer it becomes far more than that: It passes through the understanding and goes on to become nourishing food for the soul. The inspired writers were men of like passion with us, dwelling in the midst of life. What they learned about God became to them a sword, a shield, a hammer; it became their life motivation, their good hope, and their confident expectation. From the objective facts of theology their hearts made how many thousand joyous deductions and personal applications!

Upon God's faithfulness rests our whole hope of future blessedness. Only as He is faithful will His covenants stand and His promises be honored. Only as we have complete assurance that He is faithful may we live in peace and look forward with assurance to the life to come.

Every heart can make its own application of this truth. The tempted, the anxious, the fearful, the discouraged may all find new hope and good cheer in the knowledge that our heavenly Father is faithful. He will always be true to His pledged word. The hard-pressed sons of the covenant may be sure that He will never remove His lovingkindness from them nor allow His faithfulness to fail.

DAY
318

Happy the man whose hopes rely
On Israel's God; He made the sky,
And earth, and seas, with all their train;
His truth forever stands secure;
He saves the oppressed, He feeds the poor,
And none shall find His promise vain.
Isaac Watts

A. W. TOZER

A powerful impact on the world

For no matter how many promises God has made,
they are "Yes" in Christ. And so through him the "Amen"
is spoken by us to the glory of God.

(2 CORINTHIANS 1:20)

T he Bible contains thousands of precious promises from God, and at least one of them will have application to every conceivable situation we can possibly encounter—financial reversal, terminal illness, the loss of a loved one, family tensions, or anything else. A faithful God can be trusted to keep every promise.

Paul makes this astounding statement: "For no matter how many promises God has made, they are 'Yes' in Christ. And so through him the 'Amen' is spoken by us to the glory of God" (2 Corinthians 1:20). Jesus Christ is the absolute certainty that all God's promises will be fulfilled. A God who loves us enough to give us His Son will certainly keep all His other promises. Christ's coming was as though God had written beside every promise in the Bible, "Yes, so be it, I will keep My Word." When we believe His promises, our lives bring glory to Him.

DAY
319

People in the world today are fed up with empty religious claims. They want to see something that does what it says it will do. Few things give evidence to the reality of life in Christ more powerfully than a believer who exhibits genuine peace in difficult circumstances. That is the by-product of knowing a faithful God and believing His promises. When we are assured that He cares because He is loving and good; when we are convinced that He is in control because He is omnipotent; when we believe that He is with us and knows all about the problem because He is omnipresent and omniscient; when we believe that He is working everything together for good because He is sovereign and wise; then we will have peace when things around us are falling apart. And that will make a powerful impact on the world.

RICHARD STRAUSS

The Battle of the Tenses

As I was with Moses, so I will be with you.

(JOSHUA 1:5)

We are sometimes told there is no such thing as the present; before our thought has grasped it, it has already slipped into the past. But we can think of the past and cast longing glances back to the days of long ago. And we can think of the future, sometimes with happy anticipation, sometimes with feelings of foreboding and anxiety.

Joshua knew what this felt like. He looked to the past with pride and admiration: There was Moses, the all-but-invincible leader of God's people, the lawgiver, the administrator, the seer and prophet. And the future! A desert and a leaderless people. A cantankerous, stubborn, defenseless people surrounded by innumerable foes. Truly these two tenses could fully occupy Joshua's thoughts—a past of splendor and a future of anxiety and strife.

Just then God appeared on the scene and linked the past and future by a word of promise: "As I *was* with Moses, so I *will* be with you." Here was the great "I Am," the ever-present One, by His abiding faithfulness binding the past and the future into one. As He was faithful to Moses in the past, so He would be faithful to Joshua in the future, for past and future were an eternal present to Him!

We, too, are engaged like Joshua in the battle of the tenses—the past and the future. The past has had its joys and sorrows, its health and sickness, its failure and triumph, yet we have been brought safely through. But the future is causing us anxiety—conflict, strife, suffering are ahead of us. Yet here is One who can say not only "I was," but with equal authority, "I will be." His faithfulness links past and future in one.

R. A. FINLAYSON

god Remembers

But while he was still a long way off, his father saw him
and was filled with compassion for him; he ran to his son,
threw his arms around him and kissed him.

(LUKE 15:20)

Y ou have had high moments when God was very close: the day your mother died, the first day in a home of your own, or when a little one was born to you. Your heart was touched and tender, and you swore you would be faithful. You made a covenant with God and He with you. It is long ago and you had quite forgotten—but God remembers. His promises still hold and are open to you. He remains faithful, even if we fail.

That is the dominant note of Scripture—the amazing, persistent loyalty of God. You hear it everywhere. "Repent!… Why will you die, O house of Israel?" (Ezekiel 18:30–31). "All day long I have held out my hands to a disobedient and obstinate people" (Romans 10:21). Paul says God haunts us like a begger not to be turned away. He keeps following us and breaking in on us whenever He sees any chance of gaining our attention. He pleads with us to be reconciled to Him who has nothing but love in His heart for us.

The prodigal son forgot all about the father, but the father always remembered him. His eyes were always searching the road, and he was always slipping out to look for him. "That's him," he cried, when at last he saw a far-off, shabby, hesitating, limping figure. "That is surely him," and he ran to him.

This is a wonderful reading of God's heart, and oh, the splendor of the fact that it is true! We sin, and God's answer is love; we heap up more sin, and He gives more love; we make our sin inexcusable, and His answer is Calvary. Though we are faithless, He remains faithful to His own nature. He cannot be untrue to Himself.

ARTHUR JOHN GOSSIP

something to rely on

*The virgin will be with child and will give birth
to a son, and will call him Immanuel.*

(ISAIAH 7:14)

*When the time had fully come, God sent
his Son, born of a woman.*

(GALATIANS 4:4)

S cripture abounds in illustrations of God's faithfulness. More than four thousand years ago He said, "As long as the earth endures, seedtime and harvest, cold and heat, summer and winter, day and night will never cease" (Genesis 8:22). Every year that comes furnishes a fresh witness to God's fulfillment of this promise.

In Genesis 15 the Lord declares to Abraham, "Know for certain that your descendants will be strangers in a country not their own, and they will be enslaved and mistreated four hundred years.... In the fourth generation your descendants will come back here" (15:13, 16). Centuries ran their weary course. Abraham's descendants groaned amid the brick kilns of Egypt. Had God forgotten His promise? No, indeed. Read Exodus 12:41, "At the end of the 430 years, to the very day, all the Lord's divisions left Egypt."

Through Isaiah the Lord declared, "The virgin will be with child and will give birth to a son, and will call him Immanuel" (7:14). Again centuries passed, "But when the time had fully come, God sent his Son, born of a woman" (Galatians 4:4).

God's Word of Promise is sure. He may be safely relied upon. No one ever yet trusted Him in vain. We find this precious truth expressed almost everywhere in the Scriptures, for His people need to know that faithfulness is an essential part of the Divine character. This is the basis of our confidence in Him.

But it is one thing to accept the faithfulness of God as a Divine truth; it is quite another to *act* upon it. God has given us many "very great and precious promises" (2 Peter 1:4). But are we really counting on His fulfilling them? Are we actually *expecting* Him to do for us all that He has said?

ARTHUR W. PINK

Build upon it

Those who know your name will trust in you,
for you, LORD, have never forsaken those who seek you.

(PSALM 9:10)

A generation after the promises of the books of Moses had been recorded, Joshua was able to say that God had proven Himself true. "Not one of all the LORD'S good promises to the house of Israel failed; every one was fulfilled" (Joshua 21:45).

God's faithfulness, however, endures more than a generation. The wisest man known to the ancient world was wise because he knew God and had built upon His Word. At the dedication of the temple, Solomon was able to say to the people, "Not one word has failed of all the good promises" (1 Kings 8:56).

Finally, after Joshua's witness of a generation and Solomon's witness of centuries, came the Lord Jesus, the source of Joshua's strength of leadership and the spring of Solomon's wisdom. He sealed all God's Word with the seal of finality and gave Himself, not only as the sacrifice for sin, but as the pledge that there should fail "not one word" of all that had been promised and given. The Holy Spirit tells us, "No matter how many promises God has made, they are 'Yes' in Christ" (2 Corinthians 1:20).

Why do we not believe God more? Not one word of all His good promise has failed; not one soul, trusting Him for salvation, has ever been lost; not one stumbling saint has missed the undergirding of His power. The foundation of God stands sure. He must be faithful or He would cease to be God, and we cannot conceive of God's becoming "not God." His Word is settled in heaven, and though heaven and earth pass away, it shall never cease. His Word is as eternal in the past as is God and as enduring for the future. Build upon it without fear.

DONALD GREY BARNHOUSE

when Doubt comes

Can a mother forget the baby at her breast and have no compassion on the child she has borne? Though she may forget, I will not forget you! See, I have engraved you on the palms of my hands.

(ISAIAH 49:15–16)

O ne of the times we are most tempted to doubt God's faithfulness is when suffering strikes our lives. It often makes no sense to us and we see no reason for it. We begin to think that He has forgotten us or really does not care about us.

The people of Jerusalem in Isaiah's day were beginning to think that way. Israel was a tiny nation surrounded by giant powers which were continually menacing her. Listen to her complaint: "But Zion said, 'The LORD has forsaken me, the LORD has forgotten me'" (Isaiah 49:14). But the LORD was right there with words of encouragement: "Can a mother forget the baby at her breast and have no compassion on the child she has borne? Though she may forget, I will not forget you! See, I have engraved you on the palms of my hands; your walls are ever before me" (verses 15–16).

God had allowed them to suffer, but He could never forget them in their suffering because He is faithful. And He does not forget us. He really does care.

How can we appropriate this great doctrine of God's faithfulness and enjoy calmness and contentment when hard times come? The only way is to do what Peter suggested: "So then, those who suffer according to God's will should commit themselves to their faithful Creator and continue to do good" (1 Peter 4:19). As the Creator, God has the power to carry out His perfect plan for our lives and to accomplish His perfect purposes through our suffering. And as the *faithful* Creator, He can be counted on to do it. Therefore we can entrust ourselves to His care with complete confidence, believing that He will do what is best. Then we will have peace in the midst of adversity.

RICHARD STRAUSS

DAY
324

faithful in suffering

*So then, those who suffer according to God's
will should commit themselves to their
faithful Creator and continue to do good.*

(1 PETER 4:19)

I recently met a successful salesman who was struck totally blind at the age of forty-four. Not only was his sales ability hindered but his enjoyment of sports and his capacity to appreciate the great outdoors seemed to be terminated. His anger with God was intense. On one occasion he laid on the floor and cried, begging God to take his life and threatening to commit suicide. It seemed as though God said to him, "Don, trust Me. I have a great plan for your life." But still the resentment lingered.

A short time later he insisted on going for a walk. When no one in the house was free to take him, he angrily fumbled around and found his cane, located the front door, and against his wife's protests made his way down the front steps and across the yard, determined to prove something to himself and his family. He crossed the road, and in a state of disorientation accidently stumbled into a creek. As he sat there waist-deep in the water, it seemed as though God were saying, "Are you cooled down now, Don? Trust Me. I have a great plan for your life."

That was the moment he entrusted himself to his faithful Creator. A few years later he was serving the Lord effectively as a representative for a mission to the blind, finding more joy and satisfaction in his Christian life than he had ever known before. God is faithful in sustaining us through suffering.

RICHARD STRAUSS

an Anchor in the storm

God is our refuge and strength, an ever present help in trouble. Therefore we will not fear, though the earth give way and the mountains fall into the heart of the sea.

(PSALM 46:1–2)

Because God is our steadfast Anchor amid the storms and stresses of life, our future rests securely on His solid foundation. We can live peaceably in calm assurance because our God is faithful to His Word. God does not promise one thing today and change His mind tomorrow. What He promises today, He will do.

But does God always come through for us in the way that we want Him to? Does God always arrive to rescue us from our problems, as the cavalry in the movies always arrived just as the Indians were about to take the fort?

At first it may sound like a contradiction to say that God is faithful to His Word, even though He does not always do what we ask. But this is no contradiction. If God says He will do something, He does it. But if we ask Him to do something, He answers us in the way that is best for us—and His answers are not always our answers.

Paul wrote, "I can do everything through him who gives me strength" (Philippians 4:13). This does not mean that just because we ask God for something, what we have requested will automatically be ours. God gives us the strength to face up to those moments and times when life is not what we want it to be. God often has a higher purpose for our lives than we are able to understand.

We must remember that God is not our servant, answering to our beck and call. This is not what we mean when we say God is faithful. God is faithful to His Word, but He is not a genie in a bottle who will spoil us by granting all our wishes.

JOHN BISAGNO

DAY
326

no matter what

I will sing of the LORD'S great love forever; with my mouth
I will make your faithfulness known through all generations.

(PSALM 89:1)

Sometimes we see God's faithfulness in how He removes a problem and gives us what we've longed for. Other times His faithfulness is seen in how He does not give us what we request, but sustains us and molds us through the suffering. We need to hear both sides of His faithfulness.

The birth of my daughter Elizabeth is a story of the first kind. I didn't discover I was pregnant until I was three and a half months along. What I had assumed was normal each month was in fact hemorrhaging from a detached placenta. We were told a miscarriage was likely.

DAY 327

During those months I experienced many stages of emotional highs and lows, times of gripping fear and despair, times of great peace and rest in God. Most of all, it was a time of learning to trust. I poured out my fears and deepest desires to God. The Scriptures that helped me most were those that dealt with His faithfulness.

When the time came to deliver, I went through every stage of labor in sixty minutes. Afterward, as I lay there holding our daughter, I realized our baby was demonstrable proof that God is faithful.

A friend of mine has a different story. She has endured six miscarriages, one at six months, and three failed adoptions. But she says, "Becky, don't feel sorry for me. God *has* been faithful to me. In the toughest times His comforting presence saw me through. He has given me spiritual children and a life far better than I could have imagined. He's always proved Himself worthy of my trust."

God is God. His faithfulness does not depend on our goodness or gimmicks. His grace is available to strengthen us so we may live as a faithful people in a faithless generation no matter what.

REBECCA MANLEY PIPPERT

He shall lose none

*I have come down from heaven not to do my will
but to do the will of him who sent me. And this is the will of him
who sent me, that I shall lose none of all that he has given me.*

(JOHN 6:38–39)

T hough we fail, God will stand behind His covenant! It is our only hope. I have fallen from grace a thousand times. I have grown cold and hard and apathetic—sick of the whole business. But it is strangely difficult to escape from God. He follows us, haunts us, hems us in, will not be repulsed nor take refusal. Once in the flock of the Good Shepherd, we have at our back an immensity of sleepless skill and patience that, however often we may slip through each inviting gap in every hedge, finds us again.

The most comfortable passage in the Bible is that in which Christ tells us that His own good name and honor are bound up in His getting us home safely: "I have come down from heaven not to do my will but to do the will of him who sent me. And this is the will of him who sent me, that I shall lose none of all that he has given me" (John 6:38–39). If you are not there at the end, Christ's glory will be dimmed. "But," God will say to Him, "did I not tell you I must have that soul of Mine? Where is it?"

"One of the most convenient hieroglyphics of God," says Donne in a more Christian place, "is a circle; and a circle is endless; whom God loves, He loves to the end; and not only to their own end, to their death, but to His end; and His end is that He might love them still."

"Often and often," says Samuel Rutherford, "I have in my folly torn up my copy of God's covenant with me. But, blessed be His name, He keeps the original in heaven safe; and He stands by it always."

ARTHUR JOHN GOSSIP

confident, peaceful, secure

If we are faithless, he will remain faithful,
for he cannot disown himself.

(2 TIMOTHY 2:13)

A wonderful aspect of the security we enjoy in God rests in the fact that His faithfulness to us is not conditioned by our faithfulness to Him. That God is continually faithful to us, no matter what we do, provides an important basis of our confidence in Him.

Someone may say, "What do you mean—God is faithful? Look at the situation I am in! How does *that* show His faithfulness to me?"

Sometimes our emotions or the way things appear to us at the moment make it difficult for us to see God's faithfulness. But be assured, God sees the total picture and His actions are perfect. God is at this very moment being absolutely faithful to you, for He can do nothing else.

DAY
329

When we place our trust in God's faithfulness—when we consciously and willingly put our full confidence in Him—we will enjoy personal security and inner peace unlike anything the world can provide. Despite our raw emotions and regardless of what the surrounding circumstances may seem to tell us, our trust can rest in the fact that God *is faithful*. And if that is true, what can rock us? We stand confident, peaceful, secure.

Are you worried, discouraged, afraid, or tempted? Be encouraged! God is faithful to *you*.

The Old Testament prophet Jeremiah banked on this truth, and that is why he could write the following precious words, despite horrors on his right and calamities on his left:

Yet this I call to mind and therefore I have hope: Because of the LORD's great love we are not consumed, for his compassions never fail. They are new every morning; great is your faithfulness. I say to myself, "The LORD is my portion; therefore I will wait for him." (Lamentations 3:21–24)

MYRNA ALEXANDER

τrying to be like you

*As surely as God is faithful, our message
to you is not "Yes" and "No."*

(2 CORINTHIANS 1:18)

T hose who truly feel the significance of God's faithfulness will shape their words accordingly and act so that they will not fear that His pure eyes might see in them either hypocrisy, or insincerity, or vacillation, or the hidden things of dishonesty, or any of the skulking meannesses of self-seeking. We ought to be able to say, "I swear by the Lord and call Your faithfulness to witness that I am trying to be like You."

DAY
330

That is what we ought to do, if we call ourselves Christians. If we have any hold at all on Him, and on His love, and on the greatness and majesty of His faithfulness, we will try to make our poor, little lives like dewdrops reflecting the sun—both radiant and both of the same shape.

That is exactly what the apostle Paul in 2 Corinthians does. He says, "Just because God is faithful, do you Corinthians think that, when I told you that I was coming to see you, I did not mean it?" He brings the greatest thought he can find about God down to the resolution of this very little matter, his vindication from the charges of vacillation and insincerity.

The greatest thoughts should regulate the smallest acts. Though our maps are but a quarter of an inch to a hundred miles, let us see that they are drawn to scale. Let us see that God is our pattern and that the truthfulness and faithfulness upon which we rest are copied as much as possible in our own lives. Those who are trusting the God of faithfulness must live in all integrity and godly sincerity. Their yes will be yes, and their no, no.

ALEXANDER MACLAREN

Let Us Be Encouraged

Your love, O LORD, reaches to the heavens, your faithfulness to the skies.
Your righteousness is like the mighty mountains, your justice like the great deep.

(PSALM 36:5-6)

e may place full confidence in the stability of God's mercy and faithfulness to His people. He never forsakes His inheritance and He remembers His covenant to them through all generations.

With infinite reason the Lord could say through the prophet Isaiah, "For the moth will eat them [the ungodly] up like a garment; the worm will devour them like wool. But my righteousness will last forever, my salvation through all generations." And now we may see abundant reason for the name of God which the Lord revealed to Moses: "God said to Moses, 'I AM WHO I AM'" (Exodus 3:14, NASB)—that is, "I am the same Person I was when I entered into the covenant with Abraham, Isaac, and Jacob, and I will always be the same. I will keep covenant forever. I am self-sufficient, all-sufficient, and immutable."

DAY
331

We do not need to wonder that the writer of Psalm 136 so often repeats the phrase, "His love endures forever." It is as if he were in an ecstasy at the thought of the perpetuity of God's love to His people. He delighted to think of it and could do nothing but express it continually.

Let us with the same kind of pleasure and joy celebrate the everlasting duration of God's mercy and faithfulness to His church and people, and let us be comforted by it despite any present dark circumstances of the church of God and all the uproar and confusions that are in the world and all the threats of the church's enemies. And let us be encouraged to pray earnestly for those glorious things which God has promised to accomplish for His church.

JONATHAN EDWARDS

feed on His faithfulness

Trust in Jehovah, and do good;
Dwell in the land, and feed on His faithfulness.

(PSALM 37:3, ASV)

The King James Version of Psalm 37:3 reads, "Trust in the LORD, and do good; *so* shalt thou dwell in the land, and verily thou shalt be fed," but I doubt whether it brings out the original Hebrew to best advantage in the last clause. I think the American Standard Version does a much better job of rendering the verse: "Trust in Jehovah, and do good; Dwell in the land, and *feed on His faithfulness.*"

Yes, "feed on His [God's] faithfulness"! That is the best diet for the soul at all times, especially in times of trouble. So the apostle Peter writes, "those who suffer according to God's will should commit themselves to their faithful Creator and continue to do good" (1 Peter 4:19).

DAY
332

What mental relief and repose it brings, to know that back of our human suffering and back of the staggeringly vast universe in which our own planet is an almost imperceptible speck, there is a "faithful Creator"! This prodigious universe can be frightening if we view it apart from some such guarantee as that; but when we are assured that its infinite Architect is the "faithful Creator," then the frightening becomes friendly. Every dark cloud has a silver lining, and every thunderstorm has a rainbow arching it. Every mystery holds a hidden benediction, and every permitted teardrop glistens with a gracious new meaning. A streak of powerful light strikes even across the monster problem of sin, suffering, and death, so that we sense a divine fidelity even beneath *that.*

As the celebrated hymn writer Frances Havergal reminded us so well:

Every joy or trial Falleth from above,
Traced upon our dial By the sun of love;
We may trust Him fully All for us to do—
They who trust Him wholly Find Him wholly true.

J. SIDLOW BAXTER

A Happy Ending after All

And I heard a loud voice from the throne saying, "Now the dwelling of God is with men, and he will live with them. They will be his people, and God himself will be with them and be their God. He will wipe every tear from their eyes. There will be no more death or mourning or crying or pain, for the old order of things has passed away." He who was seated on the throne said, "I am making everything new!" Then he said, "Write this down, for these words are trustworthy and true."

(REVELATION 21:3–5)

W e are given few details about the future world, only a promise that God will prove Himself trustworthy. When we awake in the new heaven and new earth, we will possess at last whatever we longed for. Somehow, from all the bad news, incredible Good News emerges—a good without a catch in it somewhere. Heaven and earth will again work the way God intended. There is a happy ending after all.

DAY
333

Fantasy writer J. R. R. Tolkien invented a new word for this good news: It will be a "eucatastrophe," he said. A scene from his trilogy, *The Lord of the Rings,* expresses it well:

> "Is everything sad going to come untrue? What's happened to the world?" [asked Sam].
>
> "A great Shadow has departed," said Gandalf, and then he laughed, and the sound was like music, or like water in a parched land; and as he listened the thought came to him that he had not heard laughter, the pure sound of merriment, for days upon days without count. It fell upon his ears like the echo of all the joys he had ever known. But he himself burst into tears. Then, as a sweet rain will pass down a wind of spring and the sun will shine out the clearer, his tears ceased, and his laughter welled up, and laughing he sprang from his bed.

For people who are trapped in pain, or in a broken home, or in economic misery, or in fear—for all those people, for all of us, heaven promises a time, far longer and more substantial than the time we spent on earth, of health and wholeness and pleasure and peace. If we do not believe that, then there's little reason to believe at all.

PHILIP YANCEY

the promise-keeping god

The LORD will fulfill his purpose for me;
your love, O LORD, endures forever.

(PSALM 138:8)

I believe the happiest and truest of Christians are those who never dare to doubt God, but who take His Word simply as it stands, and believe it, and ask no questions, just feeling assured that if God has said it, it will be so.

I bear my willing testimony that I have no reason, nor even the shadow of a reason, to doubt my Lord, and I challenge heaven and earth and hell to bring any proof that God is untrue. From the depths of hell I call the fiends, and from this earth I call the tried and afflicted believers, and to heaven I appeal, and challenge the long experience of the blood-washed host—and there is not to be found in the three realms a single person who can bear witness to one fact which can disprove the faithfulness of God or weaken His claim to be trusted by His servants. There are many things that may or may not happen, but this I know *shall* happen—

> *He shall present my soul,*
> *Unblemish'd and complete,*
> *Before the glory of His face,*
> *With joys divinely great.*

All the purposes of man have been defeated, but not the purposes of God. The promises of man may be broken—many of them are made to be broken—but the promises of God shall all be fulfilled. He is a promise-maker, but He never was a promise-breaker. He is a promise-keeping God, and every one of His people shall prove it to be so. This is my grateful, personal confidence, "The LORD *will* fulfill his purpose for me"—unworthy *me,* lost and ruined *me.* He will yet save *me;* and—

> *I, among the blood-wash'd throng,*
> *Shall wave the palm, and wear the crown,*
> *And shout the loud victory.*

CHARLES H. SPURGEON

SURPRISE!

NO EYE HAS SEEN,

NO EAR HAS HEARD,

NO MIND HAS CONCEIVED

WHAT GOD HAS PREPARED FOR

THOSE WHO LOVE HIM.

1 CORINTHIANS 2:9

living by god's surprises

See, I am doing a new thing!
Now it springs up; do you not perceive it?

(ISAIAH 43:19)

M y mind is on God's surprises. Sometimes they explode into our lives like a startled ruffed grouse. Other times things happen to us and we squint into the woods, searching and wondering if it really is an albino deer or just the trunk of a white birch.

Surprises!

The earth is a bizarre, alluring, terrible, beautiful place, and its Creator answers prayer on His own terms.

Including surprises!

Scripture is full of them.

"Say, Noah, build an ark. I'm going to flood the world."

Quite a surprise!

DAY
335

We're told Christ will come "like a thief in the night." Watch out! Surprises good and bad are coming. Which do we get? Depends.

Jesus tells a story about a boss away and the people play. They do selfish things; then the boss comes back.

Surprise! Payday!

Is your lamp trimmed? Watch out! The bridegroom's back!

Suddenly there's a burning bush out in the desert. Watch out, Moses! This will lead to more surprises—bloody plagues, millions of frogs, and forty years of tramping around a desert. But it will also bring the Ten Commandments and the glory of God glowing on you so brightly people are blinded by it.

"We live by God's surprises," said Helmut Thielicke, speaking not from some safe little Sunday school class but standing in his half-bombed-out church in World War II Germany, knowing he and his war-ravaged listeners might have to run for shelter any minute at the next wave of Allied bombers.

"God packs our lives with surprises all the time," said the tough-minded debunker Oswald Chambers who, despite wanting a career in the arts, ended up preaching out of a tent in World War I. He both warned and promised that we have to be ready for God's "surprise visits" all the time.

HAROLD MYRA

His unorthodox way

The LORD said to Joshua, "See, I have delivered Jericho into your hands, along with
its king and its fighting men. March around the city once with all the armed men.
Do this for six days. Have seven priests carry trumpets of rams' horns in
front of the ark. On the seventh day, march around the city seven times,
with the priests blowing the trumpets. When you hear them sound a
long blast on the trumpets, have all the people give a loud shout; then the
wall of the city will collapse and the people will go up, every man straight in."

(JOSHUA 6:2–5)

I
t's happened to you. You're in a tough situation, you pray about it, and the Spirit of God answers—but *not* in the way you had expected. You find the Lord Jesus asking you to handle your tough situation in a way you never imagined.

DAY
336

Isn't that just like the Lord? We think God should have us manage a sticky job situation or domestic tangle one way (the "obvious" way, the "logical" way). After all, handling the matter with simple common sense improves the odds that everything will turn out right…right?

Wrong! God often calls us to ignore the odds, asking us to face our problems His way. And His way is sometimes most unorthodox.

Have you ever considered General Joshua's dilemma, described in Joshua 6? The Lord met with Joshua prior to the battle of Jericho, identifying Himself as "the commander of the army of the Lord."

Joshua received a battle plan from the Lord, but it certainly couldn't have been what he was expecting. God instructed Joshua and his army to silently march around Jericho for six days. Then on the seventh day, they were to make the circuit seven times, listen for a trumpet blast, and then yell real loud!

Now I ask you, does that sound like common sense?

The book of Joshua, however, records that the Israelites followed God's instructions to a T. In the face of ridiculous odds, they simply did as the Lord had said. The result was one of the most dazzling victories in Israel's long history.

What is God asking you to do today that seems a little unorthodox? Has the Commander of the Lord's army presented you with a highly unusual battle plan?

Ignore the odds and obey. In the long run, you can't lose.

JONI EARECKSON TADA

I DIDN'T EXPECT THIS!

*You did awesome things
that we did not expect.*

(ISAIAH 64:3)

A salesman returning home discovered he would reach Chicago too late to work in the office, so he decided to stop off at a small town to visit an old friend. Upon reaching his home, he found the house locked up; neighbors said his friend had gone away for three weeks. What a disappointment!

The next train wasn't scheduled for five hours, but he determined to make the best of it and walked into the countryside to pass the time. He soon met an old man in a field who was slowly turning hay, preparing it for the barn. After exchanging greetings, he began a conversation, but soon discovered that while the farmer was very courteous and kind, he kept at his work. *Why not help him?* he thought. So he grabbed a fork and side by side they worked and talked. By the time the hay was all raked up, it was time for him to return to the station. Extending his hand to say good-bye, he said his disappointment had been turned into genuine pleasure.

Grasping his hand, the farmer replied, "Let me tell you something before you go. This morning, mother and I talked about getting up this hay. I said that I was feeling so bad I feared I would be unable to accomplish the task; but mother encouraged me and assured me that the Lord would help me. At family prayers we both asked our heavenly Father for His help. I arose feeling refreshed and felt sure that in some way He would help—but," he added, pressing the man's hand tighter while a tear glistened in his eye, "I really did not expect the Lord to send a man from Chicago with kid gloves and patent leather shoes to help me do it!"

JOHN T. FARIS

gasp-and-gulp city

Listen, I tell you a mystery: We will not all sleep, but we will all be changed—
in a flash, in the twinkling of an eye, at the last trumpet. For the trumpet
will sound, the dead will be raised imperishable, and we will be changed.

(1 CORINTHIANS 15:51)

The highs and lows of our lives are usually triggered by surprises. Within split seconds we are sobbing or laughing like crazy...staring in bewildered confusion or wishing we would wake up from a dream.

Ever stopped to trace the surprises through the Bible? That Book is *full* of them. Like when Enoch's footprints stopped abruptly. When aged Sarah said, *"Ze angel vasn't kidding, Abe!"* When Moses' ears heard words from a bush that wouldn't stop burning. When manna first fell from the sky. When water first ran from the rock. When Jericho's walls came tumbling down. When a ruddy runt named David whipped a rugged warrior named Goliath. When a woman from Samaria had a Jewish Stranger tell her all her secrets. When the only perfect One who ever lived was nailed to a criminal's cross. When Mary saw Him through the fog that epochal Sunday morn.

And that's just a quick review of the snapshots. If we had time to enjoy the whole album, we'd be up 'til midnight. It's gasp-and-gulp city right to the end.

And speaking of the end, that last page will be the *greatest* shock of all. Talk about "the flash of a mighty surprise"! How does "like a thief in the middle of the night" grab you? How about "in a moment...in the twinkling of an eye?" Gives me the willies just writing those words. Imagine all those open mouths, eyes like saucers, spine-tingling chills high up in the clouds!

Jesus' return will be the absolute greatest surprise. Well, maybe I had better not say *that*. The *greatest* surprise is that people like us will be included in the group, stunned and dumb with wonder. That won't be just a surprise or a dream. That'll be a flat-out miracle.

CHARLES R. SWINDOLL

And more to follow

*The Almighty...blesses you with blessings of the
heavens above, blessings of the deep that lies below,
blessings of the breast and womb.*

(GENESIS 49:25)

A benevolent person gave a Mr. Rowland Hill a hundred pounds to dispense to a poor minister a little bit at a time, thinking it was too much to send him all at once. Mr. Hill forwarded five pounds in a letter, with only these words inside the envelope: "More to follow."

A few days later, the good man received another letter; this second messenger contained another five pounds, with the same motto: "And more to follow."

A day or two later came a third and then a fourth envelope, with still the same promise, "And more to follow." Until the whole sum had been received, the astonished minister was made familiar with the cheering words, "And more to follow."

Every blessing that comes from God is sent with the same message, "And more to follow."

"I forgive your sins, but there's more to follow."

"I justify you in the righteousness of Christ, but there's more to follow."

"I educated you for heaven, but there's more to follow."

"I give you grace upon grace, but there's more to follow."

"I will uphold you in the hour of your death, and as you are passing into the world of spirits, My mercy will still continue with you; and when you land in the world to come, there will still be *more to follow.*"

CHARLES H. SPURGEON

DAY
339

Astonishing Even in Miniature

How great are his signs, how mighty his wonders!

(DANIEL 4:3)

Think how astonishing are God's acts even when set forth in miniature!

A particle of radium, so small we have to see it through a microscope, is so powerful it will ring a bell for thirty thousand years.

Think of the bee and its work. A red clover blossom contains less than one-eighth of a grain of sugar; seven thousand grains are required to make a pound of honey. A bee, flitting here and there for sweetness, must visit 56,000 clover heads for that pound of honey; and there are about sixty flower heads to each clover head. When a bee performs that operation 3,360,000 times, it secures sweetness enough for but a single pound of honey.

DAY 340

Think, too, of the ruby-throated humming bird—the only bird that hibernates at night. So beautiful are the colors of these little birds that Audubon called them "glittering fragments of the rainbow." These humming birds are the only land birds that can reverse their wing action, moving backwards and forwards. Their wings move so rapidly that one can see them only in a blur. They vibrate over two hundred times per second—which is five or six times as fast as an airplane propeller usually spins. Because of this, these birds can appear to stand still in midair, or can support themselves while they dip their beaks into a flower for nectar. They travel at fast speed—one hundred feet per second, more than a mile a minute.

God's astonishing acts manifest themselves in miniature, just as He numbers the hairs of our heads, counts our footsteps, knows our down-sitting and uprising, and keeps acquainted with all of our ways at all times and in all places. How great are His signs, how mighty His wonders—even the tiny ones!

ROBERT GREENE LEE

what we're in for

Be perfect, therefore, as your heavenly Father is perfect.

(MATTHEW 5:48)

I magine yourself a living house. God comes in to rebuild that house. At first, perhaps, you can understand what He is doing. He is getting the drains right and stopping the leaks in the roof and so on: You knew that those jobs needed doing and so you are not surprised. But soon He starts knocking the house about in a way that hurts abominably and does not seem to make sense. What on earth is He up to? The explanation is that He is building a quite different house from the one you thought of—throwing out a new wing here, putting on an extra floor there, running up towers, making courtyards. You thought you were going to be made into a decent little cottage; but He is building a palace. He intends to come and live in it Himself.

The command *be perfect* is not idealistic gas. Nor is it a command to do the impossible. He is going to make us into creatures that can obey that command. He said (in the Bible) that we were "gods," and He is going to make good His words. If we let Him—for we can prevent Him, if we choose—He will make the feeblest and filthiest of us into a god or goddess, dazzling, radiant, immortal creature, pulsating all through with such energy and joy and wisdom and love as we cannot now imagine, a bright stainless mirror which reflects back to God perfectly (though, of course, on a smaller scale) His own boundless power and delight and goodness. The process will be long and in parts very painful; but that is what we are in for. Nothing less.

C. S. LEWIS

most Richly Blessed

Who has ever given to God, that God should repay him? For from him
and through him and to him are all things. To him be the glory forever! Amen.

(ROMANS 11:35–36)

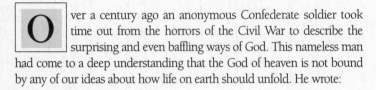ver a century ago an anonymous Confederate soldier took time out from the horrors of the Civil War to describe the surprising and even baffling ways of God. This nameless man had come to a deep understanding that the God of heaven is not bound by any of our ideas about how life on earth should unfold. He wrote:

DAY
342

> I asked God for strength, that I might achieve; I was made weak, that I might learn humbly to obey.
>
> I asked for health, that I might do greater things; I was given infirmity, that I might do better things.
>
> I asked for riches, that I might be happy; I was given poverty, that I might be wise.
>
> I asked for power, that I might have the praise of men; I was given weakness, that I might feel the need of God.
>
> I asked for all things, that I might enjoy life; I was given life, that I might enjoy all things.
>
> I got nothing that I asked for—but everything I had hoped for. Almost despite myself, my unspoken prayers were answered. I am among all men, most richly blessed.

How can we do anything but marvel at the unforeseen ways God takes the venom of hell and transforms it into the balm of Gilead? And how can we respond in any other way than to fall at His holy feet in astonished wonder and proclaim with the apostle,

> *Oh, the depth of the riches of the wisdom and knowledge of God!*
> *How unsearchable his judgments, and his paths beyond tracing out!*
> *Who has known the mind of the Lord?*
> *Or who has been his counselor?*
> *Who has ever given to God, that God should repay him?*
> *For from him and through him and to him are all things.*
> *To him be the glory forever! Amen.*

STEVE HALLIDAY

angels and lice

*He will command his angels concerning
you to guard you in all your ways.*

(PSALM 91:11)

T he Nazis were emptying jails everywhere! Male prisoners were sent in one division, women prisoners in another. My sister Betsie and I, herded together with thousands of other women, were marched into Ravensbruck. It was called a work camp.

When we first came into this concentration camp, they took all our possessions. It was a real miracle that I was able to keep my Bible.

At great risk, I hid it on my back under my dress, and I prayed, "Lord, will You send Your angels to surround me?" Then I thought, *But angels are spirits, and you can see through spirits. I don't want these people to see me!* So I prayed then, in great fear, "Let Your angels *not* be transparent. Let them cover me."

DAY 343

And God did it! As we passed through the inspection, the woman in front of me was searched, then my sister, directly behind me, was searched—but I walked through unsearched.

Our barracks was built for four hundred women, but they packed fourteen hundred of us inside. Bunks were stacked all the way to the ceiling, and we each had a sleeping space only a few inches wide. When they were all working, we had eight toilets for the entire barracks.

In Ravensbruck it was dangerous to use the Word of God. If you were caught teaching the Bible, you were killed in a cruel way, but the guards never knew that I had a Bible meeting twice each day in Barracks 28. The one jammed room was filthy, crawling with fleas and lice, and the guards never came inside the door. So the Lord used both angels and lice to keep my Bible in our possession!

CORRIE TEN BOOM

wonderfully privileged

We are therefore Christ's ambassadors, as though God were making his appeal through us. We implore you on Christ's behalf: Be reconciled to God.

(2 CORINTHIANS 5:20)

DAY

344

Questions about God's fairness and silence and hiddenness launched me on a search through the Bible. When I began that search, I wanted a more active God, one who would on occasion roll up His sleeves and step into my life with visible power. At the least, I thought, I wanted a God who did not stay quite so hidden and silent, one who worked in slightly *less* mysterious ways. Surely that wasn't asking too much.

But the Bible contained some surprises: notably that such times of frequent miracles usually did not foster long-term belief. Just the opposite—most of them stand out as examples of faith*less*ness. The more I studied the Bible, the less I longed for the "good old days" of daily manna and fireballs from heaven.

Most important, in the Bible I caught a glimpse of God's point of view. God's "goal," if one can speak in such terms, is not to overpower all skeptics with a flashy miracle; He could do that in an instant if He wished. Rather, He seeks to reconcile: to love, and to be loved. And the Bible shows a clear progression in God's efforts to break through to human beings without overwhelming them: from God the Father who hovered parentally over the Hebrews; to God the Son who taught the will of God "from the bottom up," rather than by fiat, from above; and finally, to the Holy Spirit who fills us with the literal presence of God. We who live now are not disadvantaged but wonderfully privileged, for God has chosen to rely primarily on *us* to carry out His will on earth.

PHILIP YANCEY

He Must Do More

But some of them said, "Could not he who opened the eyes
of the blind man have kept this man from dying?"

(JOHN 11:37)

C ould not Christ have saved Lazarus from dying? Of course He could, for He holds the power of life and death. But Jesus must do the absolutely best thing, not merely the second best. If it were best for Lazarus to die, then Christ could not have prevented his death. Behind how many of our unanswered prayers lies this divine reality!

Oh, how we make God a method, a law, a habit, a machine, instead of a great, dear, live, loving Nature, all afire with affection and radiant with light! How we have taken that great word *faith* and made it to mean the holding of set dogmas, when it really means the wide openness of a whole life to God! How we have limited and stereotyped the range and possibility of a miracle until only what God *has* done we think God *can* do, and so do not stand ready for the new light and mercy and salvation which the Infinite Love and Power of God has to give!

DAY
345

Open your heart today. God cannot merely do for you over and over again what He has done in the past; He must do *more*.

When Lazarus at last sat with them all at Bethany and the house was solemn with his resurrection life, how good then it seemed that Christ had not kept this man from dying! And the day will come when you, too, will be eternally thankful that your Lord refused merely to repeat the old familiar mercies of the past, but forced you through everything to let Him do for you the larger and larger mercies which your soul required. When He so tries to bless you with His largest blessing, may He also make you ready to submit to be blessed!

PHILLIPS BROOKS

The god of Turnabouts

Now I want you to know, brothers, that what has happened to me has really served to advance the gospel. As a result, it has become clear throughout the whole palace guard and to everyone else that I am in chains for Christ. Because of my chains, most of the brothers in the Lord have been encouraged to speak the word of God more courageously and fearlessly.

(PHILIPPIANS 1:12–14)

DAY
346

O ur God delights in taking the worst circumstances of life and transforming them into stunning triumphs for His people. In a word, He is the God of turnabouts.

The Lord not only brings good out of evil, He turns evil on its head. He not only overcomes the outrage, He turns it inside out. God will use the most unlikely scenarios to display His own omnipotence and the powerlessness of His enemies. God is often exactly where we do not expect to see Him, bringing good out of bad, turning evil inside out.

When our world is caving in, when things look as grim as they possibly can, when it seems as though Satan has applied the *coup de grace* to our fondest hopes and greatest desires—at precisely that point the Strong One steps in and brandishes the evil for His glory.

Now, *that* is a God to worship! *That* is a God to adore! And that is the God who fills the universe with His splendor—not some shuffling, half-dead, powerless deity who's in it way over his head.

As you focus your attention on the everlasting God, you, too, may see your worst nightmares fade and vanish into the shadows as the blinding brilliance of God's perfect plan for you takes shape. You, too, may be surprised at the unorthodox ways God chooses to bring Himself glory. Just when you think you have this business of turnabouts figured out, another one hurtles through your back door in a form and guise unlooked for. Just when you believe you know how God must act in a certain situation, the turnabout shifts shape before your unbelieving eyes.

But always the same God is behind them all.

STEVE HALLIDAY

only HE could DO It

The voice of the LORD twists the oaks and strips the forests bare.
And in his temple all cry, "Glory!"

(PSALM 29:9)

T he plain truth is, none of us is qualified to manage God's glory. None of us is wise enough, godly enough, mature enough, or imaginative enough to predict how, when, where, or why God will bring glory to His name.

Elisabeth Elliot skillfully pointed this out in *Through Gates of Splendor,* an account of the events leading up to January 8, 1956, the day five young missionaries (including Elliot's husband, Jim) would be speared to death trying to bring the gospel to a savage tribe of South American Indians called the Aucas. Nearly three years after this tragedy, Elliot found herself within ten feet of one of the seven men who killed her husband. She and her three-and-a-half-year-old daughter had returned to the Aucas' territory to point these men to the Lord. And they were listening.

DAY
347

"How did this come to be?" Elliot asked. "Only God who made iron swim, who caused the sun to stand still, in whose hand is the breath of every living thing—only this God, who is our God forever and ever, could have done it."

She wrote that the Aucas told them their attack was a mistake; they thought the white men were cannibals, and they now regarded the killings as an error. Elliot, however, saw it another way: "But we know that it was no accident. God performs all things according to the counsel of His own will. The real issues at stake on January 8, 1956, were very far greater than those which immediately involved five young men and their families, or this small tribe of naked 'savages'".... God is the God of human history, and He is at work continuously, mysteriously, accomplishing His eternal purposes in us, through us, for us, and in spite of us."

STEVE HALLIDAY

Hell Never Knew such a surprise

By his death he might destroy him who holds the power of death—that is, the devil—and free those who all their lives were held in slavery by their fear of death.

(HEBREWS 2:14–15)

DAY
348

What the devil had schemed and labored to accomplish throughout human history, the Lord at last allowed him to achieve—to Satan's eternal ruin. When Jesus rose from the grave three days after His crucifixion, the Evil One's doom was sealed forever. Hell never knew such a surprise!

It is precisely this truth that allows us and motivates us and energizes us to go forward in the work God gives us. Our God is a God of surprises! No night is too dark to hide the Lord's glory! *The Resurrection guarantees it!*

That is why you and I can move into arenas of human devastation and expect to see God work. That is why we do not despair when disasters of nature or atrocities of mankind seem to threaten God's control of this world. As members of God's family bought by the blood of Christ, we are the sons and daughters of an almighty Savior who brings good out of evil and victory out of defeat. The devil does not have the final say. He has already pulled the switch for his own electrocution.

When we find ourselves in the depths of some personal agony, all we can see are the boiling, black clouds of catastrophe. All we can hear are the snappings and growlings of the wolfpack nipping at our heels. All we can imagine is a bleak future devoid of anything good and filled with everything bad.

When that describes you, there is only one cure: Remember the Resurrection! Remember the empty tomb! If God can take Satan's most devastating attack and reverse it 180 degrees, no situation is so dark or hopeless that it outstrips His limitless ability to surprise.

Not even yours.

STEVE HALLIDAY

An Explorer of unknown Lands

Many are asking, "Who can show us any good?"
Let the light of your face shine upon us, O LORD.

(PSALM 4:6)

What a different aspect life would present if our attitude were always one of expectant waiting to discover what God has in store for us as the result of personal trials. What blessing is to be born of every one of our sorrows and disappointments and griefs? How little attention has been paid to this greatest of all fields for discovery—our own lives!

The future is a closed book. Sometimes we wish that we might read that book and so know the events of years to come. But we seldom think how God is foreshadowing our future, that each event of every day has its own meaning and its own bearing on our lives.

Why, then, don't we enter each day in the spirit of an explorer of unknown lands? We can look on everything that comes to us, whether duty or success or misfortune, as a treasure laden with vast possibilities of blessing. We do not need to resign ourselves to thinking, *We do not know what this day may bring,* as though that truth holds out a forecast only of disappointment and defeat. We can open our eyes to see the ultimate good which God will bring to us through the events whose meaning is now so uncertain.

We have every reason to live in hope and certainty. When our lives are yielded to God's leading, there will be good and only good. We must expect it. It will come.

JOHN T. FARIS

DAY
349

paris in the the spring

Open my eyes that I may see wonderful things in your law.

(PSALM 119:18)

I t was a rainy Saturday morning and the children were reading inside. Bob, a reader of Charlie Brown and old Archie comics, sauntered up and handed me a comic book. "Read this, Mama," he said, pointing to a sign at the top of the page.

"Paris in the spring," I read.

He grinned. "Read it again."

I looked at the words. "Paris in the spring!"

His smile grew. He looked like a cat with feathers on his face. "Look close and you'll be surprised."

I'd been had. I knew it, but I wasn't sure how. But when I opened myself to the possibility of surprise, I saw something else in the sign. What it really said was "Paris in the the spring"! An extra "the" had been slipped into the sentence, so that the first line ended with *the* and the second line began with *the*. I was positively amazed. It took me three tries to see what was there. Why? Because I saw only what I expected to see.

We do the same thing with God. We see Him in precisely the same old ways we've always seen Him. We see what we've come to expect. Nothing more. We are so selective. We shut out what we don't choose to see. We aren't willing to be surprised.

And so we won't be—unless perhaps God knocks hard on our door! To see Him as He really is requires that we pay attention to the unexpected…because if we don't expect to see God, the chances are, we won't.

SUE MONK KIDD

The Moment of "Ah!"

Stop and consider God's wonders. Do you know how God controls the clouds and makes his lightning flash?

(JOB 37:14–15)

e can begin to see the world around us with new eyes by practicing looking at everything with a sense of wonder. Tilden Edwards has listed five "responses on seeing a flower":

"Ah!"

"Oh, beautiful—I want it, but I will let it be!"

"Oh, beautiful—I want it, I will take it!"

"Oh, beautiful—I can sell it!"

"So?"

The response that opens us to see God in the world is the first one, the "Ah" response. The other responses make us increasingly impervious to God's presence in His creation, blind to His wonders, deaf to His voice.

Dr. Ernest Campbell once told his congregation at Riverside Church in New York, "Our television sets have progressed from black and white to color, but our daily lives have regressed from color to black and white!" He suggested that we are so mesmerized by technology, so wrapped up in our drive to produce and our need to succeed, make, acquire, amass, display, that our faculty for awe has been anesthetized. We no longer notice how the pavement of our streets glistens after a rain.

I heard an old story about a farmer and a child who were standing at the edge of the Grand Canyon for the first time. Dancing with wonder, the child threw out his arms and cried, "Look! Oh, look!"

"Yep," muttered the farmer, scratching his beard. "That's a heck of a place to lose a cow."

Whether it is a seed pod or a canyon wall, falling snow or a drop of water, the voice that spoke it into being still resounds inside it. If you listen lovingly enough, stand before it in awe, you may hear it. The moment of "Ah!" will come.

SUE MONK KIDD

A freshness of vision

All mankind will fear; they will proclaim
the works of God and ponder what he has done.

(PSALM 64:9)

O ne of the tragedies of growing up is that we get used to things. It has its good side, of course, since irritations may cease to be irritations. But there is immense loss when we get used to the redness of the rising sun, and the roundness of the moon, and the whiteness of the snow, the wetness of the rain, the blueness of the sky, the buzzing of bumble bees, the stitching of crickets, the invisibility of the wind, the unconscious constancy of heart and diaphragm, the weirdness of noses and ears, the number of the grains of sand on a thousand beaches, the never-ceasing crash crash crash of countless waves, and ten million kingly-clad flowers flourishing and withering in woods and mountain valleys where no one sees but God.

I invite you to seek a "freshness of vision," to look, as though it were the first time, not at the empty product of accumulated millennia of aimless evolutionary accidents (which no child ever dreamed of), but at the personal handiwork of an infinitely strong, creative, and exuberant Artist who made the earth and the sea and everything in them.

O, that we would open our eyes even wider to the glory of God in the world around us! With the late Wheaton College scholar Clyde Kilby, I invite you to believe (like the children believe) "that today, this very day, some stroke is being added to the cosmic canvas that in due course you shall understand with joy as a stroke made by the Architect who calls Himself Alpha and Omega."

JOHN PIPER

The Higher the Mountain, the Longer the Shadow

Can you fathom the mysteries of God? Can you probe the limits of the Almighty?
They are higher than the heavens—what can you do?
They are deeper than the depths of the grave—what can you know?

(JOB 11:7-8)

Not only are mysteries an inseparable part of all religion—indeed, they are its very substance—but it is absolutely impossible that a true religion should fail to present a great number of mysteries. If it is true, it ought to teach more truths respecting God and divine things than any other, or even all others together. Each of these truths has a relation to the infinite and therefore borders on mystery. How could it be otherwise here, when nature itself follows the same pattern?

DAY
353

Behold God in nature! The more He gives us to contemplate, the more He gives to astonish us. To each creature is attached some mystery. A grain of sand is an abyss!

Now, if the demonstrations which God has made of Himself in nature suggest a thousand questions which cannot be answered, how will it be when another is added—that is, when God the Creator and Preserver reveals Himself anew as God the Reconciler and Savior?

Will not mysteries multiply with discoveries? With each new day will we not see a new night? And every time we gain some new bit of divine knowledge, will we not also gain some new expanse of human ignorance? Has not the doctrine of grace—so necessary, so consoling—by itself opened a profound abyss into which, for long centuries, rash and restless spirits have been constantly plunging?

It is, then, clearly necessary that Christianity, more than any other religion, should be mysterious, simply because it is true. The higher mountains rise, the larger the shadows they cast. In the same way, the gospel is all the more mysterious because of its grandeur.

ALEXANDER VINET

what was god up to?

My ways are far beyond anything you could imagine.

(ISAIAH 55:8, NLT)

W hen God began to reveal His plan of redemption, He started with a lowly peasant couple trudging to Bethlehem to pay taxes, a baby born in a stable and cradled in a manger. That boy grew up to be the Savior of the world—but spent most of His thirty-three years on earth in a carpenter's shop!

What was God up to?

What if we had masterminded that Advent? Would we not have sent Him to Rome, Alexandria, and Athens? What a chance for press agents when the boy Jesus confounded the sages in the Temple! What the news media of today could have done blowing up that boy preacher into a world celebrity! It is enough to make all reporters weep.

When Jesus finally began His public ministry, it was a matter of walking around in Galilee with a few fishermen disciples. His brothers urged Him to go up to Jerusalem and get before the public, but He was thumbs down on that. When He healed people, He sometimes said, "Don't tell about it." When He rose from the dead, He missed the greatest opportunity of going before Pilate and the priests to show Himself. We've been trying to prove to this day that He rose, and that would have settled it once for all! He put on no show, just said "Mary" to a weeping woman, broke bread in the home of two grieving disciples, and, to other sad followers, He merely said, "Throw your net on the right side of the boat and you will find some [fish]" (John 21:6). What commonplace ways of breaking the greatest news ever made known to man!

God didn't do it our way.

VANCE HAVNER

A spectacular thing

In the sixth month, God sent the angel Gabriel to Nazareth, a town in Galilee, to a virgin pledged to be married to a man named Joseph, a descendant of David. The virgin's name was Mary. The angel went to her and said, "Greetings, you who are highly favored! The Lord is with you." Mary was greatly troubled at his words and wondered what kind of greeting this might be. But the angel said to her, "Do not be afraid, Mary, you have found favor with God. You will be with child and give birth to a son, and you are to give him the name Jesus. He will be great and will be called the Son of the Most High. The Lord God will give him the throne of his father David, and he will reign over the house of Jacob forever; his kingdom will never end." "How will this be," Mary asked the angel, "since I am a virgin?" The angel answered, "The Holy Spirit will come upon you, and the power of the Most High will overshadow you. So the holy one to be born will be called the Son of God. Even Elizabeth your relative is going to have a child in her old age, and she who was said to be barren is in her sixth month. For nothing is impossible with God."

(LUKE 1:26–38)

DAY
355

A s moments go, that one appeared no different than any other. If you could somehow pick it up off the timeline and examine it, it would look exactly like the ones that have passed while you have read these words. It came and it went. It was preceded and succeeded by others just like it. It was one of the countless moments that have marked time since eternity became measurable.

But in reality, that particular moment was like none other. For through that segment of time a spectacular thing occurred. God became a man. While the creatures of earth walked unaware, Divinity arrived. Heaven opened herself and placed her most precious one in a human womb.

The omnipotent, in one instant, made Himself breakable. He who had been spirit became pierceable. He who was larger than the universe became an embryo. And He who sustains the world with a word chose to be dependent upon the nourishment of a young girl.

God as a fetus. Holiness sleeping in a womb. The creator of life being created.

God was given eyebrows, elbows, two kidneys, and a spleen. He stretched against the walls and floated in the amniotic fluids of His mother.

God had come near.

MAX LUCADO

why did he come?

Since the children have flesh and blood,
he too shared in their humanity.

(HEBREWS 2:14)

Why did Jesus come to earth? Theologians tend to answer that question from the human perspective: He came to show us what God is like, to show us what a human being should be like, to lay down His life as a sacrifice. I cannot help thinking, though, that Incarnation had meaning in other, cosmic ways.

God loves matter. You can read His signature everywhere: rocks that crack open to reveal delicate crystals, the clouds swirling around Venus, the fecundity of the oceans (home to 90 percent of all living things). Clearly, according to Genesis, the act of creation gave God pleasure.

DAY 356

Yet creation also introduced a gulf between God and His subjects. Moses, David, Jeremiah, and other bold wrestlers with the Almighty flung this accusation to the heavens: "LORD, You don't know what it's like down here!" Job was most blunt: "Do you have eyes of flesh? Do you see as a mortal sees?" (Job 10:4).

They had a point, a point God Himself acknowledged with the decision to visit planet Earth. Of the many reasons for Incarnation, surely one was to answer Job's accusation. *Do you have eyes of flesh?* Yes, indeed.

I, a citizen of the visible world, know well the struggle involved in clinging to belief in another, invisible world. Christmas turns the tables and hints at the struggle involved when the Lord of both worlds descends to live by the rules of the one. In Bethlehem, the two worlds came together, realigned; what Jesus went on to accomplish on planet Earth made it possible for God someday to resolve all disharmonies in both worlds. No wonder a choir of angels broke out in spontaneous song, disturbing not only a few shepherds but the entire universe.

PHILIP YANCEY

christ's downward mobility

Christ Jesus…being in very nature God, did not consider equality
with God something to be grasped, but made himself nothing,
taking the very nature of a servant, being made in human likeness.

(PHILIPPIANS 2:5-7)

Christ's path to greatness was not a typical one. The Bible makes it clear that He came "down" into the world—and He came down from the very top. Philippians 2 states that Christ was equal with God, the ultimate object of praise in the universe. Given His high position, the violence of the Incarnation and the depth of Jesus' descent takes on astonishing dimensions. He voluntarily sacrificed His divine prerogatives. The One worthy of all worship and the Source of all power was born as a helpless baby in a dirty animal stable.

Once His life on earth began, Jesus never stopped descending. Omnipotent, He cried; the owner of all things, He had no home. The King of kings, He became a bondservant; the source of truth, He was found guilty of blasphemy; the Creator, He was spit on by the creatures; the giver of life, He was crucified naked on a cross—bleeding, gasping for air. With His death, the descent was complete.

With His life and death as a man, Christ violated every tenet of the world's system. The Highest came to serve the lowest. The Creator and Sustainer of all things came to pour Himself out. The One who possessed everything became nothing. From the world's perspective, the cross became the symbol of foolishness. Yet in God's eyes, Christ became the greatest of the great. He had accomplished totally the purpose for which God had sent Him; He had pleased His Father and advanced God's kingdom on earth. And Philippians states that because of Christ's downward mobility, God highly exalted Him, and gave Him a name above every name. That's the twist. Jesus Christ descended into God's greatness.

BILL HYBELS

with terror and trembling

Beyond all question, the
mystery of godliness is great.

(1 TIMOTHY 3:16)

T he birth of Christ provides a strong reason for us to experience holy fear and trembling, for only because of that birth could Christ become man and later die. Even though He was free from sin, He took upon Himself a mortal body—and that should make us marvel. That He who is God was willing to become man, that He accommodated Himself to our weakness and came down to our level, is too great for our minds to grasp. It makes us shudder with the deepest holy fear; it fills us with terror and trembling.

This is what amazed Paul when he said, "Beyond all question, the mystery of godliness is great" (1 Timothy 3:16). How great? "God appeared in a body." And again in another place: "For surely it is not angels he helps, but Abraham's descendants. For this reason he had to be made like his brothers in every way" (Hebrews 2:16–17).

This is why I especially greet and love this day. This is why I set before your eyes His love, so that I may help you share in it. And this is why I ask all of you to be in church for that celebration, with all zeal and alertness. Let each of us leave our house empty so that we may recall our Master wrapped in swaddling clothes and lying in a manger. It is incredible and beyond our every expectation.

The magi were strangers and foreigners from Persia, yet they came to see Him lying in the manger. Can you, a Christian, not bear to give a brief measure of time to enjoy this blessed sight? If we will present ourselves in a spirit of faith, there is no doubt but that we shall truly see Him as He lies in the manger.

ST. JOHN CHRYSOSTOM

we would not have it otherwise

While they were there, the time came for the baby to be born,
and she gave birth to her firstborn, a son. She wrapped him in cloths
and placed him in a manger, because there was no room for them in the inn.

(LUKE 2:6–7)

T he face in the sky. The child born in the night among beasts. The sweet breath and steaming dung of beasts. And nothing is ever the same again.

Those who believe in God can never in a way be sure of Him again. Once they have seen Him in a stable, they can never be sure where He will appear or to what lengths He will go or to what ludicrous depths of self-humiliation He will descend in His wild pursuit of man. If holiness and the awful power and majesty of God were present in this least auspicious of all events, then there is no place or time so lowly and earthbound but that holiness can be present there too. And this means that we are never safe, that there is no place where we can hide from God, no place where we are safe from His power to break in two and recreate the human heart. Because it is just where He seems most helpless that He is most strong, and just where we least expect Him that He comes most fully.

This birth means that God Himself is never safe from us, and maybe that is the dark side of Christmas. He comes in such a way that we can always turn Him down, as we could crack the baby's skull like an eggshell or nail Him up when He gets too big for that. God puts Himself at our mercy not only in the suffering that we can cause Him by our blindness and coldness and cruelty, but the suffering that we can cause Him simply by suffering ourselves. Because that is the way love works, and when someone we love suffers, we suffer with him, and we would not have it otherwise.

FREDERICK BUECHNER

DAY
359

HOW MUCH MORE COULD HE DO?

Glory to God in the highest, and on earth
peace to men on whom his favor rests.

(LUKE 2:14)

 Tis the season to be jolly because, more than at any other time, we think of Him. More than in any other season, His name is on our lips.

And the result? For a few precious hours our heavenly yearnings intermesh and we become a chorus. A ragtag chorus of longshoremen, Boston lawyers, illegal immigrants, housewives, and a thousand other peculiar persons who are banking that Bethlehem's mystery is in reality, a reality. "Come and behold Him," we sing, stirring even the sleepiest of shepherds and pointing them toward the Christ-child.

DAY
360

For a few precious hours, He is beheld. Christ the Lord. Those who pass the year without seeing Him, suddenly see Him. People who have been accustomed to using His name in vain, pause to use it in praise. Eyes, now free of the blinders of self, marvel at His majesty.

Emmanuel. He is with us.

In a few hours the cleanup will begin—lights will come down, trees will be thrown out. Size 36 will be exchanged for size 40, eggnog will be on sale for half price. Soon life will be normal again. December's generosity will become January's payments, and the magic will begin to fade.

But for the moment, the magic is still in the air. I want to savor the spirit just a bit more. I want to pray that those who beheld Him this season will look for Him next August. And I can't help but linger on one fanciful thought: If He can do so much with such timid prayers lamely offered in December, how much more could He do if we thought of Him every day?

MAX LUCADO

god working in mystery

Great is the LORD, and most worthy of praise;
his greatness no one can fathom.

(PSALM 145:3)

Man can send an electric current through a copper wire at sixty degrees below zero, and at the other end of the wire, heat a platinum wire to one thousand degrees. Where was that heat? From whence did it come? God—working in mystery!

A fifty pound storage battery, fully charged, will lift one hundred pounds until its "soul" has been discharged. Still the battery has lost none of its fifty pounds. Why and how? God working in mystery.

Black carbon and colorless oxygen are both tasteless. Hydrogen is a colorless, tasteless, odorless gas, fourteen and one-half times lighter than an equal volume of air and 11,160 times lighter than water. We combine this hydrogen with black carbon and oxygen and get sweet white sugar. God working in mystery.

The neutrino is an unbelievably tiny part of a cosmic ray particle. Yet it has such great energy it could drive through two hundred quadrillion miles of solid lead. God working in mystery.

Toluene, a coal tar distillate, smells like gasoline. Combine it with chlorine, a poisonous gas, and by treating it with another deadly poison, cyanide, we get a wonderful-smelling, non-poisonous, health-aiding substance which is a harmless medicine for children. God working in mystery.

Water weighs eight hundred times more than air, yet to have rain, it must be lifted against the force of gravity, held in suspension above the earth, moved to definite locations, and brought down. It has been estimated that approximately sixteen million tons of water fall every second. God working in mystery.

Looking up to the universe, with its billions of stars and millions of light years—looking down into the depths, scaling the heights, delving into the bosom and bowels of the earth, who cannot but exult in and worship our great God!

ROBERT GREENE LEE

His glory, our glory

It is the glory of God to conceal a matter.

(PROVERBS 25:2)

Goes against the grain a little, doesn't it? *It is the glory of God to conceal a matter.*

Consider the life of Amy Carmichael. She went to India in 1895, never realizing that country would become her home, the children of India her family. Nor did she know when she left home that many beautiful, intelligent little girls in India were taken from their homes and trained to become temple women to satisfy the lusts of men in the worship of Hindu gods. She learned of this horrible custom when a seven-year-old who had escaped from a temple was brought to her house.

From that day on the Lord placed the desire in Amy's heart to save these girls from moral ruin and train them to do the will of the heavenly Father.

Yet early in her ministry, Amy slipped into a pit, permanently crippling her leg. For the next twenty years she remained in bed, rarely leaving her room. On the morning of the accident she had prayed, "Do anything, Lord, that will fit me to serve You better."

That accident was the answer. But in her confinement she went on to write thirteen books which have blessed generations of sufferers around the world.

It is a glorious thing for a man or woman to be God-sufficient and not seek human explanations for His actions in his or her life. Even when those circumstances are totally mysterious. It is a glorious thing to know that your Father God makes no mistakes in directing or permitting that which crosses the path of your life.

It is the glory of God to conceal a matter—and it is *our* glory to trust Him, no matter what.

JONI EARECKSON TADA

A FUTURE YOU DO NOT KNOW

You have not passed this way before.

(JOSHUA 3:4, NASB)

T hese words were spoken to the children of Israel just before they entered Canaan. For three days their camp had stretched along the low hills which skirt the Jordan River, and on the fourth day the officers of Joshua issued their final commands. Joshua himself said to the people, "Sanctify yourselves, for tomorrow the LORD will do wonders among you."

As he spoke, the Jews became solemn. Their long journey in the desert was over, and the mystery of an unknown country and life lay before them. When they looked across to the Promised Land, all their pettier life was hushed and they grew serious and thoughtful. It was the impressiveness of a new experience, the departure from the familiar, that made them serious.

In our own lives, it is the discovery of God in life and the certainty that He has plans for us that gives us a true, deep sense of movement, and lets us always feel the power and delight of unknown coming things.

It is good to come to a future which you do not know. It is good if God brings you to the borders of some promised land. Do not shrink from any experience merely because of its novelty. Do not draw back from any way just because you never traveled there before. Oh, my friend, go into it today without fear! Only, go into it with God, the God who has been always with you. Remember what He has already done for you, and the new life to which He leads you shall open its best richness to you. For he who most humbly accepts what God already has given him and taught him is surest of the best and deepest blessings which God has yet to give.

PHILLIPS BROOKS

HOPE HAS ITS REASONS

May the God of hope fill you with all joy and peace as you trust in him,
so that you may overflow with hope by the power of the Holy Spirit.

(ROMANS 15:13)

C hristians are people of hope and not despair because we know that God, who had the first word, will have the last. He is never thwarted or caught napping by the circumstances of our lives. To have faith in Jesus does not mean we try to pretend that bad things are really good. Rather we know that God will take our difficulties and weave them into purposes we cannot see as yet. And when He is done, the day will be more glorious for our having gone through the difficulties. We are not unmindful of the difference between what is evil and what is good. We know that if the logic of His love nailed Jesus to the cross, we have no right to go another way.

DAY
364

But our lives can be lived well, with courage and with joy, because we live by the hope of the Resurrection. So no matter what life lands in our laps, if we will only trust God and wait, and never lose heart, the song we sing one day will be of victory. And then, with battles over, the time will come when faith becomes sight and hope fulfillment and our whole beings are united with the God we love. Joy of all joys, goal of our desire, all that we long for will be ours for we will be His.

For the moment, though, we are still on the road. The gap between promise and performance is still the tension of our faith. Yet hope in Christ is the most compelling incentive in the world. Hope has its reasons after all.

REBECCA MANLEY PIPPERT

The wonder of it all

*Show the wonder of your great love, you who save by
your right hand those who take refuge in you.*

(PSALM 17:7)

Several years before his death, a remarkable rabbi, Abraham Joshua Heschel, suffered a near-fatal heart attack. His closest male friend was at his bedside. Heschel was so weak he was only able to whisper: "Sam, I feel only gratitude for my life, for every moment I have lived. I am ready to go. I have seen so many miracles during my lifetime." The old rabbi was exhausted by his effort to speak. After a long pause, he said, "Sam, never once in my life did I ask God for success or wisdom or power or fame. I asked for wonder, and He gave it to me."

I asked for wonder, and He gave it to me. A Philistine will stand before a Claude Monet painting and pick his nose; a person filled with wonder will stand there fighting back the tears.

DAY
365

We should be astonished at the goodness of God, stunned that He should bother to call us by name, our mouths wide open at His love, bewildered that at this very moment we are standing on holy ground.

Let us ask God for the gift He gave to this unforgettable rabbi. And let us pray: "Dear Lord, grant me the grace of wonder. Surprise me, amaze me, awe me in every crevice of Your universe. Delight me to see how Your Christ plays in ten thousand places, lovely in limbs, and lovely in eyes not His, to the Father through the features of men's faces. Each day enrapture me with Your marvelous things without number. I do not ask to see the reason for it all; I ask only to share the wonder of it all."

BRENNAN MANNING

STEVE HALLIDAY is a freelance writer, editor, and speaker, as well as the author of *No Night Too Dark: How God Turns Defeat into Glorious Triumph*. He holds a master of divinity degree from Western Conservative Baptist Seminary in Portland, Oregon. Steve and his wife, Lisa, live in Hillsboro, Oregon.

WILLIAM G. TRAVIS is professor of church history at Bethel Seminary in St. Paul, Minnesota. He holds a Ph.D. in American history from New York University and a master's degree in church history from Boston University School of Theology. He is the coauthor of *Religious Traditions of the World* and the two-volume edition *American Evangelicalism: A Bibliography*. He lives with his wife, Lucille, in Arden Hills, Minnesota.

Multnomah Publishers®

The publisher and author would love to hear your comments about this book. *Please contact us at:* www.multnomah.net/howgreatthouart

SOURCES

Sources for the readings in this collection are listed by the number of each entry. Every effort has been made to provide proper and accurate source attribution; should any attribution be found to be incorrect, we welcome written documentation supporting correction for subsequent printings. For material not in the public domain, selections were made according to generally accepted fair-use standards and practices; we gratefully acknowledge the cooperation of publishers and individuals granting permission for use of certain excerpts. For permission to reprint any of the selections, please direct requests to the original source listed below.

1. Adapted from *The Confessions Of St. Augustine*, revised from a former translation by Rev. E.B. Pusey, D.D. (New York: John B. Alden, 1885).

2. Adapted from Novatian in *Ante-Nicene Christian Library, Vol. XXIII* (Edinburgh: T & T Clark, 1869).

3. Taken from John Piper, *The Supremacy of God in Preaching* (Grand Rapids, MI: Baker Book House, 1990). Used by permission.

4. Adapted from David Needham, *Close To His Majesty* (Portland, OR: Multnomah Press, 1987). Used by permission.

5. Taken from *Knowing God* by J.I. Packer. Copyright 1973 by J.I. Packer. Used with permission from InterVarsity Press, P.O. Box 1400, Downers Grove, IL 60515. Also reproduced by permission of Hodder and Stoughton Limited.

6. Taken from *The Pursuit of God* by A.W. Tozer (Camp Hill, PA: Christian Publications, Inc., 1982). Used by permission.

7. Adapted from *The Treasury of David, Vol. 1* by Charles H. Spurgeon (New York: Association Press, 1913).

8. Adapted from *From the Edge of the Crowd* by Arthur John Gossip (Edinburgh: T & T Clark, 1924).

9. Adapted from *The Works of John Wesley, Vol. 3* (London: Wesleyan Methodist Book Room, 1872).

10. Taken from *Close To His Majesty* by David Needham (Portland, OR: Multnomah Press, 1987). Used by permission.

11. Adapted from *The Complete Works of John Bunyan, Vol. II* (New York: Georg Olms Verlag, n.d.).

12. Adapted from *Embracing God* by David Swartz (Eugene, OR: Harvest House Publishers, 1981). Used by permission.

13. Taken from *Knowing God* by J.I. Packer. ©1973 by J.I. Packer. Used with permission from InterVarsity Press, P.O. Box 1400, Downers Grove, IL 60515. Also reproduced by permission of Hodder and Stoughton Limited.

14. Adapted from *The Trivialization of God*, ©1995 by Donald McCullough. Used by permission of NavPress, Colorado Springs, CO. All rights reserved. For copies call (800) 366-7788.

15. Taken from *The Sense of His Presence* by David Mains (Waco, TX: Word Books, 1988). Used by permission.

16. Taken from Ronald L. Jones in *The Christian Life for the Kindred in Spirit* (Gresham, OR: Vision House, 1994. Used by permission.

17. Taken from *Enjoying Intimacy With God* by J. Oswald Sanders (Chicago, IL: Moody Press, 1980. Used by permission.

18. Adapted from *The Trivialization of God*, ©1995 by Donald McCullough. Used by permission of NavPress, Colorado Springs, CO. All rights reserved. For copies call (800) 366-7788.

19. Adapted from *The Trivialization of God*, ©1995 by Donald McCullough. Used by permission of NavPress, Colorado Springs, CO. All rights reserved. For copies call (800) 366-7788.

20. Taken from *Close To His Majesty* by David Needham (Portland, OR: Multnomah Press, 1987). Used by permission.

21. Taken from *The Pursuit Of God* by A.W. Tozer (Camp Hill, PA: Christian Publications, Inc., 1982. Used by permission.

22. Taken from *The God You Can Know* by Dan DeHaan (Chicago, IL: Moody Press, 1982. Used by permission.

23. Taken from *Close to His Majesty* by David Needham (Portland, OR: Multnomah Press, 1987). Used by permission.

24. Taken from *Embracing God* by David Swartz (Eugene, OR: Harvest House Publishers, 1994). Used by permission.

25. Taken from *Glorious Intruder* by Joni Eareckson Tada (Portland, OR: Multnomah Press, 1989. Used by permission.

26. Taken from *Secret Strength* by Joni Eareckson Tada (Portland, OR: Multnomah Press, 1988. Used by permission.

27. Taken from *A Godward Life* by John Piper (Sisters, OR: Multnomah Publishers, 1997. Used by permission.

28. Taken from *Enjoying Intimacy With God* by J. Oswald Sanders (Chicago, IL: Moody Press, 1980. Used by permission.

29. Taken from John Piper, *The Supremacy of God in Preaching* (Grand Rapids, MI: Baker Book House, 1990). Used by permission.

30. Excerpted from: *The Soul's Quest for God*. By R.C. Sproul,©1992. Used by permission of Tyndale House Publishers, Inc. All rights reserved.

31. Taken from *The Pursuit Of God* by A.W. Tozer (Camp Hill, PA: Christian Publications, Inc. 1982.) Used by permission.

32. Taken from *The Beauty of God's Holiness* by Thomas L. Trevethan. Copyright 1995 by Thomas L. Trevethan. Used with permission from InterVarsity Press, P.O. Box 1400, Downers Grove, IL 60515.

33. Taken from *Foundations of the Christian Faith* by James Montgomery Boice. ©1986 by InterVarsity Christian Fellowship/USA. Used with permission from InterVarsity Press, P.O. Box 1400, Downers Grove, IL 60515.

34. Taken from J.I. Packer, *God's Words*. Published by Baker Book House, copyright 1981. Used by permission.

35. Taken from *Faith And Life* by Benjamin B. Warfield (New York: Longmans, Green, and Co., 1916.)

36. Taken from *Our God is Awesome* by Tony Evans (Chicago: Moody Press, 1994). Used by permission.

37. Taken from *The God Who Hears* by W. Bingham Hunter. Copyright 1986 by W. Bingham Hunter. Used with permission from InterVarsity Press, P.O. Box 1400, Downers Grove, IL 60515.

38. Taken from *The Whole Works of the Rev. W. Bates, D.D.* (Harrisonburg, VA: Sprinkle Publications, 1990 reprint of an eighteenth century original).

39. Taken from *In the Grip of Grace* by Max Lucado, copyright 1996. Published by Word Publishing, Nashville, Tennessee. All rights reserved. Used by permission.

40. Adapted from *The Trivialization of God*, ©1995 by Donald McCullough. Used by permission of NavPress, Colorado Springs, CO. All rights reserved. For copies call (800) 366-7788.

41. Taken from *The Best of Arthur W. Pink* (Grand Rapids, MI: Baker Book House, 1978.)

42. Taken from *Loving God* by Charles W. Colson. Copyright ©1983, 1987 by Charles W. Colson. Used by permission of Zondervan Publishing House.

43. Adapted from *The Knowledge of the Holy, The Attributed of God: Their Meaning in the Christian Life* by A.W. Tozer ©1961 by Aiden Wilson Tozer. Copyright renewed. Reprinted by permission of HarperCollins Publishers, Inc.

44. Adapted from *The Pursuit of Holiness* by Jerry Bridges, ©1978, 1996 by Jerry Bridges. Used by permission of NavPress, Colorado Springs, CO. All rights reserved. For copies call (800) 366-7788.

45. Taken from *The Gospel of the Sovereignty and Other Sermons* by John Daniel Jones (London: Hodder & Stoughton, n.d.).

46. Taken from *The God Who Hears* by W. Bingham Hunter. ©1986 by W. Bingham Hunter. Used with permission from InterVarsity Press, P.O. Box 1400, Downers Grove, IL 60515.

47. Taken from *The Practical Works of Richard Baxter, Vol. III* (Ligonier, PA: Soli Deo Gloria Publications, 1990), reprint of a nineteenth century reprint by George Virtue, London.

48. Taken from *The Pleasures Of God* by John Piper (Portland, OR: Multnomah Press, 1991). Used by permission.

49. Adapted from *The Pursuit of Holiness* by Jerry Bridges, ©1978, 1996 by Jerry Bridges. Used by permission of NavPress, Colorado Springs, CO. All rights reserved. For copies call (800) 366-7788.

50. Adapted from Jim Killion in *The Christian Life for the Kindred in Spirit* (Gresham, OR: Vision House, 1994.) Used by permission.

51. Taken from *Illustrating Great Themes of Scripture* by Donald Grey Barnhouse. ©1969 by Fleming H. Revell, a division of Baker Book House Company. Used by permission.

52. Taken from *Peace With God* by Billy Graham, Copyright 1984, Word Publishing, Nashville, Tennese. All rights reserved. Used by permission.

53. Taken from *The Best of Arthur W. Pink* (Grand Rapids, MI: Baker Book House, 1978).

54. Taken from *Foundations of the Christian Faith* by James Montgomery Boice. ©1986 by InterVarsity Christian Fellowship/USA. Used with permission from InterVarsity Press, P.O. Box 1400, Downers Grove, IL 60515.

55. Taken from *The Works of John Wesley, Vol. 3* (London: Wesleyan Methodist Book Room, 1872).

56. Adapted from George Whitefield in *The World's Great Sermons, Vol. II* (New York: Funk & Wagnalls), 1908.

57. Adapted from: *The Holiness of God*. By R.C. Sproul, ©1985. Used by permission of Tyndale House Publishers, Inc.

58. Taken from *Illustrating Great Themes of Scripture* by Donald Grey Barnhouse. ©1969 by Fleming H. Revell, a division of Baker Book House Company. Used by permission.

59. Taken from *Desiring God, Tenth Anniversary Expanded Edition* by John Piper (Sisters, OR: Multnomah Books, 1996.) Used by permission.

60. Taken from *What Luther Says*, ©1959 by Concordia Publishing House. Used by permission.

61. Taken from *Foundations of the Christian Faith* by James Montgomery Boice. ©1986 by InterVarsity Christian Fellowship/USA. Used with permission from InterVarsity Press, P.O. Box 1400, Downers Grove, IL 60515.

62. Adapted from *The Set of the Sail* by A.W. Tozer (Camp Hill, PA: Christian Publications, 1986). Used by permission.

63. Taken from *Gleanings In The Godhead* by Arthur W. Pink (Chicago, IL: Moody Press, 1975). Used by permission.

64. Taken from *Foundations of the Christian Faith* by James Montgomery Boice. ©1986 by InterVarsity Christian Fellowship/USA. Used with permission from InterVarsity Press, P.O. Box 1400, Downers Grove, IL 60515.

65. Taken from *The Place Of Help* by Oswald Chambers. ©1936 by Dodd Mead & Co., Grosset & Dunlap; ©1989 by the Oswald Chambers Publications Assoc. Ltd., and is used by permission of Discovery House Publishers, Box 3566, Grand Rapids MI 49501. All rights reserved.

66. Reprinted with the permission of Simon & Schuster, Inc., from ETHICS by Dietrich Bonhoeffer, translated from the German by Neville Horton Smith. English Translation ©1955 by Macmillan Publishing Company.

67. Adapted from *Romans: An Exposition of Chapter 5* by D. M. Lloyd-Jones (Grand Rapids, MI: Zondervan Publishing House, 1972). Used by permission.

68. Taken from *Memoir, Select Thoughts and Sermons* by Rev. Edward Payson (Portland, ME: Hyde and Lord, 1849).

69. Taken from *The Works Of John Flavel, Vol. 1* (London: W. Baynes and Son, 1820).

70. Taken from *Glad Tidings* by D.L. Moody (New York: E.B. Trent, 1876).

71. Taken from *Peace With God* by Billy Graham, ©1984, Word Publishing, Nashville, Tennese. All rights reserved. Used by permission.

72. Adapted from *Pursuit Of God* by A.W. Tozer (Camp Hill, PA: Christian Publications, Inc., 1982). Used by permission.

73. Adapted from *The Works of John Flavel, Vol. 3* (London: W. Baynes and Son, 1820).

74. Taken from *Close To His Majesty* by David Needham (Portland, OR: Multnomah Press, 1987). Used by permission.

75. Adapted from *Abide In Christ* by Andrew Murray (Chicago: Fleming H. Revell Company, n.d.).

76. Taken from *Things That Matter Most* by John Henry Jowett (Old Tappan, NJ: Fleming H. Revell Co., 1913).

77. Taken from *Close To His Majesty* by David Needham (Portland, OR: Multnomah Press, 1987). Used by permission.

78. Taken from *Glad Tidings* by D.L. Moody (New York: E.B. Trent, 1876).

79. Taken from *The Love Of God* by Bernard of Clairvaux (Portland, OR: Multnomah Press, 1983).

80. Taken from *From the Edge of the Crowd* by Arthur John Gossip (Edinburgh: T & T Clark, 1924).

81. Taken from *Abide In Christ* by Andrew Murray (Chicago: Fleming H. Revell Company, n.d.).

82. Adapted from *Glorious Intruder* by Joni Eareckson Tada (Portland, OR: Multnomah Press, 1989). Used by permission.

83. Taken from *The Love of God* by Oswald Chambers. ©1938; 1973; 1985 by Chosen Books; ©1988 by the Oswald Chambers Publications Assoc. Ltd., and is used by permission of Discovery House Publishers, Box 3566, Grand Rapids, MI 46501. All rights reserved.

84. Adapted from *The Book Of God's Providence* by John T. Faris (New York: George H. Doran Company, 1913).

85. Adapted from *Close To His Majesty* by David Needham (Portland, OR: Multnomah Press, 1987). Used by permission.

86. Adapted from *A Godward Life* by John Piper (Sisters, OR: Multnomah Publishers, 1997). Used by permission.

87. Adapted from *The Love Of God* by Bernard of Clairvaux (Portland, OR: Multnomah Press, 1983).

88. Adapted from *The Pleasures Of God* by John Piper (Portland, OR: Multnomah Press, 1991). Used by permission.

89. Taken from *The Ragamuffin Gospel* by Brennan Manning (Portland, OR: Multnomah Press, 1990). Used by permission.

90. Adapted from *The Love Of God* by Bernard of Clairvaux (Portland, OR: Multnomah Press, 1983).

91. Adapted from *The Best of Arthur W. Pink* (Grand Rapids, MI: Baker Book House, 1978).

92. Taken from *The God Who Hears* by W. Bingham Hunter. Copyright ©1986 by W. Bingham Hunter. Used with permission from InterVarsity Press, P.O. Box 1400, Downers Grove, IL 60515.

93. Adapted from *Desiring God, Tenth Anniversary Expanded Edition* by John Piper (Sisters, OR: Multnomah Books, 1996). Used by permission.

94. Taken from *The Knowledge of the Holy: Their Meaning in the Christian Life* by A.W. Tozer ©1961by Aiden WilsonTozer. Copyright renewed. Reprinted by permission of HarperCollins Publishers, Inc.

95. Adapted from *Trusting God*, ©1988 by Jerry Bridges. Used by permission of NavPress, Colorado Springs, CO. All rights reserved. For copies call (800) 366-7788.

96. Taken from *The Joy Of Knowing God* by Richard Strauss (Neptune, NJ: Loizeaux Brothers, 1984). Used by permission.

97. Taken from *Gleanings in the Godhead* by Arthur W. Pink (Chicago: Moody Press, 1975). Used by permission.

98. Taken from *Desiring God, Tenth Anniversary Expanded Edition* by John Piper (Sisters, OR: Multnomah Books, 1996). Used by permission.

99. Adapted from *The Treasury of David, Vol. 4* by Charles H. Spurgeon (New York: Association Press, 1913).

100. Adapted from *Majesty, The God You Should Know* by J. Sidlow Baxter (San Bernardino, CA: Here's Life Publishers, 1984). Reprinted by permission of Thomas Nelson Publishers.

101. Adapted from *The Sovereign Hand* by Paul H. Sheetz. Copyright ©1971 by The Evangelical Alliance Mission. Used by permission.

102. Adapted from *Majesty, The God You Should Know* by J. Sidlow Baxter (San Bernardino, CA: Here's Life Publishers, 1984). Reprinted by permission of Thomas Nelson Publishers.

103. Taken from *The Sovereignty of God* by Arthur W. Pink (Grand Rapids, MI: Baker Book House, 1965).

104. Taken from *Growing Strong In The Seasons Of Life* by Charles R. Swindoll. ©1983 by Charles R. Swindoll, Inc. Used by permission of Zondervan Publishing House.

105. Adapted from *The Unchanging Christ* by Alexander Maclaren (New York: Funk & Wagnalls, n.d.).

106. Adapted from *Silent Pain* by Kathy Olsen (Colorado Springs, CO: NavPress, 1992).

107. Taken from *Future Grace* by John Piper (Sisters, OR: Multnomah Books, 1995). Used by permission.

108. Adapted from *No Night Too Dark* by Steve Halliday (Sisters, OR: Multnomah Books, 1993). Used by permission.

109. Taken from *The Best of J. Vernon McGee* by J. Vernon McGee (Nashville, TN: Thomas Nelson Publishers, 1988). Used by permission.

110. Adapted from *Commentaries on the Book of the Prophet Daniel* by John Calvin, trans. by Thomas Myers (1948 reprint by William B. Eerdmans Co. of an 1852 original).

111. Adapted from *Sovereignty and Grace* by John B. Champion (Harrisburg, PA: The Evangelical Press, n.d.).

112. Taken from *The Gospel of the Sovereignty and Other Sermons* by John Daniel Jones (London: Hodder & Stoughton, n.d.).

113. Adapted from *Commentary on the Book of Psalms, Vol. 2* by John Calvin, trans. by the Rev. James Anderson (1948 reprint by the William B. Eerdmans Co. of an 1845 original).

114. Adapted from *Glorious Intruder* by Joni Eareckson Tada (Portland, OR: Multnomah Press, 1989). Used by permission.

115. Adapted from Timothy Dwight in *The World's Great Sermons, Vol. III* (New York: Funk & Wagnalls, 1908).

116. Taken from *Foundations of the Christian Faith* by James Montgomery Boice. ©1986 by InterVarsity Christian Fellowship/USA. Used with permission from InterVarsity Press, P.O. Box 1400, Downers Grove, IL 60515.

117. Taken from *The Gospel of the Sovereignty and Other Sermons* by John Daniel Jones (London: Hodder & Stoughton, n.d.).

118. Taken from *Foundations of the Christian Faith* by James Montgomery Boice. Copyright ©1986 by InterVarsity Christian Fellowship/USA. Used with permission from InterVarsity Press, P.O. Box 1400, Downers Grove, IL 60515.

119. Adapted from, *Majesty, The God You Should Know* by J. Sidlow Baxter (San Bernardino, CA: Here's Life Publishers, 1984). Reprinted by permission of Thomas Nelson Publishers.

120. Adapted from Newell Dwight Hillis in *The World's Great Sermons, Vol. X* (New York: Funk & Wagnalls, 1908).

121. Taken from *Gleanings In The Godhead* by Arthur W. Pink (Chicago, IL: Moody Press, 1975). Used by permission.

122. Taken from *The Knowledge of the Holy: Their Meaning in the Christian Life* by A.W. Tozer ©1961by Aiden WilsonTozer. Copyright renewed. Reprinted by permission of HarperCollins Publishers, Inc.

123. Taken from *Sermons and Discourses, 1720-1723* by Jonathan Edwards ©1992 by Yale University Press. Reprinted by permission of Yale University Press.

124. Adapted from *The Word and Works of God* by John Gill (New York: H. Dayton, 1860).

125. Adapted from *Discourses Upon the Existence and Attributes of God* by Stephen Charnock (London: James Blackwood and Co., n.d., reprinted from 1797 original).

126. Taken from *The Pleasures Of God* by John Piper (Portland, OR: Multnomah Press, 1991). Used by permission.

127. Adapted from *The Best of Arthur W. Pink* (Grand Rapids, MI: Baker Book House, 1978).

128. Adapted from *The Beauties of Thomas Boston*, ed. Samuel M'Millan (Inverness, England: 1979 reprint of 1831 publication).

129. Adapted from *A God to Call Father* by Michael Phillips (Wheaton, IL: Tyndale House Publishers, 1994). Used by permission.

130. Adapted from *Christian Apologetics* by the Rev. W. Devivier (San Jose, CA: Popp & Hogan, 1903).

131. Taken from *The Knowledge of the Holy: Their Meaning in the Christian Life* by A.W. Tozer ©1961by Aiden WilsonTozer. Copyright renewed. Reprinted by permission of HarperCollins Publishers, Inc.

132. Adapted from *The Treasury of David, Vol. 2* by Charles H. Spurgeon (New York: Association Press, 1913).

133. Adapted from *Discourses Upon the Existence and Attributes of God* by Stephen Charnock (London: James Blackwood and Co., n.d., reprinted from 1797 original).

134. Adapted from *Secret Strength* by Joni Eareckson Tada (Portland, OR: Multnomah Press, 1988). Used by permission.

135. Taken from *Library of Distinctive Sermons* by John R. Claypool (Sisters, OR: Questar Publishers, 1996). Used by permission.

136. Adapted from *Grace Grows Best In Winter* by Margaret Clarkson (Grand Rapids, MI: Zondervan Publishing House, 1972).

137. Adapted from *Grace Grows Best In Winter* by Margaret Clarkson (Grand Rapids, MI: Zondervan Publishing House, 1972).

138. Taken from *The Knowledge of the Holy: Their Meaning in the Christian Life* by A.W. Tozer ©1961by Aiden WilsonTozer. Copyright renewed. Reprinted by permission of HarperCollins Publishers, Inc.; also, Julian of Norwich, *Devotional Classics: Selected Readings for Individuals and Groups*, ed. Richard J. Foster and James Bryan Smith (San Francisco: HarperSanFrancisco, 1993).

139. Adapted from *Close To His Majesty* by David Needham (Portland, OR: Multnomah Press, 1987). Used by permission.

140. Taken from Vance Havner, *Hope Thou In God* (Fleming H. Revell, a division of Baker Book House Company, 1977). Used by permission.

141. Adapted from *The Treasury of David, Vol. 1* by Charles H. Spurgeon (New York: Association Press, 1913).

142. Adapted from *The Book of God's Providence* by John T. Faris (New York: George H. Doran Company, 1913).

143. Adapted from *The Book of God's Providence* by John T. Faris (New York: George H. Doran Company, 1913).

144. Taken from *The Best of Arthur W. Pink* (Grand Rapids, MI: Baker Book House, 1978).

145. Taken from *The First Person* by Lehman Strauss (Neptune, NJ: Loizeaux Brothers, 1967). Used by permission.

146. Taken from *The Joy Of Knowing God* by Richard Strauss (Neptune, NJ: Loizeaux Brothers, 1984). Used by permission.

147. Adapted from Augustine in *Documents in Early Christian Thought*, ed. Maurice Wiles and Mark Santer (New York: Cambridge University Press, 1977). Reprinted with the permission of Cambridge University Press.

148. Taken from Geoffrey V. Guns in *The Library of Distinctive Sermons* (Sisters, OR: Questar Publishers, 1996). Used by permission.

149. Adapted from *Glorious Intruder* by Joni Eareckson Tada (Portland, OR: Multnomah Press, 1989). Used by permission.

150. Adapted from *A Godward Life* by John Piper (Sisters, OR: Multnomah Publishers, 1997). Used by permission.

151. Adapted from *The Complete Writings of Menno Simons*, Herald Press, Scottdale, PA 15683. Used by permission.

152. Adapted from *The Works Of Saint Augustine, Part III, Sermons I* (Brooklyn, NY: New City Press, 1990). Used by permission.

153. Adapted from: *The Holiness of God.* By R.C. Sproul, ©1985. Used by permission of Tyndale House Publishers, Inc.

154. Adapted from *Lectures on Systematic Theology* by Charles G. Finney (Oberlin: James M. Fitch, 1846).

155. Adapted from *Discourses Upon the Existence and Attributes of God* by Stephen Charnock (London: James Blackwood and Co., n.d., reprinted from 1797 original).

156. Taken from *Knowing God* by J.I. Packer. ©1973 by J.I. Packer. Used with permission from InterVarsity Press, P.O. Box 1400, Downers Grove, IL 60515. Also reprinted by permission of Hodder and Stoughton Limited.

157. Adapted from *Hope Has Its Reasons* by Rebecca Manley Pippert (Downers Grove: InterVarsity Press, to be released July, 2000). Used by permission.

158. Taken from *Knowing God* by J.I. Packer. Copyright ©1973 by J.I. Packer. Used with permission from InterVarsity Press, P.O. Box 1400, Downers Grove, IL 60515. Also reprinted by permission of Hodder and Stoughton Limited.

159. Taken from *Our God is Awesome* by Tony Evans (Chicago: Moody Press, 1994). Used by permission.

160. Adapted from *A Christianity Today Reader*, ed. Frank E. Gaebelein (New York: Meredith Press, 1966).

161. Adapted from *Selected Sermons of Jonathan Edwards* (London: MacMillan & Co., 1904).

162. Adaped from *The Sermons of Matthew Mead* (London: James Nisbet and Company, 1836).

163. Adapted from L.W. Munhall in *The Fundamentals For Today*, ed. Charles L. Feinberg (Grand Rapids, MI: Kregel Publications, 1958). Used by permission.

164. Adapted from Jeremy Taylor in *The World's Great Sermons, Vol. 2* (New York: Funk & Wagnalls, 1908).

165. Adapted from R.G. Lee in Jerry Falwell, *25 of the Greatest Sermons Ever Preached* (Grand Rapids: Baker Book House, 1983).

166. Adapted from R.G. Lee in Jerry Falwell, *25 of the Greatest Sermons Ever Preached* (Grand Rapids: Baker Book House, 1983).

167. Adapted from *Selected Sermons of Jonathan Edwards* (London: MacMillan & Co., 1904).

168. Adapted from Jeremy Taylor in *The World's Great Sermons, Vol. 2* (New York: Funk & Wagnalls, 1908).

169. Taken from *What Luther Says*, ©1959 by Concordia Publishing House. Used with permission.

170. Adapted from *Ante-Nicene Christian Library: The Works of Lactantius, Vol. II* (Edinburgh: T & T Clark, 1871).

171. Adapted from *The Works Of Saint Augustine, Part III — Sermons I* (Brooklyn, NY: New City Press, 1990). Used by permission.

172. Taken from *Daring To Draw Near* by John White. ©1977 by John White. Used with permission from InterVarsity Press, P.O. Box 1400, Downers Grove, IL 60515.

173. Taken from *How To Give Away Your Faith* by Paul E. Little. © 1966 by InterVarsity Press. Used with permission from InterVarsity Press, P.O. Box 1400, Downers Grove, IL 60515

174. Adapted from: *The Holiness of God.* By R.C. Sproul, ©1985. Used by permission of Tyndale House Publishers, Inc.

175. Adapted from *Commentaries on the Book of the Prophet Jeremiah and the Lamentations, Vol. 1*, by John Calvin and trans. by the Rev. John Owen (1948 reprint of 1852 original).

176. Adapted from *The City Of God, Vol. II* by Augustine, trans. Marcus Dods (Edinburgh: T & T Clark, 1872).

177. Adapted from *The World's Hope* by Robert Boyd (Chicago: J.W. Goodspeed, 1873).

178. Adapted from J. Gresham Machen, *God Transcendent* (Grand Rapids, MI: Wm. B. Eerdmans Publishing Co., 1982). Used by permission.

179. Taken from *Illustrating Great Themes of Scripture* by Donald Grey Barnhouse. ©1969 by Fleming H. Revell, a division of Baker Book House Company. Used by permission.

180. Adapted from *The Book Of God's Providence* by John T. Faris (New York: George H. Doran Company, 1913).

181. Adapted from Ruth Senter in *The Attributes of God* (Chicago: Moody Press, 1987). Used by permission.

182. Adapted from *Fathers of the Church, Vol. 68: Discourses Against Judaizing Christians* by St. John Chrysostom (Washington, D.C.: The Catholic University of America Press, 1979). Used by permission.

183. Adapted from *Sermons on Several Occasions* by John Wesley (London: Wesleyan Conference Office, 1872).

184. Taken from *Flashes of Thought; being One Thousand Choice extracts from the Works of C.H. Spurgeon*, reprinted as *1000 Devotional Thoughts* (Grand Rapids, MI: Baker Book House, 1976).

185. Adapted from *Future Grace* by John Piper (Sisters, OR: Multnomah Books, 1995). Used by permission.

186. Taken from *Purifiying the Church* by Stuart Briscoe. ©1987 by Regal Books, Ventura, CA 93003. Used by permission.

187. Taken from *Great Verses Through the Bible* by F.B. Meyer (Grand Rapids, MI: Zondervan Publishing House, 1972).

188. Taken from *Future Grace* by John Piper (Sisters, OR: Multnomah Books, 1995). Used by permission.

189. Adapted from *Grace, Prayer, and Work* by D.L. Moody (London: Morgan and Scott, n.d.).

190. Adapted from *Comfort for Christians* by Arthur W. Pink (Grand Rapids, MI: Baker Book House, 1976).

191. Adapted from *Faith At the Frontiers* by Carl F.H. Henry (Chicago: Moody Press, 1969). Used by permission.

192. Taken from *The Works of St. Augustine, Sermons, II (20-50) on the OT* ed. Edmund Hill (Brooklyn, NY: New City Press, 1990). Used by permission.

193. Taken from *Glad Tidings* by D.L. Moody (New York: E.B. Treat, 1876).

194. Adapted from *Great Joy* by D.L. Moody (New York: E.B. Treat, 1877).

195. Adapted from *Great Joy* by D.L. Moody (New York: E.B. Treat, 1877).

196. Taken from Karl Barth in *The Living Testament* (San Francisco: Harper & Row, 1985).

197. Adapted from *Gospel Remission* by Jeremiah Burroughs (Morgan, PA: Soli Deo Gloria Publications, 1995, from a 1668 original).

198. Adapted from *Transforming Grace*, ©1991 by Jerry Bridges. Used by permission of NavPress, Colorado Springs, CO. All rights reserved. For copies call (800) 366-7788.

199. Adapted from *Transforming Grace*, ©1991 by Jerry Bridges. Used by permission of NavPress, Colorado Springs, CO. All rights reserved. For copies call (800) 366-7788.

200. Adapted from *Gospel Remission* by Jeremiah Burroughs (Morgan, PA: Soli Deo Gloria Publications, 1995, from a 1668 original).

201. Adapted from *The Treasury of David*, Vol. 2, by Charles H. Spurgeon (New York: Association Press, 1913).

202. Adapted from *The New Life* by Andrew Murray (New York: H.M. Caldwell Co., 1871).

203. Taken from *Does It Matter That I'm Saved?* by Millard J. Erickson. ©1978 by Millard J. Erickson. Reprinted by permission of Baker Books.

204. Adapted from *Able To The Uttermost* by Charles H. Spurgeon (reprint; Pasadena, TX: Pilgrim Publications, 1985).

205. Taken from *The Works of President Edwards* by Jonathan Edwards (New York: 1869).

206. Taken from *The Autobiography of Charles H. Spurgeon* (Philadelphia: American Baptist Publication Society, 1897).

207. Adapted from *Memoir, Select Thoughts and Sermons* by the Rev. Edward Payson (Portland, ME: Hyde and Lord, 1849).

208. Adapted from *A Testament to Freedom: The Essential Writings of Dietrich Bonhoeffer* by Geffrey B. Kelly and F. Burton Nelson (Eds.) ©1991 by Geffrey B. Kelly and F. Burton Nelson. Reprinted by permission of HarperCollins Publishers, Inc.

209. Adapted from Curtis W. Freeman in *The Library of Distinctive Sermons* ed. Gary W. Klingsporn (Sisters, OR: Questar Publishers, 1997). Used by permission.

210. Adapted from *Grace, Prayer, and Work* by D.L. Moody (London: Morgan and Scott, n.d.).

211. Adapted from *Devotions and Prayers of Richard Baxter,* Leonard T. Grant, ed. (Grand Rapids: Baker Book House, 1964).

212. Adapted from *The Complete Writings of Menno Simons*, Herald Press, Scottdale, PA 15683. Used by permission.

213. Adapted from *The Sermons of Matthew Mead* (London: James Nisbet and Company, 1836).

214. Adapted from *Discourses Upon the Existence and Attributes of God* by Stephen Charnock (London: James Blackwood and Co., n.d., reprinted from 1797 original).

215. Taken from *One Holy Passion* by R.C. Sproul (Nashville, TN: Thomas Nelson Publishers, 1987). Used by permission.

216. Adapted from *Close To His Majesty* by David Needham (Portland, OR: Multnomah Press, 1987). Used by permission.

217. Adapted from *The Works of John Flavel, Vol. 3* (London: W. Baynes and Son, 1820).

218. Adapted from *The Works of John Flavel, Vol. 3* (London: W. Baynes and Son, 1820).

219. Taken from *I Believe: Understanding And Applying The Apostle's Creed* by Alister McGrath. © 1991 by Alister McGrath. Used by permission of Zondervan Publishing House.

220. Adapted from *To All People* by D.L. Moody (New York: E. B. Treat, 1877).

221. Adapted from *A Godward Life* by John Piper (Sisters, OR: Multnomah Publishers, 1997). Used by permission.

222. Adapted from *Our God is Awesome* by Tony Evans (Chicago: Moody Press, 1994). Used by permission.

223. Adapted from *The Power of the Cross* by Tim LaHaye (Sisters, OR: Multnomah Books, 1998). Used by permission.

224. Adapted from *The Works of John Flavel, Vol. 3* (London: W. Baynes and Son, 1820).

225. Taken from *No Night Too Dark* by Steve Halliday (Sisters, OR: Multnomah Books, 1993). Used by permission.

226. Taken from *Foundations of the Christian Faith* by James Montgomery Boice. ©1986 by InterVarsity Christian Fellowship/USA. Used with permission from InterVarsity Press, P.O. Box 1400, Downers Grove, IL 60515.

227. Taken from *Hudson Taylor's Spiritual Secret* by James Hudson Taylor (London: China Inland Mission, 1935).

228. Adapted from *The Potency Of Prayer* by Thomas C. Horton (New York: Fleming H. Revell Company, 1928).

229. Taken from C. Samuel Storms, *The Grandeur of God* (Grand Rapids, MI: Baker Book House, 1984. Used by permission.

230. Adapted from *Desiring God, Tenth Anniversary Expanded Edition* by John Piper (Sisters, OR: Multnomah Books, 1996). Used by permission.

231. Adapted from *The Potency Of Prayer* by Thomas C. Horton (New York: Fleming H. Revell Company, 1928).

232. Adapted from *The Power Of Prayer* by Herbert Lockyer, copyright 1982 by Word Publishing, Nashville, Tennessee. All rights reserved. Used by permission.

233. Taken from *Desiring God, Tenth Anniversary Expanded Edition* by John Piper (Sisters, OR: Multnomah Books, 1996). Used by permission.

234. Adapted from *The World's Hope* by Robert Boyd (Chicago: J.W. Goodspeed, 1873).

235. Adapted from *The Potency Of Prayer* by Thomas C. Horton (New York: Fleming H. Revell Company, 1928).

236. Adapted from *The God of the Amen & Other Sermons* by Alexander Maclaren (New York: Funk & Wagnalls Co., n.d.).

237. Adapted from *The Best of J. Vernon McGee* (Nashville, TN: Thomas Nelson Publishers, 1988). Used by permission.

238. Adapted from *The Best of J. Vernon McGee* (Nashville, TN: Thomas Nelson Publishers, 1988). Used by permission.

239. Adapted from *When God Was Taken Captive* by Willard Aldrich (Portland, OR: Multnomah Press, 1989). Used by permission.

240. Adapted from *Discourses Upon the Existence and Attributes of God* by Stephen Charnock (London: James Blackwood and Co., n.d., reprinted from 1797 original).

241. Adapted from *Discourses Upon the Existence and Attributes of God* by Stephen Charnock (London: James Blackwood and Co., n.d., reprinted from 1797 original).

242. Taken from *God: Coming Face to Face with His Majesty* by John MacArthur, Jr. (Victor Books, 1993). Used by permission.

243. Taken from *No Night Too Dark* by Steve Halliday (Sisters, OR: Multnomah Books, 1993). Used by permission.

244. Adapted from *Memoir, Select Thoughts and Sermons* by the Rev. Edward Payson (Portland, ME: Hyde and Lord, 1849).

245. Taken from *Our God is Awesome* by Tony Evans (Chicago: Moody Press, 1994). Used by permission.

246. Taken from *The God Who Hears* by W. Bingham Hunter. ©1986 by W. Bingham Hunter. Used with permission from InterVarsity Press, P.O. Box 1400, Downers Grove, IL 60515.

247. Adapted from *The Attributes of God* by Arthur W. Pink (Swengel, PA: Reiner Publications, n.d.).

248. Adapted from *Discourses Upon the Existence and Attributes of God* by Stephen Charnock (London: James Blackwood and Co., n.d., reprinted from 1797 original).

249. Adapted from *Discourses Upon the Existence and Attributes of God* by Stephen Charnock (London: James Blackwood and Co., n.d., reprinted from 1797 original).

250. Adapted from *The First Person* by Lehman Strauss (Neptune, NJ: Loizeaux Brothers, 1967). Used by permission.

251. Taken from *The Living God* by Richard W. DeHaan. ©1967 by Zondervan Publishing Co. and is used by permission of Discovery House Publishers, Box 3566, Grand Rapids, MI 49501. All rights reserved.

252. Adapted from *Glorious Intruder* by Joni Eareckson Tada (Portland, OR: Multnomah Press, 1989). Used by permission.

253. Adapted from *Discourses Upon the Existence and Attributes of God* by Stephen Charnock (London: James Blackwood and Co., n.d., reprinted from 1797 original).

254. Adapted from *The World's Hope* by Robert Boyd (Chicago: J.W. Goodspeed, 1873).

255. Taken from *The Joy of Knowing God* by Richard Strauss (Neptune, NJ: Loizeaux Brothers, 1984). Used by permission.

256. Taken from *Foundations of the Christian Faith* by James Montgomery Boice. ©1986 by InterVarsity Christian Fellowship/USA. Used with permission from InterVarsity Press, P.O. Box 1400, Downers Grove, IL 60515.

257. Taken from *The God Who Hears* by W. Bingham Hunter. Copyright 1986 by W. Bingham Hunter. Used with permission from InterVarsity Press, P.O. Box 1400, Downers Grove, IL 60515.

258. Adapted from *Who Art In Heaven* by H. Phillip Hook (Grand Rapids, MI: Zondervan Publishing House, 1979). Used by permission.

259. Adapted from *Close To His Majesty* by David Needham (Portland, OR: Multnomah Press, 1987). Used by permission.

260. Taken from *The Living God* by Richard W. DeHaan. ©1967 by Zondervan Publishing Co. and is used by permission of Discovery House Publishers, Box 3566, Grand Rapids, MI 49501. All rights reserved.

261. Taken from *The God Who Hears* by W. Bingham Hunter. ©1986 by W. Bingham Hunter. Used with permission from InterVarsity Press, P.O. Box 1400, Downers Grove, IL 60515.

262. Adapted from *Sermons and Discourses, 1720-1723* by Jonathan Edwards (New Haven: Yale University Press, 1992).

263. Adapted from *Discourses Upon the Existence and Attributes of God* by Stephen Charnock (London: James Blackwood and Co., n.d., reprinted from 1797 original).

264. Adapted from *Discourses Upon the Existence and Attributes of God* by Stephen Charnock (London: James Blackwood and Co., n.d., reprinted from 1797 original).

265. Adapted from *A Heart For God* by Sinclair Ferguson. ©1985 by Sinclair Ferguson. Reprinted by permission of Banner of Truth.

266. Adapted from *The First Person* by Lehman Strauss (Neptune, NJ: Loizeaux Brothers, 1967). Used by permission.

267. Taken from *Knowing God* by J.I. Packer. ©1973 by J.I. Packer. Used with permission from InterVarsity Press, P.O. Box 1400, Downers Grove, IL 60515. Also reprinted by permission of Hodder and Stoughton Limited.

268. Adapted from *A Heart For God* by Sinclair Ferguson (Colorado Springs, CO: NavPress, 1985).

269. Adapted from *Discourses Upon the Existence and Attributes of God* by Stephen Charnock (London: James Blackwood and Co., n.d., reprinted from 1797 original).

270. Adapted from *Discourses Upon the Existence and Attributes of God* by Stephen Charnock (London: James Blackwood and Co., n.d., reprinted from 1797 original).

271. Adapted from *Discourses Upon the Existence and Attributes of God* by Stephen Charnock (London: James Blackwood and Co., n.d., reprinted from 1797 original).

272. From: *When God Doesn't Make Sense.* By Dr. James Dobson, ©1993 by Tyndale House Publishers, Inc. Used by permission. All rights reserved.

273. Taken from J.I. Packer, *God's Words.* Published by Baker Book House, ©1981. Used by permission.

274. Taken from *What Luther Says*, ©1959 by Concordia Publishing House. Used with permission.

275. Adapted from *A Heart For God* by Sinclair Ferguson. ©1985 by Sinclair Ferguson. Reprinted by permission of Banner of Truth.

276. Adapted from *Institutes Of The Christian Religion, Volume 1* by John Calvin (Philadelphia: Presbyterian Board of Publication, 1813).

277. Adapted from *Trusting God*, ©1988 by Jerry Bridges. Used by permission of NavPress, Colorado Springs, CO. All rights reserved. For copies call (800) 366-7788.

278. Taken from *Love Is Always Right* by Josh McDowell and Norm Guisler, ©1996. Published by Word Publishing, Nashville, Tennessee. All rights reserved. Used by permission.

279. Adapted from Minucius Felix in *The AnteNicene Fathers, Vol. IV*, ed. Rev. Alexander Roberts, D.D., and James Donaldson, L.L.D. (Grand Rapids, MI: William B. Eerdmans reprint of 1885 original).

280. Adapted from *The City Of God, Vol. I* by Augustine, trans. Marcus Dods, (Edinburgh: T & T Clark, 1872).

281. Adapted from *The Beauties of Thomas Boston*, ed. Samuel M'Millan (Inverness, England: 1979 reprint of 1831 publication).

282. Adapted from *Selected Writings of Benjamin B. Warfield* (Nutley, NJ: Presbyterian and Reformed Publishing Company, 1970).

283. Taken from *The History Of Redemption* by Jonathan Edwards (London: Religious Tract Society, 1837).

284. Adapted from *Spiritual Maturity* by J. Oswald Sanders (Chicago: Moody Press, 1962). Used by permission.

285. Adapted from St. Cyril in *A Select Library of Nicene and Post Nicene Fathers of the Christian Church, Vol. VII* (Edinburgh: T & T Clark, 1886).

286. Adapted from *Doing Theology With Huck & Jim* by Mark Shaw (Downers Grove, IL: InterVarsity Press, 1993). Used by permission.

287. Adapted from *The Works of John Flavel, Vol. 4* (London: W. Baynes and Son, 1820).

288. Adapted from *The Works of John Flavel, Vol. 4* (London: W. Baynes and Son, 1820).

289. Adapted from *The World's Hope* by Robert Boyd (Chicago: J.W. Goodspeed, 1873).

290. Adapted from *The Works of John Flavel, Vol. 4* (London: W. Baynes and Son, 1820).

291. Adapted from *Selected Writings of Benjamin B. Warfield* (Nutley, NJ: Presbyterian and Reformed Publishing Company, 1970).

292. Adapted from *The Invisible Hand* by R.C. Sproul, ©1996. Published by Word Publishing, Nashville, Tennessee. All rights reserved. Used by permission.

293. Adapted from *The Works of John Flavel, Vol. 4* (London: W. Baynes and Son, 1820).

294. Taken from *Evangelical Preaching* by Charles Simeon (Portland, OR: Multnomah Press, 1986).

295. Taken from Vance Havner, *Fourscore: Living Beyond the Promise* (Fleming H. Revell, a division of Baker Book House Company, 1982). Used by permission.

296. Adapted from *The Book of God's Providence* by John T. Faris (New York: George H. Doran Company, 1913).

297. Adapted from *Remarkable Providences* by Increase Mather (London: John Russell Smith, 1856).

298. Adapted from *Flashes of Thought; being One Thousand Choice extracts from the Works of C.H. Spurgeon*, reprinted as *1000 Devotional Thoughts* (Grand Rapids, MI: Baker Book House, 1976).

299. Adapted from *The Works of John Flavel, Vol. 4* (London: W. Baynes and Son, 1820).

300. Adapted from *The Works of John Flavel, Vol. 4* (London: W. Baynes and Son, 1820).

301. Adapted from *The God of the Amen* by Alexander Maclaren (New York, Funk and Wagnalls Co., n.d.).

302. Adapted from Steve Halliday, *No Night Too Dark* (Sisters, OR: Questar Publishers, 1993). Used by permission.

303. Adapted from *St. Augustine on the Psalms, Vol. 1* [Ancient Christian Writers vol. 29], ©1960 by Johannes Quaster and Walter J. Burghardt. Reprinted by permission of Paulist Press.

304. Adapted from Novatianin *Ante-Nicene Christian Library, Vol. XIII* (Edinburgh: T & T Clark, 1869).

305. Adapted from *The Word and Works of God* by John Gill (New York: H. Dayton, 1860).

306. Adapted from *The God of The Amen and Other Sermons* by Alexander Maclaren (New York, Funk and Wagnalls Co., n.d.).

307. Adapted from *Fathers of the Church, Vo. 26: Saint Ambrose, Letters 1-91* (Washington, D.C.: The Catholic University Of America, 1954). Used by permission.

308. Adapted from *All Truth Is God's Truth* by Arthur F. Holmes (Downers Grove, IL: InterVarsity Press, 1983). Used by permission.

309. Taken from *The Practical Works of Richard Baxter, Vol. III* (Ligonier, PA: Soli Deo Gloria Publications, 1990 reprint of a nineteenth century reprint by George Virtue, London).

310. Adapted from *The Joy Of Knowing God* by Richard Strauss (Neptune, NJ: Loizeaux Brothers, 1984). Used by permission.

311. Adapted from *A Slow and Certain Light* by Elisabeth Elliot (Waco, TX: Word Books, 1973). Used by permission.

312. Taken from *Illustrating Great Themes of Scripture* by Donald Grey Barnhouse. ©1969 by Fleming H. Revell, a division of Baker Book House Company. Used by permission.

313. Taken from *Talking With My Father* by Ray Stedman. ©1997 by Discovery House Publishers, Box 3566, Grand Rapids MI 49501. All rights reserved. Used by permission.

314. Adapted from *Special Sermons* by George Sweeting (Chicago: Moody Press, 1985). Used by permission.

315. Adapted from *Majesty, The God You Should Know* by J. Sidlow Baxter (San Bernardino, CA: Here's Life Publishers, 1984). Used by permission of Thomas Nelson Publishers.

316. Taken from *Behold Your God* by Myrna Alexander. Copyright ©1978 by Myrna Alexander. Used by permission of Zondervan Publishing House.

317. Adapted from *The Best of Arthur W. Pink* (Grand Rapids, MI: Baker Book House, 1978).

318. Taken from *The Knowledge of the Holy: Their Meaning in the Christian Life* by A.W. Tozer ©1961by Aiden WilsonTozer. Copyright renewed. Reprinted by permission of HarperCollins Publishers, Inc.

319. Taken from *The Joy Of Knowing God* by Richard Strauss (Neptune, NJ: Loizeaux Brothers, 1984). Used by permission.

320. Adapted from R. A. Finlayson in *Sermons I Should Like To Have Preached*, ed. Ian Macpherson (Fleming H. Revell Company, 1964). Used by permission of *The Monthly Record*.

321. Adapted from *From the Edge of the Crowd* by Arthur John Gossip (Edinburgh: T & T Clark, 1924).

322. Adapted from *The Best of Arthur W. Pink* (Grand Rapids, MI: Baker Book House, 1978).

323. Taken from *Illustrating Great Themes of Scripture* by Donald Grey Barnhouse. ©1969 by Fleming H. Revell, a division of Baker Book House Company. Used by permission.

324. Adapted from *The Joy Of Knowing God* by Richard Strauss (Neptune, NJ: Loizeaux Brothers, 1984). Used by permission.

325. Taken from *The Joy Of Knowing God* by Richard Strauss (Neptune, NJ: Loizeaux Brothers, 1984). Used by permission.

326. Adapted from *God Is* by John Bisagno (Wheaton, IL: Victor Books, 1983). Used by permission.

327. Adapted from Rebecca Manley Pippert in *The Attributes of God* (Chicago: Moody Press, 1987). Used by permission.

328. Adapted from *From the Edge of the Crowd* by Arthur John Gossip (Edinburgh: T & T Clark, 1924).

329. Taken from *Behold Your God* by Myrna Alexander. ©1978 by Myrna Alexander. Used by permission of Zondervan Publishing House.

330. Adapted from *The God of the Amen* by Alexander Maclaren (New York, Funk and Wagnalls Co., n.d.).

331. Adapted from *The History Of Redemption* by Jonathan Edwards (London: Religious Tract Society, 1837).

332. Taken from *Majesty, The God You Should Know* by J. Sidlow Baxter (San Bernardino, CA: Here's Life Publishers, 1984). Used by permission of Thomas Nelson Publishers.

333. Taken from *Disappointment With God* by Philip Yancey. ©1988 by Philip Yancey. Used by permission of Zondervan Publishing House.

334. Adapted from *The Autobiography of Charles H. Spurgeon* (Philadelphia: American Baptist Publication Society, 1897).

335. Taken from *Living By God's Surprises* by Harold Myra, ©1988. Published by Word Publishing, Nashville, Tennessee. All rights reserved. Used by permission.

336. Adapted from *Glorious Intruder* by Joni Eareckson Tada (Portland, OR: Multnomah Press, 1989). Used by permission.

337. Adapted from *The Book of God's Providences* by John T. Faris (New York: George H. Doran Company, 1913).

338. Taken from *Growing Strong In The Seasons Of Life* by Charles R. Swindoll. ©1983 by Charles R. Swindoll, Inc. Used by permission of Zondervan Publishing House.

339. Adapted from *Feathers For Arrows* by Charles H. Spurgeon (New York: Robert Carter & Brothers, 1883).

340. Adapted from *Great Is The Lord* by Robert Greene Lee. Published by Fleming H. Revell, a division of Baker Book House Company, 1955. Used by permission.

341. Taken from *Mere Christianity* by C.S. Lewis (London: HarperCollins Ltd., 1952). Used by permission.

342. Adapted from *No Night Too Dark* by Steve Halliday (Sisters, OR: Multnomah Books, 1993). Used by permission.

343. Taken from Corrie ten Boom, *He Sets the Captive Free* (Fleming H. Revell, a division of Baker Book House Company, 1977). Used by permission.

344. Taken from *Disappointment With God* by Philip Yancey. ©1988 by Philip Yancey. Used by permission of Zondervan Publishing House.

345. Adapted from *The Light Of The World And Other Sermons* by Phillips Brooks (New York: E.P. Dutton and Company, 1890).

346. Adapted from *No Night Too Dark* by Steve Halliday (Sisters, OR: Multnomah Books, 1993). Used by permission.

347. Taken from *No Night Too Dark* by Steve Halliday (Sisters, OR: Multnomah Books, 1993). Used by permission.

348. Adapted from *No Night Too Dark* by Steve Halliday (Sisters, OR: Multnomah Books, 1993). Used by permission.

349. Adapted from *The Book of God's Providence* by John T. Faris (New York: George H. Doran Company, 1913).

350. Taken from *God's Joyful Surprise* by Sue Monk Kidd. ©1987 by Guideposts Associates, Inc. Reprined by permission of HarperCollins Publishers, Inc.

351. Taken from *God's Joyful Surprise* by Sue Monk Kidd. ©1987 by Guideposts Associates, Inc. Reprined by permission of HarperCollins Publishers, Inc.

352. Adapted from *The Pleasures Of God* by John Piper (Portland, OR: Multnomah Press, 1991). Used by permission.

353. Adapted from Alexander Vinet in *The World's Great Sermons, Vol. IV* (New York: Funk & Wagnalls, 1908).

354. Taken from Vance Havner, *Hope Thou In God* (Fleming H. Revell, a division of Baker Book House Company, 1977). Used by permission.

355. Adapted from *God Came Near* by Max Lucado (Portland, OR: Multnomah Press, 1987). Used by permission.

356. From *Finding God In Unexpected Places* by Philip Yancey. ©1995 by Philip Yancey. Reprinted by permission of Ballantine Books, a Division of Random House Inc.

357. Taken from *Descending Into Greatness* by Bill Hybels and Rob Wilkins. ©1993 by Bill Hybels. Used by permission of Zondervan Publishing House.

358. Adapted from *Fathers of the Church, Vol. 72:On The Incomprehensible Nature of God* by St. John Chrysostom (Washington, D.C.: The Catholic University Press of America, 1984). Used by permission.

359. Taken from *The Hungering Dark* by Frederick Buechner. ©1969 by Frederick Buechner. Reprinted by permission of HarperCollins Publishers, Inc.

360. Adapted from *God Came Near* by Max Lucado (Portland, OR: Multnomah Press, 1987). Used by permission.

361. Taken from Robert Greene Lee, *Great Is The Lord*. Published by Fleming H. Revell, a division of Baker Book House Company, 1955. Used by permission.

362. Adapted from *Glorious Intruder* by Joni Eareckson Tada (Portland, OR: Multnomah Press, 1989). Used by permission.

363. Adapted from *The Light Of The World And Other Sermons* by Phillips Brooks (New York: E.P. Dutton and Company, 1890).

364. Adapted from *Hope Has Its Reasons* by Rebecca Manley Pippert (Downers Grove: InterVarsity Press, to be released July 2000). Used by permission.

365. Adapted from *The Ragamuffin Gospel* by Brennan Manning (Portland, OR: Multnomah Press, 1990). Used by permission.